THOMAS B. REED

PARLIAMENTARIAN

THOMAS BRACKETT REED

THOMAS B. REED

Parliamentarian

By

WILLIAM A. ROBINSON

Illustrated

DODD, MEAD & COMPANY

New York   *1930*

PRINTED IN THE UNITED STATES OF AMERICA
BY THE VAIL-BALLOU PRESS, INC., BINGHAMTON, N. Y.

PREFACE

"Anything but the truth," is reported to have been Speaker Reed's reply to a congressman who sought his advice as to what to include in a memorial address on a deceased colleague. It is safe to say, however, that in his own case Reed would have demanded "the truth, the whole truth, and nothing but the truth."

In the following study, admitting the difficulty of ascertaining the truth about any man, and especially about one whose life was spent in political controversy, the author has endeavored to let Reed tell his own story, explain his own course, and give his own opinions on the issues of the day. He has also attempted to show him as he appeared to his contemporaries. It is hoped therefore, that the reader may be enabled to make a truthful estimate of one of the great Americans of the last century.

The author takes this opportunity to express his appreciation of advice and assistance from many persons interested in the subject. In addition to Mr. Allan Nevins, whose services as editor of this series have been invaluable, he is especially indebted to the Hon. J. Frank Aldrich of Chicago, Ill., Dr. E. N. Allen and Mr. William A. Jones of Boston, Mass., Messrs. J. C. Hamlen and Frank D. Marshall of Portland, Me., Mr. John E. Lodge and Dr. Allen Johnson of Washington, D. C. Mr. Gerald G. Wilder, Librarian of Bowdoin College and Miss Ethel P. Hall of the Maine Historical Society have given valuable aid. He is also greatly indebted to his sister for clerical assistance, to his colleagues Professor Emeritus James F. Colby and Professor James P. Richardson for advice and criticism in the course of preparing the manuscript, to Professor Frank M. Anderson for calling his attention to certain sources of information, and to Professor Arthur H. Basye for assistance in reading proof.

CONTENTS

vii

CONTENTS

ILLUSTRATIONS

THOMAS B. REED

PARLIAMENTARIAN

On Monday December 8, 1902, the House of Representatives met as usual at 12 o'clock. The Chaplain prayed, reminding the members of those great souls, the leaders among men, "who have breathed their spirits into the institutions of our country," one of whom had unexpectedly passed away the day before. The Journal was read and approved; the Speaker laid before the House some routine messages from the President; leaves of absence were granted, and then James S. Sherman of New York rose to make formal announcement of the death of Thomas Brackett Reed. "He was so great, his service to his country so valuable," declared Mr. Sherman, "that it seems to me we may fitly depart from what is the usual custom of the House when one not in public life dies." He thereupon offered a resolution that the House adjourn in honor of the dead. "A distinguished statesman," so ran the last clause of the resolution, "a lofty patriot, a cultured scholar, an incisive writer, a unique orator, an unmatched debater, a master of logic, wit, satire, the most famous of the world's parliamentarians, the great and representative citizen of the American Republic has gone into history."

"They have their exits and their entrances."

Such was Reed's exit. His entrance was unobtrusive enough. He was born October 18, 1839, in a small two-story frame tenement on Hancock Street, Portland, Maine. Almost next door stands the birthplace of Henry Wadsworth Longfellow. His father, Thomas Brackett Reed, Sr., was also a native of Portland and his mother, Mathilda Prince Mitchell, was born in the neighboring town of North Yarmouth. There were two children

1

in the family, a younger sister, Harriet, being born in June, 1846.

Both the Reed and Mitchell families had been resident in New England from its beginnings in the early seventeenth century. Thomas Reade, the founder of the line in New England, had come to Massachusetts with John Winthrop in 1630. Reed's mother traced her decent from Experience Mitchell and Jane Cook, both of whom were identified with the establishment of the Plymouth colony, the latter having been a passenger on the *Mayflower*.

His paternal grandmother, Mary Brackett, was a direct descendant of George Cleve, who played a leading part in the settlement of the Portland region. There has been a good deal of historical controversy regarding the principles and performances of Cleve, but he appears in any event to have been a man of great ability and unusual force of character. He doubtless had both the virtues and defects of the pioneer, and pioneering at every stage of American development was a rough occupation. On the basis of heredity Reed was certainly a thorough-going Yankee. He had in full measure the shrewdness, humor, and essential honesty characteristic of the best of his type. In his political development he eventually transcended both state and section, but he was always a type of the "down-Easter" in the eyes of his countrymen and his political prospects sometimes suffered as a result.

Except for George Cleve, none of Reed's ancestors seems to have made a name in history. They were the inconspicuous hard-working people who, as Reed himself always contended, really shape the course of events regardless of "ostentatious actors here and there, who stride the stage with panoply or with clanging arms." They were of the tough fiber, physical and moral, which could alone have laid the foundations of new commonwealths and wrested a precarious living from the ocean or from the unfriendly soil of the north Atlantic seaboard.

"My father," he once told a newspaper interviewer, "my grandfather, as well as all my great grandfathers back two hundred years, have one and all been fishermen and sailors and sea-goers and comers of various sorts. I never heard of any of them being rich either. My father was a fisherman. At one time he was captain of a little coaster. When the steamboat drove out the coasters he was mate on an ocean-going boat, and made deep-water voyages to all parts of the map." [1]

When he gave up the sea Thomas Brackett Reed, Sr., became watchman in a sugar warehouse near the Portland waterfront. He was not in any sense a conspicuous figure in the community, but he owned his own home, was apparently devoted to his family, and made considerable sacrifices to assist his son in obtaining an education. The testimony of friends and neighbors is to the effect that his wife was of a decidedly superior type and that Thomas Brackett Reed, Jr., derived from her not only his physical characteristics but his acute mentality, his shrewdness, his philosophical viewpoint and his sarcastic tongue. Her photograph taken in advanced years shows her to have been a strikingly handsome woman, with intelligence and force of character apparent in every feature.[2] New England neighbors in a small town—and Portland was still such in Reed's youth, having a population of but 20,000 in 1850—may not have known much about scientific principles of heredity, but their judgments are likely to be trustworthy in such a matter.

Reed's boyhood, judging by the scanty information available, seems to have been much the same as that of countless other young Americans of similar condition. If he escaped the squalor and hardships on the frontier, such as Abraham Lincoln or Andrew Jackson encountered, he had, on the other hand, no unusual advantages. Certainly the family possessed no luxuries.

[1] Washington *Post,* September 6, 1895.
[2] S. W. McCall, *Life of Thomas Brackett Reed,* 4.

He was brought up in an atmosphere of thrift, self-denial, and hard work, but his inborn intellectual capacity and educational opportunities were sufficient to offset the narrowing influences which such environment frequently produces.

Years later when he had become famous, old friends and neighbors recalled Tom Reed the boy in various phases. One remembered "a tow-headed little fellow with fat cheeks and eyes as round as buttons" appearing at school for the first time as a visitor in the custody of two little girls of the neighborhood. Another recalled him when a little older climbing the wall of the Brackett Street school yard and taking a tumble which necessitated the doctor's attention.

Judge Henry Carter, who presided at the municipal court in Portland on the occasion of Neal Dow's well known arraignment for alleged violation of the liquor laws in 1855, remembered him as "a tall, gawky, round-faced, florid-complexioned boy" who "shuffled up" after adjournment of court and spoke to him "in a peculiar drawling voice," expressing admiration of the magistrate's statement rendered on discharging the defendant. Reed was at this time, as we know from his own recollections, becoming more and more interested in public affairs, and the popular interest in the case, in which Henry Clifford, afterward a member of the United States Supreme Court, and William Pitt Fessenden were opposing counsel, may well have drawn him to the court room.[1]

All accounts of Reed's boyhood agree that he read incessantly, devouring popular story papers, history, the English classics—anything he could get his hands on. As the birthplace of Longfellow, N. P. Willis, James and Erastus Brooks, and

---

[1] Interesting items regarding Reed's boyhood may be found in the Washington *Evening Star*, December 2, 1889; New York *Tribune*, June 23, 1907; "When We Were Playmates Together," by G. H. Field, Lewiston *Journal*, July 27, August 1, 1901; McCall, *Reed*, 7-12.

John Neal, Portland had many literary associations. He attended the public schools and eventually entered the Boys' High School. In an address delivered at the unveiling of the Reed memorial at Portland, August 31, 1910, his distinguished friend and classmate Joseph W. Symonds, former member of the Maine Supreme Court, declared that it was in this school that Reed first realized his own possibilities and "half-awoke from his early dreaming and from a sense of loneliness that I think attended his boyhood." "To the last of his life," continued Judge Symonds, "he was accustomed to speak in a hushed and intense way of what he owed to his severe teacher there, Moses Lyford." Judge Symonds's testimony is valuable, for, as he said, he was able to speak of Reed from the intimacies of early childhood. "We were boys together, always friends, classmates in school, classmates in college, young lawyers with adjoining offices in the old, happy, careless, briefless days when the expense of repairing the office-chairs which broke down under him, or which betrayed signs of infirmity after he was gone, was a consideration not to be regarded by either of us with entire indifference."

While still in school Reed joined the State Street Congregational Church and members of that society afterwards remembered that he passed through a period of considerable devotional enthusiasm. His religious promise apparently induced the women of the church to raise money to assist the boy through college with a view to his entering the ministry. There are various versions of the story, but that given by the Rev. Francis E. Clark, the founder of the Christian Endeavor movement, who was long an intimate friend and neighbor of Reed, and with whom he talked frankly on religious topics, is probably correct. The money was raised and accepted; Reed subsequently changed his religious views; he requested his dismissal from the church, and after graduation repaid the donors whatever had been received.[1] Whatever the details of the story, the interest of the church is evidence that he had made an impression as a promising youth deserving a college education.

Reed's course in the Portland High School led directly toward admission to Bowdoin College at Brunswick, twenty-five miles away. The entrance requirements as laid down in the college catalogue of 1856 show that the "strictness of discipline" under Lyford, to which Symonds and Reed alike paid tribute, must have stood the boys in good stead on the day of examination. "Candidates for admission will be required to write Latin grammatically, and to be well versed in Geography, Arithmetic, six sections of Smyth's Algebra, Cicero's Select Orations, the Bucolics, two Georgics, and nine books of the Aeneid of Vergil, Sallust, Xenophon's Anabasis, five books, Homer's Iliad, two books, together with Latin and Greek Grammar and Prosody. They must produce certificates of their good moral character."

Reed, one of the youngest freshmen in a class of fifty-eight members, entered college on August 28, 1856. Bowdoin College at that time had an enrollment of less than two hundred, drawn largely from within the boundaries of the State. Prosperous mercantile and professional families in Portland and other towns were represented, but a greater proportion of the students came from the farms and villages. Few had more than enough money for the very modest expenses of that day—two hundred dollars a year was sufficient—and the great majority were obliged to earn part of their own expenses. As at most New England colleges, the long winter vacation enabled students to teach school in the country districts, that experience itself, as many have testified, having no small educational value.

A college education was still an exceptional privilege which placed a man somewhat apart from his neighbors and imposed a corresponding obligation. Entire neighborhoods watched the

[1] "Thomas B. Reed as a Neighbor," *The Independent,* January 8, 1903.

boys who had gone out from their midst, boasted of their ability when they succeeded, or found explanation in the delinquencies of parents, the evils of environment, or in natural shiftlessness and depravity when they failed. That the graduating classes of Bowdoin College, year after year, throughout its first seventy-five years contributed an unusual number of distinguished men to American life may be attributed to the fine New England stock from which they came, to the special opportunities available to the college-trained man in a busy land which, in general, was still in the pioneer stage, and to the intrinsic merit of the training which it offered. It had been only some thirty years since Longfellow, Hawthorne, John S. C. Abbott, William Pitt Fessenden, and Franklin Pierce had all been at the college together.

The elective system had not yet made its appearance and most of the students pursued the same studies throughout the four year course. Latin, Greek and mathematics constituted the backbone of the work for the first three years and at the conclusion of the course in the latter subject there was a celebration at which textbooks in calculus were cremated amid general rejoicing, a ceremony in which Reed is recorded as "Bearer of the Ashes" on July 26, 1859. "Forensic disputations" were a regular feature of the work of junior and senior years, as well as weekly exercises in declamation. English composition was a required subject for the three upper classes. Judging by the number of graduates who gained distinction by voice or pen, this part of the course must have been an especially effective feature.

The theological influences of an earlier day, when training men for the ministry was the primary function of institutions of higher learning, still made themselves felt. Frank L. Dingley describes the curriculum at this time as "twenty per cent theological." Paley's *Natural Theology* and *Evidences of Christianity* were required textbooks, and in President Woods's course in theology in Senior year Butler's *Analogy* was the basis of intensive study. Several of Reed's contemporaries remembered that he was a shining light in this class and he himself, many years later, declared that he could still recite whole pages of Butler's classic from memory. "I have a very vivid remembrance of his never having once been corrected in his statement of the meaning of the author," wrote his classmate Augustine Jones. "When Reed was called I always sat a silent, wondering witness at the perfect exhibition of intellect, and its steady magnificent work. I never observed its equal in power in any other person." [1] The natural as well as the social sciences, judged by later standards, had no adequate place in the curriculum, but the course as a whole was sound and thorough. It was not perhaps "liberal" in a modern sense, but neither had it any flabbiness or superficiality, and a vast amount of twentieth century educational "liberalism" is merely a euphemistic disguise for the latter qualities.

Decades of experimentation and tinkering with undergraduate courses of study have not disturbed the basic fact that a college curriculum is no stronger than the faculty which conducts it, and the Bowdoin faculty in the fifties was a remarkable body. It consisted of only ten men, but they were almost without exception great teachers and able scholars.

President Leonard Woods, while an object of suspicion to many contemporaries because of his pronounced opposition to the abolitionist movement, was an inspiring teacher and a man of unusual breadth of scholarship and culture. "We admired him," wrote Augustine Jones, "as the one very great man in our acquaintance, of infinite tact and grace. He was a master, with deep wells of knowledge, never sounded to their depths, a great orator, a marvelous conversationalist, and in prayer had no equal

[1] MS. fragment, *Reminiscences of Hon. Thomas B. Reed,* in possession of William Augustine Jones, Boston, Mass.

in our memory for elegant periods or reverent, weighty words."
Parker Cleveland was one of the great mineralogists of
America; Alpheus S. Packard, a noted classicist; Charles Carroll
Everett, professor of modern languages, afterwards had a long
and distinguished career as professor of theology at Harvard.
Egbert Coffin Smyth is still remembered as one of the great
figures at Andover, where he went after distinguished service
at Bowdoin. Thomas C. Upham, Warren Johnson and William
Smyth were notable figures in their day and generation. Joshua
L. Chamberlain, then professor of rhetoric and oratory, was
later to become a general in the Civil War, governor of the
State, and president of the college. There is a curious irony in
the fact that in 1864, while Professor Chamberlain was leading
his brigade in the last bloody campaign in Virginia, President
Woods should have been fearlessly defending the institution of
negro slavery and declaring his opposition to the war. It may
also, however, be evidence of the greater tolerance and liberality
of the New England of this period.

Four years on the Bowdoin campus under such instructors
could not but have been a powerful formative influence, especially when the great majority of the students were there for
some serious purpose. "I believe," Reed once remarked at a
gathering of Dartmouth alumni, "that a large part of what New
England has done—and what she has done has been almost
boundless in its influence—has risen from her small colleges,
where her students went to become educated men. In my day it
cost the student very serious discomfort to get through college.
The young man then used up all he earned on his education,
and when he returned to college after a vacation spent in hard
work, he was determined to get the worth of his money." [1]

Reed lacked the manifold opportunities for campus celebrity
which are open to the modern collegian and, unlike William Pitt

[1] New York *Tribune*, January 27, 1900.

Fessenden, he escaped the measure of immortality which accompanies formal action by the powers that punish. Here and there his name appears in the records. He was a member of his class crew, of a chess club, and of the board of editors of the college annual *The Bugle*. The literary society was still a flourishing institution and the two organizations at Bowdoin, the Peucinian and the Athenaean, played an important part in undergraduate life. Reed was a member of the former and his success as a debater gave a forecast of the distinction he later attained at the bar and on the floor of the House of Representatives.

We are fortunate in having the recollections of several friends and classmates to supplement the bare records of Reed's undergraduate days. Amos L. Allen, afterwards his clerk and eventually his successor as Representative from the First Maine District, Augustine Jones, teacher and author, Judge Symonds, Edward Stanwood, editor and historian, Frank L. Dingley, editor of the Lewiston *Journal*, and others have recorded their impressions of Thomas B. Reed of undergraduate days.

Stanwood, of the class of 1861, states that Reed was unpopular except with a few close associates, of whom Samuel Fessenden, also of '61, was one. He also mentions that he bore for a time the nickname of "Biddy," although it was never generally used and was apparently forgotten in after years by classmates and associates. He had the same sharpness of tongue that was later to make him famous. "I myself happened to be a favorite target for his witticisms, for I was the youngest and most immature freshman in college and was so sensitive that I was his easiest mark." In appearance Reed, he remembers, was "a big, flabby, overgrown boy" who matured steadily, mentally and physically, while in college.[1]

Reed's tongue on one occasion got him into trouble with William L. Crowell, a classmate, and the latter knocked him down,

[1] *Bowdoin Orient,* January 15, 1903.

an incident which is reported to have had a wholesome influence on his manners. The difficulty was soon made up, however, and the two became friends. Crowell went to California after graduation and it may have been due to his reports that Reed afterwards migrated to that State for a brief sojourn of one year.

Reed did not join a fraternity until his senior year. Amos L. Allen, his life-long friend and a member of Psi Upsilon, attributed this to his youthful prejudice against secret orders in general and also to the fact that Reed's scholastic record, which was not distinguished in the earlier part of his course, had not rendered him an especially attractive acquisition from the fraternity standpoint. This, be it remembered, was long before the day of "campus activities." Augustine Jones states that he was "turned down" by several societies in the early part of his course, but, he adds, "I firmly believe that at the beginning of the junior year there was not a secret society in college which did not most earnestly desire him, and I know how vigorously some of them struggled in vain to obtain him. He had learned then to live without them." In his senior year, however, he became a member of Chi Psi, largely, it appears, through the influence of Samuel Fessenden, with whom he roomed in Appleton Hall during his last year in Brunswick. "He would have jumped in the river if Sam had asked him," records Edward Stanwood.

Reed's friendship with Fessenden deserves more than passing mention. Samuel Fessenden was the youngest son of Senator William Pitt Fessenden, one of the ablest statesmen and noblest characters New England ever gave to public life. Young Fessenden was a boy of brilliant ability and remarkably winning personality. He had given his family great anxiety by running off to Kansas at the time of the great disturbances there, recorded in a letter to his father which gives a vivid picture of one of the typical episodes in the border warfare of 1856. One year after graduation, a lieutenant of field artillery, he was mortally wounded in his first battle, the Second Bull Run, dying at Centreville, Virginia, September 1, 1862. Reed never forgot him and in his address at the Portland Centennial of 1886 paid glowing tribute to both father and son. Of the latter, "the quiet associate of the studious hours, the bright companion of the days of pleasure," he said: "He can only live in my memory, but he lives there, sublimated in the crucible of death from all imperfections, clothed upon with all his virtues and radiant with all the possibilities of a generous youth. Other companions have failed in their careers, but not he. All the world has grown old, but he is forever young."

Reed, throughout his life, was never given to indiscriminate friendships. He always had a limited number of intimates to whom he was devoted; of course there were many with whom he was cordial and friendly, but those who were really close to him were never numerous. His college associations appear to have been of much the same character. Augustine Jones remembered that most of the Portland boys held themselves somewhat aloof from him, "and a feeling spread over the college or class that he was not companionable, except to certain favorites whom he had selected for his own reasons, and who had succeeded in placating his majesty." Several non-fraternity men, he added, "formed a coterie of their own, with Reed as the central Johnsonian figure. They were dwellers in the cave of Adullam and every one that was discontented gathered himself unto him, if he was permitted to do so. Every now and again a stinging remark labeled with well known authorship would go hissing through the class. This sprang from that irresistible smartness, that brilliancy in epigram which in after years sent his fame and his spirit everywhere."

Next to Fessenden, probably the closest of Reed's college friends was Frank L. Dingley, also of the class of 1861. To him we are indebted for numerous glimpses of Reed as an under-graduate.[1] Dingley tells how on a hot August afternoon in 1857 he and numerous other homesick freshmen arrived in Bruns-wick, objects of simultaneous interest to "fishers of men from the fraternities and to sophomores planning to put us under the pump." He had his first view of Tom Reed as a member of a band of sophomore bandits, who after howling under the dormi-tory windows invaded their quarters, subjected them to sundry humiliations, and devoured the pies and other provender brought from home.

Later on the two became firm friends. When Reed was teach-ing in one of the town's outlying districts, Dingley tells how his friend often tramped the six miles of snowy road to spend Sun-day with him in Brunswick. In Dingley's attic room with its slant roof, furnished with a hard bed, a table and "a small air-tight stove which warmed one side of him only"—the standards of student life were then primitive—the two read and talked. Doubtless the same "phantoms of fame like exhalations rose and vanished" for them as for Longfellow and the successive gen-erations of students frequenting the same haunts.

"Reed once read aloud to me on a winter's night from Car-lyle's *French Revolution*," Dingley recalls. "We read Carlyle, Goethe, Macaulay's *Essays*, Thackeray and Charles Reade." It was in this room on a Sunday evening that Egbert Coffin Smyth, "to whom the new theology had not been revealed," once visited them in his capacity as "caretaker of student souls." Reed sat on the bed and expounded a merciless natural law, the inadequacies of revealed religion, and the need of a God of mercy, his opin-ion being derived probably from "allopathic doses of Tom

---

[1] "Reminiscences and Comments of a Bowdoin College Student of the Sixties, touching the Life of Thomas Brackett Reed, incidental to reading McCall's Biography of the Great Speaker," eight articles in Lewiston *Weekly Journal*, January–March, 1915.

Paine and Voltaire." "The professor," Dingley adds, "was yet to develop a sense of humor to relieve such dreadful exigencies in the religious life of his wards," and finally took his departure "without offering to pray with us as was his custom."

On January 8, 1887, Reed wrote to Augustine Jones expressing regret at his inability to attend an alumni dinner in Boston, especially as Professor Smyth was to be present. "There would," he wrote, "be a fine opportunity to repay to him two bad quarters of an hour he gave me because I staggered a little at a point or two in Westminster Shorter. Then I didn't quite dare to declare the whole counsel of the Lord, but I might now." When this epistle was read at the dinner Professor Smyth was equal to the occasion with the apposite remark: "I am very glad to learn that in Washington they know the whole counsel of the gods. That is farther than we have gone on Andover Hill."

Reed had been well prepared in the Portland High School and this fact, combined with his natural ability, enabled him to make a fairly creditable record in his first years in college without undue exertion. He was, in fact, frequently regarded as indolent and careless, but his failure to secure a place in the list of distinguished scholars in the junior class is said by his friends to have been a humiliation which brought about a decided change in his last year. He had, however, been reading widely and incessantly in the college library and testimony is unanimous that his personal habits, then as throughout his life, were irreproachable. In later years he recalled that as an undergraduate he had read *Amadis of Gaul*, old English romances, and queer, out-of-the-way volumes which seldom came within the student purview. "When I was at college I was an omnivorous reader. I read every style of literature." [1]

His funds were always scanty and while his father was able

---

[1] "What Statesmen Read," a symposium to which Reed, Ingalls, Allison and other prominent men contributed, Washington *Post*, June 3, 1888.

to give him some small assistance it was entirely inadequate. The struggle became harder, but he was able in his later years to invest it with a humorous aspect. "I managed to get through the first two years at Bowdoin by doing odd jobs here and there, and not eating any more than the student's allowance advised by Horace, 'a bit of something and plenty of fresh air.' " Toward junior year, he continues, finding that his college yell was growing faint, he said to himself, " 'Tom, you are not getting enough to eat. You must get regular meals!' So I went to work teaching. I taught the village school, and so I got along until the senior year, when I suddenly discovered that I was going to stand so low in my class at graduation that I might not graduate at all, so I dropped every other thought than that of study. I worked early and late, and I wrote a graduating essay with tears of fearful brine and drops of heart blood. It was on 'The Fear of Death,' and I almost dropped dead when I got the prize for it. It was in the form of an oration." [1] His resources had, as a matter of fact, given out completely at the end of junior year and he was enabled to complete his course only by means of a loan from Senator Fessenden. Later on he repaid this sum, clearing off the last of his indebtedness while assistant paymaster in the navy.[2]

Reed's commencement oration seems to have disappeared and repeated searches in subsequent years have failed to trace it. One production of his undergraduate days, however, has survived. In the *University Quarterly,* a publication dealing with college affairs in general, which appeared for a few years and was apparently snuffed out by the outbreak of the Civil War, the names of Thomas B. Reed and Samuel Fessenden are found in the list of contributors. For the April number in 1860, Reed wrote the story of "The May Training," dealing with an episode

[1] Quoted, Lewiston *Journal,* December 8, 1902.
[2] McCall, *Reed,* 23.

in the earlier history of the college, when, under the Maine militia law of 1836, the students were required to train.

The story of what followed the enactment of this law is well told and through it all runs a strain of irony and satire which is reminiscent of his later work. "Our people must become citizen soldiery. It is the only safety for a free people, the only bulwark of our free institutions." There was commotion in college and irrefutable arguments were forthcoming against the requirement. "But it is a singular fact, that even irrefutable arguments do not always hold sway in this world, nor prevent warrants from coming." The selectmen were determined to do their duty "having an eye likewise to the fines." At last came the momentous training day and the student contingent marched to the mustering ground clad in uniforms and armor of all lands and ages, armed with "claymores, cimeters, poleaxes, scythes, brooms, bayonets, spears, case knives and saws," headed by a squalling band and bearing a banner with the strange device of a gorgeously uniformed officer riding a hog. He goes on to describe the scene which followed and concludes: "Of its consequences, it suffices to say that it was the prime cause of that utter contempt into which general musters soon sank within the bounds of Maine."

Reed led his class during his senior year. He made a record so remarkable that it did much to offset the less satisfactory work of his earlier years and gave him fifth place in the graduating class. He received the degree of bachelor of arts on August 1, 1860. Next day he was elected to Phi Beta Kappa. President Nathan Lord of Dartmouth, a graduate of Bowdoin in the class of 1809, delivered an oration before the society on "the responsibility which Christianity imposes on educated men," and Reed's college days were over.

Thirty years later, in the midst of the great contest in the 51st Congress, he returned to receive the honorary degree of

PORTLAND DURING REED'S BOYHOOD

Doctor of Laws. He retained an interest in the college affairs, attended alumni gatherings, and delivered his last important public address at the centennial of 1902. Unlike George Evans, William Pitt Fessenden, Melville W. Fuller, William P. Frye, and other graduates of Bowdoin eminent in public life, he never served on its governing boards, and he was not a frequent visitor in Brunswick. "It is the heavy sadness that comes," he said at the Washington alumni dinner in 1898, "that makes my visits so rare. Joe and Bill and Charlie are gone, and the river, the hill, the pines and the bridge at Maquoit are too lonesome."

He had now abandoned all thought of the ministry. His name appears on the roll of the college "Praying Circle," but as his mind matured he found himself unable to accept many of the ordinary tenets of belief. A letter to his former pastor, February 3, 1863,[1] shows that his mind was of the rationalistic type which cannot accept many of the ordinary doctrines of the Christian Church. It is probably true, as Symonds pointed out, that "whatever changes of intellectual belief may have occurred later," Reed's early religious experience "was not without lasting effect upon his character, and what was vital in it retained its hold upon his mind and character." Francis E. Clark in later years noted the absence of anything "flippant, cynical, or skeptical" in his attitude toward religious matters. Political opponents, however, distorted the story of his connection with the State Street Church and circulated the report that he had been "excommunicated."

After graduation, Reed spent five years in a variety of places and pursuits. He taught school for a year at Portland, and began the study of law, but in 1861 went to California, where at Stockton he taught for a few months, and at San José continued his preparation for the bar. How he escaped the impulse of patriotism and adventure which sent so many of his college friends and classmates into the army will probably never be

[1] McCall, *Reed,* 27.

known. His California experience seems to have been unsatisfactory. He has left on record his disapproval of the California climate and inhabitants and his belief that "nature never intended any man to live there, only to dig gold and get himself out of it; and to shudder in dreams ever afterwards." California was still in the pioneer stage, although he observed the perennial tendency of its inhabitants to rave about the climate and the greatness of the country, and Reed was a Yankee. He belonged in New England of shady streets, white houses and green shutters, law, order, and social stability. It is interesting to note how much of his later pungency of statement went into the account which he wrote of the Pacific Coast while there:

Everyone praises the climate. Now I am forced, though reluctantly, to admit that the climate is not so bad. To smoke the pipe of peace in the midst of January weather is certainly comforting. But I have noticed that while all Californians are gratifyingly unanimous in chanting the glories of the climate of the Pacific slope in general, each one refreshes himself by cursing in particular the spot which the wrath of God has condemned him to help populate. The programme of the weather during the summer months is as regular as the rascality of the stockbrokers. In the morning about ten o'clock the heat is tempered by a wind which sets in from the ocean. Alone, by itself, this would be grateful. But it is fated that all pleasant things should have their compensations. And, as it is, this refreshing breeze serves to fill the air with clouds of blinding dust. . . . In the interior the mornings are pleasant but the afternoons most intolerably hot, giving one a lifelike idea of the feelings of a wet rag. The dust lies foot-deep all summer long. What clothes you wear is a matter of sublime indifference; for a half-mile walk makes black and white all one color. . . . In the winter the rain falls in torrents till the whole State is one vast sea of mud.[1]

He was admitted to the bar at San José on September 8, 1863, being examined by the eminent lawyer William P. Wallace.

[1] McCall, *Reed,* 33.

When Reed, in answer to a question, declared that he thought the Legal Tender Act constitutional, Wallace remarked that another candidate that morning had asserted that it was not. "We will recommend you both favorably," he said, "as we think that all young men who can answer great constitutional questions off-hand ought to be admitted to the bar." Reed returned to Maine soon afterwards, making the long voyage in the steerage. He later recalled that for the first and only time in his life he suffered a violent attack of sea-sickness as the vessel neared Portland harbor. He resumed the study of law in Portland in the office of Howard and Strout, but in April, 1864, joined the navy.

He was appointed acting assistant paymaster on the recommendation of Senator Fessenden and served until honorably discharged late in 1865. The greater part of this service was on the gunboat *Sybil* on the Mississippi and Tennessee Rivers; "level water and the most delightful time of my life," as he described it twenty years later.[1] A "war record," Union or Confederate, was to be an important element—perhaps a liability in the second instance at least—in the political life of the next forty years, but Reed with his eminent good sense refused to take his own at all seriously. "Tell them I kept a grocery on a gunboat down in Louisiana in wartime," he told one of his supporters who called his attention to the fact that the war services of McKinley, Henderson and Grosvenor were being played up by his opponents during the canvass for the speakership in 1889. "The gentleman need not be the least afraid," he once retorted to an ex-Confederate member in course of debate on American shipping and naval construction, "I never was under fire any more than he was; I was as safe during the war as he himself." [2]

[1] McCall, *Reed*, 31.
[2] *Cong. Record*, 47 Cong., 2 Sess., 1026.

REED returned to Portland in the fall of 1865, and like thousands of other young officers after demobilization, had little to show in a material way for the preceding four years. He had, however, seen a great deal of the country, had increased his knowledge of men and affairs, and was out of debt. His law studies had been repeatedly interrupted, but the requirements for admission to the bar at that time were far from exacting.

He was admitted to the Maine bar in October, 1865, and began practice in Portland. Competition was keen and like other young lawyers he began practice with the usual petty civil and criminal business. In 1867, however, a professional friend and associate named Nathan Webb, then county attorney and afterwards United States District Judge, secured his nomination as representative in the legislature. The story goes that Webb acted in the caucus without Reed's knowledge and had to exert all his persuasive powers to induce the candidate to accept, at last convincing him that practical political and legislative experience would be of great professional advantage to a young lawyer, a view which Reed himself repeatedly indorsed in later life. The Republicans controlled Portland; his election followed as a matter of course, and he was reëlected in 1868. In 1869 he was chosen senator from Cumberland County.

Not long before Reed's death Josiah H. Drummond, a prominent lawyer and party leader of Maine, giving some of his recollections of this period remarked of Reed's legislative service: "In my judgment, and I had an opportunity to observe him while a member of the House, he then showed all the great qualities for which he is now distinguished." [1] While there is

[1] Quoted in *Eastern Argus,* December 8, 1902.

always a tendency to estimate the earlier career of a statesman in the light of subsequent success, there is considerable evidence to support Drummond's statement.

Throughout his three legislative terms Reed served on the Joint Standing Committee on the Judiciary, his selection to this post in the first instance being a distinct compliment to the young lawyer. Debates were seldom reported and while the *Kennebec Journal* on January 15, 1869, offered to publish the remarks of any member who would pay the cost of setting the type, few seem to have availed themselves of the privilege.

One of the great events of his legislative service was the contest in 1869 between Hannibal Hamlin and Lot M. Morrill for the United States senatorship, which in view of the overwhelming Republican strength in the legislature was dependent on the result of the nomination in the party caucus. Reed supported Morrill and made what was probably his first speech on a question of parliamentary law by assailing the validity of the blank ballot which finally broke a tie and gave Hamlin the nomination by a vote of 75 to 74.[1]

During this same term, the subject of capital punishment was arousing great interest throughout the State, due to the fact that, after a long period when the infliction of the death penalty had been in abeyance, it was to be revived in the case of an especially atrocious offender. There were sundry legal technicalities involved, and in February Reed introduced a bill, brief but comprehensive, abolishing the death penalty in the future and by a retroactive clause forbidding the Governor to issue his warrant for the execution of criminals already sentenced. "Mr. Reed's well known ability and acknowledged influence," said the Portland *Press,* which was urging abolition, "afford gratifying assurance that the matter will be pushed with the vigor that its great importance demands."

[1] C. E. Hamlin, *The Life and Times of Hannibal Hamlin,* 518.

Reed spoke at considerable length in support of his bill on February 19, 1869, pointing out that for thirty years the governors had construed the statute in such a way that this punishment had been practically abolished. Why should it be revived? It was an unsatisfactory penalty because of the uncertainty of its infliction, and this uncertainty greatly reduced its value as a deterrent, all experience going to show that certainty rather than severity of punishment was most effective. Juries were seldom willing to follow the laws of the Old Testament. "You do not hold up before the murderer the certainty of death; you hold up only the chances of death, dependent upon the thousand contingencies of detection, trial and conviction." The most interesting feature of this speech, however, was the vigor with which he condemned the resolutions of a ministerial association of his own county which had upheld capital punishment as "consonant with the revealed will of God." For a rising young politician in 1869 to attack the utterances of such a body and to declare that "God's laws as given by Moses were given to conform to the situation of the people at that time," showed courage and independence.[1] The bill failed, however, as did another of Reed's measures, a bill permitting the organization of railroad corporations without special acts of the legislature.

An editorial in the Portland *Press*, March 15, 1869, discussing the services of the local delegation during the recent session, offers some significant comments on Reed. They could be applied almost without alteration to his services in the 47th Congress twelve years later, when for the first time in his congressional career the Republicans were in control of the House:

Mr. Reed's second term has more than satisfied the warmest anticipations of his friends. His position has been in several respects a trying one. He is one of the youngest members of the

[1] Portland *Press*, February 26, 1869, contains speech in full.

House, and at the same time the actual though not the nominal leader of that body. Besides, his views are several decades in advance of those of the majority of the members on several of the most important topics that came before the House for consideration. But his readiness and skill in debate, his solid legal acquirements and general culture together with his strong personal influence have given him beyond controversy the leading position which we have assigned to him.

While in the State senate he vigorously opposed an act authorizing the city of Portland to help construct the Portland and Rutland Railroad, and on March 15, 1870, secured its indefinite postponement. His course was consistent with the attitude which he maintained on the relations of government and private business throughout his career. On January 14, 1870, he presented a resolution in commemoration of Senator William Pitt Fessenden, whose death had occurred on September 9, 1869. The great senator, whose services during the Civil War had been of inestimable importance, and whose report as chairman of the Joint Committee on Reconstruction is one of the great state papers of American history, had closed his career with an act of courage and fidelity to principle which posterity has regarded as one of the few creditable incidents in the disreputable post war era. His vote of "not guilty" at the conclusion of the impeachment trial of President Johnson had aroused a tremendous storm of disapproval in his own State, but his death occurred before there was an opportunity to submit the matter to the test of another reëlection to the Senate. Reed had defended Fessenden's course, as might be expected in view of his personal relations with the senator and his family, and his own views that judicial questions should be settled on the basis, not of politics, but of the law and the evidence. In his brief speech in support of the resolution there was much that might, more than thirty years later, have been said of his own career:

Here were the scenes of his earlier triumphs. . . . It was
here that he first showed those great qualities that made him in
that large arena as easily without a superior as he was among
us without a peer.

If the high positions he filled and the deeds he did, do not
preserve him much longer than most men from the oblivion
which sooner or later awaits the mightiest, it will be because
he always preferred to fame the consciousness within himself
of doing with all his might what his hands found to do for the
safety and stability of his country. . . .

He was tried on many critical occasions and was equal to all,
and at last crowned a long life of service by steadfastly enduring, for what he thought right, the reproach of friends and the
praise of foes. The example of his stainless character and of the
steady courage with which he met obloquy for the sake of conviction, in its effects upon the lives of those who will come
after him, will carry his influence and power to centuries which
his name may never reach.[1]

Reed's legislative services in Maine ended with the session
of 1870. The Republican caucus on January 5 nominated him
for the office of attorney-general, one of the unsuccessful candidates, in a motion to make the nomination unanimous, describing him as "a gentleman who will see that the laws which we
may pass are faithfully and impartially executed, tempering the
stern requirements of justice with the utmost degree of mercy
which a due regard to his official obligations will permit." His
election followed as a matter of course a few days later, but his
official duties did not begin until after the session closed.

The floor experience of three legislative sessions, together
with the active party work involved, must have been invaluable
for a politically ambitious man. Unfortunately, the sessions were
brief; there was a dearth of constructive legislation; and the
journals show that much of Reed's activity consisted merely in

---

[1] Portland *Press*, January 17, 1870.

reporting amendments—frequently technical—to the existing statutes. Twenty years later, defending the revolutionary changes which he had brought about in congressional procedure, he declared that the greatest service of his early days in the Maine legislature was securing the passage of a bill improving the organization of the courts of Cumberland County, greatly reducing the time necessary for bringing cases to final adjudication. In both instances, he declared, the motive was the same, the efficient transaction of public business.

It was during this session that on February 5, 1870, he married Mrs. Susan P. Jones, oldest daughter of the Rev. S. H. Merrill, a prominent Congregationalist clergyman of Portland. Mrs. Reed was a woman of great tact, kindliness, and general good sense. In later years she proved able to meet the exacting responsibilities of an important place in Washington society, although the Reeds, unlike the Blaines, restricted their social activities to the necessary minimum. As a member of Congress, Reed never had the financial means necessary to maintain a place in the fashionable life of the national capital, and unlike some of his contemporaries, he scorned the expedients by which such funds were easily procurable. Their restricted means and plain living, however, were apparently never seriously felt by either husband or wife. During his long service in Washington Reed never acquired a permanent residential property in that city. He eventually purchased a comfortable home in the beautiful and much-loved city of Portland, and it was here that his social life and home interests really centered.

Reed held the office of attorney-general for three years and when defeated for renomination in 1873 by General H. M. Plaisted, it was because precedent seemed to have set three years as the maximum term. "All those who opposed him," said the Bangor *Whig and Courier*, "not only admit his faithfulness and ability but have frankly said he was an excellent officer." While the annual salary was only one thousand dollars, the position carried a pleasant amount of prestige and the fact that he was barely thirty years of age when he was elected is further evidence that his ability impressed his contemporaries in the legislature.

During his first months in office Reed came before the public in the most sensational prosecution of his entire three years' service, that of *The State vs. Edward H. Hoswell* for the murder of John B. Laflin at Hallowell. Though the case was intrinsically less significant than several others in which he represented the State, the fact that the crime grew out of an illicit love affair aroused extraordinary interest. "All the parties immediately concerned in the tragedy," said the *Kennebec Journal* in an editorial of December 8, 1870, "were obscure persons known only to a small circle and in humble circumstances," but, it continued, its similarity to the famous trials of Sickles, Cole, and McFarland, still fresh in the public mind, served to draw the interest of the entire State. In the absence of a scandal in high life, the itinerant mill hand, his erring wife and the village barber furnished a reasonably satisfactory substitute.

Reed's summation of the State's case had one characteristic note. After analyzing the evidence carefully, he turned to the arguments of the lawyer for the defense. "Now, while all this Scripture was being read to you, I make no doubt that it may have occurred to you that Brother Pillsbury was a man more given to searching the Scriptures than you had supposed before. This is not the first time that the livery of Heaven has been 'stolen to serve the devil in.' On the pages of a report of the Sickles trial, I find all the Scripture authorities that have been cited in this case." He then proceeded to demolish the doctrine of the Sickles case that a wronged husband had the right to take the law into his own hands. Judge Charles W. Walton charged the jury that the cases of Sickles, Cole, and McFarland owed their notoriety to the fact that they were decided wrongly and "intelligent and honest juries should know them to shun them." The jury returned a verdict "guilty of manslaughter," and the defendant was sentenced to nine years in the penitentiary.

The murderer Hoswell was, apparently, a most unpleasant person, and his character gained nothing in attractiveness under Reed's cross examination. His technique, furthermore, had been decidedly defective, for although possessing a Colt revolver of potent caliber he had used a knife on the guilty pair—used it vigorously, repeatedly and indiscriminately—and the American jury has always shown a decided predilection for the use of firearms in such affairs. Nevertheless, although Reed had asked for a verdict of first degree murder, the result was generally regarded as an unusual success for a prosecuting officer.

Of greater importance in Reed's career was his suit on behalf of the State against the sureties of Benjamin D. Peck, a former treasurer of the State who had defaulted to a considerable amount. The bond was dated January 28, 1858, but although the defalcation had occurred not long after, no action had yet been taken, apparently because political pressure had been brought to bear in the proper quarters. Reed pushed the case vigorously, secured judgments against the bondsmen to the amount of almost forty thousand dollars, and saw the judgments upheld by the Supreme Court. One of the bondsmen was Neal Dow and this move was a somewhat striking instance of political temerity. In later years when Reed became involved in a protracted feud with Frederick N. Dow, the trouble was attributed by many to his action as attorney-general against the father. There were other factors involved in this quarrel, but in any case it illustrates the courage and independence displayed in undertaking a suit against one of the powerful figures in his own party.

In 1871, in obedience to the requirements of an earlier statute, he commenced an action against the Portland and Kennebec Railroad Company under a writ of *quo warranto* to test the validity of its consolidation with the Maine Central. The case was dismissed the following year when the legislature recognized the validity of the lease, but the suit has some interest in view of the fact that in 1894, when railroad pooling had become a national issue, Reed declared that his action against the Portland and Kennebec had been a mistake and that Maine had found it much more advantageous to have a united system, furnishing adequate facilities, than two or three rival railroads cutting each other's throats. "I opposed the consolidation, having at the time certain ideas on the subject which are now quite prevalent in this House, but I watched the result, and I found that the combination, instead of turning out to the public disadvantage, resulted in better stations, better trains, better transportation facilities of every kind." These later views, after a vast amount of costly—at times ruinous—legislative and administrative experiment, have apparently become the basis of our national transportation policy.

Reed could not write anything dull and his reports as attorney-general, with their pungency of statement and wholesome common sense, are interesting reading. The Hoswell case had drawn forcible attention to the fact that under the laws of Maine a wife was unable to give evidence against her husband. Hoswell had had his own way as far as direct testimony was concerned, inasmuch as he had killed the only other witness, and his objection was sufficient to prevent his wife offering her evidence when she attempted to testify. The recurrence of such a situation should, Reed argued, be prevented. He also pointed out the urgent need of reform in the system of bail bonds, and recommended that the State be given a greater number of peremptory challenges in the selection of jurors.

He took up the matter of the testimony of husband and wife at still greater length in his second annual report. "The result of the trial of any cause where the facts are disputed, necessarily depends upon the evidence presented. Evidence, for the most part, is derived from individuals cognizant of the facts. If then we know that any individual is cognizant of facts bearing on the cause, and refuse to inquire of him when there is no sufficient reason for such refusal, we are liable not to get at the truth and consequently to do injustice. The unmistakable tendency of modern legislation has been towards the admission of all classes of persons as witnesses." His comment on a decision of the Supreme Court of Massachusetts, where under the same rule the wronged husband was held incompetent as a witness because his testimony would implicate his own wife, has the characteristic Reed touch. "Of course this was done to preserve his domestic felicity. It may look like an extreme measure for that purpose, but it was an extreme case. When a man has caught his wife in the act of adultery, his domestic harmony does seem to need all the protection it can get. This was the gratifying result in that State, where a law-abiding citizen, instead of shooting the adulterer, as has been the fashion of late years, appealed to the court for justice."

The Maine legislature, as many another prosecuting officer has found, was not greatly interested in the more efficient ad-ministration of criminal justice, and Reed reverted to the sub-ject in his final report. "These suggestions have met with an opposition which was anticipated. As the legislature is consti-tuted members naturally turn to the lawyers of the House and Senate when any change of law is suggested, and feel disposed to accept their views. Unfortunately prosecuting officers are excluded by their office from membership, while the lawyers who are members, having to do with criminal law only in the

way of defending criminals, are insensibly biased against anything which tends to render the punishment of their clients more
certain."

In the same report he urged an amendment of the statute
authorizing the recovery by indictment of not more than $5000
by the dependents of a person losing his life through the negli-
gence of a railroad company. "There is no reason in the world
why the State should concern itself with a private injury, further
than to provide the parties with a remedy. The present system
tends to embarrass what is really an action for damages, with all
the technicalities of the criminal law. . . . The remedy which
ought to be provided is an action on the case by the executor or
administrator of the deceased, and the amount of damages left
with the jury as in cases of injury not fatal. With the damages
for loss of life limited to five thousand dollars, it will be frequently cheaper for the railroad company to kill a man than to
hurt him."

Although the recommendations of the attorney-general did
not become law immediately, most of them eventually found
their way into the statutes of Maine. They are worth consideration, showing as they do his realization of the true objectives of
law and rules of procedure and his impatience with forms which
had outlived all practical usefulness. These same traits were
much in evidence during his protracted contest for the reform
of congressional procedure.

On retirement from office he resumed practice in Portland,
his success as chief law officer of the State having considerably
increased his personal business. He was an able attorney and is
described by those who knew him at this period of his career as
"assiduously devoted to any branch of the law that interested
him, but not prone to take up subjects as to which he had not
been thoroughly aroused." He was furthermore "a hard hitter,
who gave sledge-hammer blows and cared little for the science

of fencing . . . always a student of literature as well as of law . . . thoroughly honest in his instincts . . . somewhat intolerant of the ordinary artifices of the profession. His method was to master the crucial point of his case. He troubled himself little about the minor questions. . . . His forte was in the trial court, where his wit and readiness were of especial effect in the cross examination of witnesses, and where, when his feelings were aroused by sympathy or by attempted wrong, he was mighty in his wrath and fierce in his sarcasm and invective." [1]

For three years, 1873–76, he served as city solicitor of Portland, but his reports do not disclose any important litigation in that capacity. He defended the interests of the city in personal injury suits, and engaged in condemnation proceedings and similar routine business. In ten jury trials during his term of service, growing out of suits relating to defective highways, there were, he pointed out in his final report, only three verdicts against the city, and two of these were for very small amounts. The same report covering the official year to March, 1877, states that "the number of cases left on the docket is smaller than for very many years."

Before this final report was made Reed had been nominated and elected to the 45th Congress. He owed his nomination in large part to a disagreement between John H. Burleigh, then representing the First District, and the Blaine-Hamlin organization which completely dominated the Maine Republicans. Burleigh had made enemies by exposing corruption in the Kittery navy yard and was reported to have quarreled with these senators over questions of patronage. Reed was an organization man, popular and respected throughout the district, well known

[1] Quoted by Thomas H. Hubbard, "Memorial of Thomas Brackett Reed," *Annual Report of the Association of the Bar of the City of New York*, 1904. Hubbard was a graduate of Bowdoin in 1857 and long a friend of Mr. Reed.

on the stump, and confident of his ability to secure the nomination.

He also had the backing of a group of vigorous and enthusiastic young associates, among them his classmate Amos L. Allen. A circular distributed in Portland just before the caucuses in that city urged his nomination because "he is able, honest, fearless, and if in Congress would have something of the influence that the member of the district had in the days of Fessenden. They invite your aid because Mr. Burleigh, by his money and the control of Federal offices, is doing his utmost to carry the district against the will of the people. The friends of Mr. Reed have no money to expend for votes, and no offices to promise to active workers."

Reed carried the Portland caucuses by a handsome majority but in the district convention the contest was close and exciting. There had been considerable rivalry between its component counties, York and Cumberland, and Burleigh as a resident of York had strong local support. When Reed won the nomination on June 29, 1876, by a narrow majority there were threats of a bolt. His supporters, however, pointed out that Cumberland had 82,000 people as against York's 60,000 and yet in the past twenty years the Republican congressional nominations had been evenly divided between the two. Early in July, the recalcitrants held a meeting at Biddeford and later in the month an anti-Reed address was printed and circulated, urging opposition to the nominee. The claims of York County were set forth at length, "outside interference" in the canvass was denounced, and the Blaine-Hamlin machine was charged with a desire to dictate the affairs of the state. The fifth count in this indictment, attacking the methods by which the nomination had been secured, stated that "the nominee of the Portland convention has spent much of his time for the last two years in undignified solicitation of personal influence to secure this nomination. . . . He has deplored

BOWDOIN COLLEGE IN 1860

Mr. Burleigh's lack of influence in Congress and pointed to himself as the intellectual Goliath who would make Maine the envy of all her sister states. . . ."

As for the circular distributed by Reed's friends, "its truthfulness is on a level with its impudence." Then followed some comment and prediction which are admirable illustrations of the stupidity of partisanship and the danger of political prophecy:

We believe that the First District, with its population of 150,000, its valuation of about 75 millions, with its large manufacturing interests, its extensive shipping and the chief commercial city of the State, should be represented in Congress by a man of intelligence, ability and influence. Mr. Reed is not such a man. He is not a Fessenden, and never will be, let his friends boost him ever so hard. He is a comparatively young man, with but limited experience. He is not directly connected with either of the great business interests of the district. In his own profession he does not stand preëminent. . . . He is not the leader we need in these days of dismay and disaster, when incompetency and dishonesty have brought country and party both to the brink of ruin.[1]

Two minor incidents in this campaign should be mentioned. Reed's friends felt it desirable to publish a circular addressed to "the temperance men of the Republican party" declaring the candidate sound and orthodox on the questions of temperance and prohibition. When the *Eastern Argus* published an editorial on September 5, denouncing Robert G. Ingersoll, then campaigning on Reed's behalf, for his ridicule of the Bible, religion, and the church, and declaring that the candidate himself was understood to sympathize with, "if he does not fully concur with Ingersoll's opinions," the *Press*, Reed's chief journalistic supporter, felt obliged to contradict this charge, for on September 11, there appeared in blackface type: "The statement

[1] This address was printed in full in *Eastern Argus,* July 29, 1876.

that Thomas B. Reed is an atheist is an utter, baseless and wicked falsehood." It was a charge, however, which occasionally cropped up in his local campaigns for the next ten years.

Political campaigns still showed the influence of war psychology. In this district, as in most others throughout the North, there were thousands of voters who had served in the Union armies. It was easy for the campaign orator in a few words to evoke memories of the long blue columns toiling wearily along the dusty roads or through the Virginia mud, the crackling flash that ran along the stone fences on Marye's Heights, or the stench of the stockade at Andersonville. "Vote the way you shot" was a slogan calling for much less mental exertion than discussion of tariff, currency, and civil service reform. The Democratic party still suffered from its association with slavery, disloyalty and rebellion. Oliver P. Morton a few years earlier had described it as "a common sewer and loathsome receptacle into which is emptied every element of treason, North and South, and every element of inhumanity and barbarism which has dishonored the age." The Republicans, on the other hand, enjoyed eminent respectability throughout New England, and at one of Reed's campaign meetings Colonel Ingersoll, after describing the alleged attempts of the Confederates to introduce smallpox and yellow fever into New York City during the war, delivered himself of the following:

The Republican party depends upon reason, upon argument, upon education, upon intelligence and upon patriotism. The Republican party depends upon schools not upon brothels. It makes no appeal to ignorance or prejudice. It wishes to destroy both. It is the party of humanity, the party that hates caste, that honors labor, that rewards toil, that believes in justice. It appeals to all that is elevated and noble in man, to the higher instincts, to the nobler aspirations. . . . The horizon of the past is filled with the glory of Republican achievement. The monuments of its wisdom, its power and patriotism crowd all the fields of conflict.[1]

And the bulk of his hearers really believed it!

Conditions, however, were beginning to change in 1876. The abominations of Reconstruction, the gross maladministration under Grant, and the panic of 1873 had given the Democrats a majority in the lower branch of the 44th Congress, elected in 1874. The woes of the negro were beginning to pall on Northern audiences and many were inclined to ask if attacks on the Specie Resumption Act were not, after all, more significant from the practical standpoint than the Kansas-Nebraska Act or the Fugitive Slave Law, and whether the machinations of free traders and inflationists were not more menacing than those of the Knights of the Golden Circle or the Ku Klux Klan.

The Biddeford meeting had discussed the possibility of another convention and a second nomination. There was some talk by the dissenters of trading with the Democrats, but as the campaign progressed the rumblings of the dissatisfaction gradually subsided and on September 9, 1876, Reed was elected by a plurality of approximately 1000 in a total vote of over 30,000. In the course of the campaign an event in a neighboring county passed almost unnoticed, the appearance in Maine of the Greenback party, its first convention meeting at Paris Hill in August. The Greenback movement in this State was destined to have a decisive influence on the careers of many Maine politicians, and also to exercise no small influence on the course of national affairs.

When Reed won his seat in Congress, the exciting Hayes-Tilden campaign was nearing its close. The presidential election of 1876 is one of the great landmarks in American history. For four months the controversy over the returns absorbed public

[1] Portland *Press,* August 23, 1876.

attention. There were times when disaster seemed to loom near, but the final result, the seating of Rutherford B. Hayes, whatever the merits of the decision, meant the opening of a cleaner and more wholesome era in American politics. The Democrats had again won control of the House of Representatives. It is interesting to remember that William McKinley, with whose career Reed's was destined to be so closely involved, was also elected in this year for his first term in Congress. The Maine attorney, thirty-seven years of age, was now to enter a larger arena.

THE 45th Congress met in special session on October 15, 1877, and Reed for the first time took his place in the great hall where he was soon to become a powerful, and eventually a dominating, influence. The House of Representatives pays scant attention to the newcomer. The principle of rotation in office and the ordinary uncertainties of State and district politics have always tended to shorten the average term of service, and these influences were even more potent in the last three decades of the nineteenth century than in our own day. The natural result has been to place on the incoming member the burden of proving that he is entitled to a hearing ere an ungrateful constituency consigns him again to private life.

Success at the bar, on the stump, or in executive office furnishes no indication of probable success on the floor of a great legislative assembly, a fact which biographers and historians have often pointed out with respect to the House of Commons and which is equally true of its American counterpart. "Distinction won in other fields of endeavor will gain a man a hearing for the first time, but not afterward," Reed himself wrote in later years, with the experience of more than twenty years of legislative activity behind him. "If he wishes to talk and be listened to, he had better have something to say and know how to say it. Most men are not listened to."

While seniority has always been a potent factor in carrying long-service members into places of real power and responsibility in the House organization, and while Reed and his Maine colleagues, Nelson Dingley, Seth L. Milliken and Charles A. Boutelle—to say nothing of Senators Frye and Hale—represented constituencies which believed in rewarding faithful servants with repeated terms in Washington, until even New York and Pennsylvania cast envious eyes at the authority wielded by the little delegation from the Pine Tree State, nevertheless, Garfield's dictum is probably true that "there is no place where a man finds his true level so certainly and so speedily as in the House of Representatives."

Reed had the advantage of beginning his congressional service at one of the turning points in American history. The inauguration of President Hayes brought to an end both the more flagrant abuses of Reconstruction and much of the corruption and maladministration which had characterized the Federal government during the preceding eight years. The Southern question was pushed into the background, and as leading issues of the day prosaic matters of political economy rapidly replaced exciting speculations on the rights of man, the nature of the Union, and the penalties of rebellion.

It was not a smooth, imperceptible transition. President Hayes was savagely assailed for his conciliatory policy, alike by those who honestly believed with Senator George F. Edmunds that the Reconstruction measures "were not measures of cruelty or tyranny, but of justice and hopefulness," and by those fishers in troubled waters who realized the infinite possibilities of personal and party advantage in a continuance of the corruption and demoralization of the South. There is something naïve in the lamentations of Wendell Phillips over the Republican party's betrayal of the negro, and its failure to divert attention from "material questions" like the Greenback issue, by keeping the Southern question to the fore.[1]

Away from the political scene in Washington, and often unperceived by the leading actors there, however, the mighty forces of social and economic change were at work. Banking and currency, tariff and taxation, public regulation and control of

[1] "The Outlook," *North American Review,* July–August, 1878.

private business and the promotion of governmental efficiency, products of rapidly increasing population and steadily growing industrialism, were to be the leading issues of ensuing decades. It was with such questions that Reed's public career was largely concerned, and in the development of congressional methods and procedure his work was destined to have results which are likely to endure as long as the House of Representatives itself. While he had little liking for the South and scant respect for Southern statesmanship in general, sentiments which occasionally found brief utterance in blistering sarcasm and contempt, he seldom indulged in waving the bloody shirt. But if he did not tend the fires of sectional hatred with the assiduity of many of his Republican associates, he was nevertheless profoundly influenced by those doctrines of liberty and the rights of man which figured so largely in the political philosophy of his early years in public service. "We want to forget about the rebellion," he once remarked in the course of debate on a Southern claim bill, "but we do not want to be called upon every day in the week, not to forget but to forgive." Furthermore, he added, he was becoming very weary of "discussions of the great and fine traits of generals who deserted their country in its hour of peril." [1]

He had hardly begun his first term when the rise of the Greenback party, a political phenomenon which helps to demonstrate Maine's long-standing kinship to the economic frontier with its radicalism and agrarian unrest, threatened to deprive him of his seat. When the voters of a respectable New England State suddenly deserted the faith for the strange gods of inflation and fiat money, as did those of Maine from 1877 to 1880, it was obvious that the shibboleths of Civil War days had begun

---

[1] *Cong. Record,* 46 Cong., 3 Sess., 1019, Cf. his statement that "The South is an intolerant country . . . ! They don't stop to argue with a man there. If they don't agree with him they simply shoot the top of his head off. . . . We are as much ahead of them as we are ahead of the Pilgrim fathers." Campaign speech at Auburn, Me., August 4, 1880, Portland *Press,* August 5, 1880.

to lose their potency. Reed was one of those who from the very beginning appreciated the importance of the change. His early rise to a position of influence in the Republican minority, however, was due, as will presently be seen, aside from his inherent talents and his ability in debate, to his prominence in discussing two issues before this Congress which were indisputably products of war and reconstruction.

Reed's congressional career began in a thoroughly conventional manner. He presented a few petitions and secured the passage of a bill authorizing the Secretary of the Treasury to issue a register and change the name of a schooner. He made a few remarks in support of a proposition to print the report of a monetary commission. He was appointed to the Committee on Territories, and soon after the opening of the regular session in December, to the Committee on Expenditures in the War Department, neither assignment offering any great opportunities. Years afterward, during his first term in the speakership, when an elderly Virginia member whimsically inquired why he, a life-long farmer, had been placed on the Committee on Revision of the Laws, Reed recalled his own experience. "Really," he replied, "I had so much worry in fixing up our own side that many Democrats had to be put on any committee that had room for one more man. During my first term in Congress I was placed on the Committee on Territories and I pledge you my word that I would not have known a Territory if I had met one on the Avenue." [1]

As the regular session advanced, however, Reed's name appears more frequently in the record. He was a born debater, and even at this early stage his brief remarks show that command of irony and sarcasm which was to make him famous. On January 10, 1878, when the Democratic floor leader, Fernando Wood of New York, still remembered for his proposal in 1861

[1] New York *Tribune*, February 2, 1890.

that New York be made a "free city" and for his coarse and vindictive attacks on President Lincoln, but an able and dangerous opponent in debate, was arguing for a secret investigation of certain departmental accounts, Reed secured the floor.

The House was not, he declared, "the grand inquest of the country" charged with investigating all the wickedness of the land, although the gentleman from New York seemed to have some special pet wickedness he was unwilling to have investigated. As for the secrecy of such investigations: "How secret all things are kept here in Washington! When the body at the other end of the Capitol has a secret session, how difficult it is for the community to become acquainted with their action therein!" During the last Congress, committees of investigation had actually competed with each other in furnishing the newspapers with scandalous stories about men and measures. Why, he asked in conclusion, should legislative business be neglected for investigations whose real objective was the accumulation of political capital for use against the other party? [1]

Later in the month he spoke briefly on behalf of Maine on the occasion of its presentation of the statue of William King to the nation. Like all his addresses on non-controversial topics, this speech was admirable both in form and taste. Its good qualities were the more evident in view of the fact that the recollection of King's services in the formative period of the State's history inspired Senator James G. Blaine, on the same occasion, to indulge in a somewhat tactless rattling of the Federalist skeleton in the Massachusetts closet, his comparison of the loyal spirit of Maine during the War of 1812 with the attitude of the parent State provoking considerable ill-natured controversy.

Reed's appearance in debate on the diplomatic appropriation bill, March 13, is of greater significance and his remarks indicate a point of view to which he adhered consistently throughout

[1] *Cong. Record,* 45 Cong., 2 Sess., 278.

his career. James H. Blount, of Georgia, had attacked an amendment increasing the salaries of certain ministers, with the somewhat novel argument that since improved communication would permit conduct of negotiations directly from Washington, the diplomatic service was of very questionable value to the country. "I would gladly see the time come," he added, "when we could get rid of nearly every diplomatic agent that we have. I would get rid of them because, in my judgment, we have no occasion for them; because it should be our determination not to imitate royalty in our method of administering the Government."

For this type of "hayseed statesmanship" and demagogy Reed had profound contempt. Again and again in the course of his career he ridiculed the prevalent tendency to starve essential services while wasting public funds on projects where political advantage was to be gained. His response on this occasion was prompt. More than half a century later it is still applicable to many aspects of American public service. "I apprehend," he said, "that while we are a great people, while we are a noble and magnificent people, yet there is some wisdom outside of the United States; and so long as we have a diplomatic corps . . . we ought to pay our ministers such salary as . . . will enable them to maintain themselves properly in the places to which we send them." The question of the style of living necessary in any position was a vital factor in determining what was a proper salary, and none but rich men could afford to accept posts in the diplomatic service. Persons invited to serve the government in foreign countries should be paid salaries sufficient to enable them to maintain themselves satisfactorily from the emoluments of their offices.

As Reed concluded, Otho R. Singleton, of Mississippi, with a temerity which grew less common as the Maine member became better known, rose to supply the interesting information that he could furnish enough first class gentlemen from his own State to fill all the places at the existing salaries. Reed promptly retorted that, judging by the supply of office seekers crowding around the door-keeper, the gentleman could supply candidates for all the offices in the country. "The Republican party," replied Mr. Singleton, "has inculcated the idea that people should live off the country." "It is too bad, Mr. Chairman," came the drawling reply, amid the delighted laughter of the minority members, "to charge us with corrupting the Democratic party."

The 45th Congress had convened in an atmosphere of suspicion and bitter prejudice generated by the protracted and critical dispute over the presidential election. The Republican press and politicians prophesied the dreadful calamities certain to be inflicted by another Democratic majority in the lower chamber. A renewed assault on the title of President Hayes, repudiation of the national debt, reckless inflation of the currency, and wholesale disbursements for the satisfaction of Southern war claims were among the bogeys held up to alarm the credulous. In the House itself, the atmosphere was far from conducive to important accomplishment. Reed always remembered the tension which prevailed throughout his first term. Everybody, he related long afterwards, suspected everybody else of cheating, and kept the peace largely through fear that a fight once begun would prove to be too big a one.

The House by its loose talk furnished somewhat inadequate justification for the fulminations of Republican alarmists, although its most dangerous act, the remonetization of silver in the Bland-Allison Act, marking the first success of the inflationists in what was to prove a twenty year contest for sound currency, attracted far less attention than it deserved. Reed, who was even then fighting for his political life against the Greenbackers of his own district, voted against this measure. A bill reimbursing William and Mary College for the loss of its main building during the war and the adoption of a resolution authorizing the investigation by a select committee of alleged frauds in the preceding presidential election, were sufficiently in line with Republican fears to attract widespread popular attention, and by his participation in these proceedings, Reed before the end of his first Congress acquired national prominence.

Reed's arraignment of the William and Mary bill was at once a magnificent piece of invective and a clear logical presentation of the legal principles involved in a proposal which had meritorious features and a wide sentimental appeal. By 1878 it was apparent that sectional bitterness was abating and conciliation was in the air. The old Southern college was well known and appreciated throughout the country. It had contributed much to the intellectual life of the nation. The destruction had been unauthorized by Union commanders and was merely one of the cruel and untoward incidents likely to happen in any battle area. Sponsors of the measure claimed the indorsement of eminent Union generals and leaders who could never be accused of partiality toward "rebels."

When the bill was debated on April 12, George B. Loring of Massachusetts spoke eloquently on its behalf. Technical considerations ought not to be weighed in a matter of this kind, he argued: "If an unwritten law of broad humanity and generous sympathy for those institutions which elevate and refine and ennoble society is applicable anywhere it is in a case like this." William and Mary College was a part of our national heritage. From its halls had come many of the nation's founders. "It is not for the property of Virginia but for a national monument that I speak; and when I ask that a structure whose name belongs to this illustrious roll shall be preserved by a national bounty, I am engaged in advocating no war claim for damages; I am occupied in considering no precedent; I am only calling on Congress to preserve the ancient landmarks of our national greatness and to restore the monuments around which our brightest memories cluster and at whose feet we renew our vows as citizens of a common country and heirs and defenders of a common inheritance of social equality and of civil and religious freedom."

To reply to such an address must have seemed an invidious undertaking, but Reed proved equal to the task. Expressing appreciation of the graces with which Loring had surrounded his subject, he pointed out that in view of its far-reaching consequences the measure was more important than any other before Congress at that session. It was not the first time it had been before Congress. The Committee on Claims had rejected it time and again. Today it appeared in the guise of charity. "But if you once pass it, tomorrow it will stare you in the face as a bill of rights for the whole list of Southern war claims."

Then, step by step, he proceeded to show "in the light of reason, not in the light of rhetoric," why such a proposal should be rejected "now and forever." "The greatest barrier in this world is use and wont. To say that a thing has never yet been done among men is to erect a barrier stronger than reason, stronger than discussion. Such a wall only pluck, perseverance, and, in most cases, only right can beat down. To say that we did the same thing yesterday is to strengthen the thing we want to do today. It appeals to our sense of fairness, reason, and justice. We say that if this was proper yesterday why not do it today, and the evil, of course, increases as you go on."

Establish the precedent that the nation is responsible for such war-time incidents, he reasoned, and the result will be the establishment of a principle which will make victory more disastrous to the Treasury than defeat. Precedents at that time established the contrary principle. William and Mary College had also suffered damages in 1776, and the trustees had unsuccessfully urged their claim for compensation "upon the same revolutionary fathers who did the injury and upon the statesmen who followed them, including, I have no doubt, Washington and Jefferson and Monroe, and the thirty judges of Virginia, the twenty-four admirals and other persons who have graduated from William and Mary."

Nobody, he went on, would ever be found ready to shoulder the responsibility for the consequences of such a measure while he was urging its passage, but consider the nature of some of the business before the House. "You can tell men's minds better by noticing what they are doing than by what they are saying." Look at the thousands of claim bills, ten per cent of them Southern claims arising from incidental damage during the war. Nobody will be interested in the arguments by which such a precedent is established, "while the decision will be sought for by every claim agent who loved the lost cause and a good many who did not." He closed with a word on the tendency of Southerners to provoke controversy by raiding the Treasury. "You were beaten and yet you want us to take the consequences. You come forward and insist that the victorious country shall pay for the damages inflicted upon it by its enemies." The business interests of the country, he added, would not allow such efforts to succeed, and the South owed a great deal of its liberties to the business men of the country.[1]

This speech, the best known among Reed's earlier congressional efforts, was the outstanding feature of the session and made a deep impression. On May 10, Mr. John Goode of Virginia, who had the bill in charge, announced that it would not be pressed during the current session. It came up again during the short session, when the statement of one of its supporters that the title would be changed to obviate the objection that it was a war claim drew from Reed the remark that "his friend was like the deacon who was a member of a temperance society, who said he could not drink cider, but if they would call it apple

[1] *Cong. Record,* 45 Cong., 2 Sess., 2488-90.

juice he would drink it. He says that hereafter he is going to be foremost in opposition to the payment of war claims. I tell him that the time to fight is when the battle is going on, and not after it is over." The bill was defeated in the House on January 10, 1879. Not until the 52nd Congress did the friends of the college finally secure compensation.

A more important event in Reed's career was his appointment, May 20, 1878, as a minority member of the select committee to investigate the alleged frauds in the presidential election. This committee was created by the House Democrats after an exciting four-day struggle. Clarkson N. Potter of New York, who had introduced the resolutions charging fraud and providing for investigation, was made chairman of the committee and with him were associated the ablest Democratic leaders. They were a group later described by Reed as "the bright, consummate flower, the cream, or to use a metaphor more suitable to the subject, the combined sweetness and strength, the very 'rock and rye' of the Democracy." The Republican members, besides Reed, were Benjamin F. Butler of Massachusetts, J. D. Cox of Ohio, and Frank Hiscock of New York. *The Nation* of May 23, 1878, described all the members, with the exception of Butler, as men of high character, the four Republicans being "an excellent representation of the party both as regards its honesty, acuteness and rascality." Butler was obviously the representative of the latter element. He was a shrewd, aggressive, resourceful man, but unfortunately for the Republicans he was no longer the Butler of the impeachment trial of 1868. He was already moving, by way of Greenbackism, toward the Democratic party, and his findings in this investigation, presented in an independent report, were distinctly favorable to the Tilden claims. The bulk of responsibility for the protection of the Republican interest fell on Reed and Hiscock, and more particularly upon Reed. Both performed invaluable service, and Reed secured a distinction which gave him a long start on the road to party leadership.

The lapse of more than half a century has failed to sweeten the unsavory story of the campaign of 1876, but the immediate conclusions of many contemporaries were to be considerably modified within the next three years. While the country had acquiesced in the decision of the Electoral Commission, to millions of people President Hayes was merely the beneficiary of a gigantic fraud. Even if there was no legal remedy available, even if his tenure were to remain undisturbed for the rest of his term, nevertheless—such was the confident expectation—in 1880 judgment would be rendered and fitting penalties inflicted on the Republican party. If resentment at Republican iniquity had reached such a height in 1876 that only extraordinary efforts, most of them bearing the suspicion of fraud and corruption, had sufficed to give their candidate a bare majority of one vote in the electoral college, the prospect of a decisive overturn seemed excellent. Business depression, the aftermath of the panic of 1873, was still causing serious distress. Republican solidarity was threatened by agrarian unrest. Greenbackism and similar heresies were making ominous progress.

That the party was able to rally after serious reverses in 1878 and carry the country two years later was due, apart from Democratic blunders, to the restoration of decent administration by President Hayes, to the revival of business which followed the resumption of specie payments in 1879, and to the effective dispersal of some of the clouds of doubt and legend which had already gathered about the election of 1876. In the latter process Reed played a most important part.

The returning boards of Louisiana, South Carolina, and Florida, it will be remembered, had rejected the returns of enough Democratic precincts where violence and intimidation were reported to have occurred to give the electoral vote to

WILLIAM P. FRYE

REDFIELD PROCTOR

Hayes. In Louisiana the board had unblushingly converted an apparent Democratic majority of more than six thousand into a Republican majority exceeding four thousand. That the returning boards had been shamelessly bought up, and that the reports of interference with negro voting were grossly exaggerated, were articles of Democratic faith which the party leaders actively propagated throughout the land. The work of the investigating committee covered both aspects of the question and, in addition, the vitally important matter of the "cipher telegrams," a long series of secret communications passing between party headquarters and various agents engaged in protecting the party interests in the disputed states. From the Republican standpoint, "protecting the party interests" involved sundry Democratic activities which could hardly bear the light of publicity, and it was the function of the minority investigators to turn that light upon them.

The political character of much of the investigation was of course quite evident. It was rough work. Persons appearing before the committee were bulldozed and harried. Questions were ingeniously framed so that the embarrassed witnesses might contribute a modicum of political capital to the other side. Innuendo seemed to have a recognized place in the proceedings. Reed spoke later of one Democratic member, the astute Mr. McMahon: "My friend from Ohio, keen and subtle, than whom there is no man in five kingdoms abler to dig a pit for a witness and sweetly coax him into it."

Reed's duties on the committee led him into an intensive examination of affairs in the parish of East Feliciana, La., where, as he afterwards stated in Congress, he found that a long series of murders and other crimes of violence occurring in the course of the canvass came to a sudden termination on election day, leaving the obvious conclusion that they had been primarily political in character; especially as Republicans were invariably the victims. As a result the Democrats had cast practically the entire vote.

The results of the investigation of Southern conditions, however, were far from decisive. They showed, it is true, that there had been plenty of Democratic intimidation, but also that the Republicans had made use of equally discreditable tactics. Fraudulent counting, destruction and falsification of reports, and bribery in various forms had flourished, the Hayes electors in many instances having been the beneficiaries. Reed, however, did much to demolish the lurid stories of one of the leading Democratic witnesses from Louisiana, James E. Anderson, whom he afterwards described with pardonable exaggeration as "the loftiest liar of historic Christendom." He led Anderson into a tangle of self-contradictions, and finally compelled him to admit that he had wilfully misled the Senate Committee before which he had given testimony.

In the matter of the cipher telegrams, moreover, the Republicans scored a success which may well have saved the day in 1880. A mass of telegrams had been subpoenaed from the Western Union, and part were found to be in a secret code. These were dispatches that had passed between Democratic leaders in New York and their agents in the South. As translated by two ingenious workers for the New York *Tribune,* they showed that the Democrats had been conducting negotiations in certain quarters apparently with a view to purchasing Louisiana for Tilden.

William T. Pelton, Tilden's nephew and a member of his Gramercy Park household, had handled a great deal of business for the party and many of the compromising telegrams had been sent or received by him. This disclosure was getting unpleasantly close to the man whom the party had been vociferously proclaiming the victim of a gigantic fraud. Pelton had been Tilden's military secretary at Albany; he was a poor man, who could obviously furnish nothing like the sums mentioned in the cipher messages. Reed was too shrewd a politician and too good a party strategist not to grasp the potentialities of the situation. What happened on the witness stand to the unfortunate Pelton—who denied that he had shown any of the incriminating messages to Tilden—together with the bearing of the disclosures on Tilden's claims and those of his party, and Reed's quality as an examiner, cannot be better shown than by a brief excerpt from the proceedings of February 6, 1879:

Q. Here is a telegram, numbered 3, in this pamphlet, page 25, addressed to Henry Havemeyer, and the reading in this translation is:

"Supposed you telegraphed me to come here. Did you? Board adjourned until tomorrow. Answer to question asked this morning important tonight. Where do you want you [me] to go, and when?"

Do you remember receiving a telegram of which that was the purport?—*A.* I do not remember—

Q. Please look at that dispatch. There is something to attract a gentleman's attention.

The Witness. Please let me finish my answer. I do not remember receiving that particular telegram, but I am certain that I received a telegram of that character.

Q. The only difference is, you say "character" where I say purport. Then you did receive a telegram of that character? Did you show that to your uncle?—*A.* No, sir; I don't remember about that.

Q. Don't remember?—*A.* No, sir. My own impression is about all these telegrams—

Q. Please confine yourself to my question. Did you show this telegram to your uncle?

The Witness. I was going to answer your question if you would allow me.

Mr. Reed. No, you were going off into generalities.

A. Well, I should say I did not show that to him.

Q. I suppose it was owing to that wicked sentence in it, "Answer to question asked this morning important tonight," that you did not show it to him?—*A.* Very likely.

Q. You understood that to refer to the immoral transaction which is suggested in number 1?—*A.* I understood it to refer to what is suggested there.

Q. You decline to commit yourself to the use of the term immoral?—*A.* I don't think it is best to discuss that.

Q. The telegram numbered 4 here is from you to Weed, and it says: "Telegram here. Remain with Hampton [i. e. in South Carolina] and exhaust every means to prevent trading. The expense [of] what you do will be met. Keep fully advised often." Did you send a telegram of that character?—*A.* I sent a telegram substantially like that, I suppose; I don't know how correctly it is translated.

Q. When you sent that telegram did you consult your uncle in regard to it?—*A.* No, sir.

Q. Was that on account of this wicked sentence, "The expense of what you do will be met"?—*A.* I did not consult him about any of these telegrams.

Mr. Reed. There you go off on generalities again.

The Witness. Well, it saves time to group them all together.

Mr. Reed. We don't want to save time at the expense of truth. Now, in the interest of truth, tell us what you did say in regard to that.

The Witness. You don't insist on putting that in?

Mr. Reed. Yes.

The Witness. Give me your question.

Q. Did your reluctance to consult your uncle in regard to that have its origin in the expression which you put into this telegram, "The expense of what you do will be met?"—*A.* I don't know that it did; it was not a matter that there was any necessity to consult him about.

Q. You felt that you could go on and buy a State or two without consulting him?—*A.* I never consulted him about such matters at all, sir.

.   .   .   .

Q. You consulted your uncle about innocent matters, didn't you?—*A.* I consulted him about general matters in the campaign.[1]

Soon after, Mr. Tilden appeared before the committee and in reply to Reed's searching questions, entered a general denial of any knowledge of the questionable or corrupt negotiations which had figured in the early testimony. His denials, however, could not dispel the suspicions which the examiners had already succeeded in raising in the minds of many voters of the country.

The committee, as is almost invariably the case in election contests, divided along political lines and the final reports were little more than campaign documents. The minority report, signed by Cox, Reed and Hiscock, contains one statement, the truth of which Reed had obviously been attempting to establish in course of the examination of Pelton. "The idea that this penniless man, Mr. Pelton, living in the house and seated at the very table of his wealthy uncle, Mr. Tilden, should have conducted negotiations involving such large sums without word or hint to the man most deeply interested, or to anybody else, cannot for a moment be entertained by candid men."

At one stage of the post-election crisis the treasurer of the Democratic National Committee, Mr. Cooper, had spoken to Tilden of the apparent effort of Pelton to purchase the South Carolina electors, and Tilden, expressing anger, had called his nephew back from Baltimore. With this fact, which undoubtedly goes far to exculpate Tilden, Reed's report dealt in the following fashion:

It has been urged in Mr. Tilden's behalf, that as soon as he became aware of the South Carolina negotiations he promptly suppressed them, and we are asked to draw the inference that he was guiltless of all.

[1] *H. of R. Misc.* 45 Cong., 3 Sess., No. 31, Part 3, 196.

Had these transactions ceased when Hardy Solomons went home, had Pelton been discharged from his plenary superintendence of Mr. Tilden's affairs, there might have been some show of reason in this plea. But Mr. Pelton remained in full control, the Florida negotiations went on, the attempted bribery in Oregon followed, all under the guidance of the resident nephew, Mr. Pelton. . . . Pelton says he told Cooper not to tell Tilden. That night, Cooper did not, but on reflection the next day, probably thinking that he had already over-advanced, and that if Mr. Tilden wanted the presidency in that way he had better pay for it himself, he went to Mr. Tilden. Of course Mr. Tilden could take part in no such open transaction as it had now become. Colonel Pelton was called home, a wiser and more secretive man.

"Politics," said Elihu Root on a certain occasion, "is modified war." Democrats and Republicans in this investigation were alike striving for party advantage. Each succeeded in bringing to light a mass of discreditable facts about the other. Regarded merely as a party maneuver, however, the Republicans had scored heavily. If it were not strictly true, as Reed afterwards stated on the floor, that "the public saw that Rutherford B. Hayes had not played the knave and that Samuel J. Tilden had," nevertheless it was no longer possible for the Democrats to pose as the innocent victims of an infamous conspiracy. Starting under a severe handicap, the minority members had at least succeeded in demonstrating that the rascality of 1876 had been fairly evenly distributed, and as a result, the Republicans could fight the campaign of 1880 on different and more advantageous issues.

"There never was a baser thing in the history of this or any other country than the fraud lamentation," declared Reed in the next Congress when a North Carolina member undertook to revive the issue. The Democratic attitude in the intervening four years was happily described in the same speech—frequently interrupted by the laughter of the House—with that use of metaphor of which he was master, as resembling that of a dog which he once owned. "After going out into the street and getting a complete and thorough thrashing from a bigger and worthier dog, he used to come into the house and lay down on the hearth, and then with one paw rub one damaged ear and growl, and with the other paw rub the other ear and growl, and then he would rub his scarred and unhappy nose and growl, and feel bad generally. Now, I am in hopes that time, after a sufficient lapse of it, may cure them, as it has cured him." [1] A member, interrupting, inquired: "The dog is cured now?" And Reed, amid great laughter, replied: "He is dead."

The widespread interest in the Potter committee and its work had helped to give Reed a degree of prominence seldom attained by Representatives in their first years of service. His name and his work, applauded by the Republican press and attacked by the Democratic newspapers, became known throughout the country.

[1] *Cong. Record,* 46 Cong., 3 Sess., 117.

LONG before the Potter committee had completed its labors Reed was obliged to face another campaign for nomination and election, hurrying back from New Orleans in the middle of July, 1878, to the First District. The situation was far from reassuring. Led by Solon Chase, whose combined political astuteness, Yankee shrewdness, and ordinary demagogy made him a formidable factor among the Maine farmers, the Greenbackers were making remarkable progress. The dissension in his own party had largely subsided, and on August 1, he received the enthusiastic indorsement of the district convention. The *Eastern Argus,* that oracle of the down-East Democracy, gives us a glimpse of the candidate at the conclusion of proceedings, when in response to the clamor of the delegates, "Great Thomas the Fat was seen elbowing his way to the platform and in a minute the sharp nerve-splitting notes from an unmusical Reed were sounding in the lethargical ears of the convention."

In his speech of acceptance, Reed showed that he fully appreciated the importance of the currency question and had determined to stand unequivocally for sound money. In later years, when Reed addressed his constituency, his remarks were telegraphed throughout the country, became front page news in metropolitan newspapers, and were frequently reprinted as campaign documents. His attack on Greenbackism in 1878 was just as vigorous and well reasoned as that on Free Silver in 1896.

"This has got to be a campaign of education, of instruction to all of us," he declared, "to those who speak and write as well as those who read and hear." In financial matters there had been a fluctuating and uncertain course since the war, but, "there has always been, however, one steady ray of sunlight, and that was the desire and determination of the American people to be honest, whatever it might cost." "The party," he added, had "a sound and righteous faith, but we have not so studied it ourselves as to be able always to give a reason for the faith that is in us." There had been no historical disagreement between the parties on the currency question; all hated irredeemable paper because of the evils it had inflicted; never, until the Civil War, did we have an issue of legal tender and violate our principles. Countries issuing paper money in the past had always repudiated, but he believed the United States would prove an exception. "Whether the Legal Tender Act was an act of indelible disgrace, depends upon the history of the near future." He announced his intention of canvassing the entire district. "I have always believed that this question had got to be discussed by the people before it was finally decided."

Throughout much of the nation the Greenback party seemed rising in power like some great tide. It was destined, by various fusions, to cast more than a million votes in the fall of 1878, and to elect fourteen congressmen. The need of thorough campaigning was quite evident and the appearance on Reed's behalf of such notables as James A. Garfield and Galusha A. Grow is an indication both of the intrinsic importance of his securing reelection and of Republican alarm at the growing vigor of Greenbackism. The party, albeit somewhat hesitatingly, was gradually being forced to stand up in defense of sound money. There was still much befuddlement on the issues and Reed was more than once asked to explain why he had voted against the remonetization of silver. Ben Butler went through the district proclaiming the virtues of "a dollar fixed by law, dependent on nothing, redeemable in nothing, which should be legal tender for all debts, bearing the stamp of the wealthiest nation of the earth," and Greenbackers of high and low degree made the welkin ring with denunciations of "bondholders," "national banks," and "coin."

There was much talk of trading by Democrats and Greenbackers, and the former were obviously bidding for Greenback support, but when each party decided to nominate a candidate for Congress in the First District, Reed was saved. His vote fell short of a majority, but thanks to a divided opposition, he had a plurality of more than four thousand. Considering the State-wide disaster to the Republican party, it was a notable victory. Solon Chase had predicted that the Greenback vote would strike the old parties "like a stroke of chain lightning" and results justified his expectations. In the eastern districts, Congressmen Eugene Hale and Llewellyn Powers went down before Greenback opponents; lack of a majority forced the election of governor into the legislature, and in the latter body, Greenbackers and Democrats controlled the house. The Republican Senate, by the action of the lower chamber, was promptly presented with the Hobson's choice of a Democrat or Greenbacker for the governorship. Alonzo Garcelon, Democrat, was chosen as the lesser evil.

Reed had proved his capacity on the stump. His speeches, while constituting a dignified and reasoned appeal to the voters' intelligence, were full of the Yankee shrewdness and humor which appealed effectively to his audiences. Hecklers at first appeared, but their unhappy fate discouraged this type of annoyance. Early and late in the campaign he had hammered on the currency question and in reply to Solon Chase's oft-repeated argument based on the depreciation in the value of "them steers"—the ox-team which proved such an effective stage property in his cheap money campaigns—one of Reed's aphorisms was widely quoted: "You won't have any more potatoes if you call them 4000 pecks than if you call them 1000 bushels."

It was to take another twenty years to drive home to the American people this elementary lesson as to the relationship of money and wealth, but he had at least secured his own district. "The prevalence of the heresies we have fought," he told a crowd of Portland admirers on election night, "would do this country greater injury than either war or pestilence."

After the Maine election, Reed took part in the campaign in the West. The results were unfavorable for the Republicans and when the returns had been tabulated early in November it was seen that both branches of the 46th Congress would be under Democratic control. Fourteen Greenbackers had been elected to the House, among them a future Vice President, Adlai E. Stevenson. Among the new Republican members were two of great future importance, Nelson W. Aldrich and Levi P. Morton. At the first session, Samuel J. Randall was again chosen Speaker over Garfield and Reed was appointed to a place on the Committee on the Judiciary. This was an important promotion.

In spite of the popular interest in new issues, Congress still devoted much of its time to certain aspects of the Southern question. Federal control of elections, one of the post-war humiliations most bitterly resented by the South, was the object of a sharp and long-sustained attack by the Democrats. The Democratic House in the 45th Congress had already attempted, by means of riders attached to the essential military, legislative, executive and judicial appropriation bills, to prevent the use of United States troops or special election supervisors and deputy marshals at the polls. This was an effort to coerce the Administration by misuse of the House's power over money bills. The Republican majority in the Senate resisted stubbornly. President Hayes was a determined opponent of both the object and method of such legislation, declaring that it was contrary to the whole spirit of the Constitution; and when adjournment came on March 3,1879, the army and other great public services were left without provision for the ensuing fiscal year through the failure of the appropriation bills. The President summoned the new Congress to meet in special session on March 18.

Defying Hayes, the Democratic majority promptly renewed the attack on the Federal election laws. Several of the former bills were re-introduced and passed by both houses, only to encounter a veto by the President. There was a sharp flaring up of sectional animosity, and in view of the character of the preceding campaign, a special significance and timeliness attached to the remarks of General James B. Weaver, leader of the National Greenback group, when on April 4 he rose to present his party's demands for unrestricted coinage of silver, the substitution of greenbacks for national bank notes, the cessation of increases in the bonded debt and the liberation of the idle money in the Treasury. "I should think," he exclaimed, "the old parties would see that they stand sadly in need of an addition to their wardrobe. Their only garment is that sanguinary article of underwear of which we have heard so much. It reminds me of an Indian I once saw out in the far West whose entire toilet consisted of a red bandanna around his neck and a plug hat, and, like those old parties, he was perfectly unconscious of the ridiculous figure he presented."

Reed took no part in the earlier debates on Federal election laws, but on May 10 he spoke at some length on the currency question, refuting the claims of inflationists that the demonetization of the silver dollar in 1873 was a "fiendish outrage" and the taking away of the legal tender character of the trade dollar a "trick." As he pointed out, both acts had been passed openly and men who were now denouncing them had voted for their passage. So good a Democrat as Samuel J. Randall had introduced the bill depriving the trade dollar of its legal tender quality, and it had been reported by another Democrat, S. S. Cox. Party lines were not clearly drawn where the currency question was concerned, but Reed, in addition to his campaign services in Maine, thus placed himself on record as a staunch supporter of sound money. Only by a general agreement of nations, he pointed out, could a bimetallic system ever be maintained.[1]

In the meantime, stimulated by the successful operation of the Specie Resumption Act which had been in effect since January 1, 1879, business had greatly improved. Revenue was pouring into the Treasury in constantly growing volume, and it was apparent that Congress would soon be called upon to deal with the problem of an accumulating surplus. Important fiscal and political policies were involved. The absorption of the public in the Southern question, the corruption and inefficiency of Federal administration, and protracted business depression had served for the past eight years to prevent adequate support of necessary governmental functions. National defense had been badly neglected since the close of the Civil War. The navy and coast defenses were obsolete. There was genuine need of public buildings, river and harbor improvements, and similar projects of internal betterment, although this was accompanied by the usual clamor for improvements which were not needed but politically expedient. The demand for pensions was growing.

The parties tended to assume the historic alignment on these questions, Republicans, committed to support of the protective tariff, proposed to maintain, for the most part, the existing revenue system and to spend the resulting income. The opposing policy was well stated by Speaker Randall on December 15, 1880: "Our policy should be to take off all taxation that we can take off, modify our revenue and our internal taxation laws, and relieve the people, instead of taking steps which will increase the burdens."

[1] *Cong. Record,* 46 Cong., 1 Sess., 1231–33.

In the ten years which followed the meeting of the 46th Congress in 1879, the Democrats were in control of the House in all but the 47th Congress (1881–83) and while there was no very important modification in the protective tariff—Randall himself was a protectionist—Randall's policy of economy, ably supported by such lieutenants as William S. Holman, "the watch-dog of the Treasury," did much to shape national appropriations. Then came a violent reaction in the 51st Congress, "the Billion Dollar Congress" with which Reed's name was destined to be forever associated.

Reed had none of the truculence and jingoism which were such offensive characteristics of many leaders of the period. He believed, however, that war was a possibility which, in the existing international order, could not be safely ignored. He therefore became a powerful advocate of a modern fleet. On April 14, 1880, he denounced the existing policy of naval construction in unsparing terms as an inexcusable waste of public money on the repair and upkeep of obsolete and worthless vessels. It had been possible, he declared, "to build a ship around an old hawse-hole instead of being able to get an appropriation to build a new ship." [1]

Again on December 15, 1880, he made an able speech on the same subject. Attacking the Democratic policy of economy as unwise and short-sighted, he argued that conditions in the world at that time precluded any idea of universal peace. The country now had an opportunity to establish its defenses and when war came it would be too late. The sea coast and its wealthy cities lay open to attack; their defenses had been built before the era of armored ships and high power rifled cannon; the losses of a single successful raid would be infinitely greater than all the proposed outlays for defense. The surplus revenue was available

[1] *Cong. Record,* 46 Cong., 2 Sess., 2417.

for both naval construction and harbor defense, and it would be the part of wisdom to formulate and carry out such a program.[1]

During the second session the question of Federal election laws was still under consideration, and on April 22, Reed spoke at length in opposition to an amendment on a deficiency appropriation bill providing for the appointment of deputy marshals for election duties by the United States circuit courts, the appointees to be drawn from both parties. Reed denounced the amendment as "contrary to the spirit and intent of the Constitution" and calculated to drag the courts into political controversies by requiring of them the performance of a duty which really belonged to the executive branch of the government.

This speech, continued on the following day, was bitterly partisan in tone. It was, in fact, a dissertation on the vital necessity of partisanship in American government. From this he passed to a review of the work of the Potter committee, already referred to, describing in mock heroic style the expectations of its organizers, "the household troops" ordered up for the assault, and the final disastrous repulse. "Time would fail me," he exclaimed, "to give an Homeric catalogue of all the great souls of heroes who went down to dusty death."

Scattered through this speech, one of the very few lengthy addresses of Reed's congressional career, were characteristic items. To some opponents who had voted on constitutional grounds against a certain measure, only to see the same principles, almost immediately thereafter, upheld by a Supreme Court decision, he remarked that "seven and seventy of you had only shown your ears where you had thought you were showing your minds." The Democratic party was roughly handled. "For the last thirty years," he declared, "it has not had an honest heartbeat north of the Mason and Dixon's line." Toward the close of

[1] *Ibid.*, 46 Cong., 3 Sess., 162–3, also 168.

his speech came an incident which is still remembered. E. B. Finley, an Ohio member, asked a somewhat irrelevant, or at best unimportant question regarding the Louisiana election of 1874, and in spite of Reed's expressed reluctance to admit interruption insisted on an answer. He got it. "Now," continued the speaker, "having embalmed that fly in the liquid amber of my discourse, I wish to proceed." The embalming was effective and the unfortunate victim has been on exhibition from that day to this.

The most interesting event of Reed's second term, in view of his subsequent fame as a parliamentarian who brought about profound changes in the methods and procedure of the House, was the submission, at the regular session, of a revised code of rules. Reed, from his first appearance in the House, had devoted a great deal of time and energy to acquiring a mastery of the rules, although twenty years later he frankly admitted that there were intricacies through which, even then, he could hardly find his way. He soon acquired, however, a wide knowledge of precedents, familiarity with the legislative history and methods of the House, and, more important, a broad and philosophical outlook on the purposes and methods of legislative bodies in general. The record of this Congress shows his increasing interest in matters of procedure and it is not surprising to find that veteran Democratic leader, J. C. S. Blackburn of Kentucky referring in complimentary terms to his opponent's "store of parliamentary learning."

The scientific analytical attitude toward American governmental processes was still in a somewhat rudimentary stage in the early eighties. Woodrow Wilson's masterly analysis, *Congressional Government*, did not appear until 1885 and Bryce's *American Commonwealth* until 1888. There was, of course, interminable criticism of Congress, its leaders, and its party politics, but a somewhat inadequate realization of essential defects in methods and internal organization. All could see that the Congressional machinery worked blunderingly, haltingly, and often harmfully. Filibustering in various forms occasionally provoked public indignation and there was general and grateful appreciation of Speaker Randall's courage and determination, when, toward the close of the session in March, 1877, he had blocked all dilatory tactics and forced the counting of the electoral vote to a conclusion, thereby averting the dangerous crisis which would have inevitably ensued had no election of President been declared before March 4. In the House itself, dissatisfaction with the existing rules had been growing steadily and there was no serious opposition when, toward the close of the extra session, June 25, 1879, the Committee on Rules was authorized to sit during the recess "for the purpose of revising, codifying and simplifying the rules of the House."

This much-needed undertaking, generally recorded as "the revision of 1880," attracted considerable attention. The committee consisted of Speaker Randall, Blackburn of Kentucky, Alexander H. Stephens of Georgia, James A. Garfield of Ohio, and William P. Frye of Maine. All were men of experience and ability. The task confronting them, a really great national problem, was well described by Mr. Frye when they reported on January 22, 1880:

These rules have been growing up since the foundation of our Government down to now, and with no natural regular growth. Necessities of parties, the whims of Speakers, contradictory decisions, the practice of the House, requirements of the occasion, uncertain and doubtful language—all these have combined to make a body of rules calculated better than anything else to disturb the legislator and to obstruct legislation; a body so full of intricacies and secrets that only the most skillful and trained anatomist could by any possibility dissect it and reveal them.[1]

[1] *Cong. Record,* 46 Cong., 2 Sess., 480.

The committee chose a limited objective. It adhered strictly to the terms of reference—"revising, codifying and simplifying." "At the very outset," reported Mr. Frye, "we passed a resolution that no amendments to the rules should be made except by unanimous consent, and wherever we disagreed the old rules should be reported." Under such conditions it would have been surprising had any thoroughgoing changes been recommended. The Committee on Rules, at this stage of its development, was not the powerful political engine which it was destined to become within the next decade. In fact, it was this revision of the rules which first gave it the status of a standing committee. Speaker Randall on June 25 previous, as an argument for entrusting it with the duty of revision, had declared that the existing committee had never yet divided politically. Two highly controversial matters, both of them the source of a vast amount of mischief, were left untouched. The committee, says the historian of the House of Representatives, did useful work, justified by subsequent experience; "but by shunning 'riders' and the 'disappearing quorum' they left the real red-light district undisturbed." [1]

Both topics were debated at considerable length, and Reed's share in the discussion is of more than ordinary interest. The "disappearing quorum" which was soon to become one of the major nuisances of congressional procedure had been a sporadic vexation for many years. House practice required that the records show, for the adoption or rejection of any measure, that a quorum was not only present but actually voting. By keeping silent, a minority could block business until the majority could muster a quorum. The system frequently produced the absurd spectacle of legislation at a stand-still for lack of a quorum with most of the members in their seats, or of committee chairmen trying to induce a few opponents to vote against their measures in order

[1] D. S. Alexander, *History and Procedure of the House of Representatives*, 196.

to create the quorum necessary for passage. There was considerable filibustering in both the 45th and 46th Congresses, the
Democratic majorities in neither being large enough to insure
a smooth and uninterrupted execution of the party program.
Reed's name frequently appears in the long lists of members
present but "not voting."

The appearance of the new code of rules seemed to offer a
favorable opportunity for reform and on January 28, 1880, John
Randolph Tucker, of Virginia, moved to amend Rule VIII by
inserting after clause 1, the following:

Whenever a quorum fails to vote on any question, and objection is made for that cause, there shall be a call of the House,
and the yeas and nays on the pending question shall at the same
time be ordered. The Clerk shall call the roll, and each member as he answers to his name, or is brought before the House
under the proceedings of the call of the House, shall vote on
the pending question. If those voting on the question and those
who are present and decline to vote shall together make a majority of the House, the Speaker shall declare that a quorum
is constituted; and the pending question shall be decided as the
majority of those voting shall appear.

Disclaiming partisan considerations and declaring that the
amendment was intended to prevent non-action when a quorum
was actually present, Mr. Tucker pointed out that while many
State constitutions required that a majority of the whole House
should pass a bill, there was no such provision in the Federal
Constitution, which provided simply that "a majority shall
constitute a quorum to do business," with a natural inference that
the decision on a question shall be by the majority of that
majority. "It seems to me," he declared, "not to be in accordance
with the progress of the age we live in that we should sit here
in a condition of non-action under the self-delusion that we are
not present when we are present, and that there shall be a power

on the part of gentlemen here upon any question of remaining silent and saying, 'You cannot prove I am here unless I choose to open my mouth'." [1]

Mr. Tucker's amendment secured scant support and there is abundant evidence in the debate which followed that the House refused to take it seriously. Springer, of Illinois, it is true, pointed out the absurdity of a system which would permit the House to send to Oregon for an absent member, compel his return, and then after such an expenditure of time and money, find that he was not really present unless he voluntarily said so. Garfield in a brief but vigorous address, often quoted in later years, declared his opposition. "Who shall control the Speaker's seeing? How do we know that he may not, for his own purposes, see forty members more than there are here? What protection have gentlemen when he says he sees a quorum, if he cannot convert that seeing into a list of names on the call of a yea and nay vote? This would let in the one-man power in a far more dangerous way than has ever occurred before."

Garfield's contention was practically that of James G. Blaine, who in the 43rd Congress had declared that "there can be no record like the call of the yeas and nays; and from that there is no appeal. The moment you clothe your Speaker with power to go behind your roll-call and assume that there is a quorum in the hall, why, gentlemen, you stand on the very brink of a volcano." [2]

Reed, however, late in the discussion, added substantially new reasons for opposing the amendment. There was a stronger reason, he said, than the danger of a dishonest count by the Speaker. "The constitutional idea of a quorum is not the presence of a majority of the members of the House, but a majority of the members present and participating in the busi-

[1] *Cong. Record,* 46 Cong., 2 Sess., 575.
[2] *Ibid.,* 43 Cong., 2 Sess., 1734.

ness of the House. It is not the visible presence of members, but their judgments and their votes, that the constitution calls for. What is the practical upshot of present practices? It is that the members of the minority of this House upon great occasions demand that every bill which is passed shall receive the absolute vote of a majority of the members elected. They do this in the face and eyes of the country." The frivolous use of this minority privilege, he declared, would bring the censure of the country, and there had been no improper impeding of public business hitherto. "It is a valuable privilege for the country that the minority shall have the right by this extraordinary mode of proceeding to call the attention of the country to measures which a party in a moment of madness and of party feeling is endeavoring to enforce upon the citizens of this land. And it works equally well with regard to all parties, for all parties have their times when they need to be checked. I say that as a practical matter the results hitherto throughout all our history have satisfied the construction which those upon this side of the House have put upon this matter. . . ." [1]

In less than ten minutes Reed had given utterance to principles which were to plague him until late in his career. Ten years later, almost to a day, he was destined to deliver a death-blow to the disappearing quorum which he now defended. Incidentally, such being the curious whirligig of time and politics, Springer, who had supported Tucker, became one of the most vociferous opponents of the Speaker's "tyranny" a decade later.

It would be easy to explain Reed's attitude as that of a minority member anxious to retain a grasp on every weapon which could be used against the majority, but opposition to the Tucker amendment came from both parties. When the veteran Democrat, Alexander H. Stephens, declared that the existing rule had been made by the founders of our government, that under it

[1] *Ibid.,* 46 Cong., 2 Sess., 578–579.

there had been a long series of great achievements, and that the wisest course was to let it alone, it was evident that the amendment was doomed. On the following day, Tucker, unwilling to delay proceedings by useless discussion, consented to its withdrawal.[1]

The matter of "riders" was inseparable from the general question of the proper relationship of the Committee on Appropriations to the other committees, and those sections of the report dealing with this topic attracted much more attention than the quorum issue and provoked an acrimonious debate. In 1865 the Ways and Means Committee had been relieved of its jurisdiction over appropriations and a new standing committee for that purpose had been created. It soon became one of the most powerful in Congress and exercised a power of revising estimates and making necessary alterations in the bills framed by other committees. This power naturally aroused considerable opposition. The situation was aggravated by the adoption of the "Holman amendment" in the 44th Congress, by which, "provided it be germane to the subject matter and retrenches expenses," an appropriation bill was permitted to embody changes in existing law.

In the preceding session, April 9, 1879, Reed in Committee of the Whole had had one of his first clashes with Randall on this subject, charging that in the preceding Congress "all sorts of legislation was ingrafted on appropriation bills by means of this rule":—enumerating the transfer of the Indian bureau, the regulation of elections, the repeal of the test oath, the reorganization of the army, and similar measures, as examples of an evil which made each appropriation bill "an *omnium gatherum.*" There can be no doubt that the evil involved was very real and very grave. "The result of this matter," he added, "is this: that the country gets a great deal of crude legislation and the

[1] *Ibid.,* 604.

Committee on Appropriations gets badly overworked." The House, he declared, was becoming impatient at the absorption of its whole business by one committee, and there was a disposition to break up its work and put it in the hands of several committees, a change which if actually carried out would undoubtedly add more to expenses than the rule ever saved.[1] On the following day he assailed an attempt to foist a change in the pension law upon a pension appropriation bill, as "a degradation of the rules of the House." It had become a matter of vital importance, he argued, both to the House and the country at large. "We are taking on, under the plea of germaneness, everything that has in it the same adjective that may be in the bill before us."

The report of the Committee on Rules, however, favored continuance in power of the Committee on Appropriations; the Holman amendment was retained, and another prohibiting the adoption of river and harbor bills under suspension of the rules was added. This was directed at a practice which had recently appeared in the 45th Congress, when the Committee on Commerce had secured the passage of such a bill, under suspension of the rules, without reference to the Committee on Appropriations. Incidentally, Reed had voted in support of this proposal.[2]

These debates on revision of the rules served to bring out the existence of a sharp cleavage of opinion as to the proper division of power in the House. Should it be wielded by a few or be distributed among as many hands as possible? "There has been a gradual concentration of power in the hands of the Committee on Appropriations," declared one member, "and it has grown to such an extent that the whole House is ready to rebel against it." The amendment offered by the Committee on Rules

[1] *Cong. Record,* 46 Cong., 1 Sess., 336.
[2] *Ibid.,* 45 Cong., 2 Sess., 2716.

was rejected on February 3, and at the same time the Committee on Agriculture was given the privilege of reporting its bills directly to the House.

Garfield, whose long experience lent special weight to his opinions, predicted that this policy would prove to be a great blunder, but he also argued for a further change in the rules. There was, he declared, but one remedy for "the hobble" in which the House was caught. "Strip the Committee on Appropriations of the power supposed to be given it under the 21st rule to legislate on appropriation bills, leave it only the work of recommending appropriations strictly according to law, and let the other committees of this House have the sole right of proposing for the action of the House such legislation as they deem necessary."

Reed supported this proposal as "the only escape." It was, he pointed out, "unsafe to have a system of legislation which is founded upon loading down the appropriation bills." The Appropriations Committee was sure to attempt to legislate, and the other committees, if their power were increased, would be equally sure to exalt themselves and their work. Garfield's proposal was "philosophically correct and practically correct." [1] On February 12, he again spoke on the subject, predicting that abuses of the "rider" system would contribute to Democratic defeat in the coming election. He also offered an amendment substituting for the Holman rule, the proviso "but it shall be in order to strike out any sum of money appropriated in a bill and insert a less sum." This, he said, would have the double merit of providing opportunity for retrenchment and reform and of keeping "firebrands" out of ordinary debate.

The discussion brought out the general belief—not wholly confined to the minority—that the Appropriations Committee had the power, and was using it, to wreck administrative organi-

[1] *Ibid.*, 46 Cong., 2 Sess., 689.

zation, interfere with general policies, and pass laws affecting a wide variety of rights and duties. On March 2, however, Garfield announced that inasmuch as the Democratic majority, acting under strict party discipline, was clearly opposed to any further amelioration of the system, the minority, anxious to secure the admitted benefits of the new code without prolongation of a useless contest, would abandon further opposition.[1]

Reed's attitude toward this question, like that toward the "disappearing quorum," underwent considerable modification in the next five years, but with less fortunate results. In the end, by helping to scatter the power of appropriation among numerous committees, he contributed to an unfortunate consummation which was destined to embarrass congressional finance for almost forty years. The revised code of rules was adopted on March 2.

Politically, 1880 proved one of Reed's busiest and hardest years. During the Christmas recess of 1879-80 he had been called to Augusta by a critical situation in Maine affairs. In the state election of 1879 the Republicans, by desperate efforts, had succeeded in recovering control of the legislature. The Democratic Governor and Council, however, empowered under the constitution to canvass results, by rejecting returns from various towns on narrowly technical grounds had converted a Republican majority in the lower House into a mere plurality, with Democrats and Greenbackers, now acting together as "Fusionists," in control. There was immediate protest and the members originally chosen prepared to assert their rights.

For a few days in early January, the little New England city by the frozen Kennebec resembled New Orleans or Little Rock in the palmy days of Reconstruction. There were two rival legislatures in session; a force of militiamen confronted a posse of plug-uglies recruited to protect the rights of the Fusionists;

[1] *Ibid.,* 1256.

a Gatling gun guarded the State House steps. In the end, however the decision of the Supreme Court upholding the legality of the Republican house was accepted, and the affair ended in a grand investigation by a committee under Eugene Hale, now serving, since losing his congressional seat the year before, as representative from Ellsworth. The investigation disclosed the absurdity of most of the decisions of the canvassers and dealt also—somewhat inconclusively—with charges of bribery brought against the Republican State organization. Several Fusionists claimed to have received offers of money should they absent themselves and prevent organization of the legislature by breaking the quorum.

Politically, the struggle in Augusta resulted in a complete consolidation of Democrats and Greenbackers, who were determined to seek vindication from the charge of attempting to "steal the State." In the First District both parties united in support of Samuel J. Anderson, Reed's Democratic opponent in the last election. There was a re-appearance in a somewhat milder form of the old Republican schism of 1876 and there seemed to be a strong possibility that the September election would bring Reed's congressional career to an untimely close.

In June he went with the other Maine delegates, all pledged to support James G. Blaine, to the Republican National convention in Chicago. The dramatic struggle there between the Blaine forces and the Conkling-Cameron-Logan coalition which demanded the renomination of Grant ended in the triumph of a dark horse, James A. Garfield. To Reed, who knew Garfield well and admired him warmly, it was a pleasing nomination. He at once returned to his Portland district for the hardest election campaign of his entire career. The fusion that year of the Greenbackers and Democrats proved unusually effective throughout the State, electing the governor and two congressmen. Reed brought his utmost powers into action against the

Greenback arguments, and with splendid effect; but he went to bed on election night believing himself beaten and eventually squeezed through with a plurality of only 109. Two hundred-odd votes had been thrown away on a third candidate. There has been a persistent story that the Democrats sent a large sum into the district for the express purpose of defeating the man who, in the Potter investigation, had done so much to change the course of the national campaign.

His opponent promptly contested the result on the ground that in various towns there had been illegal registration, that the polls had not been open for the specified hours, that selectmen had committed irregularities in tabulating results, and that employees in various mills and on public works had suffered intimidation. Reed defended his own case, attending the subsequent hearings throughout the district, examining witnesses, and finally filing a very short brief with the Committee on Elections in which he characteristically remarked of the intimidation charge: "If I could scare them as easily as the contestant seems to think and by means as inadequate as he has proved, I have certainly been recreant in a plain duty. I ought to have scared more of them."

The committee decided unanimously in his favor, pointing out that, at most, the selectmen had merely erred in judgment without any fraudulent intent and declaring that the evidence fell far short of substantiating the charge of intimidation. "It consists mostly of hearsay and rumors, and does not disclose a single instance of violence or even threatened violence." [1] Fortunately the House was Republican, and sustained the committee report; for Reed was aware that had the Democrats been in control he would probably have been ousted. Time and again equally inadequate evidence had proved sufficient to satisfy a hostile partisan majority.

[1] *House Reports,* 47 Cong., 1 Sess., 1697.

The affair made a deep impression on him, for he repeatedly expressed profound antipathy for the existing method of handling contested elections. The case, he afterwards stated, cost him $2600 for preparation and his opponent $5000, and he believed "the present method is a discredit to us all." [1] On another occasion he pointed out that the system of taking evidence ran up excessive expenses for which the congressional allowance was totally inadequate and that if election cases could be brought before a United States district judge for preliminary hearing a great mass of worthless testimony, under the rules of law, would be eliminated. The five hundred-odd pages of triviality in the record of his own case confirm this belief.

In an article on "Contested Elections" in the *North American Review* for July, 1890, he again took up the matter, pointing out the hopelessness of expecting busy members to read and study thousands of pages of testimony, the waste of time and money involved, and the frequent injustice involved in the final partisan decisions. It was a matter in which he failed to secure reform and which has remained in an unsatisfactory condition to the present day, but his attitude brings out clearly his impatience with legislative ineptitude even when sanctioned by long tradition.

The Republican defeats in the September elections in Maine caused great perturbation in the party councils, but by November the tide was running decidedly in the party's favor. Garfield won the presidency by a clear majority, and both branches of Congress passed under Republican control. For four years Reed had been qualifying for greater things. He had made a reputation as an unsparing critic of Democratic policies. He had become skilled in the parliamentary tactics of a legislative minority. He was now, for a brief period, to enjoy the greater opportunities and meet the heavier responsibilities of

[1] *Cong. Record,* 49 Cong., 1 Sess., 4149.

majority membership. Before the end of the 47th Congress he was destined to establish himself as the outstanding leader of the House Republicans.

In the last months of 1880, Maine was greatly interested in an impending vacancy in the United States senatorship due to the resignation of Hannibal Hamlin. Reed's name was frequently mentioned for the place, but in a public statement [1] he declined to become a candidate because of the narrow Republican majority in the next House and the uncertain political situation in the First District. During the next few years he was frequently suggested as a Senate possibility, but the devotion of the State to Senators Frye and Hale, both of whom began their long terms of service in 1881, precluded any likelihood of a successful contest.

He was for many years on bad terms with both men and had no great respect for the statesmanship or methods of the Senate, a feeling which became intensified during the great tariff and currency struggles of the nineties. It was, he once said, "a place where good Representatives went when they died." "A close communion of old grannies and tabby cats," was another reported definition of that august assemblage.

He once wrote, in a manuscript called "History of the United States, published in 1940," a satirical description of a presidential election under an imaginary constitutional amendment which conferred the choice of Chief Magistrate on the upper chamber. The election was by secret ballot. When the votes were collected the Chief Justice, who presided, was observed to hesitate and turn pale. The count showed that every Senator had received one vote and the American people realized for the first time that "the Senate of the United States was one level mass of wisdom and virtue, perfect in all its parts, and radiant from North to South with that light of intelligence which never shone

[1] Portland *Press*, November 23, December 3, 1880.

on sea or shore." [1] Reed was one of the very few Americans who gained eminence in public life entirely on the basis of service in the House of Representatives.

[1] McCall, *Reed*, 252.

THE elections of 1880 gave the Republican party complete control of the national government, but prospects for constructive work were blighted by the bitter factional quarrel between the Stalwarts and Half-Breeds which accompanied Garfield's election to the Presidency. Not until 1889 was the same opportunity to be offered the party again.

Congress did not meet until December 5, 1881. Garfield had died almost three months before, the victim of an assassin whose cracked brain had induced him to translate into action the reckless mouthings of the politicians which were so frequently heard when anticipated collectorships and post offices failed to materialize. President Arthur gave the country a surprisingly tactful and able administration, but during these years the White House was not a source of party leadership or congressional guidance. The 47th Congress failed to coöperate with the President, a fact made quite evident by the tone of his repeated pleas for revenue reform. He vetoed three of its important enactments, the Chinese immigration bill, a bill regulating the carriage of passengers by sea, and a river and harbor appropriation bill. His criticisms of these enactments showed again the blundering and inefficient character of congressional work. The river and harbor bill he denounced unsparingly as a tissue of logrolling jobbery, but it was promptly repassed over the veto. It is to the credit of Thomas B. Reed that he voted to sustain the President's veto. Other Republicans would have done well to follow the same course, for in the opinion of George F. Hoar it was the repassage of this offensive bill which "cost the Republican party its majority in the House."

From the standpoint of party efficiency the situation in the

House of Representatives was far from promising. The quarrel between Stalwarts and Half-Breeds was still exerting its baleful influence. The Republicans lacked a comfortable working majority, the party strength standing Republicans 152, Democrats 130, Greenbackers 9, Readjusters 2. The allegiance of some western Republicans was uncertain. Should obstruction develop it was apparent that the hands of the majority could be effectively tied with a minimum of effort.

Furthermore, and especially significant in its bearing on Reed's career, the Republicans, unlike their opponents, were handicapped by a scarcity of experienced leaders. Garfield, whatever his other shortcomings, had been brilliantly successful on the floor and in the committee room. William P. Frye, who would probably have been the strongest candidate for the speakership, had been elected to the Senate. There were men of ability among the majority members but most of them were either temperamentally or politically disqualified for leadership, or else too young in service to have acquired the necessary power and prestige.

The first result of this situation was a "scrub race" for the speakership, and on the sixteenth ballot J. Warren Keifer, of Ohio, received the nomination of the Republican caucus, with 93 votes out of a total of 144. His closest competitors on this ballot were Frank Hiscock of New York with 18 and Thomas B. Reed with 11. It is worth noting that at the beginning of his third term, Reed's capacity had been recognized by some of his colleagues as entitling him to the highest office in the gift of the House. In the light of subsequent developments there can be little doubt that he would have performed its duties with vastly greater credit to all concerned than the successful candidate.

Keifer's election was due to the operation of various obscure forces. He was a Stalwart; he had a war record, a dignified presence, and a certain personal affability. The death of Gar-

CLEARING THE ROAD
(From *Judge*)

field had transferred the presidency to New York, and according to the theory of practical politics, Ohio was entitled to compensation, a circumstance which militated against the nomination of Easterners like Hiscock and Reed. Of the high qualities which had distinguished his immediate predecessors, Randall and Blaine, he had scarcely a trace. Deficient in knowledge of parliamentary rules and practices, lacking the clear insight, judgment and balance needed to control the legislative program of a somewhat discordant party majority, and the courage, humor, and innate sense of justice which could alone command the respect of the House as a body, it is not surprising that a few weeks after election he was described by *The Nation* as "more successful than any of his predecessors in displeasing the majority of the House."

But the very lack of competent leadership and the fumbling efforts of the nominal leaders were advantageous to the aggressive member from Maine. Keifer, with one exception, to be noted later, bestowed valuable committee places on his rivals for the nomination. Hiscock was made chairman of the Appropriations Committee and Reed of the Judiciary, probably third in importance among the great standing committees. The chairmanship of Ways and Means, carrying with it—at least in theory—the majority floor leadership, went to the "father of the House," William D. Kelley, of Pennsylvania. Kelley, however, was sixty-seven years old, and the devotion to the cause of protection which had earned him the euphonious title of "Pig-iron Kelley" was hardly an offset to deficiencies in physical strength and other qualities essential for successful leadership. Almost from the start Reed, although outranked by several veteran members, became a director of parliamentary tactics, an adviser in party strategy, and a leader in debate and by the close of the session had proved himself a match for such able Democrats as Randall, Tucker, Blackburn, S. S. Cox, and Carlisle.

To his opportunities, an apparently unimportant incident contributed mightily. Godlove S. Orth, of Indiana, one of the recent candidates for the speakership, disgruntled at Speaker Keifer's failure to assign him a more desirable place on committee, resigned from the Committee on Rules, and on January 9, 1882, Reed received the vacant place. While the importance of this committee had been somewhat increased under the revision of 1880 and by various rulings of Speaker Randall during the 46th Congress, its potentialities were not yet fully appreciated. The committee consisted of the Speaker, George M. Robeson, of New Jersey, and Reed for the majority, Randall and Blackburn for the minority.

Robeson was a political veteran and was considered to be one of the members most trusted by Speaker Keifer, if not indeed the actual leader of the majority. He was, however, one of the heaviest liabilities of the Republican party. He had been charged with gross corruption as Secretary of the Navy under Grant and was to be relegated to deserved obscurity at the next election. The minority members were of high character and ability but, after all, a minority is only a minority in the transaction of parliamentary business and the Committee on Rules was rapidly becoming a powerful party organ. Could Reed dominate his two colleagues, he would occupy a place of unquestioned power. Such domination, considering the slender ability of his party colleagues, was not especially difficult.

This Congress provided several opportunities for Reed to give practical demonstrations of those principles by which he was destined a few years later, to put an end to century-old abuses and to influence profoundly the course of congressional practice. Primarily an executive and now sharing the responsibility of carrying out a majority program, he conceived of the speakership as an office of centralized power and correlative responsibility. Accordingly, when on January 17, 1882, Orth, taking advantage of the general dissatisfaction with Keifer's assignments, and smarting under his own ill-treatment, introduced a resolution providing for the selection of committees by an elective board of eleven members, Reed went into action as a defender of the Speaker's prerogative. He said:

Whatever complaint can be made against the appointment of committees as the result of pressure on the Speaker can be made with redoubled force against the appointment by a board elected by this House. Think of the speakership of this House going into commission! Think of the log-rolling there would be in order to get such a board as would favor various measures that might be presented; supposing always that in this House there is any danger of tyranny, or ruin and corruption such as is suggested by the gentleman from Indiana. What modest, good men the board would have to be! Think of the self-denying ordinance they would have to pass and how virtuous they would have to be not to shine as members of Judiciary, Appropriations, Ways and Means, and Foreign Affairs, all at once on their own suggestion! . . .

No material interest in this country is liable to be destroyed or injured by any committee to be appointed by a Speaker of this House. Every action of every committee has to undergo the scrutiny of this House, and the moment a committee is appointed which is not in accord and harmony with the wishes and desires of members, that moment that committee is such an object of suspicion that its power is utterly destroyed and lost. On the contrary, committees are always appointed by the Speaker to represent if not the individual wishes of members, at least the wishes of the country upon matters of public policy. The whole history of the Congress of the United States will bear me out in that statement.[1]

Orth had supported his proposal by arguing that the power of appointment was "a one man power" and as such in constant danger of abuse. But Reed denied this contention on the ground

[1] *Cong. Record,* 47 Cong., I Sess., 465.

that "the Speaker is not only under constant supervision of public opinion but also of the House." He also opposed a proposal for enlarging the committees as likely to reduce practical efficiency. It was his firm belief, he added, that the geographical demand for that enlargement should be disregarded. "I believe that the particular fitness of individuals, not the places where they sleep nights, ought to be the first thing to be considered in determining their positions on committees." Orth's resolution was defeated by a large and nonpartisan majority.

While the Judiciary Committee of the 47th Congress originated no general laws of far reaching importance, Reed, as chairman, was in charge of several interesting bills. In January, 1882, he successfully carried through a bill for the retirement of Justice Hunt of the Supreme Court, who was ineligible for a pension except by special act. Justice Hunt for some time had been unable to perform his duties, but his term of service did not entitle him to the usual retiring allowance. The proposal aroused great opposition among the proponents of economy, the haters of aristocracy, and the upholders of the rights of the common man. "It is perfectly amazing how much gentlemen can find in a subject," Reed remarked, "when they give loose play to their imaginations and their tongues." The judicial pension, he argued, was merely an incidental part of the compensation for which the judges served. The judge who was appointed for life, as a mere matter of contract, was entitled to draw the salary for life when obliged to retire because of disability.

More important was a bill for the distribution of the unexpended balance of the Geneva Award, which had been lying in the Treasury for some years because of the inability of Congress to determine an equitable method of distribution. This is one of the few pieces of legislation with which Reed's name is directly associated. His speech of May 10, 1882, setting forth the principles on which it was proposed to distribute the fund, is a model of exposition, especially that part explaining why marine insurance companies were not entitled to any share in it. They had adjusted their premiums to meet war risks and after all losses had paid large dividends to stock holders. In the course of debate he pointed out the moral obligation to distribute the money among those who had really suffered from the depredations of the Confederate cruisers, and remarked to Southern members who were showing signs of opposition that "it is not like your high-minded character to cause this damage and then try to put part of the proceeds in your own pockets, for that is what keeping it in the Treasury means." The bill was passed by a decisive majority in both houses and proved as generally satisfactory as such a difficult settlement is likely to be.

Late in May, however, Reed scored the greatest of his early triumphs, a triumph which not only established his reputation as a parliamentarian and floor leader, but unquestionably contributed to the formation of conclusions to which he was later to give practical effect as Speaker. He had already begun to realize the inadequacy of the rules revision of 1880; the congressional machinery was as creaky and ill-adjusted as ever; and on March 1 and 8, 1882, he presented reports from the Committee on Rules proposing amendments to Rule XXIV which would have enabled the House by majority vote to secure prompt consideration of business regardless of its place on the calendars. The majority, however, was insufficient to secure action on such a highly controversial topic and no action was taken. The obstruction and the time-wasting continued. "We could never get a quorum there," Reed remarked in the next Congress, "except for those non-partisan judicial performances which are called election cases."

On May 20, the House undertook to consider the South Carolina election case of Mackey vs. Dibble. The Democratic minority, foreseeing that the Republican claimant would be seated, began to filibuster. For seven days all attempts to take up the case were met by motions to adjourn, or endless variations thereof. The yeas and nays would be taken, while the Democrats, as an exasperated opponent described them in somewhat mixed metaphor, sat "like a set of mules with their haunches on the breech strap wagging their ears instead of answering their names." The Republican majority, narrow enough to begin with, had been still further depleted by various causes, and since they were uncertain of being able to secure a voting quorum it seemed likely that the sorry farce would continue indefinitely.

But Reed was now thoroughly aroused. He resolved on a bold stroke, and on Saturday the 27th, immediately on the opening of business, secured recognition to submit a privileged report from the Committee on Rules. All attempts to get him off the floor by motions to take a recess were ruled out by Speaker Keifer, and he accordingly moved to amend paragraph 8 of Rule XVI so as to read:

Pending a motion to suspend the rules, or on any question of consideration which may arise on a case involving the constitutional right to a seat, and pending the motion for the previous question, or after it shall have been ordered on any such case, the Speaker may entertain one motion to adjourn; but after the result thereon is announced he shall not entertain any other motion till the vote is taken on the pending question; and pending the consideration of such case only a motion to adjourn or to take a recess (but not both in succession) shall be in order, and such motions shall not be repeated without further intervening consideration of the case for at least one hour.

The significance of this proposal was obvious. The Republican majority actually proposed to stop all obstructive motions and force the matter under consideration to a decision. The Democrats took alarm and a running fire of dilatory motions greeted Reed's amendment like the popping of a skirmish line. When

Randall moved an adjournment until Thursday, Reed raised the point of order that such motions were "mere dilatory motions, and therefore, as against the right of the House to consider a proposition to amend the rules, not in order."

Further discussion of the report and the point of order went over until the following Monday, when the prospect of debate between the veteran Randall and the aggressive majority member of the Committee on Rules, together with the intrinsic importance of the issues involved, combined to fill the House. Incidentally, the Republicans appear to have rounded up the absentees, and even sick members appeared in their seats. The right of the majority to control the course of business is a commonplace today, but in 1882 the contention that the Committee on Rules should formulate, and the Speaker enforce, a rule against dilatory motions—motions which he had been putting regularly for the past eight days—and Reed's further contention, that the rules could not themselves be applied to block alterations in their own structure, seemed to many members an ominous innovation. It was presently described by Blackburn as "an entering-wedge for the abolition of parliamentary government."

The debate proved spirited. When discussion opened promptly after approval of the Journal on the 29th, Reed struck vigorously on behalf of his proposals. Under the Constitution, the House enjoyed certain expressly conferred powers, among them that of judging "of the elections, returns, and qualifications of its own members." Yet under the provision the House had been vainly trying to judge the right of a member to his seat, only to be frustrated by the rules. It was proposed to remedy the situation by changing the rules. Now these same rules, which the House admittedly had the right to change, were being used to prevent the needed changes.

Personally, he believed that under the existing rules such

dilatory motions might be overruled by the Speaker, but a more orderly way was to revise and amend the rules. And again he stated his conception of the speakership. "Whenever it is imposed upon Congress to accomplish a certain work, it is the duty of the Speaker, who represents the House, and who, in his official capacity, is the embodiment of the House, to carry out that rule of law or of the 'Constitution. It then becomes his duty to see that no factious opposition prevents the House from doing its duty. He must brush away all unlawful combinations to misuse the rules and must hold the House strictly to its work."

Precedent did not fully cover the conditions under which Reed's proposal was made. James G. Blaine, it is true, had once declared, although not in a formal ruling, that dilatory motions should not be entertained when a proposition to change the rules was before the House.[1] In the course of debate on the second Civil Rights Bill, the House by a two-thirds vote had taken steps against dilatory motions. Randall himself, in the critical days when the electoral vote of 1876 was being counted, had refused to entertain dilatory motions offered by members of his own party. When Reed called attention to this ruling, however, the ex-Speaker was quick to point out that the law creating the Electoral Commission had required such action and a mandatory provision of law was superior to the rules of the House.

"I make the proposition," declared Reed in closing, "that inasmuch as by the organic law of the United States, which is at the same time the organic law of the House, the House has a right to change its rules at any time, no member or set of members have any right to use the rules which are to be changed to prevent the change which the House desires to make. If I were to state that a great many times I do not believe that I should

---

[1] *Cong. Record,* 43 Cong., 2 Sess., 806. Quoted Alexander, *House of Representatives,* 196. For comment on Reed's work against obstruction in this Congress, 196–205, *passim.*

be able to state it more clearly. The very power which the House is exercising cannot be used to destroy that power. There is no such thing as suicide in any provision of the Constitution of the United States." [1]

From the standpoint of the minority, the implications of Reed's doctrine were as plain as they were alarming. If the power of the majority were capable of changing the rules in order to suppress filibustering in election cases, admittedly a matter of the highest privilege, in which, as several members pointed out, obstruction had never before been used, what was to prevent the majority from resorting to the same tactics in ordinary matters?

Randall himself, who in three terms as Speaker had been scrupulous in protecting minority rights, pointed out the vital importance of the rules as safeguards for the minority, reading into the record the well-known statement of Speaker Onslow of the House of Commons, that parliamentary rules formed the only safeguard by which the minority could protect itself from irregularities and abuses on the part of dominant and impatient majorities. Onslow had stated:

And whether those forms be in all cases the most rational or not is really not of so great importance. It is much more material that there should be a rule to go by than what that rule is, that there may be a uniformity of proceeding in business, not subject to the caprice of the Speaker or captiousness of the members.

But the minority view was perhaps best stated by Blackburn, who argued that the House must change the rules under the terms and conditions which it has itself imposed. "What guarantee can you give," he demanded, "that there is a single question of legislation committed to the American Congress that will

[1] *Cong. Record,* 47 Cong., 2 Sess., 4307.

not be made the victim of just such summary and arbitrary procedure, which must be determined simply by the temper in which the House may transact its legislative duties?" Reed himself, Blackburn pointed out, had once emphasized the need of guarantees for the minority, and it could be seen by any one that the present procedure would be equally effective should the majority ever see fit to attack the quorum issue. Amid ironical applause from the Democratic side he caused to be read into the record the remarks which Reed had made two years before against the Tucker amendment, which, as S. S. Cox presently remarked, "would have torn up filibustering by the roots." It was an awkward moment for Reed and he made the mistake of trying to maintain his consistency. His retort, reaffirming his position was, like his original statement, to be invoked against him in future years. "I am glad," he interrupted, "for once to have the approval of the Democratic side of this House. What has been read is sound sense today, and that is why I wonder at your approval of it."

"It is proposed," declared Blackburn in conclusion, "to turn the American Congress, or this branch of it, without any limitation, without any restraint, over to be guided by a partisan majority." This was precisely the fact. Within a few years Reed boldly took his stand in defense of this very proposition, though always maintaining that common sense and accepted rules and legislative practices assured the minority of ample protection.

After three hours of debate—debate of a kind all too rare in the drab annals of this Congress—Speaker Keifer delivered his ruling on the point of order, and completely upheld Reed:

The question here decided the Chair understands to be an important one, because it comprehends the complete organization of the House to do business, but it feels that on principle and sound precedents the point of order made by the gentleman from Maine must be sustained to the extent of holding that the motion made by the gentleman from Pennsylvania, which is in effect a dilatory motion, is not at this time in order.

Randall promptly appealed from the Speaker's decision and Reed moved to lay the appeal on the table. The Republicans were solidly behind the Speaker and the vote stood yeas 150, nays 0, not voting 141. The report of the Committee on Rules was then adopted. Reed had triumphed in his first notable effort to improve the procedure of the House.

A protest signed by one hundred minority members was entered in the record denouncing the proceedings of the majority and the rulings of the Speaker as "unjustifiable, arbitrary and revolutionary and expressly designed to deprive the minority of that protection which has been established as one of the great muniments of the representative system by the patient and patriotic labors of the advocates of parliamentary privilege and civil liberty." But this was a mere gesture.

"It was a great victory," says Alexander, "since it enabled the Committee on Rules to have its reports promptly adopted, and from that hour Reed became the real leader of his party. Ever after, so long as he remained in Congress, his voice gave the word of command." [1]

But this was only a beginning in the great work of remaking the House into a genuinely efficient body. Another stroke was needed. Reed's second foray on the obstructionists came toward the close of the second session, but is so closely related in principle and method to his successful *coup d'état* in the election case that it should be considered at this point. This attack, bolder—his opponents said more unscrupulous—in conception and execution than the first, involved action on the tariff bill.

The tariff had figured as a leading issue in the preceding presidential campaign. It had not yet, however, assumed over-

[1] *House of Representatives,* 202.

shadowing importance. General Hancock's famous remark that "The tariff is a local issue," regarded by his generation as a joke, and by ours—perhaps with a slight distortion—as a truism, is the best known utterance of this campaign discussion. The Democratic platform in 1880 had contained a plank supporting "a tariff for revenue only," and the election of Garfield was promptly interpreted by Republican protectionists as not merely a condemnation of this proposal but a demand for increased duties.

Whatever the protectionists' arguments might be, they could hardly use the fiscal situation as a justification for higher duties. Business had continued to improve and revenue was still pouring in. President Arthur stated in his first annual message, December 5, 1881, that the surplus for the fiscal year ending June 30 had amounted to more than a hundred millions, and he accompanied this with recommendations for the abolition of most of the internal revenue taxes and a revision of the tariff. The establishment of a tariff commission had already been discussed in the 46th Congress and a bill creating one had actually passed the Senate. This project was now renewed and a bill establishing a commission passed the House, becoming law on May 15, 1882. Reed voted for this measure but took only a minor part in the debate.

The commission, it was hoped, would study the needs of the country in a broad-minded, non-partisan manner and make its recommendations in a scientific spirit. This body, to which President Arthur appointed business men of high standing and protectionist views, conducted an excellent investigation in the limited period at its disposal and submitted a voluminous report to the House at the opening of the December session. Substantial reductions in many of the rates and the enlargement of the free list were recommended. These recommendations were reënforced by President Arthur's second annual message, December 4,

1882, where it was pointed out that "immediate and extensive reductions in the annual revenues of the government" were highly desirable, inasmuch as the surplus, still further increased, constituted a menace to sound finance and a standing invitation to waste and extravagance. "Large reductions from customs revenue are entirely feasible," the President added, with a further comment that the existing tariff was unjust in many respects. President Arthur's demands were frank and courageous and, so far as can be seen, represented the dominant opinion of the country.

But if the country expected prompt action on the tariff it seemed likely to be disappointed. The congressional elections of 1882 had resulted in Democratic victory and the 47th Congress had but three more months to live. A tariff bill, especially if reductions are contemplated, offers one of the most complex and difficult problems in the whole range of legislation. For a body like the existing House it seemed impossible of solution. In the previous session, however, on June 27, 1882, "an act to reduce internal revenue taxation, and for other purposes" had been passed. The Senate, giving liberal interpretation to its power of amendment, now added to this bill an extensive revision of the tariff, making a number of reductions as recommended by the commission. The House promptly raised the shout of "usurpation," and when the bill was returned from the Senate, February 20, 1883, it lay on the Speaker's table with every prospect that March 3 would find it still on that very spot.

The Democrats were determined that there should be no tariff legislation before adjournment and conducted an energetic filibuster against an independent House bill reported by the Ways and Means Committee in January. "It seems that after all this is getting to be rather a decent world," remarked Reed, February 5, 1883, when his opponents defended their obstructive tactics by descanting on liberty of speech. "Even the Democratic party pays that homage to virtue which is implied in hypocrisy." Filibustering, with the session so far advanced, seemed an invincible weapon.

Reed was naturally a protectionist. As will later be pointed out, he had a well reasoned economic philosophy of which the protective system constituted an integral part. He spoke for protection during the presidential campaign of 1880. On February 3, 1883, he delivered his first important congressional speech on the subject, arguing that protection was merely the system under which American manufacturers, laborers and farmers were given the markets of the country, and that any duty, high or low, which accomplished that object was in accordance with its principles. He ridiculed "the two Dromios from Illinois," Townshend and Springer, who proclaimed their belief that monopoly would be the inevitable result. As for Bastiat, whose free trade doctrines supplied opponents of protection with so much of their ammunition, Reed held that his arguments were irrelevant as far as American conditions were concerned. "The great sophism of Bastiat is he always argues about what would be the effect if the city of Paris were cut off from the rest of the world." The United States, on the other hand, contained almost everything needed in its own economic life. In such a country, protection offered tremendous advantages for all.

Reed saw that there was still a possibility of forcing tariff legislation through the parliamentary entanglements which appeared impassable. There was no likelihood that the House would pass its own bill, but on the Speaker's table lay the internal revenue bill of the previous session with the Senate tariff amendments attached. The bill could be taken from the table and sent to conference only under suspension of the rules, and suspension of the rules required a two-thirds vote. This obstacle, Reed perceived, however, could be overcome by the same weapon used in the election case a year earlier. Accordingly on

February 24, 1883, he presented a privileged report from the Committee on Rules under the terms of which the rules were to be suspended by *a majority vote*, the internal revenue bill to be taken from the Speaker's table, the House to declare its disagreement with Senate amendments, and a conference committee to be requested.[1] The final form of the bill would thus be dependent on the action of the conference committee, and with protectionists controlling both houses, there could be little doubt as to the outcome.

The proposal provoked a storm and the Democratic leaders denounced it as an impudent attempt to throttle the minority. It was no "rule," declared S. S. Cox, but merely "a fraud on parliamentary law," intended to gag opponents. Reed, it was charged in the course of debate, had secured written pledges of support from Republican members, but if that were the case —and it apparently was—he had a narrow escape from defeat when, late in the evening of February 26, a vote on the report showed yeas, 120; nays, 20; not voting, 151. The "disappearing quorum" was endangering the outcome. On the following morning, however, the report was adopted, yeas, 129; nays, 22; not voting 140. His bold move had after all—though very narrowly—won.

The House conferees, appointed in accordance with the terms of Reed's report, were Kelley, McKinley, Haskell, Randall, and Carlisle, all but the latter being protectionists. In combination with Senators Morrill, Sherman and Aldrich, the high tariff men had a large majority in the conference committee. Senators Bayard and Beck, objecting to the conditions of conference laid down by the House, had refused to serve. The bill when it finally emerged, although containing numerous reductions, was still staunchly protectionist in character. Certain rates were raised above those originally proposed in either House;

[1] *Cong. Record*, 47 Cong., 2 Sess., 3259.

the symmetry of the revenue system as proposed by the tariff commission was completely destroyed, and in general the enactment proved offensive to the country. Senator Sherman in his *Recollections* criticized the measure unsparingly; expressed regret that he had supported it; and declared his belief that had the report of the commission been adopted much of the subsequent tariff agitation would have been averted. Reed himself never believed it possible to frame a tariff on the basis of scientific investigation and report. Twenty years later he wrote of the commission of 1882: "Its report was not enacted into law but all its mistakes were."

The tariff measure was hurried through both Houses with a minimum of discussion, securing a bare majority in the Senate, and on March 3, President Arthur affixed his signature. It was a bad bill. But whatever may be thought of the contents of the measure, regarded strictly as a matter of party strategy and parliamentary tactics its passage was one of the most daring maneuvers of Reed's entire career, or for that matter, in the history of Congress.

The constitutional issue had been relegated to the background in the bitter controversy provoked by Reed's spectacular *coup*. John Randolph Tucker summed up this phase of the affair fairly enough in words which he put into the mouths of his opponents as the final vote was about to be taken. "We will not raise the constitutional question until we settle the fact as to whether we can get a tariff; let us manipulate the tariff first and see if we can get it. And if we can get what will suit us we will swap the Constitution for that."

The House, however, passed a resolution declaring the Senate amendments to the bill "in conflict with the true intent and purpose of the Constitution." Reed, apparently in high good humor at the outcome, supported the resolution, but contented himself with a few ironical remarks on his own generosity, alike to the present House and future generations, in omitting a speech on the constitutional questions at issue, "the more singular favor because such an opportunity in the common course of events seldom happens to a man more than once in a lifetime."

"No legislation in this Congress," declared Speaker Keifer in his valedictory a few days later, "will be found upon the statute books revolutionary in character or which will oppress any section or individual in the land." Reduced to less euphemistic terminology, the legislative accomplishments of the 47th Congress were somewhat meager. *The Nation,* on March 8, 1883, declared that the Congress just expired could not be pointed at with pride by either party, that it had excited more adverse criticism than most of its predecessors, that its debates had been exhibitions of the dreariest kind of mediocrity, its acts "the result of a helpless obedience to pushing or restraining outside forces of various kinds," and its Speaker "a sorry apparition" in the chair.

Some of Reed's work, however, deserves mention. He occasionally presided as chairman of the Committee of the Whole, and on one or two occasions, as Speaker *pro tempore.* He voted against the Chinese Exclusion Act in its first crude and offensive form, although finally supporting the bill which met President Arthur's approval. He voted for the Civil Service Law. As chairman of the Judiciary Committee he brought in a report recommending the forfeiture of a number of railroad land grants, mostly in the South, adopting the general rule that "where, after a long lapse of time, no attempt has been made to earn the grant, it has seemed as if it should be withdrawn." [1]

In the case of the Northern Pacific, however, he opposed a forfeiture. After careful study he presented a report concluding that in view of the nature of the original grant and the progress of current construction, "the sole right which remains in the

[1] *House Reports,* 47 Cong., 1 Sess., No. 1284.

United States at the present time in respect to the lands granted to that company, is the right, by its Congress, to do such acts as may be needful and necessary to insure the speedy completion of the road" and "we can conceive of no legislation which would hasten the completion of the road and therefore recommend none." The minority, dealing with the legal basis of this conclusion, reported a dissenting opinion accompanied by a resolution providing for the restoration of the lands to the public domain. For some years thereafter, Reed was assailed as altogether too friendly to the railroads, but his Northern Pacific opinion seems to have been fair.

On January 9, 1883, he spoke at some length in opposition to the proposal for "free ships," on the ground that the country should encourage the construction of ship yards, train workmen, and provide the elaborate equipment needed for modern construction. "I believe," he went on, "that the only blessed time for this world will be when the sword is beaten into the plowshare and the spear into the pruning hook, and there shall be war on earth no more." Nevertheless, war was a contingency which could not be ignored, and if it should come, ship construction would be an imperative need. Like most Maine representatives, Reed always maintained an active interest in the merchant marine, although never giving it the devoted study which made Nelson Dingley one of the masters of the subject.

In the meantime he was steadily enhancing the reputation which in the nineties gave him the title of "the Terrible Turk" of political debate. Throughout the 47th Congress his tongue fell on opponents like the lash of a whip. He was as dangerous in casual repartee as in the interchanges of regular debate. "If I could get my friend from Michigan where I could put a wick in him, I would illuminate this country," remarked S. S. Cox, who had some reputation as a wit, in the course of debate on February 3, 1883. "If the gentlemen from New York illuminates anything it will have to be by the aid of the gentleman from Michigan," interrupted Reed, "as he seems incapable of doing it alone."

When Cox, apropos of Reed's opposition to the proposed holiday recess during the congested short session, reminded him that in 1879 he had been conspicuous in extending the length of the recess, the retort came like a flash: "That was a Democratic Congress, and the country needed a rest."

When William M. Springer complained that Reed. had "made light of his remarks" he was met by the retort: "I will say to the gentleman that if I ever 'made light' of his remarks it is more than he ever made of them himself." [1] Reed at this period of his career was somewhat given to hunting small game in the House. "The gentleman never got within a decade of the present in his life, and his party surrounds him where he stands," was another retort to one of Springer's questions on a later occasion. While Springer was perhaps the favorite target for his wit and sarcasm, he was not alone in that distinction. Thus, in the 48th Congress, when two Democrats engaged in a somewhat heated exchange on the merits of a pending bill, Reed made the soothing comment: "I have listened with pleasure to both gentlemen . . . and so far as they reflect upon each other I agree with both of them. It always does take at least two Democrats to tell the whole truth about the Democratic party, and they do not always succeeded at that." [2]

The Maine representatives were chosen by general ticket in 1882, pending the adoption of a re-districting act, and the Republicans easily carried the State. Except for the election of 1884, when there was some dissension in the First Dictrict due to patronage squabbles, while the Democrats played up Reed's railroad policy and attempted to make political capital out of the

[1] *Cong. Record,* 47 Cong., 1 Sess., 5663.
[2] *Ibid.,* 48 Cong., 2 Sess., 1401.

fact that he had represented a Texas land syndicate in England during the long recess, his election troubles were practically over. The district was now fully aware of the national prestige conferred by his presence in Washington and he was assured of indefinite tenure.

For the ordinary political hack work of a party representative he had profound dislike. Once when some of his constituents desired him to secure certain condemned cannon for a soldiers' monument he brusquely replied, "I am not in the old junk business." He was, however, industrious in caring for the legitimate interests of the district and State. For many years he handled personally an enormous amount of routine correspondence. In matters of patronage he was not particularly successful. He was on unfriendly terms with Senators Hale and Frye almost from the start. "The only President I could ever get any patronage from was General Arthur, but nevertheless I have done very well," he once told Champ Clark.[1]

Democratic success in the congressional elections of 1882 had been only one indication of impending disaster for the Republicans. Grover Cleveland won the governorship of New York by an astounding majority and there were sweeping Democratic victories in Massachusetts and Pennsylvania. Within the Republican party itself, the reform element was becoming increasingly restive and there were ominous mutterings against the leadership and methods typified by James G. Blaine. With Blaine's nomination in 1884 the storm broke. The Mugwump schism of that year was the inevitable result. Reed was a party regular and not a reformer. He disliked and distrusted Blaine, but supported the party ticket in that year. His feeling toward Blaine's nomination, however, was apparent when Henry Cabot Lodge, meeting him on State Street in Boston, asked his opinion of the outlook. "Well," answered Reed sarcastically, "it is a great com-

[1] *My Quarter Century of American Politics,* I, 280.

fort to think that the wicked politicians were not allowed to pick the candidate and that the nomination was made by the people. The politicians would have been guided only by a base desire to win." But this is slightly anticipating our story. We must go back to the events in the House during the year 1883 and afterward.

CHAPTER VI

FOR six years following the close of the 47th Congress, the Democrats held control of the House, and Reed continued to do battle for reform of the rules. In its earlier stages, at least, the contest consisted for the most part of a protracted duel between the Republican leader and Samuel J. Randall. Randall had graduated from the rough and ready school of Philadelphia local politics, had served in the army during the Civil War, and was a veteran of twenty years' congressional experience. He was a man of integrity, courage, unusual parliamentary ability, and one of the ablest floor leaders in the history of Congress. As Speaker he had shown great ability and rendered important services, alike to his party and the country. Reed considered him one of the ablest Democrats of his time and once wrote that "there have been few men with a will more like iron or a courage more unfaltering." The mere fact that Randall represented a Philadelphia constituency for so many years is a sufficient index of his tariff sympathies, and in 1883 the demand for tariff reform was gaining headway. Samuel J. Randall, the protectionist and William R. Morrison, the leader of the low-tariff Democrats, were at loggerheads, and it was this feud that gave Reed such small measure of success as he attained.

Randall had served three terms as Speaker, but when the 48th Congress met in 1883 the party caucus bestowed the nomination on John G. Carlisle of Kentucky. Like Morrison, Carlisle was an advocate of a lower tariff. He was an able Speaker, but his adherence to traditional modes of procedure and his unwillingness to reform the existing rules, in the face of changing conditions and demonstrated abuses, not only discredited his speakership but prepared the way for Reed's radical reforms of 1890. "His name," says Alexander, "belongs in the short list of great Speakers. His opinions read like the decisions of an eminent judge. His impartiality and the sweetness of his manner prompted the minority members to present him a loving-cup as evidence of their affection." [1] "Carlisle is not naturally ineffective," Reed once remarked, "he is the ablest man they have on that side of the House. But no Speaker could do any better with his hands tied by the rules we are working under."

Morrison became chairman of the Ways and Means Committee, but Randall, who headed the Appropriations Committee, was still a power to be reckoned with. Not only was he an able debater, a master of parliamentary tactics and an inspiring party leader, but the Committee on Appropriations, under existing rules, held tremendous legislative power. By controlling, in large measure, the distribution of public funds, it frequently held the power of political life or death over the individual member. Under the "Holman amendment" it could attach legislation to appropriation bills, often the only method of securing passage for needed measures. This situation should be kept in mind, for it contributed to another important incident in Reed's career as parliamentarian.

The opening of the 48th Congress found the House Republicans in a somewhat embarrassing position. Keifer's real caliber was more apparent than it had been in 1881. His conduct as Speaker had multiplied his enemies. His greed for petty spoils, and especially his bestowal of places on near relatives, disgusted even his somewhat callous party colleagues. Nevertheless, in a singular exhibition of political obtuseness, the minority paid him the compliment of a renomination for the speakership.

By precedent, such a renomination carried with it the minority floor leadership, but Keifer's career in this capacity was brief. The ex-Speaker was in a parlous position from the start, and

[1] *House of Representatives*, 205.

when, on December 19, 1883, after having already been subjected to sundry annoyances and slights, he offered a resolution to prevent a North Carolina member taking his seat, only to have the minority led by Reed and Hiscock join the Democrats in rejecting it, followed by similar action on a motion to refer the case to the Committee on Elections, the action was taken as a final repudiation. "All in all," remarked the Washington *Post* next day, "it was a good day's work for the Republicans, but we are afraid the reform comes too late." Evidence forthcoming in the course of this session still further discredited the ex-Speaker, and after his defeat in the election of 1884 he passed into obscurity, to emerge twenty years later for another period of service.

Keifer and Reed were appointed to the Committee on Rules, the majority members being the Speaker, Blackburn and Randall. Reed retained a place on the Judiciary Committee, and in addition was also appointed at the close of the session to the Committee on Ordnance and Gunnery and, more important, to a vacancy on Ways and Means. The latter appointment brought him in close touch with tariff legislation, and for years to come the tariff was to be the chief issue before the country.

Now that Keifer had been deposed, Reed and Hiscock were much in the public eye, but contemporaries had little doubt as to the relative abilities of the two men. In any event, Hiscock entered the Senate in 1887. McKinley was making a reputation as a fluent speaker and an unswerving devotee of protection and, unlike Reed, was winning friends on every hand by his kindly disposition and charming manners. Nelson Dingley, whose district in Maine adjoined Reed's, and who as we have seen had begun service in the 47th Congress, was already known as an indefatigable worker whose speeches, if somewhat tedious, were based on genuine study. Joseph G. Cannon had many of Reed's qualities but had not as yet secured any great recognition. No

Republican, however, could seriously dispute the position of the Maine member, and in general throughout the eighties the Democrats enjoyed a decided advantage in the number, ability and experience of outstanding Representatives.

Reed at this time took little part in the social life of the capital, satisfying himself with an occasional dinner or card party. His financial resources were limited, and he had little assistance in handling the routine work which falls to the lot of every member. In addition, he was studying parliamentary practice, public finance, and sundry economic questions, not perhaps with the thoroughness of Nelson Dingley, but certainly with far greater industry than the ordinary member is likely to display.

The Washington correspondent of the New York *Times* gives an interesting picture of Reed and Hiscock, "the ablest men on the Republican side," as they appeared at this time. Reed was forty-five, Hiscock just under fifty years of age; both had been associated in public affairs since they appeared together in the 45th Congress; and both seemed to have a brilliant future. Reed he described as "the more brilliant of the two," "the brightest man in the House," "a master of parliamentary law," "a thorough lawyer," "a close student and a hard worker," "always well prepared upon any subject he undertakes to discuss." No man of his age in public life was better acquainted with "the minutiæ of past legislation." He was constantly, as we shall again note later, to be found in second-hand bookstalls rummaging for some rare publication.

"In personal appearance," continued the writer, "Reed disappoints at first, but the more you observe him the more he impresses you as a man of intellectual force. He is tall, large-framed and rotund. His walk is not graceful, the gait being heavy and rolling, as if he were trying to catch the roll and pitch of a vessel. His face is round and wears a jolly contented look. His forehead is high and bold, indicating fine imagination. Without knowing the fact, I would wager a round sum that he is fond of poetry and occasionally makes verses. He has a humorous vein and is witty when he wants to be. His voice is not pleasant to listen to because it is pitched high and has a nasal rasping sound. In ordinary conversation he has a deliberate expression, which with the nasal defect in utterance, instantly attracts attention and creates a disagreeable impression. His eyes are fine, and there is a roguish twinkle in them that pleases and attracts. He is a conspicuous object in the Republican side as you view the House from the gallery. There are lines of thought in his face and the evidence of reserved force which impresses the observer. If he is watching the ordinary proceedings of the House he has an indolent, listless look, which makes you think he is a lazy fellow. But the instant something interesting occurs his whole manner changes. He no longer balances on his chair, but either sits bolt upright or leans forward on his desk and is all attention. He is watching his opportunity either to let fly a keen, biting sarcasm at an egotistical speaker or to make a pertinent point in the debate. You will hear his rasping and irritating voice pierce the din of a contentious wrangle like the note of the hautboy. There is a pith in what he says that will please you notwithstanding the grating sound of utterance. He does not talk for the mere purpose of appearing frequently in the *Record*. His speeches always bristle with points. He is not an orator, but there is an earnestness and vigor in his style that sweeps you along, and you lose sight of the speaker's defects. . . . He hates shams and pretenses and delights in sticking pins in windbags." [1]

The 48th Congress had been in session but a few weeks when the contest over the rules broke out with renewed vigor. According to regular practice the rules of the preceding Congress would have been readopted, but in this instance the adoption was for

[1] February 9, 1884. For another contemporary sketch of Reed see New York *Tribune*, December 6.

twenty days only, extended early in January for a second period of the same length. On February 4, 1884, Randall on behalf of the Committee on Rules moved the adoption of the rules of the 46th Congress, thus getting rid of the innovations established by the 47th, citing in particular the amendment to Rule XVI under which filibustering in election cases had been effectively suppressed.

At once Reed was aroused by this destruction of his handiwork. He promptly moved a series of amendments, expressing the hope that he would have a careful hearing, because "the conduct of the business of a great nation" was dependent upon the action taken on these amendments. "We are authorized by the Constitution of the United States to make rules, not for the hindrance of business, but for the transaction of the business of the House and of the country." These bold amendments were identical with those he had offered in March, 1882, on which the House had failed to act.

His fight was much needed. To understand the existing situation it should be remembered that congestion of the congressional calendars, and especially those of the House, had reached an unprecedented condition. For twenty years the burdens of the national legislature had been steadily growing. The Civil War produced an incredible number of claims and similar matters which could be handled only in the form of private bills. Miscellaneous reports and petitions poured in in an endless stream. Changing economic and social conditions were reflected in the increasing activity of members and their bills threatened to choke the legislative hoppers. Doubtless much of the proposed legislation was unwise, some of it positively dangerous, but scattered through the mass were measures whose enactment was urgent.

Involved in the contest for reform of the rules was a still broader issue. It was not merely a difference in opinion as to proper methods of handling committee reports, claims, and appropriation bills. Inseparable from this were ancient differences in the philosophy of government. In the eyes of one group government was inherently evil, and its instrumentalities must be chained, weighted, placed behind a barrier of constitutional and legal entanglements so that there could be no sudden onslaught on private rights. In the eyes of another school, government, although not necessarily operating under divine sanctions, was at least a highly useful institution created by men for the accomplishment of indispensable ends. Its creators must be permitted to judge as to the method and the occasion of its use. Here lay part of the difference between the Jeffersonian and Hamiltonian schools.

While Thomas B. Reed was learned in parliamentary lore, he never made a mere fetish of the House rules. The broad principles involved, the objectives to be gained by rules of law, transcended in importance the mere formulation of procedure. He believed that government had positive as well as negative functions.

He believed in particular that Congress had grave and urgent responsibilities to meet, and that it was not meeting them. It should perform the work for which it was elected by the people or at least show adequate reasons for not performing it. Again and again he expressed his contempt for the do-nothing policy and the negative philosophy of some members of the Democratic party. "Are they but an organized 'no'?" he asked on one occasion.

The rules played an important part in the practical application of these theories of government, and Randall, whom Reed described as "the real governing force" in the Democratic party, held views as to their objects and functions which were diametrically opposed to those of his Republican opponent. "He had passed his life in the minority," Reed afterwards wrote, with special reference to the revision of 1880, "trying to prevent things from being done, and was therefore more anxious that the new machine should have perfect back action than that it should have forward movement." [1] It would be unfair to Randall, however, not to mention the fact that he had served his congressional apprenticeship during the governmental debauchery of the post-Civil War era and had gained much of his experience in manful opposition to the cruel and unwise Reconstruction legislation.

Reed's amendments of February 4, 1884, were directed chiefly at the order of business. The rules governing this subject were involved and technical and the amendments, as offered, had, necessarily, somewhat the same qualities. His explanation of existing procedure and of the general purpose of his amendments, brief, lucid, and admirably phrased, renders detailed analysis unnecessary.

"The principle of our present rules," he declared, "is that every question shall be taken up in the order in which it finds itself upon the calendars, and if the House were to transact all its business, and act upon every bill so reported, that system would be perfection itself, because it would only be a question of time as to when any measure would be acted upon." Congress, however, was unable to do all its business; in fact, not eight per cent of its business. Selection was made on the basis of place on the calendars, and it was in most instances the least important matters which were earliest reported from committee and placed on the list. This system encouraged the expedient of asking unanimous consent when measures could not be otherwise reached. "At least one half of the public building bills of the last session were passed in that way; and it is a most vicious and pernicious system of legislation."

Some business, Reed continued, was sure to get by if every-

[1] *Century Magazine,* March, 1889.

thing was dammed up; but under what conditions? "It is to depend not on the justice of the measure but on the impudence of the member." There was but one other way of doing business and that was under suspension of the rules by a two-thirds vote. The majority, however, should have control. It would undoubtedly pass bad bills, but that was one of the risks of republican government.

To remedy the existing conditions Reed proposed that the House establish a "morning hour" which should henceforth have a minimum length of sixty minutes. It should be utilized by committees for reporting and for the consideration of bills. If necessary, and the House approved, the "hour" should last all day, the committee having the privilege of concluding consideration of any bill unfinished at the close of the day, the next committee then to secure the same opportunities. He next proposed to eliminate the troublesome technicalities involved in reaching business on the calendar of Committee of the Whole—"perfect child's play" as he called them; urging that the committees be permitted to have a vote of the House on consideration of any proposition on this calendar on which they desired action. Finally, the House, subject to a few necessary restrictions, should be enabled, when it so desired, to proceed to consideration of business on the Speaker's table.

The total effect of the proposed changes would, he argued, be decisive. The House, subject to some necessary limitations, would be enabled to get to all the calendars, "take up such bills as the majority of the House are willing to take up," and proceed to transact the public business. With some additional points of minor importance he then offered his amendments for adoption, "because I believe in the government of the people, and I am not afraid of the government of the people through their representatives. . . . If the people do foolish things and suffer the conse-

quences of them, they will not be likely to repeat their foolishness." [1]

The Reed amendments received some Democratic support,
Roger Q. Mills pointing out that at the close of the last session
950 bills, favorably reported, had remained on the calendars as
unfinished business. "After you get beyond the boundary of
tariff legislation and appropriation bills and great measures of
that class, all other measures before this House come under the
head of unanimous-consent legislation." Similar in tone was the
warning of Richard P. Bland, of Missouri, that the country
expected the House to get rid of bad laws and pass good ones,
but "you never legislate except on privileged reports" from
such committees as those on Appropriations, Rules, or Ways and
Means.

There was, however, very little discussion on the part of the
Democratic majority, and on February 8, Reed closed the debate. "The single object of my amendment is to make a selection,
and I maintain the system I propose makes a selection in a better way. I doubt if there will be any more legislation passed, but
I believe a better class of legislation, one worthier of the House
will receive its attention. And I do not anticipate any great increase of legislation by it; but I do anticipate an enlargement of
the right of the members of the House to such an extent that
those bills which the House considers worthy will receive attention." [2]

Randall vigorously opposed the amendments. In this opposition he was quite consistent with one of his own rulings as
Speaker to the effect that the "morning hour," which, under
Speaker Blaine, had given each committee two days to put their
bills on passage with the privilege of continuing until finished

[1] *Cong. Record,* 48 Cong., 1 Sess., 869.
[2] *Ibid.,* 998.

with any measure pending when the second "hour" closed, really meant sixty minutes. Furthermore in 1878, as Reed remarked, "this conduit had been plugged" by restricting the use of the period to the reporting of bills.

When debate had closed, the amendments were voted down. Reed's gallant effort had failed, and he accepted defeat, remarking ironically, "The House having determined not to trust itself, let us see how far it will go." He felt that right was on his side, and that he would yet triumph.

The soundness of Reed's position was soon demonstrated by the course of events. The question of the rules would not down, and on April 17, a clash over the adoption of a pension bill allowed the principals in the February debate to state again their respective articles of belief on the basis of another two months' legislative inaction and futile debate. This debate also called attention to what was coming to be regarded as intolerable, the power of the Appropriations Committee over ordinary legislation.

An amendment to the pending bill facilitating the filing of pension claims was offered; and Randall declared it should come from the Committee on Invalid Pensions as distinct legislation, and not from the Committee on Appropriations. In fact, the former committee had already reported a similar bill and the rules, as Reed pointed out, prevented an amendment to any measure provided a bill embracing substantially the same provision was pending. The existing situation was a vivid illustration of the entanglements through which legislation was obliged to struggle. The rules, Reed declared, made legislation impossible except on appropriation bills, and then the chairman of Appropriations would not let this legislation be attached to such a bill. The rule prohibiting amendment while a bill of substantially the same effect was pending meant that amendments were restricted to matters of slight importance, as there were likely to be

NELSON A. DINGLEY

JOHN G. CARLISLE

bills on the calendars dealing with matters of genuine public concern:

Here we are, with the business of three Congresses piled upon this House and with the prospect that the business of four Congresses will be piled upon the next. . . . But once in a while there may be such a thing as an expression of judicious contempt for this condition of affairs. I am very sure, whatever may have been the feeling at the beginning of this session, that today I have in this expression the hearty sympathy of this House. We are doing no business, because under our rules we deliberately sacrifice our time in such a way that it is impossible to do business. Why, sir, we waste an hour almost every day in cataloguing the decisions which have been made by the committees. As I have had occasion to remark heretofore, with perhaps some exuberance of metaphor, the only effect of the decision of a committee is that it enables the corpse to be put in a glass case where the friends of the deceased can look upon the remains.

Reed added that there were 1200 reports of committees on the table and no business being done except by Mr. Randall's committee; "yet he, even with the assistance of Mr. Holman, is not equal to the business of the country." The country should get a chance to have its legislative needs met, but under the House rules it could not get it.

Randall replied that the rules were intended to prevent omnibus bills and save public money. Furthermore, he argued, the country was legislated to death. "If there be one evil greater than another today in this country, it is that we have too much legislation." Reed did not attempt to refute the latter statement. He did, however, declare emphatically that Congress sat for the purpose of hearing the people, regardless of the action it took when the hearing was completed. "But when we will not hear a matter we have done injustice gross and most foul. You might as well say a court of justice was doing right when it decided for the defendant by refusing to hear the plaintiff."

When the end of the short session approached the pressure for the passage of measures became terrific. The Appropriations Committee, exercising the whip hand through its control of funds and its power to accept or reject amendments to its bills, was in a position to dictate to the House. By waiting until late in the session the heads of the committee crowded the great appropriation bills through with a minimum of debate.

As Reed repeatedly pointed out, there was a mad scramble to secure the passage of a few bills out of the accumulations of a two-year period. Political expediency dictated what was done. A few members were placated by having their measures selected for passage, but the great bulk of public business merely piled up in hopeless confusion. 'We undertake," he graphically remarked, "to run Niagara through a quill. That is the effort that is made Congress after Congress since this infamous system of rules was adopted, and the result is always the same." [1]

He had no objection to being considered a fanatic on the subject, because "virtue in this world gets on not merely by sound statement but by reiteration of sound statement. It gets on by means of men having the idea driven into them that something is wrong. Everybody in this House knows from the condition of public business that something is wrong. Everybody knows it is a senseless proceeding for a body of three hundred and twenty-five men to sit here for two years and be chained as this body of men has been." [2]

The legislative farce reached a culminating point on February 26, when the House took up the sundry civil appropriation bill, containing 86 pages and 2089 lines of printed matter, involving an outlay of $22,346,749.74. It had less than a week to debate

[1] *Cong. Record,* 48 Cong., 2 Sess., 1288.
[2] *Ibid.,* 1290.

this measure, for there had been no way of forcing earlier consideration. Yet the bill, as many believed, was highly defective. Reed quite properly described the hurried debate as "an extraordinary spectacle" and ironically asked if it was what was meant by the constitutional right to originate appropriation bills—"the right to pass eighty-six pages of printed matter without examination, without reading, and without knowledge?"

But except for these recurrent and important attempts to reform the rules, the sessions of the 48th Congress were neither interesting nor productive. Reed belabored the Democrats in general and Randall in particular for their theory and practice of economy. In matters of national defense, he said, both the party and its chieftain took "a gentle refuge in the past—that home of the Democracy—the place where they live, and from which they never go."

Why, he also demanded, the efforts to starve the consular and diplomatic services? Why provide money for flags, stationery and signs and cut off the appropriation for rent? What sort of economy is it that "provides a sign for the legation and does not leave any place to stick it"? Money was being squandered in ill-advised efforts to improve the Mississippi, but "no man who has been up and down that river will doubt the fact that a work of this character is like undertaking to chain a tiger with a bullrush." Called to order stating that members of the Committee on Rivers and Harbors were more interested in congressional district expenditures than in real measures of improvement for the Mississippi, he vigorously defended the truth of his assertion.

He had two rough and tumble encounters with Democratic members during the first session. One with Townshend of Illinois grew out of Reed's unmerciful ridiculing of a Post Office appropriation bill. The Democratic member very unwisely lost his temper and denounced his opponent as the champion and defender of speculators, railroad corporations, and extravagant appropriations. Reed made a dignified but crushing rejoinder, addressed to "the only two sets of people" whose opinion he greatly valued—"the one is my constituency which knows me, and the other is this House, which knows him. And it is hardly necessary to say that I shall stand vindicated before them both."

The other incident involved a somewhat ridiculous mistake of S. S. Cox, who attributed some remarks of his own to Admiral Porter, thereby giving Reed an opportunity to liken the New York representative to George IV, who was the victim of an obsession that he had been present at Waterloo. Cox was furious and denounced "this man from Maine, with his gall bladder all reeking with meanness toward the Democratic party." After a series of unpleasant interchanges Cox sat down with the parting shot, aimed at Reed's handling of the Northern Pacific forfeiture case: "You ran the railroad business. I never did." "No," came Reed's rasping drawl in reply, "and the gentleman from New York never ran anything that required a head. The gentleman from New York pleads his size. I admit the insignificance of it. If he pleads littleness in every other respect I will admit it." Sometimes Reed, like Dr. Johnson, used the butt end of the pistol.

The tariff question was still unsettled, although with the Republicans controlling the Senate there was little chance that any House measure could become law. Morrison introduced a bill early in the first session making a general horizontal reduction in duties and placing additional articles on the free list, but it was soon apparent that the Democrats were hopelessly divided and the movement for reform degenerated into desultory wrangling which Reed not inaptly described as "staggeringly and putteringly trying to destroy the business prosperity of the country." Some members of the party were greatly agitated over "free raw materials." What is meant, he asked, by free raw materials? One representative had argued that that meant materials on which no labor had been expended. "Why, sir, it is the round earth without so much as a hole in the ground." Mr. Morrison, with his free trade leanings, would tear the whole tariff system up by the roots. "But when he can lead them to the Pisgah heights of the Morrison bill there in front of them will be the promised land of agriculture devoid of all manufactures, free from anything to trouble or molest or make the Democrat afraid." The bill, due to the defection of Randall and other protectionist Democrats, was eventually defeated.

Whether or not Reed's agitation was responsible, the 48th Congress came to a close with a wide-spread feeling abroad that changes in procedure were needed. Carlisle's valedictory, devoted very largely to a discussion of the existing pressure for legislation and the unprecedented congestion, contained a hint that procedural changes might be found necessary.

In the meantime, in 1884–85, Grover Cleveland had been elected and inaugurated. To millions of good people the presence of a Democrat in the White House was of sinister omen, but the President took up his duties in much the same fashion as his predecessors. The Constitution remained unimpaired. In the ensuing contest with the Senate over the exercise of the power of appointment and removal, Cleveland maintained the dignity and independence of his office in a manner which impressed the country. The reformers, as always, were disappointed at the President's handling of the civil service problem, but improvement was unquestionably made and the earlier gains were never entirely lost.

Reed's congressional speeches during the next two years were on other matters, but when renominated in 1886 he made some characteristic comments on the new administration, which, he pointed out, after twenty-five years of denunciation was conducting the government much as the Republicans had done.

By careful attention to Republican precedents, by following in our footsteps, the administration has received and deserved some praise. By this they have shown that they mean well. Meanwhile the party is not happy. They realize now that the present administration, though Democratic, is mortgaged. The first mortgage to the Mugwumps is ostensibly in favor of civil service reform; but it is one of those mortgages put on to deceive creditors. When the wrong kind of a Democrat demands office, reform heads him off. When one comes who has friends at court, civil service reform is but a nebulous ghost through which the properly recommended Democrat walks unharmed. . . .

This first mortgage, he said, would be lifted, but the second would not be. "It was given to the Eastern financiers and the title was well looked up. I do not complain of this, and yet I feel sympathetic. It moves the coldest heart to see the Western and Southern democracy, which through good report and evil report —mostly through evil report—have struggled for twenty years for an administration, to find itself put off in the very hour of victory by a mere equity of redemption."

He concluded this speech with a few remarks on the situation in the House. He pointed out that the Republicans at the outset had coöperated with the majority in changing the rules. There had been no thwarting of action by dilatory tactics and yet nothing had been accomplished. "A Democratic House and a Democratic administration, and both in power for fifteen months! The newest of new brooms and not even a back entry swept out yet." [1]

The attempts of the 49th Congress to reform procedure constitute another interesting episode in Reed's parliamentary career, which must now be considered.

When Congress met in December, 1885, it was apparent that an attack would be made on the power of the Appropriations Committee. The manner in which Randall had dominated the

[1] *Kennebec Journal,* June 4, 1886.

affairs of the preceding Congress rendered him a conspicuous target alike for honest reformers of the rules, disgruntled opponents within and without the Democratic party, and dissatisfied hunters of pork and privilege. His attitude on tariff reform had also aroused great opposition among his party colleagues. Congress, asserted the Washington *Post*, December 1, 1885, had too long "consisted of the Senate and Sam Randall." Randall saw the approaching storm and in published articles and an Associated Press interview pointed out that jobbery, raids on the Treasury, waste, and loss of control of the executive departments would be inevitable consequences of the proposed alterations.[1]

The caucus of the House Republicans met on December 5. Reed was placed in nomination for the speakership by William McKinley, receiving 63 votes as against Hiscock's 42, whereupon the latter moved to make the vote unanimous. Reed's position as floor leader, long recognized in actual practice, was thus given formal sanction. The Committee on Rules consisted of Carlisle, Randall, Morrison, Reed and Hiscock. Randall was thus placed in a position where he was practically helpless. His party colleagues were ready to combine with the Republican members in stripping his committee of its power.

Carlisle, Morrison, Reed and Hiscock joined in reporting the revised rules on December 14, 1885, Randall bringing in an extremely able minority report in which he repeated his views as to the evils involved in the proposed changes, citing in evidence the growth in river and harbor appropriations since they had passed from control of the Appropriations Committee. The majority report proposed to give additional committees on Foreign, Military, Naval and Indian Affairs, Post Offices and Post roads power to report appropriation bills directly to the House with the same privileges as the Appropriations Committee, which, be it remembered, included that of reporting to

[1] Washington *Post,* December 3, 6, 1885.

the House at all times, and still greater, that of demanding consideration of their reports at such times as the committee itself
might suggest. The committees on Agriculture and Rivers and
Harbors, it will be remembered, had already received similar
powers. The "Holman amendment" was to be abandoned.

In addition to distributing the appropriating power, the
majority report provided a second "morning hour" for consideration of bills placed on the calendars by committee reports. Furthermore, procedure in Committee of the Whole was somewhat
simplified. These changes soon proved to be entirely inadequate
and obstructionists could still prevent action which the majority
of the members might desire.

In debate next day, Reed urged the adoption of the majority
report. The last three Congresses, he argued, had been in irons,
"allowed to transact no public business except at the dictation
of a small coterie of gentlemen, who, while they possessed in-
dividually more wisdom than any of the rest of us, did not possess all the wisdom of this world." These gentlemen of the Committee on Appropriations, he added, in a statement which was
not altogether fair or accurate, had left the country without for-
tifications or navy, and had failed to respond to its other needs.
After all, the virtue and intelligence of its representatives must
be the country's chief reliance and under the proposed system
they would be better informed as to the public needs.

He expressed some doubt as to the effectiveness of the proposal for a second "morning hour" and the related changes in
procedure. But if they failed to furnish relief, "I shall be found,
as I always have been, in favor of the largest liberty which gives
a majority of this House, representing a majority of the people
of this country, a right to control." The rules as now proposed
were not a panacea; no system would enable 325 men to work
like a board of aldermen. He had already, as a matter of fact,

re-introduced on December 9, 1885, the amendments which had been defeated in 1884.

Reed had made some remarks during debate on the revision of 1880 in support of the centralized power of the Appropriations Committee, and Randall had not only appended them to his report, but other members had quoted them. "Some gentlemen have been kind enough to resuscitate a youthful effort of mine, made when I was a member of the Forty-sixth Congress . . . why, that is not half the extent of my offending against good sense. I actually believed that our old rules, adopted in the Forty-sixth Congress, were going to furnish a sensible way of transacting business; and I would hang my head in shame today if I had not had such good company at that time." He went on:

I do not promise the members of this House whenever they listen to me to give them wisdom of adamant. I do not promise them I shall not change my opinion when I see good reason for doing it. I only promise that I will give them honestly what my opinion is at the time. They must take their chances at its being for eternity.[1]

This speech in support of the "scatter" policy was certainly not "wisdom of adamant." Nor can the entire episode be considered one of the brilliant features of his career. This revision of the rules failed to deal with the essential defects in House organization and procedure which he himself had repeatedly pointed out. From the fiscal standpoint, the weakening of the power of the Appropriations Committee turned out to be thoroughly bad and for more than thirty-five years the change was to be used as an illustration of American backwardness and

[1] *Cong. Record,* 49 Cong., 1 Sess., 210.

shortsightedness in budgetary procedure. "It will not require the voice of a prophet," remarked William S. Holman in the course of the debate, "to foretell that you yourselves will in the end admit a great and vital mistake was made." Reed himself eventually admitted it. Apparently he was actuated at the time by a belief that the "backing up" of measures, the attempts "to pour Niagara through a quill" would be lessened and that other considerations were of secondary importance.

There was some opposition to the change among the Republicans. McKinley, Cannon, and John D. Long were among those speaking and voting against it, the latter making an admirably lucid and effective address in opposition to the "scatter" proposal. He admitted that under the existing system only three classes of measures could be passed: bills of such utter insignificance as could secure unanimous consent; those of such overwhelming necessity that they went through under a two-thirds vote for suspension of the rules; and those which by the grace of the Committee on Appropriations were carried through in the form of riders or amendments to general appropriation bills.

What was the remedy? First, said Representative Long, give each committee "full, fair, equal opportunity to present its business to the House and have the majority determine whether it becomes a law or not." Second, "shear the Appropriations Committee of every vestige of power of enacting general legislation in the form of riders or amendments to appropriation bills, thereby absorbing, and in the absence of other means of legislating actually controlling the action of the House." In view of the fact that the Senate rules in regard to the latter practice were diametrically opposed to those of the House, disagreements had been aggravated and conference committees had acquired undue power and importance. Furthermore the Appropriations Committee should be compelled to report its bills earlier. There changes should stop, for nothing was to be gained by annihilating the committee. Divided responsibility as proposed meant no responsibility at all.

The opinion of the House, however, was overwhelmingly behind the report and on December 18, it was carried by a vote of 227 to 70. Next day the newspapers carried an announcement that "Randallism" was dead.

While the changes made in December, 1885, failed to produce any revolutionary improvements, and the filibustering nuisance—with Reed participating—appeared sporadically, the 49th Congress accomplished more than its immediate predecessors. It passed the Presidential Succession Act, the Interstate Commerce Act, and repealed the Tenure of Office Act. Reed opposed all three, but took little part in debate. He supported the Edmunds Act penalizing polygamy in the Territories, although, as he declared, he strongly believed in local self-government. The case of the Mormons, however, was "an entire and complete exception to the general rule," their polity being such that they could not be permitted to run their own institutions.

The accomplishments of this Congress, however, seemed to be the result of cumulative pressure rather than well formulated design. The 46th Congress, Reed pointed out on February 5, 1885, had spent its time discussing the rules, and the same rules, once adopted, had proved a fatal handicap to transaction of business by its successors. The legislative current had been dammed up for the last seven years.

Bills and resolutions had piled up like a log jam in a Maine river. By determined efforts the drivers of the 49th Congress succeeded in extricating a few pieces and putting them on their way. In a short time, however, the jam was worse than ever. Three years later Reed placed the necessary dynamite, applied the spark, and the obstructions went out with a crash that shook the government.

At the time of Reed's death, the Louisville *Courier-Journal*, in an editorial which bears all the marks of Henry Watterson's authorship, remarked that "there was no duty in life from playing Republican Czar to a lot of obstreperous Democrats in Congress to the gentlest offices of the fireside, which this Yankee Titan did not fill to the brim. . . . He was by no means democratical in his private walks and ways; a picker and chooser of his company; not in the least effusive as to his personal outgivings; always self-contained, always self-respecting, yet—beneath the rock-ribbed exterior—a man every inch of him—loving the good things of the earth earthy, like the rest of us, self-indulgent to the point of duty, never beyond it; sublimated in nothing. . . ."

The intense activity of Reed's political life, the frequency and bitterness of the controversies in which he was involved, his reputation for blistering sarcasm and savage invective, all combined to divert attention from a very different personality—the Reed whom his intimates knew as a delightful companion and steadfast friend, or the Reed who appears occasionally in the memoirs of his contemporaries or his own writings as the student and philosopher with wide and varied interests in life and letters.

By 1884 Reed had won a secure place in congressional affairs. Before considering his subsequent career, in which he became the outstanding figure in the public life of his generation, the more personal qualities and interests of the man should receive some consideration.

In their earlier years in Washington the Reeds lived simply and inexpensively, first in a boarding-house, and for a longer period in a quiet family hotel, the Hamilton. In a little room under the roof, barely furnished and cluttered with books and papers, Reed worked and read. Occasionally he was seen dining with a group of his cronies at Harvey's restaurant, but for the most part he attended strictly to his public duties and it was not until he was the recognized leader of the House Republicans that he became a well known figure in Washington society. When he became Speaker in 1889 he moved to the Shoreham Hotel and resided there during the remainder of his congressional service. He was known as one of the most brilliant conversationalists of his time and was much sought after as a dinner guest. For the remainder of his life the presence of Tom Reed at a dinner party was regarded as sufficient to guarantee its success. Reed himself preferred small informal dinner parties and had no special liking for those formal state functions which his official position frequently obliged him to attend. Stories of his wit and repartee, which on such occasions lacked the barbs that characterized his public utterances, occasionally found their way into print, and some have been preserved in memoirs of the period; but for the most part they have vanished with the contemporaries who surrounded him.

He was not a total abstainer, but always abstemious in his habits both in eating and drinking, although it is of record that the Gridiron Club once presented him with a leather medal as the champion beefsteak eater. Frank L. Dingley declared that fewer dinner parties and more outdoor exercise would have given Reed a longer life. He loved a good cigar, and after an exhausting session in the chair or on the floor was frequently to be found smoking and chatting with his intimates.

The importance of physical training was not so much appreciated in Reed's day as a generation later. People were less concerned with expanding waistlines and dietary antidotes for them. Reed was a giant in stature, standing six feet three, and weighing from two hundred and fifty to two hundred and seventy-five pounds. His great frame was covered with muscular flesh, although in the nineties he tended toward obesity and became more careful of his diet. His bulk was undoubtedly an asset both on the floor and in the chair. It served not only to make him the center of attention, but conveyed a certain sense of physical mastery over the House. His slow movements and drawling speech sometimes gave strangers an impression of indolence or outright laziness. This impression was always short-lived. His mental alertness, quickness in retort, and pointed wit were in striking contrast to his physical qualities. Incidentally, a member once remarked that it was fortunate for Reed that dueling was no longer the vogue in Congress, as his tongue would surely have got him into trouble and his huge figure would have been too good a target to miss.

He had no interest in games, although he is said to have tried golf on one or two occasions without becoming sufficiently fascinated to follow it up. In Washington he walked a good deal, and in good weather was often to be seen on his way to and from the Capitol on foot. While fond of walking alone, he frequently made the trip with one or more companions and the contrast between Reed's giant figure and that of the diminutive Robert R. Hitt, who often accompanied him, always attracted amused attention.

His gait was characteristic and often the subject of comment; "a combination of pudgy roll and lurching stride, terminating in a jolting shrug of the body every time his heel meets the sidewalk," as one writer has described it. Others noted its resemblance to that of men accustomed to the motion of a ship's deck. Even the newspaper writers fell into nautical metaphors when describing him. "Aside from what is superficial," said one, "there's something of the sea in his nature; something salty, invigorating; while the expanse, the depth, the billow-like power and lucid strength of the man are suggestive of nothing so much as blue water." [1] The spectacle— "entertaining if not impressive" —of Reed negotiating the icy sidewalks of Capitol Hill on his way to the street car, was described by a vigilant reporter in similar terms. "He resembles, when he launches himself upon the ice, one of those Dutch luggers that bear down against the wind with the ease and rapidity of a Potomac River sand scow. He rolled and pitched. His ponderous bulk swayed from side to side as if in imminent danger of capsizing. It tacked here and fell off there." [2]

He enjoyed walking alone whether in the city or country, and store windows had a fascination for him. It was often noted that a display of haberdashery would hold him spellbound for minutes at a time. When traveling abroad or when campaigning in various parts of the United States he relished wandering about the various places visited, watchful, observant and enjoying himself to the full. He once mentioned after a prolonged and arduous campaign tour how much pleasure he had derived from riding on the street cars in San Francisco.

When in Europe Reed was always interested in national traits of character. The contrast between French and British habits and thought always appealed to him. He was a student of British and continental institutions, and naturally was especially familiar with their parliamentary practices. But judging by a letter which he wrote to Henry Cabot Lodge from Paris on May 27, 1891, he found that legislative bodies were much the same everywhere. He had, he wrote, visited the Italian chamber when in Rome. The deputy who had the floor resembled one of their own Alabama members. "He kept on and on. Nobody paid any attention to him but he never stopped as far as I know. It had such a homelike look, such a familiar sound that I felt as if I

[1] Washington *Post*, December 1, 1895.
[2] *Ibid.*, January 15, 1893.

were in my native jungle and as if it were really Herbert himself." [1]

While always generous in recognizing the merits of foreign governmental institutions and repeatedly paying tribute to the methods and traditions of the House of Commons, he was not impressed, like some of his contemporaries, with the possibility of adapting foreign institutions to American use. On his return from Europe in 1899 he was asked whether he had discovered anything in the parliamentary institutions of the countries visited which could be profitably grafted on to those of the United States. "No," he replied. "In each the conditions are different from ours, and I do not think that their methods could be successfully adapted to our needs. Of course if we are going into the colonizing and empire-building business we shall need a new outfit." [2]

Unlike Hannibal Hamlin, who was an expert hunter, or William Pitt Fessenden, who could forget the heavy responsibilities of war administration and lighten the burden of personal bereavements by whipping the trout streams of his native state, Reed never seems to have had the instincts of the sportsman which were so common in Maine men. He did, it is true, indulge in deep sea fishing—a poor substitute from the angler's standpoint—and enjoyed boating and sailing in Casco Bay. He had a summer cottage at Grand Beach and could be seen strolling along the shore or in the neighboring woods and bypaths. It was here that he delighted his neighbors by his efforts to learn bicycle riding. Wearing a white sweater which made his huge figure even more conspicuous, he was often seen pedaling clumsily and uncertainly along the paths or the hard sand of the beach, and on one occasion, according to observers, when the machine got out of control on a declivity he escaped going out

[1] *Lodge Papers.*
[2] New York *Tribune,* August 13, 1899.

REED AT VARIOUS STAGES OF HIS CAREER

to sea only by ignominiously throwing himself into a sand drift. It was here also that for a time he became absorbed in photography, though with no marked success as measured by technical standards. A friend who induced him to get into a canoe for a short trip up river long remembered Reed's labored response when cautioned not to rock the frail craft in a stretch of swift water: "Ira, you have insulted me. You are insinuating that I am a damned fool."

Reed was devoted to his family, although he kept his personal interests out of the public eye and disliked the intrusion upon privacy which is the inevitable accompaniment of prominence in public life. He was popular with children, and Miss Grace H. Boutelle, daughter of his Maine colleague, has recorded some childhood impressions of Reed at their Washington rooms, participating in a doll's party, amusing a children's gathering by his comments on an exhibition of "magic lantern" pictures, and in general displaying a characteristic side which was unknown to the public. "He never talked down to children," she recalled. "People who knew Mr. Reed in public life," writes one of his former neighbors, "I do not think ever realized his lovable character. Oftentimes, when at our summer home on the shore, he used to take my children in the woods nearby, and talk as if he were one of them." [1]

Reed regarded Portland as his home in spite of the fact that so much of his life was spent in Washington. In the eighties he purchased a three-story brick dwelling at the corner of State and Deering streets. It was a double house, the other half being occupied by William L. Putnam, for many years a judge of the United States Circuit Court. Visitors have described Reed's home as characteristic of the occupants in its simplicity, comfort and good taste. Most of them noticed the abundance of books. "Books," one of them wrote, "are scattered through the rooms

[1] Mr. J. C. Hamlen, Portland, Maine, letter to author September 23, 1929.

on every floor; books bought not for binding or editions, but for the contents, ranging from miscellaneous novels to the dryest historical treatises, from poetry to philosophy."

His home life, all his contemporaries agree, was singularly happy. Mrs. Reed was deeply interested in his work and he relied on her judgment in many matters, frequently submitting his set speeches or magazine articles to her criticism. It is said, however, that her presence in the House gallery was the only thing that ever made him nervous and that she seldom was a witness of his forensic triumphs. Two children were born, of whom his daughter Katherine became well known in Washington in the later years of his congressional service, and one of her father's valued assistants. His son died in early infancy.

A commonplace domestic incident gave rise to a well known story. His small daughter on one occasion was horrified to see her father about to seat himself in an armchair in which a favorite kitten was sleeping peacefully. It needed no vivid imagination to picture what his two hundred and fifty pounds would do to the innocent victim, and her action was prompt and effective. The chair was jerked abruptly from under him, and Reed's huge bulk hit the floor with a crash. The catastrophe was averted from the animal to the man. The results for all concerned might have been serious, but Reed, recovering his breath, got slowly to his feet, and closed the incident with the pained admonition: "Remember, Kitty, it is easier to get another cat than another father."

A letter to Henry Cabot Lodge, June 19, 1889, gives an interesting glimpse of Reed at his Portland home.

"But if you think we are leading an idle life here let me hasten to unfold a tale of sorrow. Our house is getting painted and papered and plumbed and we are camped in the midst of it all. We wake up at five, at which time it seems the beastly sun rises or has risen or something disagreeable of that kind. Heretofore the appliances of civilization, shades and blinds, have saved me from any knowledge of the disgusting facts of astronomy. Let me repeat to you that ignorance is bliss.

"After getting up at five, at seven I interview the laboring classes. Then we try to decide on papers and paints. At nine commences the deputations on Post Offices and things until I can't get time to answer your letter." [1]

He was not active in the social life of the city and positively refused to pose as the great man of the community. He enjoyed entertaining intimate friends at his own house and his hospitality was genuine and delightful. He never attempted to "nurse his constituency," confining most of his local political efforts to formal campaigning, but had a wide circle of acquaintances in all walks of life to whom he was always accessible. He could make satirical comments on his Portland neighbors, when occasion arose, quite as effectively as in Washington. "Have you ever noticed how narrow Squire So-and-So makes the street look?" was his comment on a pompous and conceited member of the Portland bar.[2]

But it was in the Cumberland Club that Reed was to be seen at his best, and it is around that old Portland organization that his memory will always linger. Here he spent a great deal of his time when in the city. The members, he once said, were for the most part friends from boyhood, had attended school together, and addressed each other by their first names; "indeed, there is no place like it." "This is where the old turtle can shed his shell," was another of his appreciative remarks. Here he loved to loaf, play cards and talk. The formal entertainments of

[1] *Lodge Papers.*

[2] Holman F. Day, "Tom Reed among his Neighbors," *Saturday Evening Post,* January 3, 1903.

the club had less attraction for him, and one of the members thirty years later still remembered how he once walked up the alley, climbed a fence, and slipped in the kitchen door to avoid a reception in progress in the front rooms.

In this environment he talked with the utmost freedom on men and affairs, sure that the members would never betray his confidence; and occasionally with more intimate friends he fell into the philosophical vein in which he displayed the deeper and more serious side of his nature. But for the most part, as Day describes him in this environment, "Happiness and ease and deep content radiated from his broad smile and rippled in his laugh. He would lead along some argumentative friend step by step and those sitting about 'could see it coming' with delighted anticipation. Thus when the unsuspecting one was at last in full range, bang! went both of the Reed barrels and down would go the adversary with the Reed roar leading all the rest of the laughter."

Reed was always a wonderful conversationalist in any environment. "In places where men congregate," one writer recorded, "he made himself a source of pure delight or apprehension and uneasiness according to his mood. To laugh with him was a joy, to be laughed at another matter." But there was no apprehension among his intimates. "No more agreeable companion ever lived," wrote Henry Cabot Lodge. "Like Doctor Johnson, he loved to sit and have his talk out, and no one was ever better to listen to or a better listener, for his sympathies were wide, his interests unlimited, and nothing human was alien to him. With the friends he cared for, and he was himself the most loyal of friends, he would sit or walk by the hour, talking of everything; the talk was always fresh, keen, and suggestive, and the great, hearty, contagious laugh would come at intervals and carry every one with it."

One of his most striking comments on Philippine policy was

recorded by a couple of Portland friends with whom he discussed the matter on a railroad train. What would happen, one had inquired apprehensively, if the American troops were withdrawn? "You don't think those Filipinos would chase our soldiers seven thousand miles, if they start for home?" rejoined Reed. When objection was offered that withdrawal would constitute humiliation in the sight of other nations, he added: "I have always observed that with individuals the fear of humiliation is exactly in proportion as they deserve it, and I believe the same principle holds good with a nation and with a party. Some people seem to be afraid that these Filipinos will put their tongues in their cheeks at us. They have done that already. They have watched our failure as others have . . . I conceive that freedom is just as dear to them as it is to us, and they will fight for it just as long." [1]

"He wore no shell," wrote Mark Twain. "His ways were frank and open and the road to his large sympathies was straight and unobstructed. His was a nature which invited affection—compelled it, in fact—and met it halfway. Hence he was 'Tom' to the most of his friends, and to half the nation. The abbreviating of such a man's name is a patent of nobility, and is conferred from the heart."

His friends did not escape his friendly banter. He once came to the relief of Robert R. Hitt, then a new member and later one of his trusted lieutenants, when the latter found himself obliged to offer on a Washington street car a larger bill than the conductor was able to change. Reed paid the fare and added, "Do you work this racket on the conductors as a regular thing?" Another story has frequently been told, with sundry variations, of an incident occurring during one of his visits to England, when a small group of friends gathered after dinner and a discussion on human destiny drifted into a somewhat serious vein. As it

[1] New York *Tribune,* September 13, 1899.

progressed, Joseph H. Choate was moved to remark, "I think I can say that I have lived a clean and decent life. I have none of the vices and a good many of the virtues, and I think I average up pretty well."

"I wish I could say that," said another member of the party.

"Well," said Reed, "Why don't you say it? Choate did."

He had much of the wag in his make-up and took delight in teasing Nelson Dingley. The latter, for whom he had great affection and the highest esteem, was devoid of humor and his temperament undoubtedly gave added zest to Reed's efforts. Dingley was a leader in the total abstinence movement and Reed therefore deemed it fitting on one occasion to look under the table in quest of his colleague at the conclusion of a public dinner. At another time, approaching Dingley's seat on the floor of the House he surveyed him with an intensity and solemnity that made the occupant fairly writhe with embarrassment. Then in apologetic tones he remarked: "I was merely thinking how respectable you are, Dingley. Actually, Dingley, there are times, as I sit and muse over you, when it seems as if you were respectable to a degree absolutely incompatible with human existence."

When Holman F. Day was a cub reporter on the Lewiston *Journal* he once visited Reed in his Portland office. "Do you and the rest of the devoted young men of the Lewiston *Journal* office realize that you are working for an awfully good man?" asked Reed with his characteristic drawl. "But probably you don't fully realize how transcendentally good a man he is." He then directed him to convey a message to his chief. "Tell him I still think he is an awfully good man. He always likes to hear that I think so. It always gratifies him to know that such a lost and wayward creature as I am appreciates his goodness." The reporter faithfully delivered the message and found that Dingley utterly failed to see the joke, as Reed undoubtedly expected he would.

A reporter once ran across him in the barber shop of a Washington hotel "looking like an aproned Buddha far plunged in contemplation." The negro barber tried to draw him out with a question about his baldness. His success was startling and the Speaker delivered one of his characteristic short speeches, beginning: "I came into the world that way. Then I had an interval of comparative hirsute luxuriance, but it was not enduring. I have long since emerged from the grief of the deprivation. It no longer affects me. Do not permit it to weigh upon you," and so forth at some length. The barber, breathless and dismayed, quickly subsided. "Speakuh! I should say he was a Speakuh," he was heard to remark as Reed took his departure.[1]

In a somewhat different category is an anecdote of the days of the Cuban agitation. While American newspapers were playing up Spanish atrocities on that island a South Carolina mob proceeded to demonstrate American culture and white supremacy by murdering a negro postmaster. Reed saw the story, clipped it from the morning paper and ordered his clerk to paste it on a sheet under the caption:

Another Outrage in Cuba
Body of a Patriot Riddled with Bullets and Thrown through
the Burning Rafters of his Dwelling

He then handed it to a South Carolina member who had been particularly blatant in demands for intervention. The latter began to devour the article greedily. "Why, this isn't Cuba," he exclaimed suddenly as he proceeded with the story. Reed turned away with the remark, "No, it isn't," but in tones of contempt that rasped like a file.[2]

[1] Washington *Post*, February 20, 1898.
[2] *Ibid.*, December 21, 1902.

While dignified and observant of all the proprieties in his official duties, Reed was simple and unaffected in personal relations. He did not, like some of his colleagues, consider it necessary to dress for the statesman's part. The linen suit which he wore during the sweltering summer sessions in Washington was practical and comfortable and that was sufficient for him even if its untidiness and bad fit amused the spectators. On June 13, 1894, the Washington *Post* reported among the congressional items of the day that Mr. Reed's favorite suit of "Kentucky tow" had been freshly pressed, and that the minority leader was apparently attempting to set a new fashion, inasmuch as the trousers were creased at the sides instead of in front. "The result was very funny. Mr. Reed's capacious legs looked as if they had wings on them, for the creases stood out conspicuously and with generous expansion."

He rarely, if ever, appeared in a silk hat, and his dislike of conspicuous clothing or jewelry was well known. He himself was satisfied with a modest scarf pin and an unobtrusive watch chain. On one occasion when admirers in Providence presented him with a cane, gold headed and adorned with filigree work, he was observed carrying it somewhat gingerly on board the train, and when at a safe distance from the donors, wrapping it in a newspaper and secreting it under his seat.[1]

Occasionally, however, he appeared with a red necktie, and in the course of the angry debates in the special session of 1893 a waggish reporter attributed the bad temper displayed on a certain occasion to the unhealthy influence of Reed's red tie—"one of those aggressive, bull-baiting reds, unsafe, offensive, and suggestive of a remnant of the bloody shirt elevated beyond its proper station."[2]

One of his Grand Beach neighbors, years later, still retained

[1] New York *Tribune,* January 29, 1895.
[2] Washington *Post,* September 17, 1893.

a vivid recollection of Tom Reed, clad in a torn shirt and old suit, busy at odd jobs about the premises. When he undertook to paint his fence, as he frequently did, the results were striking, as he invariably emerged, after an hour's work, dedaubed from head to foot. On another occasion, when Reed accompanied the neighbor on a sailing trip in the bay, a sudden gale obliged them to land at Portland. Reed had left that morning in his shirt sleeves, carrying one of Mrs. Reed's old fashioned waterproof cloaks with a hood as additional protection. His friend succeeded, as he thought, in smuggling him into the smoking car of a homeward bound train only to find the Speaker a few minutes later holding an informal levée for friends and constituents on the train, entirely unabashed by his ridiculous appearance. Mrs. Reed's horrified expression when he at length arrived home added to the humor of the occasion.[1]

He was fond of card games and played frequently, sometimes at the Washington home of Joe Cannon. According to reports, he was a poor player and his partners at whist sometimes urged him to undertake a revision of the rules. He loved the great American game of poker, but was very moderate and conservative—a fortunate circumstance, for he was a notoriously bad player, paying little attention to the methods of his opponents or the number of cards drawn. According to D. S. Alexander, Reed was utterly incapable of any form of deception, unable "to appear serene when he is cross, nor indifferent when he is interested," and these qualities always cropped out when he played poker with members of the New York delegation. Invariably he had nothing left at the end of the game. "They knew when he was bluffing." [2] Those who remember his games with cronies at the Cumberland Club corroborate this testimony.

[1] Mr. J. C. Hamlen, letter to author, September 26, 1929.
[2] *Bowdoin Quill,* January, 1900.

His fondness for poker at times perturbed his straight-laced colleague Nelson Dingley. During the preparation of the Wilson tariff, in response to Reed's advice that Dingley had better get a Democrat to introduce him to the Ways and Means Committee if he had anything for which he wished to secure protection, the latter was moved to inquire, "Have they put that tax on poker yet?"

"Dingley," responded Reed in his most solemn and portentous manner, "I am sorry to have you betray your anxiety so early in the game. I was hoping that your interest in not having this tax put on would be kept from the public, so that you would make a telling speech in opposition, but I am afraid it is too late. Your only salvation lies in the fact that your constituents will think that the poker tax has something to do with the steel and iron schedules."

Throughout his life Reed derived a vast amount of recreation and comfort from books. At his Portland home he accumulated what was said to be the largest private library in Maine. There were few men in the public life of that generation who read as widely or had better literary taste. He bought many volumes annually and the second hand bookstores on Pennsylvania Avenue knew him as a regular customer. He enjoyed rummaging among their stock, occasionally purchasing some odd book, pamphlet, or engraving which caught his fancy. He once told with great glee how the eccentric elderly proprietor of one establishment, with whom he frequently haggled, terminated an argument as to the price of a book entitled "Scruples." Reed had objected that it was not worth what was asked. "Take it or leave it," retorted the store keeper. "What does a congressman want of a book with that title anyway?" Reed took it. "I have spent a lot of time hunting books," he wrote Lodge from Paris, July 2, 1891, "and I think have near two hundred volumes to add to my library, mostly things I don't need but which I wanted." [1]

He was a thorough student of American history and biography and read widely in the field of government and comparative legislation. Acknowledging the gift of Lodge's *Washington*, July 14, 1889, the first volume of which he had read at a sitting, he wrote: "Upon my word, I am pleased with the *George Washington*. It comes to me like a discovery. He has always been classed in my mind with St. Paul and John M. Mead and Adoniram Judson and other like persons with whom I wished always to be on respectful terms but with whom I never intended to associate." And a few days later, having completed the second volume, he added: "Your rescue of his character as an American from the phrase mongers had a vigor which stirred my blood. . . . It has given me two days of real pleasure." Lodge, apparently, did not appreciate the reference to Mead and Judson, for two weeks later Reed wrote: "It seemed probable that you would not, for a Unitarian education blunts the perceptive faculties greatly as to facts connected with true religion. I flung in St. Paul so that you might know that the others were pious." [2]

He retained some of his early interest in religious writings, and possessed a number of well-used commentaries on the Scriptures, but gave an increasing amount of time to philosophy and general literature as the years passed. He delighted in *Punch*, of which he came to own thirty-five bound volumes. He was always fond of novels. "It is surprising," he once wrote, "how much there is in the modern swarm of novels, how much of study and research. They do a part in the education of the world of which the schools and colleges might well be proud." [3]

[1] *Lodge Papers.*
[2] *Ibid.*
[3] *Illustrated American,* September 11, 1897.

He was fond of poetry and read Burns, Byron, and the Victorian poets, especially Tennyson, constantly and with great enjoyment. Some of the men who knew him best always declared that Reed had a deep vein of sentiment in his make-up, and that he concealed it, for the most part successfully, by the somewhat cynical and sarcastic side which he displayed to the world.

A. Maurice Low noticed the difference between Reed, "the Achilles of his party," and "Reed the scholar and the student, Reed quietly sitting in his little room in his hotel reading poetry or philosophy, examining into causes, trying to solve for his own satisfaction the eternal why and wherefore, the same eternal questions that every man who thinks must ask himself—that is, unless he can cast the burden of thought on the back of religion, and Reed's religion was not broad enough to carry the burden of his brain." He has described one occasion on which he visited Reed in search of political news only to find him poring over Burton's *Kasidah*. Reed refused to discuss politics, but read from the poem and "talked with marvelous power and force and insight" of "all that lay before him and what he had been forced to overcome."

When he was more than forty he took up the study of French and acquired not only an effective reading knowledge but a fair command of the spoken language. He took a vast amount of enjoyment in reading both the older French memoirs and histories and modern French literature, and accumulated some five hundred volumes in French. "There is a pleasure in the study of the style of a language," he wrote, "which becomes measurably exhausted when we become acquainted with its literature. Then we must seek pleasure in the study of some other language; in studying the style in which its phrases are turned. It is for this reason that I read so much of the French. I read a great deal of the light literature of our own language at times. I find a great deal of pleasure in the works of Thackeray and Dickens. Charles

Lever is another of my favorites, and there are three or four of his works which give me pleasure at all times. I like Charles Reade very much; in fact, I think he is the best story writer in the English language today. I do not devote much time to tariff literature. Most of my reading is done during the vacation." [1]

A vigilant reporter has recorded an interesting glimpse of Reed riding up to the Capitol on a street car during the protracted and dreary summer session of 1888. Reed seated himself ponderously on a front bench, surveyed the neighboring occupants cautiously, and apparently satisfied by his scrutiny, drew from his pocket "Theophile Gautier's very wickedest story," *Mademoiselle de Maupin,* to the perusal of which he devoted himself for the rest of the trip. [2]

He had a deep admiration for Balzac. "His closeness to nature and life hold you in spite of yourself because there is hardly a book of his which is not sad beyond tears." Take, he said, the wonderful delineations of character in *Eugènie Grandet, Le Peau de Chagrin,* or *Père Goriot.* "How sad they all are, and the sadness of a life that toils not nor spins. Verily to be happy we must take no note of the flying hours, and live outside of ourselves. Is not the condition of joyous life to forget that we are living? Here most of the characters are so entirely selfish that one sometimes thinks there is not one single friendly heart in the entire story. All are so conscious of living—even those in the higher sphere—and are so anxious to appear other than they are, that their entire lives are only ignoble struggles, with nothing of serene repose. When the strife is not for gold or position it is for love, which is thus degraded." [3]

For practice he kept a somewhat fragmentary diary in French,

---

[1] Washington *Post,* June 3, 1888.

[2] *Ibid.,* August 26, 1888.

[3] Quoted, Robert P. Porter, "Thomas B. Reed of Maine. The Man and his Home," *McClure's Magazine,* October, 1893.

and the excerpts available show the wide range of his reading and general interests in addition to interesting comments on every day affairs in Washington.

Reed was a superb debater who excelled in brief pointed speeches. He once stated to Representative John Russell of Massachusetts: "Russell, you do not understand the theory of five minute debate. The object is to convey to the House in the space of five minutes either information or misinformation. You have consumed several periods of five minutes this afternoon without doing either." [1] As might be expected, his own speeches were too condensed and pointed for any display of erudition and literary allusion. His command of the mother tongue was remarkable. His epigrammatic sentences went into the record as they fell from his lips, and he practically never revised or edited them before printing. He rarely quoted and always insisted that the House was no place for mere rhetorical display. Nevertheless, here and there in the course of his career on the floor, random comments or stray bits of curious and unusual information show how broad was the range of his reading and information.

One of Reed's speeches during the second session of the 47th Congress, for example, gives a glimpse of this other personality, strikingly different from that of the parliamentarian, the protectionist, the partisan leader of rough and tumble debate. The Congressional Library, then housed in the basement of the Capitol, had long since outgrown its quarters and various proposals had been made from time to time for a new and adequate structure to care for collections which had been growing steadily for almost a century. "Economy," however, was always popular unless home politics stood to benefit by a generous expenditure of public funds, and the library project immediately became a target for members who had a burning desire to protect the Treasury from such wanton extravagance.

[1] Lodge, "The Democracy of the Constitution," *Thomas Brackett Reed*, 199.

In support of an amendment limiting the cost to two million dollars, William S. Holman, the indefatigable "watch-dog of the Treasury," declared his unshakable opposition to all embellishments for such a building. It should be plain, solid and substantial, in harmony with American institutions. The people, he declared, "have demanded a plain, frugal government, such as excited the pride of their fathers, not one embellished after the models of government which we have long left behind. Great isolated institutions fostered by government belong to the old ideas of government not to the new." Others urged that Washington, populated by government employees, and the resort chiefly of casual visitors and persons having business with the courts and public offices, had no need of a general library. A Maryland member went so far as to suggest that more than half of the volumes in the present library "might be with advantage destroyed or distributed to other libraries."

Among the utterances of these Bœotians Reed's brief speech of December 12, 1882, fairly sparkles. It reveals for a brief instant Reed the man of letters, the lover of good literature, the philosopher, and the legislator with a vision of greater and better things than post offices, pensions, and river and harbor appropriations. To the great host of readers and scholars who year in and year out avail themselves of the vast collections of the Library of Congress it should be of appealing interest.

The nation, he pointed out, had treated its store of literature and learning with a contempt which could not but arouse indignation and sorrow among all who had any regard for learning or any love for books. As for burning half of the collection, who would decide which half? What was useless to one person, was invaluable to another. Macaulay's great history owed "its very existence, its strength, its picturesqueness and power," to the author's use of pamphlets which other men had discarded as ephemeral and useless. There should be one library on the continent where everything could be found, and the question of cost was not the paramount consideration.

If the nation had such a collection, it should be properly housed in a building "fitted for the treasures a library building ought to inclose." Members opposing such a project could not "look down the centuries and see the wants of this country for future times," but books would always be collected, knowledge would continue to spread, and provision must be made for ever growing needs. "Let us," he concluded, "be worthy of the nation we belong to; let us be worthy of the civilization we believe in; let us make a building worthy not only of ourselves but of the object for which we build it." [1] The bill failed at this session, but long before Reed had finished his career in Washington, the library had been provided with quarters which on the whole were "worthy of the object."

Reed's letters were for the most part as brief and pointed as his remarks in the House. His characteristic humor is always in evidence. "How did this happen?" runs a note in the scrapbook of the Cumberland Club, addressed to the treasurer and inclosing a small check in payment for cigars and playing cards. "I took so much trouble to pay up fully before I departed that I am grieved over this renewed charge of card playing and smoking. It lumps me up with bad men again, after I had abandoned their society."

Much of his correspondence was conducted in longhand, and when hurried, was written in large sprawling characters. Sometimes he supplemented his remarks with crude pen and ink drawings on the margins of the page. He was careless as to spelling and punctuation. "That was very low down in you to criticize my spelling," he once wrote to Lodge, who had twitted him with his having deviated from the accepted spelling of "cynical"—"cyn-

[1] *Cong. Record*, 47 Cong., 2 Sess., 221–2.

icle" was Reed's version—"because it is universally admitted to be beyond criticism. It is mighty lucky that I got as near as I did. You have the most untranslatable writing I ever saw. If we both of us wrote by typewriter, I would spell well and you would be legible." [1]

[1] *Lodge Papers.*

WHEN Reed became Republican nominee for the speakership of the 49th Congress, it was formal acknowledgment of the fact that he was now one of the leaders of American public life. While several years were to pass before the country at large realized his capacity as his colleagues had long since done, and while he was destined to fail in his ambition to secure the highest honor in the gift of the party, he was from 1885 until his retirement fourteen years later a tremendous influence in congressional affairs and after 1889 his opinions on public questions commanded nation-wide attention. It is worth while, therefore, before taking up in sequence the events of his later career, to consider the political and economic principles for which he stood and the underlying philosophy which shaped his conclusions as to both throughout a long career of public service.

In an introduction contributed to Calvin Colton's edition of the works of Henry Clay, Reed once pointed out that "the speeches of a statesman who is under the inexorable necessity of bringing things to pass, suffer much with the lapse of time." Subsequent generations seldom appreciate the power and importance of the prejudices he has to meet, the personal rivalries which embarrass him, the varied extraneous factors which he is obliged to consider. "It is here that reformers and men of letters have so manifest an advantage." Unlike the statesman, obliged continually to deal with men "who have both their own prejudices and those of the people they represent," they "can utter truths of all time regardless of the prejudice of the hour." "We all like criticism," he wrote on another occasion, "it has so few conditions. It is temporary emancipation from the thraldom of time and space. Therefore there are fewer limitations on its brightness." [1]

Thomas B. Reed was a statesman. In what is perhaps his most famous aphorism he once defined a statesman as "a successful politician who is dead," but his own career, taking "politician" in its ordinary American usage with all its implications, was a refutation of the definition. He was a man of letters, and had he given himself fully to that work, he might have been a great one. Except in the field of parliamentary procedure, he was not a reformer and there is ample evidence that he regarded reformers in general sometimes with sympathetic concern, but more often with cynical suspicion.

"One, with God, is always a majority, but many a martyr has been burned at the stake while the votes were being counted," was one of his comments when opponents seemed unduly confident of divine inspiration and protection; and the remark is indicative of the cynicism with which he was inclined to view "causes," "missions," and enthusiasts in general. Senator W. E. Chandler can hardly be considered a reformer, but one of Reed's remarks is characteristic of his general attitude. "I see the dear Chandler will not willingly let bimetallism die," he wrote to Senator Lodge, August 27, 1897. "Isn't William trying to make the world better in more spots than he can visit and oversee?" [2] He was fond of Theodore Roosevelt, but he viewed the latter's crusading spirit with a certain tolerant amusement and on one occasion was moved to remark: "Theodore, if there is one thing more than another for which I admire you, it is your original discovery of the ten commandments."

But if a man ever knew his own mind and spoke it in pungent language, Reed was such a man. Intellectual honesty was one of his outstanding traits, hardly questioned during thirty years of

[1] "Critics and Leaders," *Illustrated American,* October 23, 1897.
[2] *Lodge Papers.*

partisan warfare. He was a student, a thinker, a sound reasoner, and he preferred his own opinions to those of party colleagues or the general public. From his speeches and published writings it is possible, therefore, to form an accurate judgment as to his views of the great issues before the country in the last quarter of the nineteenth century, and as to the school of political thought of which he was such an outstanding representative.

He had, to an unusual degree, the ability to see beyond the immediate project before the House and to estimate its ultimate effects. "Reed," says William Allen White, who knew him well in his later years, "was a scholar of wide and judicious reading. He knew things at the base; and understood the ultimate philosophy of them." [1]

The philosophical tone is in evidence throughout his career, but especially so in the speeches which he made or the articles which he wrote in the last decade of his public life—the days of his fame—when the public crowded to hear him and editors bid eagerly for contributions from his pen. But it appears also in casual remarks in the course of debate, in comment on a petty appropriation, in some sarcastic fling at an opponent whose inflated confidence in the efficacy of a legislative nostrum aroused his ire. Or, now and then some friend listened to one of the monologues to which he was given in his later years, and was impressed with its objectivity. One such occasion is of record, when, on the day of McKinley's funeral, he sat with William Allen White at a window of the Century Club in New York and "for three long hours discoursed most beautifully upon life, its uncertainty, its real rewards, and its checks and balances; upon fame and its accidents and its emptiness; upon death and immortality, and God and all His ways and works."

Constantly influencing his attitude on concrete questions, and undoubtedly accounting in part for the frequency with which

[1] Emporia *Gazette*, December 8, 1902.

contemporaries regarded him as a fatalist or a cynic, was his
philosophical outlook on human progress in general. There was,
he argued, no such thing as continuous progress "so many inches
to the mile, so many miles to the year, and all without jostle or
push, comfortable and serene from dawn to dark." [1] Advances
were often followed by violent reactions when all that had been
gained seemed lost.

Social improvement of any kind was a slow process. "This
is a world that goes slowly," he once remarked in an address to
the Young Men's Republican Club of Philadelphia, "because
it has an eternity to go in. . . . We are supposing that whenever we have decreed that the millennium shall come that it will
come, and are always forgetful of the years which are absolutely
necessary to intervene between the good that we intend and the
good we actually accomplish." [2] Furthermore, as he pointed out
in his last important public address, at the Bowdoin College centennial in 1902, the real beneficiaries of social action had often
been the very ones who most bitterly opposed it. But if the people were often intolerant of innovations it was well to remember
how frequently learned men had led the attack on new dis-
coveries.

Mankind, he continued, reasoned differently in matters of
public right and wrong as distinguished from personal. It took
a long time for truth to penetrate to the depths of the human
race, but only when it did so could it prevail. "The reason why
truth is given the eternal years of God is because she needs them
every one." Also, "with wide knowledge come doubt and difficulties. Ignorance has no hesitations. Philanthropy does noble
work, but there is very little of it. Human self interest is constant and perpetual. It is untiring." Habits were likely to prove
barriers to progress. "Intellect is the great pioneer. It points the

---

[1] "Historic Political Upheavals," *North American Review*, January, 1895.
[2] Washington *Post*, April 10, 1890.

pathway. Habit treads it every day. For the ordinary business of life, an ounce of habit is worth a pound of intellect." There was too much reverence for the past. "We weep over lost causes which were fortunately lost, and mourn over pretenders whose attributes and adventures are the life of literature and the grave of fact."

All social progress was dependent on the people taken as a whole. Leave any portion of them a prey to ignorance, and the consequences affected everybody. Mere leadership counted for very little. "If human progress had been merely a matter of leadership we should be in Utopia today," he declared in a notable address at Colby University, June 30, 1885. "War would have ceased long ago, and perhaps government by the people would have become automatic in all its branches."

Great movements like the Puritan revolt or the French Revolution were not created by leaders. "The men who are at the top of these great waves get mistaken in the popular mind for the wave itself." One of these transformations, he pointed out, was even then in progress in the United States. Criticisms of Abraham Lincoln—so common in his lifetime—were disappearing. "But to say that without him we could not have worked out the problem would be to do, not justice to him, but injustice to all the others."

Public sentiment, "in its essence nothing more or less than the expression of the average intelligence and average ignorance of mankind," constituted "the ever present regulator and police of humanity." It was public sentiment—not the Revised Statutes —which governed the American people. It made the Revised Statutes; it executed them, "with due abatement if they seem harsh, and puts in an occasional Bill of Attainder or lynching if they seem not adequate." Public sentiment distrusted innovation. Whoever invented the table fork undoubtedly offended the sentiment of his day and it was a long time ere that useful implement came into general use. "Let a man proclaim a new principle. Public sentiment will surely be on the other side."

But in spite of the fact that raising the level of public sentiment was a slow and laborious process, and retrogression only too common, Reed was not a pessimist. He might ridicule projects of reform, but he was confident that in spite of local failures and temporary set-backs, humanity was moving forward. We were not, he declared in his Bowdoin centennial oration, "governed by the spirit of the hive," nor "victims of destiny, with our lot marked out for us beyond our will and ken." "Justice, equality and the rights of man have an ever increasing sway." The influence of mere physical strength was declining. "Whatever contribution any man makes to humanity and justice will not be lost, but will be gathered up and be among the treasures of the Almighty."

What was the use, he argued in the House, of educating a few Indians here and there, if nothing were done to raise the general level of the race? Whites, negroes and Indians were all alike in one respect. "We hate to see people standing too much above ourselves; we never endure it patiently. In practical life we never submit to it. We either grow up to the advanced people, or we pull the advanced people down." [1] Congress could accomplish no more than the conflicting interests and political intelligence of the American people permitted. "A representative body," he declared, "has to do the best it can to reconcile with the terms of its proposed action all the prejudices of the whole people and to take into account their wrong views as well as their right views."

He believed, naturally enough in view of such a philosophical basis for political doctrine, in the traditional democratic methods of the country. Social progress might be slow, but he was adamant in opposing proposals to speed it up by depriving any part

[1] *Cong. Record*, 52 Cong., 1 Sess., 1525, also June 13, 1894.

of the community of political power. He even expressed disapproval of educational requirements for suffrage. He began his public career in the midst of the emotional enthusiasm for the rights of the downtrodden and oppressed which followed the Civil War and he closed it in disgust at the new policy of exporting what he contemptuously described as "canned freedom" to colonial dependencies.

Throughout the thirty years which intervened he had stood loyally by his views of democracy and human rights. He believed that the negro had a right to vote and was never entirely reconciled to the abandonment of the freedman to the mercy of State suffrage restrictions. "We would like all our citizens to be learned, we wish they were all rich," he declared while arguing for the Federal Election bill at Pittsburgh, "but until they are both we will take the average of them as they are." [1] The rule of the majority was the safest and most satisfactory method of government. "John Stuart Mill knew more than any of us," he once remarked in a political address to his own constituents, "but I would not want to be governed by John Stuart Mill."

But if some of Reed's views on suffrage and democratic control seem unsound to a later generation—and it is well to keep in mind the influence of the "inferior races" concept which spread throughout our political consciousness after 1899—in one matter, woman suffrage, he was decidedly in advance of his time. Unlike many of his contemporaries who bestowed the ballot on the freedmen and were willing, if necessary, to order out United States troops to protect them in its exercise, but who considered the enfranchisement of women a dangerous innovation, Reed was a firm believer in their political capacity and in their inherent right to participate in the government of the country.

The Committee on the Judiciary of the 48th Congress made

[1] New York *Tribune,* April 27, 1890.

an adverse report on a proposed constitutional amendment providing for woman suffrage. Reed, then a member of the committee, dissented in characteristic terms. Years later this minority report was reprinted in connection with the suffrage movement which culminated in the adoption of the Nineteenth Amendment. The original bore the date April 24, 1884.[1]

"No one," he began, "who listens to the reasons given by the superior class for the continuance of any system of subjection can fail to be impressed with the noble disinterestedness of mankind." The good of the African was always the main object of slavery and when children were considered "little animals who had no rights," it was their own good and not the bad temper of parents which was used to excuse severity of treatment. Political equality for women was opposed by reasons "drawn almost entirely from a tender consideration for their own good," and this anxiety "would be an honor to human nature were it not an historical fact that the same sweet solicitude has been put up as a barrier against every progress which women have made ever since civilization began."

The Turk or Algerine, he continued, would consider the liberties already enjoyed by Western women as exceedingly dangerous, "a violation of the divine law which in the opinion of all conservative men, always ordains the present but never the future." When women received the right to own their own property and to keep the earnings of their own labor, dire results were predicted. It was argued that "the only real safety for women was the headship of man" and such innovations threatened the integrity of the family. Nevertheless, the emancipation of women had continued and they were proving their usefulness in a constantly growing sphere. Why not approach the question without trepidation? "We can better leave the sphere

[1] *House Reports,* 48th Cong., 1 Sess., No. 1330.

of women to the future than confine it in the chains of the past."
As for the vague talk about "nature" it meant only "that the
thing we are opposing has not hitherto been done."

There was no reason on earth for extending suffrage to men
and not to women. Our government was founded on the rule
of all, "the ignorant, the learned, the wise and the unwise, the
judicious and the unjudicious are all invited to assist in governing." Women should share in political life and profit from its
educational advantages. They had influence at present, but it
would be wiser to give them responsibility.

He was a bitter partisan and believed, naturally enough, that
the political party was all important in the machinery of popular
government.

"There is no such thing as a non-partisan republic," he argued
in his speech on Federal election laws April 22, 23, 1880, "and
the moment you get a non-partisan republic that republic is
tottering to its fall." Parties, he continued, grew out of the necessities of mankind. The dominance and responsibility of one
party was the basis of the elective system. Non-partisan expedients had never proved satisfactory in the United States. In the
municipalities they had proved a source of corruption. "The
best system is to have one party govern and the other party
watch." Naturally, he considered the Democrats better qualified
for watching than governing. Men associated in their respective
parties because progressive, honest, interested in public improvement, or because conservative, hostile to progress, and on the
average insufficiently enlightened. Every party, at the polls, expressed its average intelligence. The Democratic party might
have brilliant leaders but he believed that its average of intelligence was lower than the Republican.

He never wholly outgrew the Civil War sentiment that "the
worst Republican is better than the best Democrat." He was
generous in his tributes to individual opponents but had scant

respect for their party. He once wrote, arraigning it for the failures of the 52nd Congress, that the Democratic party was "a
hopeless assortment of discordant differences, as incapable of
positive action as it is capable of infinite clamor." [1]

Reed was a conservative but he detested the Bourbon type of
conservatism which dominated the opposing party. "Hanging
on to old traditions is the business of the Democratic party, and
it does that business well; we can never rival it." [2] "That is so,"
he retorted to an opponent who boasted that the Democratic
party would last forever, "there has always got to be a hind end
of things." "I hail every advance of the Democratic party with
very great satisfaction," he remarked on another occasion, "because I am a sincere believer in the doctrine that in order to
have an army take a new march the rear guard must be got up."

He saw no necessity for innovations in governmental methods.
"I look upon many of the tendencies—temporary I hope—of
modern times with great distrust," he declared in the course of
a speech on the Edmunds Act, "for instance, the tendency to take
from the people of this country their power of frequent examination into the acts of their officials. I believe that biennial elections and quadrennial governorships are inventions which deprive the people of power, and at the same time offer prizes to
be captured by the corruption of political life."

He opposed the amendment of the Maine constitution substituting biennial for annual elections, and when Massachusetts
was considering a similar change, a letter which he wrote to
Adin Thayer was read into the records of a legislative committee,
stating that he considered the action of Maine "a great mistake"
and the whole project merely "one of the many expedients
which are always starting up to carry on a government of the
people without the people." The people in the long run would

[1] "Two Congresses Contrasted," *North American Review,* August, 1892.
[2] Speech before Americus Club, Pittsburgh, April 26, 1890.

get just the sort of government they deserved, and nothing had ever proved more satisfactory than the New England system of town government. It would be better appreciated after all experiments "for avoiding elections, concentrating power in the hands of mayors, governors, and presidents," had broken down.[1]

Good laws and good administration could only be brought about by a good people. A temporary conquest by a minority, even if its enactments were theoretically good, was rarely effective, in spite of the fact that minorities often made up by zeal what they lacked in numbers. Laws made by minorities were likely either to be imperfectly administered, or if they were rigidly enforced they would be overturned. Legislation, he frequently pointed out, should, to be most effective, "represent the average sentiment of the people, neither the best nor the worst." If it was impossible to secure such legislation, "the best foundation for law is the consensus of the largest majority, and the best preparation for good law is universal education of the people. If the educated desire better laws—those more suited to them— there is one sovereign way, and that is to lift the majority to their heights, and then the laws will not only be abstractly right, but practically right." [2]

Jeffersonian sentiments may seem anomalous in the Republican leader who was denounced as a despot and tyrant and whom the cartoonists loved to portray as "Czar" with crown, robes, and scepter. Nevertheless, the reader who has followed his arguments on parliamentary procedure in his earlier years in Congress or who follows the reasoning by which he justified his drastic reforms in 1890, or the reasoning of his opponents when they adopted the most unpopular of those same reforms in 1894, will find no inconsistency. In both cases the governmental machinery had to be adapted to the necessity of executing the public

[1] Quoted in full, *Kennebec Journal,* January 29, 1886.
[2] "Historic Political Upheavals," *North American Review,* January, 1895.

will as expressed in duly constituted process of popular election.

Except in connection with the rules, discussion of constitutional questions plays but a minor part in Reed's speeches. As a good Republican he was a liberal constructionist, but he was likewise a thorough-going conservative, and while his life ended before the new nationalism of the Roosevelt era had fully developed, he viewed its early manifestations with suspicion. In spite of this, however, he despised those who, as he described the opponents of Henry Clay, "were struggling with their own inertia and mistaking it for the Constitution." "For my part I beg leave here and now," he remarked in the course of debate on April 12, 1886, "to protest against this everlasting putting up of the Constitution of the United States against every proposition which is presented in this House," a practice which he described on another occasion as "this hackneyed degradation of the Constitution by making a mop-broom of it to sweep up everything that gentlemen think they do not believe in." As for constitutional lawyers, he had observed two kinds, "the constitutional lawyer pure and simple . . . and the political constitutional lawyer. The one always tries to give some reasons for the faith that is in him; the other does not think it necessary." [1] Strict constructionists often roused his ire. "I wish I could give to the words 'sovereign State,'" he once remarked, "the dignity and magnificence with which it fills the mouth of a Southern gentleman while he is trying to perpetrate some outrage upon the Union."

He viewed some Democratic applications of constitutional theory with sardonic humor and concluded that "public welfare gets taken care of by the insistence of majorities whenever the demand is sufficiently imperative." He disliked two famous enactments because of their partisan origin and because they also involved what he regarded as an unwise interference with pri-

[1] *Cong. Record,* 48 Cong., 1 Sess., 1401.

vate business: "If by the aid of any witch of Endor one of our forefathers could have been beguiled from the New Jerusalem to listen to Mr. Reagan expounding the Inter-State Commerce Act, he would have returned heavenward in a paralysis of amazement, after learning that all that millennium was to be accomplished under the power to regulate commerce between the States. Or if he had been present when the needs of our farming community demanded protection against oleomargarine, he would have been startled to find that adulteration of food could be dealt with by the Union, and that too, under the taxing clause." [1] Nevertheless, he was entirely willing to support the exercise of national power or the expenditure of national funds, under proper conditions, for public improvements. He knew, however, when projects were merely raids on the Treasury intended to favor a locality and when they should be considered matters of actual general concern.

He defended appropriations for irrigation on the ground that such outlays, while local in some respects, were really for the benefit of the whole nation. Vast areas of the West, now unproductive and apparently useless, could be made to blossom like the rose and the entire country would benefit. River and harbor expenditures likewise could be defended on no other ground but that indirectly everybody would share in the benefit.[2] His long congressional experience, however, had made him only too familiar with the wretched system of pork barrel appropriations, and his contemptuous distrust for promoters of public improvements, the cynical wit with which he treated proposals which occasionally had genuine merit and which were nearly always honestly believed in by the localities concerned, did nothing to increase his popularity. The country at large forgot that he had protected the Treasury. On the other hand, his attitude con-

[1] "Mr. Speaker," *North American Review*, January, 1892.
[2] *Ibid.*, 50 Cong., 2 Sess., 1229.

tributed to strengthen a widespread sentiment that he was indifferent to the welfare of the common man and disdainful of the struggling communities of the South and West.

Stories of the treatment which, as Speaker, he accorded requests for local expenditure are common. Thetus W. Sims, of Tennessee, once related how, soon after his election to Congress, he was introduced to the Speaker of the House. He told Mr. Reed that as the Tennessee River ran through his district he would like to go upon the Committee on Rivers and Harbors. Mr. Reed with great gravity, turned to him and inquired in his characteristic drawl, "How big a steal do you want?" [1] During the first session of the same Congress, Representative Davis of Florida, went to the Speaker with an appeal. He wanted to get consideration for a bill making some improvement in a river in his State. Speaker Reed looked at him with a bland smile.

"I am sorry," he said, "to see you joining the procession which is not happy unless it is taking money out of the Treasury."

"But this is only $50,000," pleaded Mr. Davis.

"Well," drawled the Speaker, "that is a good deal for a district where alligators form the largest part of the population."

Why, he once argued, should not river and harbor appropriations be dealt with as facts and figures instead of "with mouth-filling discourses" about "the necessity of giving everybody everything for as nearly nothing as possible?" Why should this be thought especially patriotic? "What a folly this always is! Why, an aruspex looking an aruspex in the face could not smile as we must do here when we are making this talk among ourselves."

It is a matter of regret that Reed did not comment on a wider variety of purely governmental problems, some of which were assuming great importance before he left office. He supported civil service reform, but his comments on the general

[1] Washington *Post*, February 6, 1898.

topic were largely confined to sarcastic remarks on the failure of his opponents to live up to their professions in regard to it. He used the patronage for political purposes in the First District as his contemporaries everywhere did in theirs, but he had no liking for that aspect of party politics. The election of President Cleveland, he once told some friends, had a measure of consolation since it assured him four years' relief from "those infernal postmastership squabbles."

A quarrel over patronage brought him into serious collision with President Harrison in 1890. The collectorship of the port of Portland, the most important and lucrative Federal office in the State, had been a frequent source of trouble in the past, and Reed insisted that inasmuch as it was in his district he was entitled to select the appointee. On this occasion, Secretary of State James G. Blaine, still the head of the State Republican party, and the two Senators supported Colonel F. N. Dow for the position. Reed, for some time on bad terms with Blaine and the Senators, opposed Dow. Soon after Reed had been reëlected in September, 1890, Dow was appointed and there was a buzz of excitement in political circles, inasmuch as it seemed to be a deliberate affront to one of the outstanding party members. "The Dow business makes a lovely vacation," he wrote to Senator Lodge, "but B. H. would hardly be human if he loved me." [1]

Party regularity was an important tenet in Reed's political creed, and he made no public statement. His attitude toward Harrison was well known, however, and his scorching comments in private on the Chief Executive delighted the latter's enemies, who were both numerous and vindictive. Harrison's pardon of the cashier of the First National Bank of Portland, a relative of Dow convicted of embezzlement under the national banking laws, added to his resentment. Reed had steadfastly refused to

[1] *Lodge Papers.*

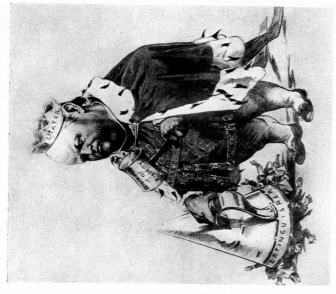

REED AS THE CZAR, 1890

REED'S REELECTION, 1890

(From *Judge*)

recommend a pardon on the ground that the offender had used his church affiliations and the cloak of piety in sundry fraudulent schemes—an unforgivable offense from the Speaker's viewpoint. Clemency had also been refused by President Cleveland. The incident, however, gave Reed opportunity for a remark which is still remembered in both Maine and Washington. "I never had but two personal enemies in my life. One of these Mr. Harrison has pardoned out of the penitentiary and the other he has just appointed Collector of the Port of Portland."

If Reed's views of American government and institutions were conventional, displaying no particular originality, they were at least the product of a wide reading of history and general literature. He had also a keen insight into human nature and its political manifestations, while his characteristic ability in the art of exposition raised his discussions above the commonplace level. In the field of parliamentary procedure, moreover, he certainly made a unique contribution to the development of American polity.

It was to be expected that Reed, guided by a sober philosophy of government and politics, would take a conservative attitude on the great economic issues which divided the public sentiment of his day. Conservatism, he remarked in the course of his report on woman suffrage, "is essential to the stability of mankind, of government, of social life. To every new proposal it rightfully calls a halt, demanding countersign whether it be friend or foe." "Most new things are not good," he wrote in his last published article, "and die an early death; but those which push themselves forward and by slow degrees force themselves on the attention of mankind are the unconscious productions of human wisdom, and must have honest consideration, and must not be made the subject of unreasoning prejudice." [1]

[1] "What shall we do with the Tariff?" *North American Review*, December, 1902.

It was a period when reckless exploitation of men and resources was a commonplace, when the beneficiaries of public favor solemnly proclaimed and probably believed that their activities were all for the common good. Tariff favors, land grants, subsidies, tax immunities, were all defended on the ground that general prosperity was thereby promoted, and everybody shared in the result. The first fumbling ineffectual efforts at public regulation and control of private business aroused an amount of hostility which is hard to understand at the present day.

Throughout Reed's public career there were active parties of discontent and it is not hard, at this later day, to realize that their discontent had a real justification and that governmental policies only too frequently did nothing to allay their sense of injury and injustice, especially in the West. Unfortunately, their proposed remedies were in many instances economic absurdities which would have further aggravated the evils they were supposed to cure, and nearly always the suffering agrarians exaggerated the efficacy of legislative panaceas.

Reed's views were not essentially different from those of a majority of the Republican leaders of the East. He was quick to see the political aspects of the situation and assailed the Democratic party for its readiness to take up the cause of the discontented, regardless of its nature and the possibility of finding a remedy. He made ironical remarks about the absence in his Cedar Rapids audience in the 1890 campaign of "the sad-eyed, poorly clad men covered all over with mortgages and Democratic pity," but he did not always appreciate the bitter day-to-day struggle which the settler was conducting on the prairie or in the mountain valleys of the new states or the genuine hardship, and the frequent tragedy which overhung the sod-built houses or log-cabins of the frontier. The soil might indeed be "so rich that if we had had an acre of it in Maine we would have sold it by the bushel," but that fact was small consolation to the man who was paying usurious interest rates, who sold his grain for a song after a two or three-day haul to the railroad, or who felt that under the protective tariff he was paying tribute to the Pennsylvania or New England manufacturer every time he bought a plow, a set of harness, or a cotton work-shirt.

In the long run, Reed's views were for the most part correct. Conditions throughout the West were due to a combination of causes which legislation could do little to reach. Given sufficient time many of them would be remedied by the inherent vitality of the American people, their capacity for organization, their inventiveness, and above all by their ability to utilize the incalculable natural resources which were available at their feet. Encourage private initiative; secure foreign capital by adhering to sound currency and high standards of financial integrity; remember that the corporation was a necessary instrumentality of modern business and that, like the individual, it had its legal rights; diversify industry under the benign influence of protection; avoid governmental meddling. Follow such a policy, and American conditions, already, in spite of temporary set-backs, the envy of the world, would—Reed firmly believed—continue their improvement and we would attain a level of well-being unprecedented in human history.

He began his congressional career in the midst of the widespread depression which was the aftermath of the panic of 1873 and witnessed the restoration of prosperity which followed the resumption of specie payments in 1879. His last years in Congress were spent under similar conditions. The panic of 1893, the subsequent depression, the gradual improvement of conditions and the tide of prosperity which began to flow with the settlement of the currency issue in 1896, were all strikingly similar to the course of events in earlier years. He had a distinctly fatalistic attitude on the whole matter.

In his great speech for repeal of the Silver Purchase Act, August 26, 1893, he declared that crises like that through which the United States was then passing were common phenomena; they seemed to be essential to human progress; they arose from the characteristics of human nature, periods of buoyant confidence and expansion being regularly followed by periods of distrust and depression. "If we could have had that perfection of wisdom which is exhibited, so far as I have ever known, only in a greenback oration, we should have the human race proceeding on the upgrade steadily, without faltering and without relapse." Such alternations of prosperity and depression, he wrote on another occasion, probably antedated the Pyramids of Egypt, and Joseph's dream of the fat and lean kine was symbolic of a fundamental economic law. Waste and extravagance, aggravated by the eternal hope of escaping the penalties of "overstaying prosperity," were followed by economy, reduced costs of production, and renewed activity of invention; and good times were gradually restored.[1]

Prosperity was dependent on having all the people at work, and with productive processes requiring a vast amount of cooperation, general confidence was an imperative requirement. "After a great smash like that of 1893 or that of 1873 there is nothing to do but wait and let the business of the world settle itself, carefully keeping meanwhile the medicine men of finance with their feathers and rattles out of the way of the sick man." The medicine men of 1896 were to be found in 1897 explaining in apologetic tones why their noisy utterances had not been justified by the course of events. In a short time they would be silent—"the signal that the world has settled one other financial problem in the only way it can be settled, and that is, in the minds of the people."[2]

[1] *Illustrated American,* August 28, 1897.
[2] "Prosperity," New York *World,* September 12, 1897.

Protracted periods of depression, he held, led to attacks on private property, vested rights and wealth in general. Greenbackers, Populists and sundry minor political sects were constantly assailing "the menace of wealth" and exalting the merits of the patient and long-suffering poor. Reed was intensely conservative on all questions affecting private property, and regarded such efforts as mere demagogy. Their success, however, would cause general ruin.

"For my part, sir," he declared in the course of debate on May 14, 1884, "I am heartily tired of this continual talk about this being a land where the poor man can flourish and the poor man is honored. It is neither a credit nor a discredit to a man to have been born poor. Nothing stands in the way of his advancement. He has an equal chance and fair opportunity in the race with every other citizen; and these repeated declarations are born of a suspicion on the part of some gentlemen that the poor man is not equal to the rich. I maintain that neither in our constitutions nor in the practical working of the government is there any superiority on the part of the rich over the poor man that needs the orations of Congressmen to equalize the citizens of this country."

Writing for a popular magazine years later, he expressed his disdain for "the vague fear of penalties attached to the increase of wealth." Wealth, he pointed out, meant education, increased leisure, and the spread of intelligence, not merely for those who become wealthy but for the entire community. Wealth, for example, had ameliorated the general condition of women by such commonplace improvements as running water, kitchen conveniences, and better light.

He repeatedly declared that the material conditions of human life were constantly improving. The country was becoming more prosperous every year. Replying to John Randolph Tucker during a tariff debate he expressed surprise "to hear a sensible man like the gentleman from Virginia tear himself into tatters over the dreadful condition of the poor man. He knows as well as anybody here that there never was a time in the history of the country when the poor man's wants were so thoroughly supplied. I say to you today that he has wants supplied which nobles and princes three hundred years ago could not have supplied with all their wealth."

The heavy indebtedness of the farmers, to his mind, did not indicate depression but confidence in the future on the part of men who were willing to buy more than they could pay for at the time. "In my own State I have seen the farmers' buildings getting better every year. The very cattle are better housed than their owners were fifty years ago. Yet men who reside in agricultural districts come here and for mere political effect undertake to perpetrate what I say is a slander upon their own constituents."

Such comfortable conclusions were hardly justified by the facts of life in Kansas and the Dakotas, and to state them in such bald and sweeping terms was certainly not good political strategy on the part of a man whose ambitions were as far-reaching as Reed's. It was undoubtedly due to a long series of such utterances that he came to be regarded in many quarters as the great defender of the interests of predatory capital, and the representative merely of the interests of the Atlantic seaboard.

His discussions of Mississippi River improvement may still be read with profit by a generation which almost half a century later is still struggling with the problem. He condemned the tendency to "scatter money all up and down the river" instead of completing work on a single reach, whereby total costs might be estimated and the actual value of the work ascertained. But of far greater interest and timeliness is his analysis of the value of water transportation in the American economic system. Commerce, he argued in 1886, was beyond the control of the government, and invariably took its own course.

It is our business to notice the movements of trade. We can help them; we cannot change them; that is beyond our utmost power. What is the tendency of modern mercantile transportation? It is upon the lines of shortest time. The great merchant of today makes his money by small percentages upon great transactions, and, therefore, he wishes to eliminate from his business every element of loss. He demands the element of time, in which losses may happen and fluctuations may take place, shall be cut off and as far as possible annihilated with space. That is his object. Hence it is that the movement of commerce in this country is from east to west, and largely by railroads, because they save time, eliminate loss, and enable the merchant to calculate his small percentages on his great transactions.

The result, he continued, was that the products of the entire world were made available at a minimum cost. A great economic law was working in favor of the consumer, apparently without any cognizance or knowledge on the part of Congress, judging by the speeches of members. The great laws of trade would persist and the money spent on the Mississippi would for the most part be wasted "not in a change, but in a futile attempt to make a change":

I am well aware that the public mind is filled with that old idea of the great highway of commerce. It is astonishing how this mouth-filling language doth beguile the people. Let us sit down and look at it with sense in our heads and light in our eyes, and ask ourselves if we are willing year after year to earn the opprobrium of the country by adding this sum to our bill without any more proof of its righteousness and wisdom. Let us cut loose this great question from the general river and harbor appropriation bill and let it stand upon its own merits—it is big enough to do it—if there are merits in it. Surely this is a wise course.

Such opinions were easily distorted in many localities into evidence of indifference or active hostility toward the Mississippi valley, dictated by undue friendliness for railroads and "robber barons" of finance. Reed, however, was confident of the essential unity of the country, economic and political, in spite of local differences and conflicting interests, and when William Jennings Bryan in the course of debate in the House threatened the East with a union of West and South, he was quick to point out that such projects had always failed in the past and would continue to fail in the future. "We of the East not only send our property West, but we send our children there, and no man who crosses from East to West can fail to be struck by the fact that there is after all a unity of sentiment between the two sections of the country that no language will ever blot out or destroy." [1]

During the period of Reed's congressional career there were repeated outbreaks of industrial warfare, but there is little evidence that he was seriously disturbed thereby. In 1886 a bill providing for arbitral settlement of controversies between common carriers and their employees, one result of a great strike which had demoralized the railroads centering in St. Louis, gave him an opportunity to state several of his governmental and economic theories. The country, he admitted, was faced with grave problems, but he was inclined to adopt the same comfortable, laissez-faire attitude with regard to the labor question that he maintained in regard to the problems of the farmer.

"One of the greatest delusions in the world," he said, "is the hope that the evils in this world are to be cured by legislation. I am happy in the belief that the solution of the great difficulties of life and government are in better hands even than that of this

---

[1] *Cong. Record,* 53 Cong., 3 Sess., 2198.

body, which I respect very much." He acknowledged that the
law did not always keep pace with changing economic and social
conditions. There was little likelihood that such problems, "the
complications of which have no parallel on the face of the earth,"
could be solved out of the inner consciousness of congressmen.
But by watching the workings of organized bodies of workers,
their methods of reaching conclusions, their discussions among
themselves, their experiences and errors, much could be learned
which would assist in formulating a sound public policy.

Laboring men, he went on, wanted a fair share of the joint
products of capital and labor. Capital required fair treatment as
well, for if the incentive to accumulate should be lost, work
would stop and all would suffer. "Is the solution to be found
placarded on every fence?" It was possible to provide better
facilities for comparing the views of both employers and em-
ployed, and this would be a forward step. "For if men know
alike they are sure to act alike." There was nothing new in this;
in various forms it had been in progress for years. If we had
the means to ascertain the facts and provided arbitration for the
unreasonable parties, that was all that could be done. Compul-
sory arbitration worked both ways and had distinct limitations.

Arbitration was going on all the time and yet there was no
legal machinery for enforcing decisions on either employers or
employees. What then, did enforce them? "Why, that ultimate
tribunal which is master of us all, the public sense of all the human beings of this country. Public sentiment governs. What is
it today that is having the greatest influence in controversies that
are going on within our knowledge? Is it the one side or the
other? No, it is the general community and their feeling that
one side is right and that the other side is wrong, or that both are
wrong and must arbitrate. And that public sentiment ultimately
will govern the matter." The present bill, he concluded, was no
panacea, but it could be supported if it were honestly presented

as merely offering an opportunity to lay the results of arbitration before the common sense of the country.[1]

The prosperity of the country, he always maintained, was dependent on the condition of the wage earner. His views of the tariff were those of the practical politician, not the economist, but it is worth noting at this point that in his tariff arguments he always stressed the matter of wages. His emphasis on the interrelation of high wages, high consumption and general prosperity had a distinctly modern note. In the great debate on the Wilson tariff bill in the 53rd Congress he had a memorable clash with Bourke Cockran when the latter in fiery terms contrasted the distress of the wage earner with the porcine prosperity of the tariff beneficiaries.

Wages, argued Reed, depended on the condition of the market and also upon the nature of the workingman himself. Under protection it was possible to elevate the market by paying higher wages, "thereby constituting a market as broad as our production." The world was a selfish place, everybody was seeking his own good, everybody was endeavoring to obtain the best he could out of life. Human nature was the same, regardless of free trade or protection. "Men in this country and men abroad are endeavoring to obtain what they can for wages and what they can for profit, and in this struggle there are certain underlying fundamental principles, among which is this: that when they reach a certain stage of civilization—supply or demand, or what not—they are going to have their wants supplied or they are going to make difficulty and trouble."

Wages were more secure under the protective tariff, but there could be no arbitrary fixation of their amount. Growth in the intelligence and in the desires and wants of the laborer would force a rise of wages in time. "What is the direct means by which the laboring men reach this result? By labor unions, by com-

[1] *Cong. Record,* 49 Cong., 1 Sess., 2966.

bining, by making manufacturers understand that they must give higher wages. By increasing their product, which increase can only take place by the larger market which comes of these larger wages." Invention and improved methods of production enabled the manufacturer to meet demands for better wages but there was, of course, a temporary limit to the load which new invention and the enlargement of markets could carry. "In this country, with the laborer seeking to obtain higher wages and fewer hours of work and the demand of the public for lower prices, there is going on a tremendous struggle; and that is all the struggle that the inventive power of this country can sustain." Why make it more difficult by bringing its industries in competition with a lower scale of civilization?

In an address at Cooper Union on October 13, 1894, Reed defended protection with great ability, although in terms which were distinctly conservative when compared with many Republican utterances in that year. Comments on the attitude of labor in the election of 1892, however, show some of Reed's limitations. He admitted that laboring men had generally voted the Democratic ticket in that year. "Minor grievances" had bulked large. "This human nature of ours is queerly made up. A man cares infinitely more for a little thing which is present than for a great thing afar off, and as he thinks, contingent. A man will be set wild by sand in his shoes and give no thought to the question of a final place of punishment for the wicked." Unhappily, the story of the Homestead strike, the industrial warfare in the Cœur d'Alenes, and the indifferent attitude of the Harrison Administration toward corporate abuses, can hardly be considered mere "sand in the shoes" by any reasonable person.

He had a good word to say for the corporation. "It is sometimes customary here," he remarked while arguing for repeal of the Silver Purchase Act, "to make remarks indicative of great contempt and hatred of banks and of corporations. I expect during the next year or two to hear a great many such declarations. In this country corporations are sometimes brutal. They are difficult to approach. You can not reason with them, and they must have ironclad rules, and very few men have dealings with corporations without having their tempers ruffled and their feelings hurt."

"Nevertheless," he continued, "a fundamental purpose and object of all corporations is to gather together the odds and ends of money in such quantities that large business operations can be carried on by wealth which is aggregated out of small sums; and in the main, large corporations represent little holders." This was especially true of banks, and regardless of the vituperation visited upon them they were doing an invaluable service for the country and constituted its mainstay against disaster. Again and again in the course of his career he pointed out that the corporation was a natural development and the most effective instrumentality for the conduct of modern business.

"Monopoly" became the object of an hostility which steadily increased throughout the eighties and nineties, culminating, after Reed passed from the scene, in the "trust-busting" activities of the Roosevelt administration; but he refused to become excited on the subject. "I suppose," he declared in the course of his speech on the Mills tariff bill of 1888, "that during the ten years last past I have listened to more idiotic raving, more pestiferous rant on this subject than all others put together . . ." And yet outside the Patent Office there were no monopolies in this country, and there never could be. As for "the great new chimera 'trust,' " "with tongue of lambent flame and eye of forked fire, serpent headed and griffin clawed," why be alarmed? The belief that a dozen men could fix prices for sixty million was utterly unreasonable. "They can never do it. There is no power on earth that can raise the price of any necessity of life above a just price and keep it there. More than that, if the price is raised and maintained for even a short while, it means ruin for the combination and still lower prices for consumers. Compared with one of your laws of Congress, it is a Leviathan to a clam."

In his *North American Review* article on the tariff which appeared a few days before his death he again took up the matter of the trusts. The movement of concentration in business, he pointed out, was a natural one and changes in the structure of business organizations, produced as the trusts had been, by gradual experience, were most likely to be right. In this case the consolidations had been brought about by wasteful competition. They were impressive because of their size, but no new principle was involved. Prices could be controlled only by producing and selling more cheaply than everybody else. Natural forces would correct any serious evils in the situation and the public eventually would determine the real value of their stocks in the open market. "Providence has not left us to the stump orator or the newspapers."

Here again his laissez-faire principles were cropping out, but while the attitude of the present generation toward trusts and consolidations in general is more friendly and tolerant than in the days of Roosevelt and Wilson, there has been a vast amount of restrictive governmental action in the intervening years, and Reed's complaisant attitude has by no means been fully justified by the test of time.

He defended railroad consolidation. Unrestricted competition, he pointed out in a brief and impromptu speech on December 6, 1894, was bad for the community. "It ought to be the object of legislation to benefit all the people of the country, and in order to do that there ought to be a full understanding of the ramifications and permeations of business." Railroads were vital to the community, and they should be kept in good condition.

It was not enough, he thought, merely to have lower freight

rates. "Another question is, are you preserving your instrumentality for transportation in such a shape that it will do your work more advantageously than it can be done in any other way?" Stockholders also had their rights and unrestricted competition might ruin them, without conferring any lasting advantage on the other interested parties. But he showed no enthusiasm for regulatory action by the government, and while our national transportation policy has accepted the desirability of consolidation and recognized the evils of unrestricted competition, the corollaries have been stringent supervision and regulation of the entire business.

Reed's economic doctrines were of course those of the practical partisan leader and not those of the scholar formulating learned treatises in his study. Considered from the scientific standpoint they were vulnerable, but as he once said: "We have got to do practical business in this House. Statesmanship does not consist in doing the best thing, but in doing the best possible thing. We have got to do what the resources of the country and, above all, what the sentiment of the country will support and sustain." They had at least the merit of frankness and honesty. In stating them he often injured his political prospects. If they display his limitations as a thinker they at least show that he was never a time-server or a demagogue.

REED was reëlected in 1886 without serious difficulty and the Washington *Post,* commenting on the outcome of the Maine elections in an editorial of September 15, 1886, welcomed the result as follows: "All the Republican Congressmen are elected. Even Tom Reed comes back to Washington. That sentence might be set to music. He is a joyous creature, and we shall be glad to see his bald head once more, and hear his resounding baritone. To the casual observer he seems to be perpetually inebriated. He never drinks whisky. Or hardly ever. But he takes great quaffs of ozone, and the divine ichor of existence exhilarates him till his carryings-on are often fantastic, not to say grotesque. When he is at his best he is as officious as a second trombone, as inflammatory as a pack of fire crackers under a barrel, and as busy as a bumblebee in a boy's trousers. Without him we should suffer greatly from ennui. We are glad that he is coming back."

The 50th Congress contributed little, in a legislative sense, to American history. Exemplifying the futility and paralysis caused by existing procedural methods, however, it has an important place in our parliamentary history. Its sessions produced some ennui, but more indignation, and gave Reed an admirable opportunity to show his ability in what were once described as his chief rôles, "mentor of the Republicans, and tormentor of the Democrats."

When Congress assembled on December 5, 1887, the party strength stood Democrats 168, Republicans 152. There were also two Labor members and one Greenbacker. Reed was again the Republican candidate for the speakership, receiving 143 votes to Carlisle's 163. The Republicans controlled the Senate and there was little likelihood that partisan measures could secure adoption. The record of the House proved worse than that of any of its recent predecessors. Not only was its legislative output meager and unimportant, passage of the usual routine measures being secured only with the greatest difficulty, but members staged a series of filibusters which made the entire body appear both odious and ridiculous in the eyes of the country.

In many respects this Congress and its successor constitute a single chapter in Reed's parliamentary experience. As leader of the minority in the 50th Congress he had unlimited opportunity to observe the futility of existing rules of procedure. The pitiable situation of Speaker Carlisle, especially during the second session, could not but have strengthened his oft-expressed determination to end such abuses at the earliest opportunity, and that opportunity was to come in the 51st Congress —the first Congress under President Harrison—only two years later.

Although outranked by William D. Kelley, of Pennsylvania, Reed really led the minority in the Committee on Ways and Means, and retained his place on the Committee on Rules. With a presidential campaign impending and revenue legislation the subject of a vast amount of partisan discussion, the former post was a strategic position of the highest importance. Under Carlisle's able leadership the Committee on Rules had been growing in power, but the 50th Congress was to demonstrate that the defects of the existing system were too deep-seated for that committee, or any similar body, or any group of leaders however able and determined, to exercise adequate guidance and control over the course of business.

The tariff, after the abortive efforts of the last two Congresses, was to be the leading issue of the campaign of 1888, both in Congress and on the stump. President Cleveland, with his usual straightforward courage and fine indifference to the political hazards involved, devoted his annual message to revenue reform. It was a frontal attack on the protective principle, its vigor and audacity offsetting deficiencies in the strategical conception. Carlisle, in acknowledging his election to the speakership, also spoke vigorously on behalf of tariff reduction. The Democratic party, accordingly, was definitely committed to a lowering of the tariff; but in view of the complications involved, including the disposal of the surplus, the incidental necessity for a revision of internal revenues should the existing tariff be continued, and the hostility of important elements in the party to any alterations in the existing system, there seemed scant probability that the President's recommendations would be enacted into law.

The House majority, however, at least had an opportunity to make a demonstration on behalf of tariff reform. Democratic success in November would undoubtedly mean popular indorsement of such a policy and definite action could no longer be prevented. Roger Q. Mills of Texas headed the Ways and Means Committee, and the bill produced a few months later bears his name in tariff history. While destined to fail of enactment, this measure produced one of the finest debates in the annals of revenue legislation.

Mills reported his bill on April 17, 1888, in an able speech arraigning Republican fiscal policy and emphasizing the imperative need of a reduction in customs duties. The bill itself was far from meeting the wishes of low tariff members and was well described by the Washington *Post* of the same date as "a compromise in which reform gets a thin slice and protection the rest." Hemp, flax, lumber and wool went on the free list; the duty on pig-iron was reduced; sufficient reductions were scattered through the schedules to lend plausibility to protectionist claims that the industries of the country were endangered.

Reed took little part in the earlier stages of the debate, but on May 19 he closed for the Republican side in one of the greatest speeches of his career. Carlisle, who had not spoken from the floor during the preceding Congress, appeared as the leading champion of his party. The prospect of such a forensic battle was sufficient to crowd the House. A brilliant audience packed the galleries and the Senate chamber was empty while the members moved to the other end of the Capitol. "Everybody," reported the Washington *Post* next day, "felt that it was a debate of no ordinary character and an event of no ordinary political importance; everybody felt that it was a debate which set the keynote for the coming presidential campaign, and besides, it was expected that the closing speeches by the leaders would be charged with something of consequence to the bill."

Reed seldom spoke for more than ten or fifteen minutes and in his whole congressional career made barely half a dozen set speeches of any length, but on this occasion he spoke for almost two hours. He made no searching examination of the pending bill, confining himself entirely to a presentation of the broad economic issues involved; but as an argument for the protective principle, although perhaps not so analytical and less carefully reasoned than that on the Wilson Bill six years later, his speech left little to be said. In its clarity of exposition, its brilliance of statement, its sarcasm, its wit and epigrammatic force, it showed Reed at his best. Again and again his delivery was interrupted by laughter and applause.

Assailing President Cleveland's thesis that domestic prices were raised to consumers by the amount paid in customs duties, he then struck at the weakest point in the Democratic position. "Protection is either in its essence a benefit or a curse." If the latter, why compromise? "Tariff for revenue only, goes down before the same arguments which are used against protection." Why not come out for the only alternative, direct taxation? Yet the proposed bill would permit the same oppressions, the same robbery of consumers, while its supporters stood "higgling about the amount of the tribute" instead of sweeping them away.

The theories of Bastiat, who had "furnished the other side with most of its brains and all of its dialectics," could not stand against a hundred years of practical experience which had made the republic great and prosperous. He knew the feeling which was behind some of the arguments. He himself had experienced that feeling when walking past the brownstone fronts of "that Democratic importing city of New York," trying to understand "why the virtue which I know is on the side walk is not thus rewarded. . . . But when I feel that way I know what the feeling is. It is good, honest, high-minded envy. When some other gentlemen have the same feeling they think it's political economy." Tariff reformers, he continued, had charged the protective tariff with the creation of monopolies and trusts. Ridiculing this aspect of revenue reform in a brilliant mock-heroic passage, he pointed out the impossibility of establishing monopoly under American conditions. Inexorable economic law was working for the protection of the people.

Next came the problem of the tariff in relation to agriculture. "But if the revenue-reform orator on the monopoly is terrible, like an army with banners, there is a theme on which he can take up the notes of the dying swan. How we do love to hear him on the impoverished farmer! Then he is not sublime, but he is pathetically great. I heard him first ten years ago." But, compare "the woe-begone, down-trodden, luckless, unsuccessful, dispirited devil" depicted by the congressional orator, with what he discovered when in the fullness of time he traveled West himself. There he beheld the vast fields of corn, the comfortable homes, and everywhere a general appearance of prosperity.

Should the tariff be lowered in order to open the markets of the world to American products? "The markets of the world! How broad and cool these words are. They stretch from the frozen regions of the northern pole across the blazing tropics to the ice bound shores of the antarctic continent. All this we can have if we will but give up the little hand's breadth called the United States of America." What were the real possibilities of the situation? "To hear these rhetoricians declaim you would imagine the markets of the world a vast vacuum, waiting till now for American goods to break through, rush in, and fill the yawning void."

At this point he introduced his famous application of Æsop's fable of the dog who lost his succulent shoulder of mutton by greedily jumping for the reflection in the stream. "He trotted along and looked over the side of the plank and he saw the markets of the world, and dived for them. A minute after, he was crawling up the bank, the wettest, the sickest, the nastiest, the most muttonless dog that ever swam ashore." This illustration made a great impression on the audience and later on the country at large, where it soon became a recognized part of the Republican stump speaker's stock in trade.

He closed by calling attention to the marvelous growth and prosperity of the country during twenty-seven years of protection. Its benefits had not been confined to any section, social class or economic group and the chief beneficiaries had been the plain, ordinary people of the country.

It was a great speech. McKinley, Kelley, Carlisle, Mills and others displayed ability in the course of the protracted debate, and made notable addresses, but the honors were generally accorded to Reed. Years later the editor of *Harper's Weekly* remarked of his speech on the Mills Bill that "Webster himself could not surpass him in the art of lucid, cogent and fire-tipped demonstration."

The tariff debate dragged on until well into the summer and Reed spoke briefly from time to time on various aspects of the question. As the end of the protracted discussion approached he ridiculed the tariff reformers for their apparent apprehensions as to the effects of their handiwork. Throughout the debate there had been constant demand for free trade. Why were they now trying to explain away previous utterances? "Why, is it that this change has come over their feelings?" he asked. "Why are detachments sent over to New York to give reassurance to the doubtful brethren?" That lofty and courageous citizen of Texas, the chairman of Ways and Means, had been explaining in New York that they need not fear any free trade from him:

Why is it that he has swallowed words that are only four years old, and why is it that he comes back here where he is known and tries neither to swallow them nor to deny them? Why is it that the entire crowd of Democratic newspapers are today endeavoring to explain that after all they have great yearning for 40% of robbery? Why is it that the gentleman from Indiana was all agog and shaken with emotion in his eagerness to show that the principle on which this bill was framed is as near protective robbery as ever we were? [1]

The Mills Bill passed the House by a strict party vote on July 21, only to die in a hostile committee of the Republican Senate. This result had been expected, but the contest did much to shape the course of the presidential campaign, and when President Cleveland was defeated by Benjamin Harrison in November, the result was taken as proof that the country had rejected the reform program. The session dragged on, month

[1] *Cong. Record,* 50 Cong., 1 Sess., 6536.

after month, with a minimum of accomplishment, and not until October 20, 1888, did adjournment take place.

It was in the 50th Congress that the House of Representatives reached the nadir of ineffectiveness. Its exhibitions of helplessness and ineptitude under existing rules far surpassed any previous displays of the sort. The hope that the changes in procedure made by the preceding Congress, whose rules had been adopted with little discussion, would expedite the course of business, had proved illusory. As the months passed, the situation attracted more and more attention throughout the country, a fact to which Reed called attention two years later, September 4, 1890, when defending, before the voters of his own district, the revolutionary reforms he had accomplished. "Great events do not turn upon one man," he commented. "The House of Representatives was ready and ripe for change, and the people stood ready to approve. What all the world wanted was easy to do."

As early in the session as January 5, 1888, *The Nation* had criticized the House for its methods and general attitude on broad questions of legislative policy, especially those which might be considered so important as to be really non-partisan in character, the Presidential Succession Act, the Electoral Count Act and similar measures, declaring that it was unable to recall a single instance in which the Senate "had not been years in advance of the House."

Public interest was a hopeful sign. On January 19, 1888, the Washington *Post,* under the caption "Slowly Doing Nothing," pointed out that the House in more than six weeks had passed only four bills, none of them important, and that matters seemed to be going from bad to worse. "The system of rules is the prime cause of the wonderful inertia of this unwieldy and self-shackled body. . . . In stalling legislation and keeping everybody else from doing anything a few members are all powerful, but when it comes to passing laws little can be done except by what is practically unanimous consent."

That matters actually were going from bad to worse received striking demonstration three months later when an attempt was made to pass a bill refunding to the States the direct tax which had been collected under the war revenue legislation of 1861. It was a proposition which broke through political lines and involved many serious complications. It aroused sectional animosities as aiding the prosperous industrial states at the expense of the impoverished South, which had not paid the original contributions. It meant a reduction of the surplus in the Federal Treasury by the old and questionable method of a distribution among the States. Nevertheless, there is no ground for questioning Reed's claim that it was a measure demanded by an overwhelming majority of the House.

The opponents of the bill, however, were determined, sufficiently numerous to force the taking of yea and nay votes, and above all well versed in the rules of the House. They succeeded in blocking all transaction of business. It was difficult to maintain a quorum, and again and again the silent members brought proceedings to a standstill while desperate efforts were made to muster a voting majority. Motions, privileged under the rules but obviously dilatory in purpose, supplemented the disappearing quorum, while the House kicked and struggled as helplessly as Gulliver in the bonds of the Lilliputians. The legislative day of April 4 lasted, with occasional recesses, until April 12, a total of 192 hours. The strain exasperated everybody and resulted in the physical collapse of several members, but the filibusterers fought on.

Finally the struggle ended. Eighty-six roll calls, according to Reed, had been taken during the contest, each consuming approximately half an hour. Further consideration of the bill was postponed until the next session, with an agreement that it should come to a vote on December 11. It was passed on that date, but encountered a veto at the hand of President Cleveland. Speaker Carlisle had been placed in a humiliating position by the prolonged filibuster, but as a stalwart defender of the existing rules, he could do nothing but follow them to the bitter end.

While Reed offered no general discussion of the situation, his subsequent comments voice the deep-seated indignation and disgust with which he regarded the whole performance. The records show that throughout the filibuster he was at his post as Republican leader, watchful, alert on points of order, and ever ready as opportunity offered to sting an opponent with his characteristic sarcasm. "I object, a judicious physician would prescribe a change of conduct," was his response to a member who requested leave by unanimous consent in order to safeguard his health by "a change of air." Unquestionably he was shaping in his mind certain conclusions of which the country was to learn ere long. There was sporadic filibustering throughout the rest of the session, but nothing which approached that of April.

But if conditions during the first session had been bad, those of the short session were worse. The Republicans had carried the country in November but would have a bare majority in the next House. There was therefore no inducement for the Democrats to coöperate in reforms which could only benefit their opponents. With Congress expiring on March 3 and business piling up continually, any determined minority was in a position to play the part of legislative highwaymen. The combined evils of the short session and the unreformed House rules were vividly illustrated in these closing days of the first Cleveland Administration.

In January, 1889, James B. Weaver of Iowa began one of the most famous filibusters in the history of the House in order to force consideration of a bill organizing the Territory of Oklahoma. His tactics were simple but effective. He commenced obstruction as soon as the chaplain finished prayer, demanding a roll call in order to assure the presence of a quorum for the reading of the Journal. Then followed a series of dilatory motions, and the resultant roll calls effectively wasted the day. If the Oklahoma Bill could not be brought to a vote—for his object was perfectly plain—no other business should be transacted.

"I have commenced this fight in dead earnest," said Mr. Weaver to a reporter of the Washington *Post* on January 10, 1889. "I reviewed the situation in the House and counted the cost before commencing. I am aware that nothing but the gravest of situations could justify a member in resorting to the parliamentary rights now invoked. This is a battle for the rights of the people against the arrogant assumptions of syndicates and corporations who are now occupying Oklahoma in defiance of law." As a matter of fact, conditions in that region were intolerable and territorial organization was imperatively needed.

For eight days Weaver, aided by a handful of sympathizers, continued to hold the House at bay and the record is little more than a dreary succession of roll calls. Efforts to induce him to desist proved unavailing. On January 10, Ezra B. Taylor of Ohio attempted to offer resolutions, which Speaker Carlisle refused to entertain, providing for a committee of five to confer with the member who had taken complete control and refused to permit performance of regular legislative duties, "to ascertain from him upon what terms and conditions and subject to what limitations he will permit the House of Representatives to resume its proper legislative functions and proceed to business."

Whether this proposal was made in good faith or not, it at

least recognized the realities of the situation. Reed suggested that the committee should be made permanent in order to treat with each member as he made his appearance, inasmuch as Weaver was only exercising a right common to every one. At length, having wasted more than one twelfth of the available working time of the session, Weaver won a decisive victory. "I have refrained from making the usual parliamentary motions this morning," he announced on his day of triumph, "because I have been waiting for a report from the Committee on Rules."

By agreement of the party leaders, action on the Oklahoma Bill was promised, and Weaver ceased from troubling. On January 21, 1889, the House adopted a special order fixing January 24 for a vote on the bill and on February 1 it finally passed the House, too late, however, to secure Senate action before the close of the session.

Weaver's tactics had given further impetus to the mounting criticism of congressional procedure, although the prospect of a Republican majority in the next House tended to lend a partisan color to the discussion. The New York *Tribune* in a series of brilliant editorials assailed the rules and demanded their amendment as "an absolute and paramount necessity" in order "to permit the majority to control the business for which it is responsible." The existing system, it declared on another occasion under the title, "Legislative Lunacy," was explainable only on the ground that "the Democratic party in Congress was quite aware that it could not be trusted, and so went beyond all reason in providing a strait-jacket for itself," and furthermore, that the prolonged struggle between the Randall and Carlisle factions had produced a series of rulings "intended to hamper business and to make it easier for the managers to hold the mob in check." [1]

[1] January 16, 1889. See also January 7, 11, February 7.

Reed took advantage of the situation in this session to put forward a vigorous demand for reform. Under the rules, as he afterwards explained to the country, on two Mondays of each month, after the presentation of bills, the remainder of the day was "set aside to enable the House to pass bills by a two thirds vote or so to suspend other rules as to enable particular measures to be considered on special days." [1] A single member earlier in the session, desiring "to make himself equal to the whole House," and block the passage of the Union Pacific Funding Bill, had absorbed all available time by demanding the reading of a bill for the codification of the laws of the District of Columbia.

To frustrate this practice, described by S. S. Cox as "one of the worst abuses which I have ever seen in connection with parliamentary life, this puerile, small, little, uneducated idea of trundling up to the Clerk's desk a great big bill or bills to be read on Monday," Reed on January 3 reported from the Committee on Rules an amendment ending for the remainder of the session "the call of the States and Territories" on the first and third Mondays of each month. It was the opportunity for obstruction available under this "call" which blocked the passage of the Union Pacific Funding Bill.

Reed's resolution was debated at some length but on January 8 was recommitted to the Committee on Rules. The Democrats in the meantime had held a caucus, and their failure to take any action against Weaver's activity was everywhere taken as indicative of the party's attitude on the principle of filibustering. The Washington correspondent of the New York *Tribune* saw its significance and in a dispatch on January 9 pointed out that as a result of the caucus decision, there was "a discouraging prospect before the slim Republican majority in the next House, for it was inspired by the determination of the Democratic

[1] "Obstruction in the National House," *North American Review,*" October, 1889.

leaders, openly avowed in the caucus and scarcely concealed outside, to filibuster in the next House against revenue legislation, Territorial bills, contested election cases and every other measure when by so doing the minority can hope to reap a party advantage. It is clear that the Democrats in the next Congress will filibuster against any and every proposition to amend the rules so as to give the majority that control of the business of the House to which it is justly entitled."

The debate on Reed's resolution, however, showed clearly the issue between the minority leader and his opponents. He repeated the views which he had again and again declared in previous Congresses. "The rules of this House are not for the purpose of protecting the rights of the minority, but to promote the orderly conduct of the business of the House. They can have no other object. It is because in their application they have been perverted from the purpose for which such rules are intended that we have this great trouble today."

Very different were the Democratic doctrines. The governing principles of the rules, declared Randall, was the protection of the minority's rights from an arbitrary and despotic majority. "I shall adhere," he stubbornly declared, "to that principle which guided our forefathers in the formation of the rules."

"We live in this country under written constitutions," said C. F. Crisp of Georgia, then a rising parliamentarian and eventually to be Speaker, in reply to Reed's contentions. "These constitutions are made not to protect the rights of majorities but to protect the rights of minorities. They are to protect the life, liberty, and the property of the citizen—against what? . . . the unbridled acts of majorities. My idea, sir, is that the rules of this House are made not only, as suggested by the gentleman from Maine, for the orderly conduct of the public business, but there is a greater and higher object, and that is to protect the rights of the minority, to restrain, in the language of the old law writers, unbridled license of the majority, to give them time for reflection, so that when passion is allayed they may return to a sense of justice if they find they have departed from it." Carlisle's conduct in the chair was in itself an expression of the same principles.

The session at last came to an unlamented close, and Congress dispersed with a minimum of work accomplished, amid widespread resentment and disgust. The Washington *Post* in a long editorial on April 8 made a scathing attack on the "un-Democratic, un-Republican, and un-American rules of the House of Representatives which have submitted that body to a petty committee of debaters." The members, subjected to the rule of "a legislative trust contrasted with which all other existing monopolies pale into significance," were constantly degrading themselves and wronging their constituents, in pitiable efforts to secure from the arrogant objectors the privilege of a hearing. It was high time to change this situation and "the proper time to establish republican government is at the opening of the next session." The *Post* declared its intention of conducting a nation-wide canvass in order to secure expressions of public opinion on the situation. On April 22 and May 6 there appeared a mass of opinions, gathered from chambers of commerce, business men, State and Federal officials, editors, and many others, all extremely critical of the complexity, wastefulness and futility of House procedure. Together with other opinions published when the struggle for reform was at its height in February, 1890, they showed that the time was ripe for a change.

Reed himself made two important contributions to the public discussion of the parliamentary situation in the House. In the *Century Magazine* for March, 1889, under the title, "The Rules of the House of Representatives," he demanded the restoration of representative government in that body. A check on dilatory motions was imperatively needed, and, even more important, a restoration of the "morning hour," for which he had contended in the 48th and 49th Congresses, in order that the House might be enabled to select measures from the public calendars for prompt action. It would all contribute to government by the majority and there was crying need of "a deeper rooted belief in the principles of Thomas Jefferson, whose memory today seems to be most vociferously cherished by those who never act on his opinions."

More important, and foreshadowing coming events, was his article on "Obstruction in the National House" in the October issue of the *North American Review*. Comparing the analogous situation in the House of Commons, where systematic obstruction by the Irish members had forced Speaker Brand in 1881 to take the responsibility of terminating debate and the House itself to adopt a closure rule in the following year, he pointed out that in both legislatures the original rules had been formulated in the expectation that the members would do their duty and conform to the spirit of necessary regulations. In both instances the rules had been perverted from their actual intent. The constitutional provision by which one fifth of the members could have the yeas and nays entered in the Journal had the legitimate object of recording how members voted on important questions of public policy, but it was now being used on frivolous pretexts to delay business. The reading of bills was necessary and proper under certain circumstances but it was capable of abuse when done merely to waste time as in the last session.

A legislature, he continued, was not merely a law-making body. It had to decide an infinite variety of public questions and a negative decision was often quite as important as a law. Time was not wasted when cases were investigated and action refused. Half the grievances of mankind turned out to be unfounded as soon as somebody could be found to listen to them. A great many cases were of such a character that the legislature alone could handle them. It was therefore the court of very last resort. Surely, with these responsibilities, it should have such rules as would assure efficient action by the majority.

Reed included in his article some significant comments on the conditions which would confront the next House. The majority would possess only three more than a quorum, and hence would hardly be in a position for tyrannical action. There had been a great deal of talk of late about changing the rules, but this expression conveyed an incorrect idea. "No rules have to be changed, for the new House will have no rules. What should have been written is that there will be an effort to establish rules which will facilitate the public business—rules unlike those of the present House, which only delay and frustrate action."

This was a most important declaration and it was actually carried into effect when the 51st Congress assembled, the House conducting its business for more than two months under "general parliamentary law." It was under "general parliamentary law" that Reed handled that tumultuous body while the new code of rules was in process of formulation. It is worth while, therefore, to point out that four years previously he had laid down precisely the same doctrine, declaring that although different Speakers had ruled that each House adopts the rules of the preceding he had never believed such rulings to be correct. He had then said:

I never believed that any House of Representatives had the right to bind its successors. I believe that each House has got to establish rules for itself, and that no dead hand can be laid upon us. But I do not think that that conclusion remits us to chaos. I believe that in this country an assembly like this, coming together without special rules, would necessarily be re-mitted to the common parliamentary law, or what I should perhaps more properly call the common legislative law, of the country, the foundation of which is to be found in Jefferson's Manual and which has been modified by the general action of American legislative assemblies, especially by the action of this legislative assembly; and it is very possible that the rulings which have been made upon this subject by previous Speakers were, after all, intended only to cover that. . . .

He would hardly know, he admitted, what it was and the Speaker would have to evolve it out of his own knowledge.[1]

Henry Cabot Lodge had discussed the situation in the *North American Review* a month earlier, agreeing that the rules had been so perverted that "the American House of Representa-tives today is a complete travesty upon representatives gov-ernment, upon popular government, and upon government by the majority." He predicted that the coming session would be "interesting as well as important" and that drastic changes in the rules would be necessary in order to "change the condition of the House from dead rot to vitality."

"The people of this country," continued Mr. Lodge, "are, as it seems to me, thoroughly tired of the stagnation of busi-ness and the general inaction of Congress. They are disgusted to see year after year go by and great measures affecting the business and political interests of the country accumulate at the doors of Congress and never reach the stage of action. They have also waked up to the fact that this impotence and stag-nation are due to the preposterous fabric known as the rules of the House, and they are prepared to support heartily that party and those leaders who will break down these rules and allow the current of legislation to flow in its natural channel and at its proper rate."

[1] *Cong. Record,* 49 Cong., 1 Sess., 145.

HENRY CABOT LODGE

Roger Q. Mills continued the discussion from the Democratic standpoint in the December issue and charged the Republicans with initiating an attack on the rules as soon as the election returns had assured them of a majority. Why not attack the Constitution itself, which also obstructed majority action? "The demand for the removal of the limitations in rules means that the party in power are fatally bent on mischief; that they have some desperate enterprise on foot that their prophetic souls tell them is beyond the boundary of rightful jurisdiction, and that in carrying it out they will meet with stubborn opposition."

Seventeen election contests had been filed, Mills pointed out, and the Republicans undoubtedly planned to oust enough Democrats to give them a working majority and so insure the enactment of their legislative program, but—and here it seems possible to detect a certain complacent note—"the perplexing question that will not down is how to obtain a quorum." The majority had only three above the necessary number, and he proceeded to quote James G. Blaine's dictum on the responsibility of the majority for maintaining the quorum. There was no special reason, he concluded, why the barriers should be leveled and the proposal resulted merely from the Republicans' desire to entrench themselves in power. During the debates in the first session of the next Congress, opponents read into the record an interview which Mills had granted to a representative of the New York *Sun* in which the threat was made in precise terms that legislation would proceed only when satisfactory to the House Democrats.

Even more plainly than Mills, James B. McCreary, of Kentucky, a veteran member and head of the Committee on Foreign Affairs in the last House, indicated what the majority might expect. McCreary made an early return to Washington and on October 1 gave an interview to a representative of the Washington *Post*. In reply to questions as to the policy of the minority, he declared that if the Republicans attempted to commit "arbitrary, unjust, and oppressive acts," the Democrats would fight them to the uttermost and oppose every parliamentary obstacle to their attempts. If necessary, opposition would extend so far as to prevent the consideration of appropriation bills and other important legislation.

Answering a specific question as to what would be considered "the first overt act of hostility and oppression," McCreary replied: "An attempt to revise the rules of the last House, and impose on the minority an arbitrary and tyrannical code." He had studied the precedents, he continued, and would consider failure to present a resolution adopting the rules of the last House, or an attempt to limit those rules to a fixed date, as proof of an intention to revise the rules. With only three more than a quorum the Republicans would be dependent on Democratic aid and that ought to be a strong inducement toward moderation.

From such utterances it is easy to see under what handicaps the next House would begin its work. The country looked forward to the session with lively anticipation. Whatever the outcome, there seemed certain to be a battle such as had not occurred since Reconstruction days. These anticipations were not disappointed.

On November 8, 1888, when the results of the election had been compiled and it was apparent that the Republicans would control the next House, the Washington *Post* reported that the reorganization of that body was a fruitful topic of discussion wherever politicians met, and that "the speakership question was regarded on all sides as being settled" in favor of Thomas B. Reed. This statement was somewhat premature, for while the Maine Representative had been the outstanding Republican member in the lower House for at least seven years, and this leadership had been formally recognized by his nomination for the speakership of the 49th and 50th Congresses, the post was too important to be conceded without a contest. The Harrison Administration was expected to bring forward a large program of legislation, and the Speaker would be in practical control of it in the House.

It was one thing for a minority to make a complimentary nomination but an entirely different matter for the majority to place the same man in an office second only to the presidency of the United States. It was expected that the coming session would be productive of great measures. A host of personal and local interests were dependent on the action of the Speaker. Furthermore, argued others, Maine would have more than a proper share of the offices.

The duties and responsibilities of the speakership are familiar even to elementary students of American government. Reed was soon to give additional prestige to an office which had been growing in dignity and power under such incumbents as James G. Blaine, Samuel J. Randall, and John G. Carlisle. While Carlisle's administration had at times been paralyzed by the tactics of the obstructionists, this brilliant Kentuckian had, more than any of his predecessors, adhered to the principle that the Speaker was the chief representative of the majority, and as such entitled to guide and in large measure determine its legislative program. Carlisle's description of its duties is accurate and relevant:

The Speakership is certainly a very arduous position. It entails hard work from the beginning to the end of the session, and taxes the strength and tries the patience of the incumbent to the fullest extent. The work of selecting the committees, determining just what members will deal most intelligently with certain classes of questions, and the naming of chairmen, is perplexing and tedious in the extreme. When this is done the Speaker's work is only begun. He has to pass upon questions of importance almost every hour. He has to be consulted as to the time that shall be given to the various legislative measures; must carry in his mind a panoramic view of the whole legislation of the session, and must understand the merits of each measure and how it should be treated. This, of course, requires a great amount of investigation and study. He must be ready to decide upon all matters the moment they come up, and new questions of procedure and parliamentary law are always being presented.[1]

Reed's views on political and parliamentary questions were well known. He had been critical of all recent incumbents for failure to use to the utmost the powers of the office for the expediting of public business. As minority leader he had maintained party discipline with a firm hand, and although his sarcasm and invective were not used against his own followers publicly, as they were against Democratic opponents, there were undoubtedly many Republicans who could hardly view his elevation with unmixed satisfaction. His leading rival, Mc-

[1] Interview with F. G. Carpenter, Washington *Post*, December 27, 1891.

Kinley, on the other hand, was a man of great personal popularity.

It is not surprising, therefore, that from the close of the 50th Congress until the convening of the 51st there were rumors of deals, intrigues and combinations. During the autumn months public interest steadily increased. The importance of the speakership in connection with revision of the rules began to draw attention, and the prominence which Reed had acquired in discussion of that issue undoubtedly strengthened his candidacy.

From the most powerful political leaders of his own State Reed could count on little support, and every one knew it. The Boston *Herald* accurately summarized the situation when it remarked: "If the Hon. Thomas B. Reed captures the Speakership, as some shrewd prophets think he stands a good chance of doing, it will be a very remarkable personal triumph in the face of difficulties. Mr. Blaine, it is well known, dislikes Mr. Reed. Mr. Hale shares Mr. Blaine's feelings in this direction, and Mr. Frye and Mr. Reed don't speak as they pass by. All the same, Mr. Reed's good humor hasn't forsaken him." But all the New England members of the House were solidly behind him.

Reed, who had been campaigning in Virginia, arrived in Washington on November 18. He had been considerably less active in his canvass for the speakership than several of his opponents and with characteristic astuteness and independence refused, when asking his colleagues for support, to make any commitments on legislation or committee appointments. On November 29, following a dinner given by Representative Belden, the New York Republican delegation declared for Reed and the adherence of this large and influential group proved decisive. The caucus met next day and Reed won on the second ballot, receiving 85 votes out of 166. McKinley was second with 38, Cannon received 19, Henderson 14, and Burrows 10.

The selection was widely approved. There was no disagreement as to Reed's courage, integrity and parliamentary ability. Party organs, according to their complexion, predicted brilliant success or expressed misgivings at the appearance of such a famous partisan in the seat of power. *The Nation,* somewhat grudgingly, described the choice as "the best possible," the new incumbent being "a man of marked ability, with habits of thinking about public questions, and likely to take the conservative rather than the radical view of any such subject as the silver question, for example."

How Reed met expectations can best be judged by what followed. The session formally opened on December 2, 1889. While the membership had been reported as consisting of 170 Republicans and 160 Democrats, the leaders of the former party placed its maximum strength at but 168, only three more than the quorum of 165. Reed received almost a full party vote, 166, Carlisle 154, and Amos J. Cummings 1, a North Carolina member, William H. H. Cowles, "whose saber-slashed crown was familiar to the galleries," having bolted Carlisle, according to the Washington *Post,* because of an unfavorable parliamentary decision by the ex-Speaker in the last session.

The clerk declared Mr. Reed elected Speaker and William McKinley and ex-Speaker Carlisle were appointed to escort the newly-elected officer to the chair. After a short interval "the trio appeared at the north entrance and moved down the main aisle. The portly form of Mr. Reed occupied most of the passage-way, and the escort was partially invisible during the trip from the entrance to the chair. Venerable Judge Kelley had already come within the bar of the House, holding the book from which he had read the oath to Speakers-elect so often before. In a voice far less resonant than in days long ago he administered the oath, and Speaker Reed was formerly inducted into an office no less consequential than the presidency of the United States." [1]

Taking up the gavel the new Speaker, expressing his appreciation of the honor and his realization of the responsibilities and duties involved, remarked: "Under our system of government as it has been developed, these responsibilities and duties are both political and parliamentary. So far as the duties are political, I sincerely hope they may be performed with the proper sense of what is due to the people of this whole country. So far as they are parliamentary I hope, with equal sincerity, that they may be performed with a proper sense of what is due to both sides of this chamber."

The session began peacefully. On December 3, the rules of the 50th Congress were referred to the Committee on Rules for consideration and report, and business proceeded as Reed had predicted it would under general parliamentary law. On December 9, the Speaker announced the first of his committee appointments. McKinley received the chairmanship of Ways and Means, Cannon and Henderson were both placed on the Appropriations Committee, and Burrows became head of the Committee on Manufactures. The Speaker's late competitors were thus taken care of, according to the usual precedents of congressional politics. The Committee on Rules consisted of the Speaker, McKinley, Cannon, Carlisle and Randall. Randall was in ill health and took practically no part in the work of the session. The Speaker was authorized to administer the oath of office in the latter's sick-room, and the great Democratic Representative passed away on April 13. His presence in the parliamentary contest might have altered the course of events.

Prior to the speakership election, there had been a great deal

[1] Washington *Post*, December 3, 1889.

of speculation as to Reed's successor on the floor and on Ways and Means should he secure the coveted position. The appointment of McKinley had far-reaching consequences for both men and there were probably few in the House, or elsewhere, who could have realized that it marked an all-important stage in the Ohio member's progress toward the White House. McKinley was the high priest of protection. *The Nation*, comparing his tariff views with Reed's, once described him as "the ignorant and solemn fanatic, whose faith knows no wavering. Protection was something supernatural in his eyes. All foreigners were devils. Political economists were traitors."

From a strictly political standpoint, moreover, McKinley had elements of real strength. He never said bitter things of his opponents. He could talk melodiously and at great length without committing himself or the party. He enjoyed doing favors for friends and associates, although he was sometimes suspected of merely promising favors when something was to be gained thereby. Intellectually far inferior to Reed, he was much more popular. His tactfulness and genuine kindliness made him, on the whole, a successful leader on the floor, although it is hard to tell how much of his success in this capacity was due to the rigorous party discipline enforced by the Speaker. That the tariff bill of this session which eventually popularized his name throughout the country owed much to the industry of Nelson Dingley is certain, and McKinley generously acknowledged his indebtedness.[1] While the Speaker had undoubtedly taken his measure and held him in no exalted estimation, the appointment was a good one and McKinley did yeoman service throughout the turbulent sessions which followed.

On December 21, the remaining committees were announced. It was noted that the West received 29 chairmanships, the Middle States 16, New England 7, the Pacific Coast 3, and

[1] E. N. Dingley, *Life and Times of Nelson Dingley, Jr.*, 325.

the South 1, and there was some criticism of the Speaker's generosity to his Western supporters. New York, however, had also been generously rewarded for the support its delegation had given, receiving seven chairmanships. In spite of the inevitable criticism that there was unfair discrimination, the appointments were regarded as unusually good. Even *The Nation,* seldom friendly toward Reed, on December 26 admitted that "Speaker Reed's committee appointments average very well and special praise is due for the composition of the Committee on the Civil Service." Unlike some previous committees the latter was composed of friends of the civil service law.

Routine business of no particular importance filled the opening days. C. E. Silcott, the Sergeant-at-Arms, disappeared early in the session, carrying off with him most of the funds on hand for the monthly payroll. This created further diversion and forced consideration of sundry regulations intended to prevent a recurrence of such defalcations and secure the Treasury against loss. The Speaker was given charge of Silcott's safe, and one who was present when the House committee placed the key in his custody still remembers that, when some of the members began to relate how obliging and good-natured the defaulter had always been and to express astonishment that he should have proved faithless to his trust, Reed interrupted with his rasping, snarling drawl: "You needn't start singing his praises around here, with all that money gone." [1]

The Christmas recess from December 21 to January 6 also served to delay the appearance of important matters, but the press correspondents from the opening of the session were keeping a watchful eye on developments. Like the members, they were well aware that trouble was brewing, but no one outside of the inner councils of the majority had any idea when,

[1] Related to author by Dr. E. N. Allen.

or under what conditions, it was likely to boil over. The House continued under general parliamentary law, which in effect meant that as long as the Speaker was sustained by a majority he could enforce his own conclusions as to what was parliamentary.

The Washington *Post* on December 20 pointed out the growing significance of the quorum issue, and reported that the Republican leaders, uneasy over the situation, were discussing the feasibility of changing the method of establishing a quorum. It was obvious that "general parliamentary law" would collapse the moment that there was no majority to table appeals from the Speaker's decisions and the Democrats refrained from voting. The *Post* reported that a proposition was under consideration providing that when a roll call disclosed the absence of a quorum, the officers of the House should be authorized to bring enough delinquents to the bar to aggregate a quorum, and that their presence should then constitute a record that a quorum was present. Opinions from prominent members were appended to this story, together with the statement that Mr. McKinley refused to be interviewed on the subject.

Representative Lewis E. Payson, of Illinois, said in regard to the suggested change: "I favor it as a common sense basis for a quorum. In the past the procedure was absurd. Upon finding that a quorum of the House was not present, a call would be ordered. Delinquents would be arrested and brought to the House, while those present would be restrained from leaving. Yet when enough arrests had been made to complete the quorum, the very members arrested could refuse to vote and we would be no nearer a quorum than before. Now, there is no use sending out to arrest members if, when they are brought into the House, their presence does not assist in completing a quorum."

Ex-Speaker Carlisle was unqualified in his denial of the right of the House to establish any such rule. "Such a change would be a violation of the Constitution, which provides that a majority of each House shall constitute a quorum. The recorded vote on a roll-call determines whether or not a quorum was present when the business was transacted. If an attempt were made to enact legislation, unless a quorum was shown the matter could be taken into court, and the rule would be declared unconstitutional."

On January 6, under the heading, "Reed will Count Them," the same journal printed a current rumor that the new rules would authorize the Speaker to count and declare a quorum and that "even Mr. Cannon" was opposed to such an innovation. General parliamentary law, it continued, required "a great confidence in the judgment and nerve of the Speaker, but that is just the sort of sentiment the Republicans have toward him." The lack of an elaborate code of rules deprived the Democrats of the many bases for obstructive tactics which they enjoyed in the last House and in any case the majority seemed to be determined to assume responsibility and enact legislation.

On January 7, however, there was a protracted wrangle on points of order in which Carlisle and other members handled "general parliamentary law" without gloves. Several hours were consumed in this discussion before it was possible, by tabling an appeal from the Speaker's decision, to secure a few minutes for actual legislative business.

The first really serious clash occurred on January 21, when the Speaker refused Mr. Bland's demand for tellers on a motion to adjourn, on the ground that it was intended merely for purposes of obstruction. After a prolonged wrangle accompanied by many displays of bad temper, an appeal from the Speaker's decision was laid on the table by a vote of 149 to 137. The Speaker had shown his mettle, the majority had stood solidly by him, although with no great enthusiasm, and the tension was still further heightened.[1]

The Democrats held a caucus on the evening of January 24, at which Carlisle was reported to have explained the nature of some of the changes which the Committee on Rules would probably present. In spite of the secrecy of the meeting some reliable information had been given out, inasmuch as several of the rules as described on this occasion were afterwards reported in almost identical form. The alleged intention of the majority to unseat Democratic members in the pending election contests caused much indignation and threats were freely made that the House would be left without a quorum if election contests were taken up before the rules were adopted. This proved an accurate forecast.[2]

The Republican caucus met on the 27th and it was announced next day that election cases would be taken up before the rules. It was also stated that a careful canvass revealed that four members of the party could not be relied on, a serious matter in view of the extremely narrow majority. That majority, incidentally, had been still further reduced on January 9 by the death of "the father of the House," William D. Kelley. There were "indications," the Washington *Post* reported, that the Speaker would not count a quorum. The party, however, adopted a portentous resolution: "That it is the sense of this caucus that every Republican member of the House should remain in this city, except in case of sickness; and that all members should remain in this hall during the time the House is in session, unless prevented by sickness."

The legislative program of the majority depended on securing procedural reforms, and procedural reforms depended on ability to maintain a quorum. It is true that the chief re-

---

[1] *Cong. Record*, 51 Cong., 1 Sess., 749.
[2] Washington *Post*, January 25, 1890.

liance of the obstructionists, as exemplified in such famous filibusters as those against the Kansas-Nebraska Bill in 1854, when
on one legislative day there were over one hundred roll calls
on motions to adjourn, against the Force Bill in 1875, or those
in the recent sessions of the 50th Congress, had been the
dilatory motion. Motions to adjourn to a certain day and to
take a recess, both subject to two amendments upon which yeas
and nays could be demanded by one fifth of the members
present, could be repeated for hours at a stretch. As Reed well
said, it was "a system which enabled one member to hold the
whole House at bay until the going down of the sun and then
to hold it until physical exhaustion set it free and one fifth
to hold it forever." The disappearing quorum was in most cases
only temporarily effective; but in the 51st Congress, the narrow majority and the expressed determination of the Speaker
to secure reforms establishing effective majority rule and the
equally evident determination on the part of the minority to
fight such reforms to the last ditch, made it absolutely vital.
Without a quorum it was evident that little could be accomplished, and it was obvious that a voting quorum could be
maintained only with the greatest difficulty and under unusually
fortunate circumstances.

Reed, it will be remembered, had defended the disappearing
quorum against the Tucker amendment in 1880; had taken
part in this form of obstruction on numerous occasions while a
minority member; had reiterated his opinions of 1880 in debate on an election case in 1882; and a few months later barely
escaped humiliating defeat through its agency when forcing to
a vote the tariff bill of 1883. The system, however, had been
in vogue before Reed had been born. The First Congress had
adopted a rule requiring members to vote unless having some
personal or pecuniary interest in the question, but when John
Quincy Adams in 1832 refused to obey the rule and the House

found no means of compulsion or method of punishment, a new weapon of obstruction had been created, of which Adams himself soon made use. In somewhat different form it had appeared sporadically in still earlier times.

The disappearing quorum, having become a common method of obstruction in Congress, was adopted by other bodies for similar purposes in the period following the Civil War. As Reed himself wrote, "this system of metaphysics whereby a man could be present and absent at the same moment" spread until it reached States, municipalities, and churches, but when the doctrine of corporeal presence and parliamentary absence began to affect fundamental rights there was prompt revolt. "Hence when municipal bodies began to imitate their superiors and break contracts as well as quorums, the gladsome light of jurisprudence was soon shed upon them, and the parliamentary fiction that a man present could truthfully declare himself absent disappeared from every place except the Capitol at Washington."

It was still effective, however, in the House, and sanctified by "the precedents of a hundred years," a phrase which Reed described as "simply rhetoric," inasmuch as this form of obstruction had become an abuse only in recent times. It had once been used merely to call attention to pending measures, and not until recent Congresses to block measures demanded by the majority and bring legislative programs to a standstill.

The party caucuses had served to heighten the existing tension and frequenters of the Capitol and correspondents in the press gallery were constantly on the alert for something to happen. For more than a year a great parliamentary battle had been foreshadowed and when the storm broke on January 29, 1890, there was almost a sense of relief that the strain of waiting in an atmosphere sultry with suspicion and nervous strain was over at last. According to Cannon, Reed, while warning McKinley and himself to be ready for action at any time, had given them no intimation of what was about to happen and on this eventful morning they had "no premonition that before the day was over history would be written." [1]

Only 161 Republican members were in their places, several of these so ill that they were actually there at the risk of their lives. Of the absentees, several were dangerously sick, and another had been summoned to the bedside of his dying wife. A quorum under the existing practice required 165 votes. But as the *Post* reported next day, "The apparent advantage of the Democrats rested only upon the assumption that the previous practices of the House were to be observed. Speaker Reed is not an everyday Speaker. He arises to occasions and yesterday was one of them. He had a little surprise for the Democrats."

After the transaction of routine business Mr. Dalzell called up the West Virginia election case of Smith vs. Jackson. Mr. Crisp promptly raised the question of consideration against Dalzell's resolution and the Speaker put the question, declaring that "the ayes seem to have it." Crisp then demanded a division and when the result was the same demanded the yeas and nays. The yeas and nays were ordered and the clerk proceeded to drone through the roll call.

There was an ominous calm. As Representative Edward P. Allen, of Michigan, described it in debate a few days later, "It was like the silence of heaven after the seventh seal was broken, as recorded by John of Patmos, and continued for about the same length of time, half an hour. Then it was broken and broken in a way no one present will ever forget."

The roll call gave yeas 162, nays 3, not voting 163, but on recapitulation, two Democrats amid the laughter of their colleagues withdrew their votes, making the result yeas 161, nays 2, not voting 165. By all accepted practices the only course

[1] L. W. Busbey, *Uncle Joe Cannon*, 175.

open to the majority was another vote. Carlisle had held, time and again, that when the point of "no quorum" was raised it could be met only by a yea and nay vote which showed a voting quorum. On this occasion, however, precedent had short shrift. Calmly ignoring Crisp's shout of "no quorum," the Speaker announced the result as yeas 161, nays 2, and directed the Clerk to record the names of some forty members as present and refusing to vote. The battle was on.

There was an instantaneous crash of applause on the Republican side, a rising volume of protest from the Democrats, and pandemonium broke loose. Even the official record succeeded in catching something of the drama of the occasion. It could not, however, reproduce the giant figure of the Speaker as, gavel in hand, he confronted the shouting, threatening mass before him, a scene which his friends long after still loved to picture. Throughout the turbulent days which followed he displayed a gentleness and patience which amazed beholders, ignored insult and abuse, and except for occasional sarcastic interjections, betrayed no anger. The New York *Tribune,* at the time of the Speaker's election, had described him as a man "the sweetness of whose temper" was most evident when he was thoroughly enraged. In the privacy of the Speaker's room, when the strain was over, he sometimes gave full vent to his wrath. He afterwards related that during the session the House often reminded him of a wild beast leaping toward the rostrum as far as its chain permitted, but never quite breaking loose. The *Congressional Record,* however, is vivid enough:

The Speaker. On this question the yeas are 161, the nays 2.
Mr. Crisp. No quorum.
The Speaker. The Chair directs the Clerk to record the following names of members present and refusing to vote. [Applause on the Republican side.]

Mr. Crisp. I appeal—[Applause on the Democratic side]—I appeal from the decision of the Chair.

The Speaker. Mr. Blanchard, Mr. Bland, Mr. Blount, Mr. Breckinridge, of Arkansas, Mr. Breckinridge, of Kentucky.

Mr. Breckinridge, of Kentucky. I deny the power of the Speaker and denounce it as revolutionary. [Applause on the Democratic side of the House, which was renewed several times.]

Mr. Bland. Mr. Speaker—[Applause on the Democratic side.]

The Speaker. The House will be in order.

Mr. Bland. Mr. Speaker, I am responsible to my constituents for the way in which I vote, and not to the Speaker of the House. [Applause.]

The Speaker. Mr. Brookshire, Mr. Bullock, Mr. Bynum, Mr. Carlisle, Mr. Chipman, Mr. Clements, Mr. Clunie, Mr. Compton.

Mr. Compton. I protest against the conduct of the Chair in calling my name.

The Speaker (proceeding). Mr. Covert, Mr. Crisp, Mr. Culberson of Texas [hisses on the Democratic side], Mr. Cummings, Mr. Edmunds, Mr. Enloe, Mr. Fithian, Mr. Goodnight, Mr. Hare, Mr. Hatch, Mr. Hayes.

Mr. Hayes. I appeal from any decision, so far as I am concerned.

The Speaker (continuing). Mr. Holman, Mr. Lawler, Mr. Lee, Mr. McAdoo, Mr. McCreary.

Mr. McCreary. I deny your right, Mr. Speaker, to count me as present, and I desire to read from the parliamentary law on that subject.

The Speaker. The Chair is making a statement of the fact that the gentleman from Kentucky is present. Does he deny it? [Laughter and applause on the Republican side.]

Amid repeated interruptions the count proceeded. The Speaker took occasion to point out that the question of quorum had been raised, was being treated by him in orderly fashion, and after submission of his opinion, there would be an opportunity to overrule the latter on an appeal taken from the decision. The count concluded with the names of Mr. Tillman and Mr. Turner, and when, after repeated and violent objections from the members counted, the confusion had somewhat subsided, the Speaker issued his ruling on the quorum issue. It was less elaborate than some of his arguments subsequently published and omitted precedents and judicial decisions which were afterwards effectively presented in debate. He did cite, however, the ruling of Lieutenant-Governor Hill in the New York Senate in 1883 holding that members present constituted a quorum whether voting or not. Hill was a Democrat, but not the type of official whose opinions were likely to inspire general confidence. The meat of Reed's decision was contained in the statement: "There is a provision in the Constitution which declares that the House may establish rules for compelling the attendance of members. If members can be present and refuse to exercise their functions and cannot be counted as a quorum, that provision would seem to be entirely nugatory. Inasmuch as the Constitution only provides for their attendance, that attendance is enough. If more was needed, the Constitution would have provided for more." And in closing he declared: "The Chair thereupon rules that there is a quorum present within the meaning of the Constitution."

This common sense doctrine ripped through the tangle of precedents and sophistry like a scythe, but it could hardly be expected that the House would tamely acquiesce in the overthrow of a system from which both parties had so often derived advantage. Furthermore, the rules and precedents of the House had acquired a measure of sanctity in the eyes of the members which had to be reckoned with. With all their weaknesses and defects, rules and precedents alone permitted a legislative body to function, and there were many who did not realize, as did the Speaker, how completely they had been perverted from their real intent.

Mr. Crisp, amid the uproar, promptly appealed from the ruling of the Chair. It is apparent that the majority had caught the spirit of "Up Guards, and at them," and probable that Lewis E. Payson's motion to lay the appeal on the table could have been carried through in a rush of enthusiasm. Fortunately, however, the matter was submitted to exhaustive debate. Crisp made an impassioned plea for an opportunity to present the minority side of the case. It would, he declared, be "unfair, unjust, and unmanly" to deny it. "Are you afraid to permit the country to judge between you and us?" Turning toward his opponents on the Republican side he made a bid for their support by expressing "a confident assurance that there are at least some Republican members of this body who can rise above partisan prejudice, who can respect and will respect the ancient usages and customs of the House, who will respect the opinions of the fathers, and who will be regardful of that Constitution whose sacredness we all acknowledge, and in which alone are secured the rights of the American people." [1]

On the suggestion of Benjamin Butterworth, Ohio Republican, Payson withdrew his motion and debate proceeded. Reed must have realized that the situation was critical. Desertion of a few self-seeking, disgruntled, or unduly conscientious members of his own party would have subjected him to a humiliation such as no Speaker had ever experienced. It is known that he had considered such a contingency, and that in case of defeat he was determined to resign and enter the practice of law with Elihu Root in New York City. [2]

Debate then continued on the original question, "Shall the decision of the Chair stand as the judgment of the House?"

[1] *Cong. Record,* 51 Cong., 1 Sess., 956.
[2] McCall, *Reed,* 167.

Both sides were ably represented and the discussion was worthy of the best traditions of American debate. Reed's attitude on the Tucker amendment of 1880 was still remembered by those who had been present ten years before, and amid jeers and ironical applause his utterances on that occasion were read into the record, the Speaker, however, failing to betray the slightest evidence of irritation or embarrassment. His ruling had already mentioned the fact that in 1880 the matter had been less thoroughly understood and since that time the courts had repeatedly passed on the question.

Carlisle and Crisp defended the traditional practice of the House and savagely attacked the innovation, but encountered competent adversaries in Cannon and McKinley.

If Reed had opposed the Tucker amendment, prominent Democrats like Blackburn and Springer had supported it. The former was now in the Senate, but the latter, prominent in his vociferous opposition to the Speaker's rulings, could at least be forced to listen while Cannon quoted his attack of 1880 on the disappearing quorum. When a Democratic member twitted him with his own refusal to vote on an election case in the last House, Cannon made a few remarks which, after all, cover the political aspects, Democratic or Republican, of the entire performance:

The gentleman knows that in this popular body, the House of Representatives, members from time to time do, and perhaps always will do, under a supposed partisan necessity, that which lies in their power to do, and then, having done it, the desire to be sustained makes them claim a construction of the Constitution to justify that which nothing in sound sense or good morals can justify else.[1]

In effect, he argued, the claim was being made that legislation should not proceed unless the majority would allow the

[1] *Cong. Record,* 51 Cong., 1 Sess., 957.

minority to rule. "In reply, I say that a majority under the Constitution is entitled to legislate and that, if a contrary practice has grown up, such practice is unrepublican, undemocratic, against sound public policy, and contrary to the Constitution."

The House met next day, January 30, before crowded galleries, and disorder broke out afresh. "The House resembled a perfect Bedlam," wrote the correspondent of the New York *Tribune;* but Reed continued master of the situation. "In the midst of this pandemonium he remained calm and self possessed, not for an instant losing his presence of mind. He delivered his decisions in the calmest way possible, but in a voice that could plainly be heard above the din."

The proceedings opened with some parliamentary skirmishing and a vote on ordering the previous question on the motion to approve the Journal produced the familiar result; yeas 160, nays 1, not voting 167. Amid cheers from his own side and yells of execration from the Democrats, the Speaker thereupon counted enough members to insure a quorum and declared that 160 members having voted in the affirmative and 1 in the negative the previous question was ordered. He also refused to entertain Springer's appeal from the Speaker's decision and again counted a quorum on the approval of the Journal. "You are not a tyrant to rule over this House, or the members of this House," howled Bland during the roll call, almost incoherent with rage, "and I denounce you as the worst tyrant that ever ruled over a deliberative body."

Debate then continued on Crisp's appeal from the Speaker's decision of the day preceding, Representative Benjamin Butterworth of Ohio making a long and able address upholding the Speaker's contentions and denouncing the disappearing quorum as the weapon of anarchy and revolution. Butterworth had frequently chafed under Reed's leadership in previous Congresses and had he proved recalcitrant in this crisis the Speaker would undoubtedly have lost. With his support, victory was practically assured. His speech, repeatedly interrupted, consumed most of the day.

At last, late in the afternoon, McKinley moved to lay the appeal on the table. A motion to adjourn was defeated and the yeas and nays were taken on McKinley's motion. Again the familiar result, yeas 162, nays 0, not voting 167, and again the Speaker counted a score or so of prominent Democrats to make the quorum. "I am much obliged to the Speaker for recognizing me as being present," remarked Roswell P. Flower of New York. "The Chair is glad to be able to recognize the gentleman from New York as being present vocally," was the polite rejoinder.

Perhaps the most disorderly scene in the three-day contest occurred on January 31. The Speaker again counted a quorum on the approval of the Journal. William D. Bynum, of Indiana, appealed from the decision of the Chair only to encounter the Speaker's placid response: "That is a question of fact which cannot be appealed from. The vote stands, yeas 161, nays 0. Accordingly the Journal is approved." There was another outburst from the minority, members crowding to the front denouncing and threatening the Speaker. Bynum broke into a frantic tirade denouncing Republican misgovernment for the past twenty years, finally drawing from Reed's Maine colleague, Charles A. Boutelle, the advice: "As the member has denounced every department of the government, executive, legislative and judicial, he had better sit down or secede." Bynum, after inviting the Maine member to try putting him down himself, at length subsided, denouncing "the arbitrary, the outrageous and damnable rulings of the Chair."

Springer, who had described the Speaker's conduct as "tyranny simple and undiluted," now made a motion to adjourn which the Speaker promptly ruled not in order. There was great confusion, but amid noisy protests the Speaker finally made another memorable ruling which embodied many of the principles for which he had contended for nearly ten years:

There is no possible way by which the orderly methods of parliamentary procedure can be used to stop legislation. The object of a parliamentary body is action, and not stoppage of action. Hence, if any member or set of members undertakes to oppose the orderly progress of business, even by the use of the ordinarily recognized parliamentary motions, it is the right of the majority to refuse to have those motions entertained, and to cause the public business to proceed.

Primarily the organ of the House is the man elected to the Speakership. It is his duty in a clear case, recognizing the situation, to endeavor to carry out the wishes and desires of the majority of the body which he represents.

Whenever it becomes apparent that the ordinary and proper parliamentary motions are being used solely for purposes of delay and obstruction; when members break in an unprecedented way [derisive laughter and applause on the Democratic side] over the rule in regard to the reading of the Journal; when a gentleman steps down to the front, amid the applause of his associates on the floor, and announces that it is his intention to make opposition in every direction, it then becomes apparent to the House and to the community what the purpose is. It is then the duty of the occupant of the Speaker's chair to take under parliamentary law, the proper course with regard to such matters; and in order that there might not be any misunderstanding as to whether or not it is the wish or desire of the majority of the House—apparent as it seems to be—the question of the appeal from the refusal of the Chair to entertain the motion will be put to the House for its judgment and determination.

The House promptly laid Springer's appeal from the Speaker's decision on the table. There were further attempts at obstruction and the Speaker's cheeriness and good humor when he finally suppressed Mr. Springer delighted both the Republicans on the floor and the spectators in the galleries. "When will it be in order again to make that motion?" asked the Illinois member when Reed had again refused to entertain a motion to adjourn. "It will be in order at the proper time," was the pleasant response.

The ground having thus been cleared, Dalzell brought up the disputed election case and Crisp's attempts to revive the question of consideration were ruled out of order. The Chair, amid hisses from the Democratic side, refused to entertain an appeal from the decision and directed Mr. Dalzell to proceed, Crisp's persistence serving merely to bring on himself one of those brief but scorching rebukes from the Chair with which the House was soon to become familiar and under which the victims usually wilted.

"Now," said Dalzell, when at last he had undisputed possession of the floor, "let us proceed with the public business." And the House proceeded, with Springer piteously exclaiming, "Where is the appeal?" and some anonymous Republican derisively shouting, "In the air." The first stage of the great quorum battle was over and the Speaker was master of the situation. The House was being placed on the road to genuine efficiency of action.

THE three-day episode just closed was happily described by Representative Moore of New Hampshire in debate a few days later, when he predicted that some future historian of Congress —some Blaine who described events as he had witnessed them during the last week—would write: "In the tenth week of the first session of the Fifty-first Congress a very strange frenzy seized the Democratic side of the Chamber. When the Speaker ruled that members present but not voting should be counted as a part of the quorum necessary to do business, twenty members on the Democratic side jumped to their feet. Some gesticulated wildly; some vociferated loudly; some shook their fists at the Speaker; some denounced him as 'czar,' 'tyrant,' 'despot.' This frenzy lasted for three days, when, like the Russian influenza that prevailed about that time, it suddenly disappeared and the House resumed its wonted dignity and decorum." [1]

While the frantic excitement aroused by the Speaker's quorum ruling seems grotesque in view of subsequent events and the fact that within four years the Democrats themselves adopted virtually the same rule, the effects were felt throughout both sessions. While the "wonted dignity and decorum" of the House had been restored, they were again and again upset by relatively unimportant incidents, and the 51st Congress passed into the records as one of the most turbulent in American history.

The pending election case of Smith vs. Jackson consumed the next three days,[2] obstructive tactics being no more effective than

[1] *Cong. Record,* 51 Cong., 1 Sess., 1255.
[2] February 1–3, 1890.

hitherto. The evidence was strongly in favor of the Republican contestant, the case hinging chiefly on the fact that a Democratic governor had certified Jackson on the ground that a defective "o" in the word "two" was an "e" and that "twe" was an abbreviation for "twelve," the number thus altered giving the contestee a plurality. The impudence of this claim gives the case a somewhat unique place in the long and discreditable story of contested elections.

On February 3, 1890, William L. Wilson of West Virginia, one of the ablest Democrats in the House, took advantage of the opportunity to discuss the circumstances under which the case had been brought up, making a scathing attack on "general parliamentary law" which in its wit and sarcasm was worthy of Reed himself. His gentle irony was more effective than the frantic denunciations of his colleagues had been. Butterworth a few days earlier had likened the Republican party to "the great train of progress" and Wilson in conclusion delighted his party colleagues with a description of this train in motion, Butterworth riding the cowcatcher, Reed at the throttle, McKinley conductor, Cannon fireman, while Payson "from his alacrity in laying things upon the table would make a splendid grand master of the buffet." The Speaker let Wilson have his head, although a sarcastic remark at the end showed that he regarded the speech as irrelevant to the business before the House.

On the evening of February 3 resolutions unseating Jackson and giving his place to Smith were carried by a vote of yeas 166, nays 0, not voting 162. It was, Roger Q. Mills pointed out a few days later, the first occasion since organization that there had been "a constitutional quorum" in the House and he charged that the vote had been delayed "until you brought up your sick men," in order to avoid the danger of Jackson's taking his case before the courts where the quorum issue could have been tested.

The contestant was promptly sworn in and there ensued the following colloquy:

Mr. Springer. Is this a proper time to move to adjourn? [Laughter.]

The Speaker. Does the gentleman desire to make that motion?

Mr. Springer. I do if the Chair will permit me.

The Speaker. The Chair will entertain the motion. [Laughter.]

Mr. Springer. I make that motion.

The "proper time" had evidently arrived in due course, as Reed a few days earlier had said it would, and the House adjourned at 8: 30 P. M. Another stage in the struggle was over.

The next matter of business was the adoption of formal rules, "general parliamentary law" having served its purpose but having also demonstrated the need of unending vigilance by the majority leaders and the constant danger of irritating clashes over the Speaker's decisions. Reed had been at work for weeks on the new code and the revision when it appeared was everywhere regarded as his handiwork. McKinley on January 7 had stated in the House that the Committee on Rules, "for reasons satisfactory to themselves," had as yet held no meeting to consider a general plan of rules, and on February 1, during debate on the Smith vs. Jackson case, Carlisle reported that there had been but three meetings to consider the proposed rules. The first, on January 23, had lasted about an hour and two subsequent meetings about thirty minutes each. This revision, unlike that of 1880, was obviously not a product of coöperative effort and unanimous consent. It was primarily the creation of Thomas Brackett Reed.

The question naturally arises why the majority had not first adopted rules to authorize the counting of a quorum and so obviate all necessity for radical action on the part of the Speaker. The reasons are clear. The majority was small and there was certain to be sharp opposition to innovations in procedure. Furthermore, there was pending important legislation in many fields. In matters of tariff and currency, where sectional differences were likely to assume serious proportions, it was especially desirable to avoid all preliminary clashes. A protracted wrangle over the rules would have given any petty group of obstructionists within the party an unprecedented opportunity for the levy of political blackmail. The Democrats would, as a result, have been in a position to block the progress of business throughout the session.

The case of Smith vs. Jackson, where the Republicans clearly had the right on their side, had given an excellent opportunity to demonstrate the evils of obstruction. Democratic tactics on this occasion had furnished ample excuse for heroic treatment. The case was settled before it could be confused by protracted discussion of new rules, and the Speaker's ruling on the quorum assured the passage of the new code when it should be submitted.

Reed apparently had planned to meet the issue when it should arise, consolidate his party by a daring stroke, and then force the fighting to a successful conclusion. In spite of all the rumors during the weeks which elapsed between the opening of Congress and the *coup* of January 29, it is plain that the rank and file of the party were unaware of the Speaker's intention. It was a splendid exhibition of daring, and brought out the Speaker's wonderful capacity for executive office. The party members, almost to a man, stood behind him throughout the struggle. If they did not love him as the Whigs did Clay, or if he could not inspire the enthusiastic devotion aroused by James G. Blaine, in his sheer intellectual mastery of the House he surpassed both his famous predecessors.

The Republican press, many leading members of the party throughout the country, and a considerable body of non-partisan opinion supported the Speaker both in the quorum ruling and his projected reform of the rules. "It is idle to quote precedents and refer to other legislative bodies," said news dispatches to the New York *Tribune* which expressed widespread lay opinion on the subject, on January 31, 1890. "What Speaker So-and-So said, or this and that Legislature did, interests no one outside of a limited number of parliamentary bric-a-brac hunters. The country wants results, and doesn't care much in what way they are obtained. That cumbersome machinery known as the 'rules of the House,' which were the work of brooding Buddhas in the seclusion of their committee rooms, was designed to retard business rather than promote it. The barnacles which time and the fetish of precedent have permitted to surround them, have grown to the proportions of an intolerable nuisance. Everybody of sense has long ago arrived at the conclusion that it is time to remove them."

The tremendous uproar occasioned by counting the quorum should not obscure the fact that this procedure was merely incidental, although absolutely prerequisite, to the formulation of thorough-going reforms. Reed made in the next Congress a brief explanation of the contradiction between his utterances on the Tucker amendment of 1880 and his unprecedented action ten years later, although he took pains to declare that "a great constitutional question ought not to be degraded into the question whether I was consistent or not." His words "it would seem" in his original statement implied doubt and were used intentionally. A decision of the Maine Supreme Court on the quorum question as it arose in a local board of canvassers during the "State Steal" of 1880 had led him to insert these words. Furthermore, the filibustering he had then defended was defensible. "The same word is often used to describe the same animal when a harmless kitten and a ferocious animal running wild."

The old rules were the product of forces and conditions which he recognized clearly, and which he pointed out to the voters of the First District when on September 4, 1890, he opened his campaign for reëlection. "For years rule has been piled upon rule and decision upon decision to render legislation dependent upon the sufferance of the minority. Filibustering lurked in every line. The power of obstruction was without limit. You will naturally ask why it was that those who most of the time had the majority should so strengthen the minority. If you will consider the nature of the two parties the cause cannot escape you. The Democratic party wants no legislation. It is not charged with the progress of the world. All the Southern men who control the party want or ask for is to be let alone. When the Republican party comes into power it has work to do. If that action can be prevented what more should the Southern Democrats desire? Hence all their plans, whether in power or out of power, are centered in obstruction."

What was the use, he continued, of summoning an army of voters to listen to arguments on public policy, what was the use of having the great journals of the country devote their space to the discussion of current issues, what was the use of "that grand culmination of the power of the citizen"—the election itself—if nothing could be done without the sanction of the beaten party?

What statesman could there be so foolish as to battle for power with responsibility when he could have the same power without responsibility? What kind of a fight is that to go into where the victim will be victorious and the conqueror powerless? Says the Koran: "Dost thou think, O Man, that we created the heavens and the earth in jest?" Are elections a farce, and is government by the people a juggle? Do we marshal our tens of millions to the polls for sport? If there be anything in popular government it means that whenever the people have elected one party to take control of the House or the

Senate that party shall have both the power and the responsibility. If that is not the effect, what is the use of the election?

On February 5, the House Republicans held a six-hour caucus on the question of the rules, under "the most imperative injunction of secrecy," but it soon leaked out that the proceedings were exciting and the members far from unanimous. The Speaker vigorously applied his great argumentative power and dominating personality, secured the full adherence of his followers, and was ready to force the matter to an issue on the floor. Next day the Washington *Post* announced the result under the caption "The Speaker's Victory," and the "Reed rules" were reported in the House, accompanied by lengthy majority and minority reports, the latter signed by Carlisle and Randall.

A complete discussion of the "Reed rules" would involve a dissertation on parliamentary law as evolved through centuries of British and American practice. It will be sufficient here to point out that the changes made in 1890 were, for the most part, those which he had been urging ever since the 47th Congress. The last general revision in 1880, he once pointed out, had been made under apprehension of what might happen to the existing laws in which the Republican minority was deeply interested, with the result that the 46th Congress had agreed—and he admitted he was one of those who accepted the code—"to a set of rules which, for imbecility, for absolute protection against progress, never had their equal on printed white paper." The idea of obstruction was so completely dominant that "you can come across these obstructions in the most unexpected places."

The new code retained twenty-nine of the forty-seven rules in force at the close of the 50th Congress unaltered. There were numerous changes in detail throughout the remaining eighteen, usually for the purpose of bringing all the rules into conformity with the vitally important changes made in a few essential particulars, or to remove potential obstruction. An instance of the latter was the elimination of the old privilege of making verbal explanations when a member requested to be excused from voting, which obviously could be used for filibustering purposes.

The important changes were only four in number, but they were revolutionary in character. First: Dilatory motions, the evils of which had received such striking demonstration in the last Congress, were torn up by the roots. Under the old rules "a motion to fix the day to which the House shall adjourn, a motion to adjourn, and to take a recess shall always be in order." These privileged motions under which a single member, by alternation and repetition, could bring business to a standstill, were eliminated, thereby evoking raucous lamentations that the first of them had been sacred since 1789. In addition, the safe-guards against obstruction were made still more effective by incorporating a new clause: "No dilatory motion shall be entertained by the Speaker."

The second great innovation was in regard to the quorum, providing that when a roll call failed to show the presence of a quorum, at the demand of any member, or at the Speaker's direction, and before another roll call, the names of a sufficient number of members present in the hall who did not vote should be noted by the clerk and recorded in the Journal, to be counted and announced in determining the presence of a quorum.

A third important change involved the Committee of the Whole. The great increase in congressional business, the majority of the Committee on Rules pointed out in its report, had for years past rendered it desirable to reduce the quorum in Committee of the Whole. It had been a common practice for the committee in arranging its order of business to fix a quorum at less than a majority of its whole number. No constitutional or legal question was involved, inasmuch as the Committee of the Whole was a purely advisory body without power of concluding

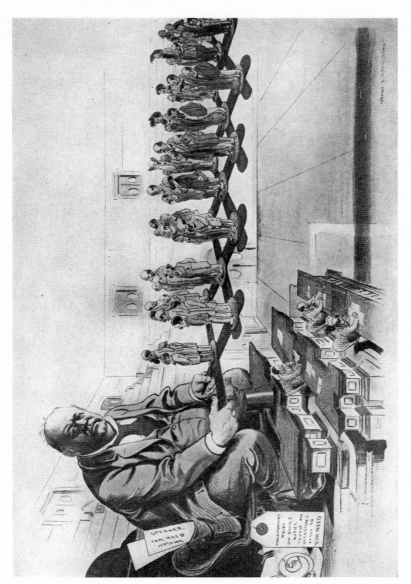

REED AS MASTER OF CONGRESS

(From *Judge*)

anything. Accordingly it was proposed that its quorum thereafter should consist of one hundred members. When the rules were debated a few days later Cannon urged this change, explaining how, when in charge of appropriation bills, he had often stood for hours at his desk imploring members not to make the point of no quorum. "I have time and again accepted amendments and bought the poor privilege of going on with the consideration of bills by accepting amendments upon condition that gentlemen would abstain from no quorum."

By a further modification of the rules, the Committee of the Whole was empowered to close debate on any section or paragraph of a bill under consideration. The minority of the Committee on Rules pointed out that this was a power never before granted, having in the past been exercised only by the House. It was, however, merely another check on obstruction and intended to promote the speedier transaction of business.

The fourth group of changes dealt with the order of business, and embodied most of the reforms which Reed had been urging during the last three Congresses. The old rules in this instance underwent almost complete reconstruction, and the result has been described by high authority as "a better system, original in its conception, satisfactory in its practice, and destined to survive new conditions arising from increased business and a larger membership." [1]

The old Monday call of the States and Territories for the introduction of bills, memorials and resolutions was abolished and such items thereafter were to be indorsed to the Speaker, to be referred by him to the proper committees, and to be entered on the Journal, reasonable opportunity for the correction of references being retained by the House. This meant in effect a mere depositing of bills with the Clerk and saved a vast amount of time, once wasted in formal introduction and reading. The old

[1] Alexander, *House of Representatives*, 220.

system, Reed declared, had been "one of the worst features of our legislative practice," a waste of time at the best and a source of obstruction when a member desired to misuse it.

Business on the Speaker's table was to be disposed of by empowering the Speaker to refer messages from the President, departmental reports, and bills, resolutions, and messages from the Senate to appropriate committees without debate. Most nonfinancial House bills with Senate amendments might now be disposed of at once, as the House determined, as might also "Senate bills substantially the same as House bills already favorably reported on by a committee of the House." The object of the rule was to enable the House either to conclude legislation or put the matter into conference. Sundry technical changes were made in the rules regarding "unfinished business," which was placed next in order after business on the Speaker's table. Under the new regulations its prompt disposal was rendered possible without the interruptions to regular business which had once been so common. Reed's reform in this particular has been described as "a master stroke." [1]

The new rules then provided that after the disposal of unfinished business there should be a period of action by the House, under the direction of committees, upon "bills of a public character which do not appropriate money." This embodied the principles regarding the use of "the morning hour" which Reed had urged so persistently in the 48th and 49th Congresses. The period under the new rules had to be sixty minutes, and at the option of the House could be extended. Reed had repeatedly urged in the past that the House be given freedom to continue the business in hand as long as necessary, to select measures from the calendars at discretion, or to pass into or out of Committee of the Whole with a minimum of delay.

The majority report declared that "in at least three fourths

[1] *Ibid.,* 221.

of the business considered by the House, from necessity we are compelled to trust the investigations, reports and recommendations of the respective committees." It will be remembered that the process of reaching bills so reported was so involved and difficult that Reed had declared that "the only effect of the decision of a committee is that it enables the corpse to be put in a glass case where the friends of the deceased may look upon the remains." All reports of committees, under the new rules, were to be delivered to the Clerk for printing and reference to the proper calendar. The waste of time involved in reporting, which Reed stated had amounted to the equivalent of one working day each week, was thus eliminated, and with the House empowered to reach bills on the calendars, the latter were no longer graveyards as they had been in recent Congresses.

The new code unquestionably meant a great increase in the power of the Speaker, and it was undoubtedly anticipation of the hostility which it would provoke that led the majority to incorporate in their report the following statement:

If the suggestion should be made that great power is here conferred, the answer is that as the approval of the House is the very breath in the nostrils of the Speaker, and as no body on earth is so jealous of its liberties and so impatient of control, we may be quite sure that no arbitrary interruption will take place, and indeed, no interruption at all, until not only such misuse of proper motions is made clearly evident to the world, but also such action has taken place as will assure the Speaker of the support of the body whose wishes are his law.

Debate on the rules opened on February 10 and continued for four days, the brevity of the discussion attracting unfavorable comment from some minority members, one of whom pointed out that the House of Commons had devoted nearly a year to discussion of a simple closure rule which was far less drastic in curbing minority rights than several of the changes here proposed. The new rules, several Democrats tauntingly reminded the majority, were to be driven through under the party lash, a reluctant acquiescence having been extorted by the recent caucus.

Cannon, in introducing the code, made an able argument in support of the changes offered. The power of the Speaker, he argued, was already very great. This was shown by the action of Carlisle in preventing the Blair Education Bill, which had passed the Senate several times, from ever being brought before the House. Other measures which members desired should at least reach debate had been withheld in a similar manner. But in spite of the Speaker's power to prevent the passage or even the consideration of measures, the minority had enjoyed a still greater power of obstruction. The new rules would have positive results and would facilitate the transaction of business.

As might have been expected under the circumstances, opposition concentrated on the quorum-counting rule, and the legal and constitutional aspects of the subject were exhaustively argued. Cannon ably defended the proposed changes, reinforcing the former Republican arguments by citation of additional court decisions in many States, supplemented by the rulings of various legislative officers, which all went to show that "the doctrine is well established that those who are present and who help to make up a quorum are expected to vote on any measure, and their presence alone is sufficient whether they actually vote or not." There was, he added, no danger of a tyrannical Speaker, for whatever he did had to have the support of the House, an effective check against abuse of power.

There was apparently little opposition to the new rules regarding the Committee of the Whole, or order of business, although Carlisle and Randall in their minority report had assailed the latter as tending to exalt the committees at the expense of the individual member. The debate dealt largely with generalities, the usurpations and dangerous powers of the Speaker, the tyranny of the majority, and the sanctity of minority rights. Throughout the discussion it is easy to trace the old cleavage between the parties. In addition to reducing the individual member, especially the newcomer, to the status of a wooden Indian, said William H. Hatch, of Missouri, the new system broke down every barrier to speedy legislation and yet the country was already suffering from too much legislation. The Speaker, he declared, was a worthy representative of the present schemes of the Republican party.

In a somewhat far-fetched comparison of the Speaker with Judge Jeffreys, William McAdoo, of New Jersey, argued that under the new rules Reed would be in a position to destroy the liberties of his countrymen. His closing attack on the rules, in spite of excessive fervor, contained a decidedly unpleasant element of truth:

What is the meaning of these rules? You obtained power in this land in 1888 by a mere scratch. You are mortgaged; you pledged the public Treasury; you promised every clique and class and interest in this land that helped you into power that you would pass legislation for their benefit, however nefarious, dishonest or unconstitutional, and you are smoothing the way to keep your promises because they threaten foreclosure of their mortgage.

The tariff had been the issue in the last election; the Republicans had had ample campaign funds, and campaign funds in a tariff controversy involve an obligation. William S. Holman, that stalwart Jeffersonian and indefatigable watch-dog of the Treasury, defended the practice of filibustering and cited instances in which it had defeated great abuses when all other methods failed. The recent filibuster against the Pacific Funding Bill had been a public service. Never had there been so many schemes of plunder afoot as at present, never such manifest preparations for a raid on the Treasury. "These schemes of plunder, often successful under even rules most favorable to the minority have, during the last twenty-five years, aided to create the enormous private fortunes which now threaten our free institutions, for the possessors of these overgrown estates, distrustful of the people, are plotting for a stronger government, which enlarged navies and armies well express." No one could fail, he continued, to understand exactly what was meant by this change of the rules:

It means that the Speaker, instead of being as for the past one hundred years, the servant of the House, shall be its master; that the Speaker and the chairmen of committees shall be a petty oligarchy, with absolute control of the business of the House. It means the striking down of the manhood and proper influence and control, in legislation, of every other member of the House on your side, gentlemen, as well as ours. It means more than all that; it means a great navy, an enlarged army, a great zoölogical park and other embellishments in this city, and all else that creates a splendid government and gives a sense of security to the owners of overgrown and imperial estates who have no faith in the people and long for a stronger government.[1]

From the Republican standpoint part of Holman's indictment was admittedly correct, and the fact was acknowledged by Byron M. Cutcheon, of Michigan, when on the following day he gave a frank and convincing statement of the necessity behind the proposed changes. In the 44th Congress there had been introduced 4708 bills and resolutions; the number had steadily increased to 12,664 in the 50th, and in two months of the 51st, 6,776 had already been introduced. Hence the need for better facilities to handle legislation. Population was growing, wealth accumulating, problems of commerce and transportation were multiply-

[1] *Cong. Record*, 51 Cong., 1 Sess., 1208–13 *passim*.

ing. The scope of legislation was broadening from day to day.

The party of strict construction, he continued, had been ordered to the rear, and the party of broad and liberal construction had been intrusted with the helm of the ship of state. Changes in the mode of procedure and of policy must inevitably follow this change of political control. Why not accept the situation? "The school of Jefferson for the time being has been retired by the people and the school of Hamilton and Washington is placed in control." [1]

The rules were adopted on February 14 by a vote of yeas 161, nays 144, not voting 23, and a momentous change had been effected in congressional procedure. While both the rules and their author were savagely assailed, and part of the gains were lost in the next Congress, most of the changes proved so reasonable and so valuable that they were soon restored.

How far the country accepted the changes with complacency it is hard to judge, inasmuch as its verdict in the elections of 1890 was complicated by a wide variety of factors, especially the excesses of the McKinley tariff bill. There was considerable perturbation at the vigorous action of the Speaker. Editorial writers, stump orators, cartoonists and miscellaneous critics denounced him as a bully and a coward, insulting and browbeating the patient and long-suffering representatives of the people. The title of "Czar" which was conferred upon him in the early stages of the quorum contest, had no pleasant connotations in the early nineties. It conveyed no picture of benevolent despots who in our own day administer the affairs of the garment industry, the moving pictures, or professional baseball with firmness and righteousness. In 1890, it brought to mind the Russian autocrat himself, together with George Kennan's descriptions of the Cossacks, Siberia, and the knout.

The Nation, best representative of intelligent and educated

[1] *Ibid.*, 1236.

opinion, on February 6 had declared that the Speaker "is doing enormous harm to free institutions by destroying the good understanding which enables free institutions to work." The Democrats, it concluded, were entitled to "every sort of opposition short of violence." "The truth is," said another editorial in the same issue, "that there never has been seen under representative institutions a display of such power as Thomas B. Reed would enjoy if things went on through his term as for the past few days. It is a power which ought not to be wielded even by a George Washington."

The same journal, two weeks later, after the revised rules had been adopted, argued that they made a change in the method of electing the Speaker highly desirable. "They demand his complete dissociation from party leadership and from partisanship in every form, and the surrounding of the chair with a thoroughly judicial atmosphere. Consequently they make the appearance in it clothed with these extraordinary powers of a man who has made such an exhibition of violence and unscrupulousness as Mr. Reed has made during the past few weeks, an absurdity as well as an outrage." At the close of the first session, October 2, 1890, in an editorial on the Speaker, it remarked: "We have seen this theoretically judicial functionary openly assuming the duties of leader of his party in the Legislature, and putting himself in direct charge of pending legislation, and seizing for the use of the majority every power, short of physical force, within his reach for the passage of such bills as he approved of, and finally abandoning his place for a stumping tour in his own State, during which he denounced the minority, and produced a full legislative programme in the character of the chief party manager. . . . We look with confidence for the judgment of the country on this wanton attempt to destroy one of its most valuable possessions—the respect within the walls of the legislature for law and justice and decency."

This criticism of the American speakership was sound neither in history nor theory, and no one would have been more ready than Reed to argue that the Speaker must always be the party manager and leader of the House. In an address delivered after adjournment of the 51st Congress he declared that "the condition of things today is the result of a natural growth of American institutions." It was impossible, he said, to govern a nation of 60,000,000 people as the fathers had governed 3,000,-000. There had been some discussion of introducing responsible government by having the President and Cabinet members in Congress, a proposal which he described as "utterly inconsistent with the principles of our government . . . a mere dream of visionaries who think that English institutions can be adopted by halves. Our government has got to be the growth of the necessities of our people, and must be worked out under the principles of our government, and can never be adopted from any other land. If you want to mark the growth of our government you will mark it, if you study the history of the country, by the action taken by each House with regard to the Speaker at its close."

When all was said and done, he closed his case as he had opened it, defending his action as necessary to establish genuine majority rule in the House. He declared to his own constituents on September 4, 1890, that "what the House has shown the country that any House can do is worth a prince's ransom. Henceforth promise cannot be excused except by performance. Henceforth great measures cannot be lost and nobody know what has become of them":

Party responsibility has begun, and with it also the responsibility of the people, for they can no longer elect a Democratic House and hope the minority will neutralize their action or a Republican House without being sure that it will keep its pledges.

If we have broken the precedents of a hundred years, we have set the precedents of another hundred years nobler than the last, wherein the people, with full knowledge that their servants can act, will choose those who will worthily carry out their will.

REED's policy, from the start, had been based on the supposition that the 51st Congress had received a mandate to legislate, and legislate it did. Not since the 37th Congress had taken up the burden of war legislation in 1861 had there been so many enactments of genuine public importance.

During the debate on the rules the minority had regularly forced a roll call on the approval of the Journal. But after their adoption on February 14, this performance, with its accompanying wrangle over the quorum and the Speaker's imperturbable use of the count, lost its zest. On February 17, Carlisle expressed the hope that the Journal would be approved without any call of the yeas and nays. "We protest, but the case must be tried elsewhere." Business was now resumed under normal conditions. Obstruction had by no means ceased, but it was to be used henceforth only against specific measures.

"Here is a very short catalogue, made by a neutral hand, of what was done by the last Congress," said Reed early in the next Congress, reading a list containing twenty-six public laws, "and I ask some of you gentlemen to say where as much was ever done before." Two measures, the McKinley Tariff Act and the Sherman Silver Purchase Act, were of major importance, and a third, not on Reed's list because of failure to pass the Senate, was almost equally so. The third deserves mention at this point.

A Federal Election Bill, sponsored by Henry Cabot Lodge, was one of the measures promised soon after Republican success in 1888. Congressional elections were to be placed under protection of the strong arm of Federal authority. While national in scope, the bill was intended primarily, to restore the ballot to the Southern negro. This measure, of the inordinate length of more than 17,000 words, was reported in the House by Lodge on June 14, 1890. Known as the Force Bill, it aroused a terrific storm.

It is somewhat difficult for a later generation to realize that in 1890 there were still men in public life who had an honest belief in the doctrines of complete racial equality and the right of the freedmen to the ballot which had been so popular at the close of the Civil War. Reed was one, and he earnestly defended the proposed legislation in a notable speech before the Americus Club at Pittsburgh, on April 26, 1890, and in a published article.[1]

The negro, he argued, had a constitutional right to vote, even if he were poor and ignorant, and the Constitution should be enforced. The Republican party, however, as opponents soon pointed out, had for some years been content to leave the negro to his fate. Why, after a dozen years, the sudden revival of interest? The answer seems to be that the power of the party in the West was threatened, and the Farmers' Alliance, determined to secure the remonetization of silver, and already turning a cold and suspicious eye on McKinley's tariff policy, was a power to be reckoned with. In the South, however, there was a great body of potential allies and in a close election a few Southern Republican congressmen might turn the scale.

Reed lent support to this view by some admissions that were scarcely in line with disinterested enthusiasm for the rights of the negro. If, he argued in his Pittsburgh speech, there were objections to negro domination in State politics, these could hardly hold true of national elections where white supremacy, taking the nation as a whole, was overwhelming. The Republicans were entitled to the Republican vote of the South. "If ignorant, we

[1] "The Federal Control of Elections," *North American Review*, June, 1890.

need it to offset the Democratic ignorance which votes in New York and other large cities. Why should they poll their ignorance and we not poll ours?" In effect, his proposal meant the separation of local and congressional elections, with registration, polling, counting and certification in the latter conducted under Federal supervision and protection. The Democrats at once raised a shout that the Federal Election Bill was intended to secure a Republican House in the 52nd Congress and so perpetuate "the Reed dynasty." The Speaker's statements, written and spoken, were quoted against him. "Now," said Amos J. Cummings, after pointing out the political motives apparent in the Speaker's statements, "there is no cant or humbug about the Speaker of this House. He has the nerve—if not the cruelty— of Oliver Cromwell. He 'talks right out in meeting,' and with a rich nasal twang." [1]

Against the "Force Bill" sectional animosity at once flared up in a manner reminiscent of Reconstruction days. In any of the half-dozen preceding Congresses its passage, or the passage of any measure of such intensely partisan character, would have presented overwhelming difficulty. The Reed rules, however, had changed the entire situation. "The Speaker," wrote Representative William McAdoo, reviewing the work of the session a few months later, in the *North American Review*, "readily assuming responsibility for all legislation, did not hesitate to cast his party and personality into the contest for any measure that he desired to succeed, and thus, under the intense pressure of the one and the forceful and imperturbable presence of the other, to coerce the weak and wavering of his own party, and challenge within the same the fears and ambitions of those who might otherwise be his rivals and opponents."

The Speaker, of course, was a dominant figure on the Rules Committee, McKinley and Cannon being merely his lieutenants

[1] *Cong. Record,* 51 Cong., 1 Sess., 6680.

on the floor. James H. Blount, of Georgia, had succeeded to Randall's vacant place and when Carlisle was promoted to the Senate, Benton McMillin, of Tennessee, became the second minority member, June 12, 1890. The latter retained a vivid recollection as to the manner in which the new system functioned. The majority of the committee would decide a pending question. "Then the Speaker would send for me and say: 'Well, Mac, Joe and McKinley and I have decided to perpetrate the following outrage, of which we all desire you to have due notice.' Whereupon he would read and give me a copy of whatever special order had been adopted by the majority of the committee. He did the same with Blount, I believe, and he never tried to catch us napping; but I can assure you that the Committee on Rules was never a debating society in which Blount and I took part after the first explosion. No, sir!" [1]

Control of business by the committee was rigorously exercised. Section 45 of Rule XI of the 50th Congress which read "All proposed action touching the rules and joint rules shall be referred to the Committee on Rules" had been amended by adding "and order of business" to its jurisdiction. When the 52nd Congress reverted to the old plan of earlier Congresses, Thomas C. Catchings, of Mississippi, described the working of the Reed system as it appeared on the floor. "We all know how the Committee on Rules would bring in a report fixing the time at which a vote should be taken on a pending measure, and at that time, before any gentleman could be recognized, Mr. McKinley, speaking for that committee, would demand the previous question upon the adoption of the report. Instantly by a partisan vote the previous question would be ordered, no debate beyond forty minutes would be allowed, the report would be adopted, and the measure would be put upon its passage at the time named and voted through."

[1] New York *Tribune*, April 23, 1899.

It was under this procedure that the Federal Election Bill was passed. It was made a caucus measure and on June 25, the Committee on Rules submitted a resolution to thrust it to passage. This resolution provided that the House should proceed to consider the bill and should debate it until July 2 at two o'clock, when the previous question should be considered as ordered. There were naturally violent objections from the Democrats and "great confusion" is recorded in the proceedings, but the resolution was carried. Strictly on schedule, the bill passed the House on July 2. The South was almost ready to take up arms against the measure, and it encountered bitter opposition in the Senate, where the liberal rules of debate were in striking contrast to the new system in the lower chamber. The first session closed without its enactment, and the opposition was renewed with even greater vigor at the second. Closure, in spite of all Senate traditions against such action, was seriously discussed as the ultimate method of securing adoption, but about the middle of January, 1891, it was laid aside in order to take up the silver question. In effect it had been killed. It is significant that Senators from several of the newly-admitted States assisted in this consummation. Free Silver and the Federal Election Bill practically destroyed each other, inasmuch as "a bill to provide against the contraction of the currency, and for other purposes," passed by the Senate on January 14, met an adverse report from the House Committee on Coinage soon after.

The "Force Bill" and the Blair Education Bill, both intended for the benefit of the blacks, were laid on the Republican shelf and the great contest over the former may properly be considered to mark the end of the Southern question. Its passage in the House had been a notable parliamentary and partisan triumph for the Speaker. The bill itself had little to recommend it and the revival of sectional hostility which it caused was decidedly unfortunate A marked rise in lynchings and racial disorders became evident in the South. Its failure was salutary and Reed's share in the matter added nothing to his reputation.

A second but equally important party measure was the Mc-Kinley Tariff Bill. While the campaign of 1888 had been waged on the issue of protection, the country was hardly prepared to accept the degree of protection which was finally accorded under the supposed mandate of the presidential election. Driven through the preliminary stages at high speed, the bill passed the House on May 21.

Secretary Blaine had been anxious to have a bill which could be used to promote the American export business, but the House had disregarded suggestions for a reciprocity clause. The matter was taken up in the Senate, where debate was hampered by the bitter contest over the Federal Election Bill. Progress ceased while, week after week, as Reed contemptuously remarked, the Senators "were pouring out waves of oratory." It should, he afterwards wrote, have been passed so that Congress could have adjourned by the middle of July.

On September 10, the bill finally passed the upper chamber with a reciprocity provision attached. "What is reciprocity?" asked Reed, and answered his own question by defining it as "commerce on paper." The revised bill threatened to cause a serious deadlock between the two Houses, but it was at length decided to let the reciprocity clause remain and with sundry amendments the measure finally passed. The President signed it on October 1.

Probably no tariff bill since 1828 has caused more violent and unreasoning opposition. Times were far from good, the agricultural West was seething with discontent, and the McKinley tariff was generally regarded as unduly favoring the industrial and financial regions. *The Nation*, of strong free-trade sympathies, on September 18, 1890, described it as "a series of minute interferences with trade and industry for the benefit of indi-

WILLIAM McKINLEY

viduals, firms and corporations," and when the November election resulted in a disastrous Republican defeat, it attributed the outcome to "the wicked and unprincipled measure which that party devised to pay the campaign debts of Quay and Wanamaker. The cash that was subscribed to elect Harrison was charged up to the American people in a gross, uncounted sum. It was to be collected by duties on tin plate, worsted cloth, carpet wool, pearl buttons, and a thousand other things that enter into the food and raiment of the people."

Reed defended the bill against what he later described as "slanders which . . . poured upon it as if the foundation of the great deep had been broken up," but in 1894 admitted that in some of the schedules protection had been carried to an extreme. He bore no small responsibility, however, and was freely criticized even in his own party for crowding the measure through without allowing adequate opportunity for debate and amendment.

Politically, the McKinley tariff had curious results. Reed himself admitted that it was largely responsible for the disastrous defeat in November following. The international financial situation, he explained, was critical, and "the whole mercantile situation at that time was a quicksand which then began to give signs of sinking." Money was scarce. Importers had stocked up in anticipation of higher duties and in need of funds, the retailers conducted a nation-wide selling campaign by warning of higher prices under the new law. Congress did not adjourn until October 1 and this propaganda had free rein until it was too late to counteract its effects. "It followed then, as night follows day, that we found a hundred counters talking against one stump. Every woman who went to a store and tried to buy went home to complain, and a wild unrest filled the public mind. The wonder is that we got any votes at all." [1]

[1] "Historic Political Upheavals," *North American Review,* January, 1895.

Nevertheless, the disastrous collapse of business three years later, the bungling of the Democrats in the next two Congresses, and the natural revulsion of public sentiment which followed, gave the McKinley law a standing when dead which it had never had while alive. Its author became the potential savior of American business and restorer of prosperity. His popularity grew by leaps and bounds. His supporters were as unreasonable as his detractors had been, but they eventually carried him to the White House, while the Speaker who had meanwhile done infinitely more to restore the prestige of the party was destined to leave public life in disgust.

The third great measure of the first session was the Sherman Silver Purchase Act, and in connection with this enactment the Speaker performed a service of tremendous importance to the cause of sound money, a cause which he consistently supported throughout his public career. The demand for free silver had been gaining ground. Its supporters controlled the Senate, most of the House Democrats were for it, and enough Republicans were sympathetic to render the situation extremely critical.

The necessity of "doing something for silver" was unavoidable. On January 20, 1890, Edwin H. Conger, chairman of the Committee on Coinage, Weights and Measures, introduced a bill authorizing the issue of Treasury notes at the current market price of silver, on the deposit of silver bullion. Nothing was done until early in June, when the committee reported a revised measure providing for the purchase of $4,500,000 worth of silver per month by the issue of Treasury notes, the latter to be legal tender. Free coinage was authorized when silver reached the ratio of 16 to 1, this provision being of somewhat dubious merit in the eyes of free silver advocates in view of the declining price of the metal.

Reed had strongly opposed concessions to the silver men and

the dissatisfaction which greeted the bill necessitated prompt action. Again the powerful machinery of the Reed rules was brought into operation. The Republicans had held a caucus on June 4, at which Reed spoke earnestly against further concessions to the silver advocates in the party. Further compromise was defeated, but the silver members were insistent and the caucus broke up with party solidarity seriously threatened and disaster imminent. Next day came the inevitable special order from the Committee on Rules under which debate was to be permitted until June 7 when "the previous question shall be considered as ordered at three o'clock."

There was a disorderly outbreak of opposition, Blount denouncing the proposal as "a wicked and shameless outrage on the minority, on fair discussion, on fair debate, on proper deliberation. It takes from this body the bare right to even vote upon a great question like that of the free coinage of silver." The order, declared Bland, prevented not only the offering of a free coinage amendment, "but any other amendment unless it comes from the chairman of the committee who wants the demonetization of silver." A vote for the order meant a vote for a gag rule and against free silver.

McKinley, in reply to Crisp's question whether an impartial Speaker would not give an opportunity to offer a substitute, provoked derisive laughter by stating that "the matter of recognition has been left to the Speaker." Party discipline still held, the silver Republicans had no chance to rally, and the order, after acrimonious discussion, was carried by a vote of 120 to 117. The bill passed two days later by 135 to 119.

The sequel was one of the most daring acts in Reed's career. On June 17, the Senate adopted a free coinage amendment by a vote of 42 to 25. The House Republicans were taken by surprise with a considerable number of members absent. Had the bill come up at once, there is no doubt but that it would have passed the House. But again it was demonstrated that Reed was no ordinary Speaker and no ordinary party chieftain.

The *Record* on June 19 begins the story. When McKinley moved that the Journal be approved and demanded the previous question, Mills objected that the entire Journal had not been read and when the clerk read the omitted portions it was found that the Senate bill had been referred to the Committee on Coinage. There was a furious outburst and Reed sustained what was probably his first and only parliamentary defeat of the session when approval of the Journal was defeated by a vote of 117 to 105. The free silver men were determined that this bill should not be smothered by being quietly handed over to a hostile committee.

There followed an angry debate on a resolution offered by Mills, striking from the Journal the part dealing with the reference of the Senate bill, Mills contending that this bill was beyond the jurisdiction of all committees except Committee of the Whole and that the question was merely one of disagreeing with the Senate. The Speaker's supporters contended that an appropriation and a new provision added by the upper chamber constituted sufficient grounds for the reference. Cannon's motion to lay the Mills resolution on the table was beaten and shortly before adjournment the resolution was carried by a majority of five votes, several silver Republicans supporting it. If the free silver measure were defeated now, it would have to be after an open battle.

All day, however, the party whips had been using messenger and telegraph in a desperate effort to collect the absent members and the Speaker was reported to have worked all night getting a majority into line. Next day, although the situation had improved, a majority was still lacking. The Journal as amended by the Mills resolution was approved by 132 to 130 and Bland moved to take from the Speaker's table "House bill No. 5381, directing the purchase of silver bullion and the issue of Treasury notes therefor and for other purposes," with the Senate amendments thereto, for immediate consideration.

Conger at once made the point of order that the bill was not on the table but in committee. Debate proceeded on this and related parliamentary questions of a somewhat metaphysical character, wasting time in a highly effective manner, while every train brought missing members to reinforce the majority. The Speaker, who must have watched proceedings with some of the same anxiety that Wellington experienced till Blucher's columns came in sight on the late afternoon of Waterloo, remained cool and imperturbable, blocking all attempts to get the bill before the House.

Next morning, June 21, he ruled that the bill was in committee, his ironical statement that "gentlemen may have noticed, within the last few days, that parliamentary law does not seem to be an exact science," doing nothing to soothe the feelings of his opponents. The depleted ranks had been filled and Bland's appeal from the Speaker's decision was laid on the table by a vote of 144 to 117.

The outcome is an old story. The House disagreed with the free silver amendment and a compromise measure—the Sherman bill—was agreed upon in conference, providing for the purchase of 4,500,000 ounces of silver by the issue of Treasury notes, purchase to be at market price. The purchased silver was to be coined into dollars until July 1, 1891, thereafter only as needed for redemption, but the notes were redeemable in gold or silver. It is obvious that the measure had dangerous possibilities, but it became law on July 14. Unlimited coinage of silver had been defeated, the act declaring for the maintenance of parity of the two metals. The party situation, however, had been so dangerous, due to the hostility of the free silver element, that its passage was secured only with great difficulty. Blount on June 24 declared that "the disciplinary process" had been steadily going on in Republican caucuses, the councils of the party leaders and the Committee on Rules in order to prevent a vote on free coinage.

With these three major enactments out of the way, the House devoted itself to other legislative business. The summer wore on and in the intense heat both House and Senate presented a picturesque appearance with the members arrayed in yachting shirts, white trousers and silk sashes. It was noted that some conservative members refused to part with "the boiled shirt with its glossy front" and that McKinley was one of them. "He has discarded his waistcoat, however, and moves around the House with thumbs hanging from his galluses, a veritable Napoleon in undress uniform."

"The illustrious Speaker Reed" is described as "the most wonderful of all," with his flannel shirt and black silk sash. According to one chronicle, a Texas member exclaimed: "Well, I'll be damned. Look at Tom Reed wearing a dude belly-band." New Englanders were said to be "guessing" and Southerners "reckoning" how many yards it contained. "Mr. Reed has not yet acquired the self-confidence which ought to accompany the wearing of a flannel shirt. His coat is drawn over his breast and fastened by the two upper buttons. It looks as though he was ashamed and as if he desired to hide as much of his shirt as possible." Henry Cabot Lodge was held responsible for the Speaker's adoption of the sash. "Lodge wears one of a dark blue color, and at times looks like a student from a tennis court. The Speaker looks like an honest rutabaga wound in a black ribbon." [1]

The Democratic lemonade-cooler was a popular institution, and its popularity was further increased when some unknown humorist or benefactor emptied three quarts of Kentucky rye

[1] Washington *Post,* July 20, 1890.

into the concoction. Several Republicans were observed to disregard party lines on this occasion, and the Speaker was reported to have gasped when observing that members from Prohibition Kansas and Iowa were among the number, "although not surprised at the seduction of the Maine members."

Reed inaugurated a number of minor reforms in the course of the first session. On May 24 he curtailed the rights of ex-members on the floor and debarred women from the use of the lobby. Both orders were directed against lobbyists, who were becoming a nuisance and interfering with the business of the House. The lobbyist, he admitted, had a necessary function, but his operations should be conducted in the open, and in such a manner as would safeguard public interests. On May 28 he ordered the manager of the House restaurant to stop the sale of beer and whisky. The latter "knew that the Speaker would entertain no points of order or appeals from his decision and gloomily took the elevator to the floor below" to make the decree effective at once. Conditions had been disgraceful and Reed's action was indorsed by practically all the members.[1]

The stirring events of the first session made the Speaker a national figure. His quality had long been known to his House colleagues, but the country was now aware of the fact that Thomas B. Reed was one of the most able and forceful characters in public life. His comings and goings were matters of general interest and newspaper correspondents sent his witty remarks throughout the country. Within a few days of the counting of the quorum, he was, according to a good American custom, discussed as a presidential possibility.

He was obliged to return to Maine early in September to conduct a brief but intensive campaign for reëlection. It was felt that the contest was of more than ordinary importance and Reed's speeches in which he defended his parliamentary reforms

[1] Washington *Post*, May 29, 1890.

and the legislative record of the 51st Congress were given wide publicity. He received a record plurality of almost 5000 votes, and returned to Washington at once, disappointing a large crowd which had gathered at the Shoreham by retiring early and sending word that he did not want to be serenaded. His success was generally taken to mean a continuance of his policy in the House and a strong likelihood that he would be a contestant for the presidential nomination in 1892.

The business of the session was still dragging and the disposal of election contests occupied a great deal of time, especially during September. The Democrats adopted new tactics, the bulk of the members absenting themselves, while Charles T. O'Ferrall of Virginia and a handful of members remained on the floor to skirmish with the Speaker. On September 18 there was great difficulty in securing a quorum, and the House officers were sent for enough members to make a quorum. This performance lasted for several days, but the work of unseating Democratic contestees could not be balked. Nine in all were eventually ousted. There was much bad feeling and occasional outbreaks of unparliamentary language, which of course does not appear in the chaste pages of the *Record*. One incident had a touch of humor. In the effort to preserve a quorum during the contest of September 18, the Speaker ordered the doors locked. C. Buckley Kilgore, of Texas, was determined to leave and kicked out the panels of a door leading into the lobby. The door crashed open, Kilgore went out, and Nelson Dingley, who had been waiting outside, came in with a damaged nose. It had not, as Cannon later remembered it, been an especially noteworthy feat, but thanks to the efforts of the newspaper correspondents, who bestowed the title "Kicking Buck Kilgore," the public, with vague notions that one of the giant portals of the Capitol was involved, came to regard the exploit as almost on a par with Samson's removal of the gates of Gaza, and the hero was henceforth an object of special interest to visitors in the galleries.

When the session closed at last on October 1, 1890, Reed joined the campaign in the West. He was received with great enthusiasm, but the tide was running strongly against the Republican party, and when the November election was over the next House was Democratic by a tremendous majority, its membership comprising 236 Democrats, 88 Republicans and 8 Farmers' Alliance men. Seldom had there been such a complete overturn. "Well," wrote Reed to Henry Cabot Lodge on November 5, "I find it a trifle difficult to put the thing into words! Don't you? It looks just for the moment as if this was a world made mostly for cowards and laggards and sneaks." [1]

The second session was a most uncomfortable one for the Speaker, but the legislative program proceeded and his conduct of affairs demonstrated a confident belief that time would justify the work of this Congress. By the end of the session an unusual number of important measures were on the statute book.

The direct tax collected under the law of 1861, a bone of contention for years past, was at length refunded to the States and as Reed ironically remarked, saved Kentucky from bankruptcy, although her representatives had opposed its passage. The Sherman Anti-trust Act was adopted. The World's Fair at Chicago was provided for, the criminal jurisdiction of the Federal courts was extended to the Great Lakes, interstate quarantine regulations were strengthened, the scope of the census was broadened, an apportionment act passed, provision was made for the inspection of meats exported from the country and for the prevention of export or import of adulterated food products. The International Copyright Bill, providing protection for foreign authors against the pirating of their works, was driven through on the last day of the short session. Immigration, the merchant marine, the agricultural colleges, the land laws, and a mass of

[1] *Lodge Papers.*

special and local business received attention. A customs administrative act of great importance was adopted to supplement the new tariff bill.

A measure of far-reaching importance and unquestioned merit was the act creating the Federal Circuit Courts of Appeal, which greatly relieved the Supreme Court and expedited the administration of Federal justice. The House passed a bankruptcy act which was much needed, but which failed to pass the Senate. The adverse effects of "original package" decisions of the Supreme Court on State prohibition laws received statutory correction. The Louisiana Lottery, long a public nuisance, received a death blow in the act prohibiting interstate carriage of lottery tickets. The regulations of the International Maritime Conference were enacted into law. Idaho and Wyoming were admitted to the Union and the Territory of Oklahoma was organized. A Dependent Pension Act was passed, described by *The Nation* as "the most reckless and indefensible on record," and by William McKinley as generous legislation which would "carry comfort and cheer to thousands of homes throughout the land." A later generation can only regard it as extravagant and ill-advised.

While the 51st Congress cleaned up a mass of outstanding claims against the government, the path of special and local legislation was far from smooth. There was bitter complaint of the Speaker's attitude toward public building bills. The Washington *Post* on July 17 related the following anecdote as illustrative of Reed's attitude. A party from Minnesota appeared to urge government aid for the Sioux Canal and Hay Lake channel. A special bill was prepared but there was no opportunity to get it before the House:

As a last hope it was decided to appeal to the Speaker for a special order. It was well understood that the Speaker is against special orders for any bills carrying appropriations, but the bulk of the Minnesota members had deserted Western friends to support Reed for Speaker, and it seemed like a very small return on his part to give them one day for a bill of such vast importance to Minnesota. Accordingly the party went to the Speaker's Room.

"Mr. Reed, we have a small request to make."

"Only too happy to oblige you," said the Speaker smilingly.

The look of doubt passed from the faces of the delegation, and smiles dwelt thereon.

"We want," said the spokesman boldly, as though ordering a ton of coal by telephone, "a day set apart for the Sioux Canal and Hay Lake Chan——"

"What!" roared the Speaker, in a voice that cracked three globes on the chandelier, the crash of glass mingling with the sounds of footsteps as the Minnesota delegation went scurrying down the corridor.

Speaker Reed is a Speaker who speaks.

Appropriations, however, reached an unprecedented total. The problem of the surplus was not likely to be troublesome in future, but Reed had never accepted the contention that the way to get rid of the surplus was to reduce taxation, and especially the tariff. Total appropriations exceeded $988,000,000, more than $175,000,000 greater than those of the 50th Congress.

Pension legislation and greatly increased outlays for the navy and coast defenses were largely responsible, but many new offices had been created. It was hard to convince the voter that the business of a nation of 70,000,000 people could not be carried on as it had been in earlier days, and there was a tendency throughout the country to regard the whole performance as a gigantic piece of jobbery. The 51st was promptly dubbed "The Billion Dollar Congress." "This is a Billion Dollar Country" was the retort almost universally attributed to Reed himself, although in an article in the *North American Review* for March, 1892, he lays no claim to its authorship and praises it as containing "both wit and wisdom" and "the best in kind ever evoked."

It is worth note, however, that Cannon, defending the policy of the 51st Congress, severely criticized the decentralization of appropriating power which had occurred in the 49th and for which Reed was in no small degree responsible. "Such a system is vicious. It divides responsibility and tends to beget extravagance in appropriations. It promotes legislation in connection with appropriations. One committee in the House should be charged with the preparation of the money bills for its consideration. Such a practice fixes responsibility, begets vigilance, and secures harmonious appropriations for the whole public service consistent with the proper demands of the same and proportionate to the revenues of the government." [1] It is apparent that the chairman of Appropriations must have had some misgivings as to the growth of the expenditures.

In spite of so much legislative activity, and the frequent outbreaks of disorderly opposition which it provoked, Reed kept his temper and his sense of humor. "We shall get a vote in about an hour. Springer has only two more pieces in his repertoire," he once told Henry Cabot Lodge with a pleasant smile, during an exciting and disorderly evening session. His retorts and sarcastic comments from the chair are scattered through the record in great abundance, accompanied by the frequent comment "laughter" or, even more frequently, "laughter on the Republican side." The point is not always clear to the present day reader and there is also undoubtedly much truth in the contemporary saying, "It's not always what Tom Reed says, but the way he says it."

When the hour of final adjournment arrived on March 2, 1891, the Speaker held aloft the battered gavel which was a fitting symbol of his rule throughout the turbulent period just closing. This gavel, it may be noted, the broken handle patched with wire, is now in possession of the Maine Historical Society,

[1] *Appendix, Cong. Record,* 51 Cong., 2 Sess., 231.

together with a letter of the Speaker, commenting in humorous vein on the bad behavior of the House. He confronted the assembly which had just refused him the usual courtesy of a unanimous vote of thanks, and declared:

After two long and stormy sessions, in some respects unparalleled in our hundred years, the House of Representatives of the Fifty-first Congress will soon pass with completed record into the history of the country, and its works will follow it. What we have done is in large measure political. Whatever is political rouses the sternest, the most turbulent, the most unforgiving passions of the human race. Political action can never be justly viewed from a near standpoint. Time and distance are needed for a ripe judgment, and the verdict of history is the only verdict worth recording. . . .

Confident, as I am, of the verdict of time on what we have done, I am still more confident that the highest commendation will be given us in the future, not for what measures we have passed, valuable as they are, but because we have taken so long a stride in the direction of responsible government. . . .

But Reed did not have to wait for posterity to give him his well-earned palm. On March 6, 1891, a body of citizens eminent in law, politics, and business gathered at the Federal Club in New York City to do honor to the ex-Speaker. Chauncey Depew presided and introduced the guest of honor. Henry Cabot Lodge and Theodore Roosevelt spoke in eulogy. Characteristically the latter, while pointing out the importance of the recent changes in the rules and declaring that future historians would have to credit the Speaker with a great victory in the cause of parliamentary government, laid chief emphasis on the adoption of the International Copyright Bill.

Senators Platt and Aldrich, said Roosevelt, had performed great services in securing its passage. "Yet if any one man more than another is entitled to the credit of its passage, that man is our guest of this evening, ex-Speaker Reed, for it was owing solely to the tremendous influence he wielded as Speaker and to his active and efficient support, and to the fact that the adoption of the new rules of the House had rendered it impossible for an unscrupulous and resolute minority to check any good measure, that the bill passed through the lower House and ultimately became a law." It would be remembered, he added, long after laws which seemed more important had been forgotten. It had long been demanded by honor and honesty and should have been enacted fifty years before. "Every American citizen has a right to lift his head a little higher and feel prouder of the country because the copyright bill has been enacted into law." [1]

Reed spoke briefly in response, enumerating the accomplishments of the recent Congress and explaining that the work of the Committee on Rules had been in reality the result of a widespread desire on the part of members themselves for such control of business. As for his own position, he said: "I am not wanting in such intellectual capacity as not to appreciate that the utmost kindness that has been done me in this world has been done me by enemies. . . . Your friends sometimes go to sleep; your enemies never do. . . . If a man's object in life is to hold offices and to wear decorations, undoubtedly the best course for him is to go softly like a cat on a carpet; but if his object is to do something, perhaps it is not undesirable for him to buy a trumpet, especially if he can get somebody who don't like him to sound it."

[1] New York *Tribune*, March 7, 1891.

REED has gone into the records of his country as a debater of the very first rank, one of its greatest Speakers, and its greatest parliamentarian. His contemporaries were fond of disputing whether he appeared at his best in the chair or on the floor. It is a debatable point, but it should be remembered that of his twenty-two years' service, only six were in the chair. For three fourths of the remaining period he was the real, if not the formally recognized leader of his party in the House. "His power as a floor leader," says Alexander, "was in his directness, his contentiousness, his ability to help men make up their minds, and to justify them in following him. He never scattered. His arguments bore directly on the issue before the House at the moment, and, though he indulged sufficiently in generalities to give force and sidelight to his views, he never fell into vagueness. No one yawned while he was on his feet." [1]

Reed occasionally indulged in careless generalizations which, misinterpreted or scarcely understood by the country, frequently came back to plague him. His oft-quoted, "Thank God, the House is no longer a deliberative body," belongs in this category. That such a remark was made by the greatest American debater of the age should have led his critics to inquire as to its actual meaning, but coming as it did in the midst of the heated controversies of the 51st Congress, it led to charges that the Speaker was an enemy of free discussion, an executive tyrant who desired a legislative body to confine itself to the ratification of decisions made in the committee room. The drastic limitations

[1] *House of Representatives,* 131. There was general agreement among contemporary legislators as to Reed's preëminent position as a debater. "The finest, the most effective debater that I have ever seen or heard," was the opinion of Henry Cabot Lodge.

imposed on debate under his speakership gave color to these charges.

Time and again, however, he stated his views as to the essential characteristics and purposes of genuine debate. What is debate, and what is it for? he wrote, and in answer declared that it was not "merely a display of the vocabularies of orators," nor "a sacred privilege of talk for no purpose." It was intended to guide an assembly to sound conclusions, to bring out the advantages or disadvantages of pending measures, to light up the subject from all directions. The "right of debate" so far as minorities were concerned was like the right of individuals on the highways, "subject at all times to the control of the community." It existed "not to enable the minority to prevent conclusions, but to enable the majority to come to right conclusions." [1]

"Many things in this world, and especially arguments," he had already written in defense of his course in the 51st Congress, "hinge upon definition." The proper definition of debate, "speaking made and listened to for the purpose of elucidating the principles of a law proposed or of settling its details, and even debate for the purpose of enlightening the outside world," was very different from that debate "which is largely in manuscript, which empties the abodes of deliberation, which has for its object the consumption of time and the frustration of public business." For debate "which meanders on through the dreary hours with oft repeated platitudes, full of wise saws without even the flavor of a modern instance, solemn repetitions of stale arguments made with owlish solemnity to empty benches," he had no tolerance whatever.[2]

There was, he often pointed out, a vast difference between speech-making and debate. "When debate becomes the rule and speech-making the exception, we shall have a better state of

[1] "Mr. Speaker," *North American Review*, January, 1892.
[2] "A Deliberate Body," *Ibid.*, January, 1891.

things in that regard; for speech-making contributes more than anything else to the ruin of debate." The desire to address the constituency was, he admitted, the same everywhere; it was not wholly for purposes of display; it had some educational value. "Still there are times when business propositions being numerous and the days few, one wishes that eloquence and speaking bore closer resemblance to reasoning and deliberation." He frankly admitted that the House of Commons, due to its differences in practice and especially in reporting, was superior to the American Congress in matters of debate. Again and again he criticized the physical conditions surrounding discussion in the House, complaining that the vast proportions of its hall imposed an insurmountable handicap on effective debate.

Reed fulfilled all his own requirements for the first class debater. He could be eloquent in his own way but had no use for the tricks and devices of elocution. Stories were often told of his comments on congressional colleagues who indulged in them. W. C. P. Breckinridge, "the silver tongued orator" from Kentucky, affected a solemn and funereal manner whatever the subject of discussion and on one occasion when his mournful periods were resounding through the chamber, Reed paused at the door and listened. Then, wiping his eyes he inquired of Cannon, "Joe, were you acquainted with the deceased?" Another story went the rounds regarding a Western orator of somewhat the same type, James B. Belford, of Colorado. According to John Allen, of Mississippi, "every time he wanted to state a fact he put it in three ways." "There he sits," he shouted on one occasion at an opponent, "dumb, mute and silent." "He ain't saying a word either," added Mr. Reed, in his piping voice, and the effect on the speaker and the audience can be readily imagined.

He could make opponents appear ridiculous by use of the mock-heroic, as in his description of "the household troops" ordered up for the Potter investigation of 1878. "There at the head was a polished and able gentleman, taken some years ago from our ranks, and who had voted with us often enough since to give the people the idea that he was respectable and to be trusted—a gentleman to whose fairness and impartiality in everything except his report I bear cheerful, cordial and willing witness. Next came my friend from Ohio [Mr. McMahon], keen and subtle, than whom there is no man in five kingdoms abler to dig a pit for a witness and sweetly coax him into it. And there to give a tone of chivalry to it was my friend from the Seventh District of Kentucky [Mr. Blackburn], then as now undallying and undoubting, and consequently undastardized and undamned. Time would fail me to give an Homeric catalogue of all the great souls of heroes who went down to dusty death."

Or, as another illustration, take his description of the tariff reformers in the great speech on the Mills Bill: "What a beautiful sight it is to see the revenue-reform orator go into action against monopoly. Nelson, as he stood blazing with decorations on the decks of the *Victory* on the fatal day of Trafalgar; Napoleon at Friedland, as the Guard went cheering and charging by; Thomas Sayers as he stripped for the championship of England when Heenan had crossed the lifting waters; the eagle soaring to his eyrie; the royal man-eating Bengal tiger in his native jungle; nay, the very bull himself, the strong bull of Bashan, as he uplifts his bellow over the rocky deserts of Palestine, are all but pale reminders of one of these majestic creatures." [1]

In the 53rd Congress, when William L. Wilson of West Virginia was Democratic floor leader, another member from that state, John D. Alderson, presented during debate on the rules a compilation of eleven cases in which Reed was alleged to have wrongly counted absent members as present during the

[1] *Cong. Record,* 50 Cong., 1 Sess., 4445.

tumultuous sessions of the 51st Congress. He had already, during the 52nd Congress, when discussing the same topic, drawn from Reed the remark that to such "general declamation" he would make no reply and "to that kind no reply can be made, from the very nature of the case." Now, in response to a concrete statement Reed rose with the characteristic introduction to his rebuttal:

Mr. Speaker, this is only another echo of the minority of the Fifty-first Congress. Those echoes are dying—not musically, but dying. In due time we shall have the end of them; because there is no method so satisfactory of disposing of anything which has passed the period of ripeness and usefulness as exposing it to the common air. [Laughter on the Republican side.] The gentleman from West Virginia is not a novice in this business. His noble voice was uplifted in the last Congress in a similar line of observations. . . .

After two years of strong mental effort, after two years of enormous examination, and by the assistance of typewriters and clerks, he has evolved the remarkable production to which you have listened this morning. [Laughter on the Republican side.] I hail the rising State from which he comes. To have two statesmen, one to lead the House and the other to bring up the rear in this manner, is too much glory for a State "made outside the Constitution." [Laughter.] [1]

But there followed—and this was true of practically all such performances—an admirably clear, frank and logical defense of the Speaker's counting during that protracted struggle. Where error had occurred, it was acknowledged, but at the conclusion, there was nothing to be offered in reply and this phase of the controversy, "exposed to the common air," now disappeared for good.

His mind was both philosophical and analytical, but he seldom indulged in minute analysis of pending measures or opponents' speeches. He could pick the weak spot in either at a

[1] *Ibid.,* 53 Cong., 1 Sess., 1116.

glance and blast it with a sarcastic sentence or two, but he was at his best in generalization. He could see a proposition in its entirety, how it bore on related matters which escaped the view of the ordinary observer, why it was wise or unwise in the light of American experience. And subsequent history has vindicated his arguments with surprising frequency. In five or ten minutes he could state the essentials of a question. Others could then argue on details, but the issue was drawn on the lines he indicated.

His speeches were therefore, for the most part, either brief general arguments for some measure or equally brief and pointed assaults on those of an opponent. He argued with rare force and ability for protection; there is nothing finer in revenue debates than some of his attacks on the Wilson Bill, but nowhere did he take up schedule and section. Even in his protracted fight for reform of the rules, where he had a wonderful mastery of history, precedents, and general detail, he never lost sight of the main objectives of reform. He knew precisely why Section X of Rule Y stood in the way of more efficient transaction of business, exactly where it stood in the general scheme of procedure; and he could present a convincing demonstration of the alterations needed.

In his ability to state a proposition in brief and pointed form Reed was unequaled. Randall had much of the same ability and when the two leaders confronted each other, as Alexander says, "they could brighten the driest details, inspire implicit confidence in their views, and arouse the admiration of the indifferent until their appeals divided members into two hostile camps; but they could also hold their alignment without the loss of a vote and crush a less confident man who dared to offend." [1] With the passing of Randall, Reed's supremacy was unquestioned.

[1] *House of Representatives,* 309.

As an example of Reed's ability to brush away the irrelevant and sentimental and to concentrate attention on essentials, take a sentence on the William and Mary indemnity question in the 45th Congress. "You may bring together Bunker Hill and York-town, Massachusetts and Virginia, and tie them together with all the flowers of rhetoric that ever bloomed since the Garden of Eden, but you cannot change the plain, historic fact that no nation on earth ever was so imbecile and idiotic as to establish a principle that would more nearly bankrupt its treasury after victory than after defeat." The essential question involved was a both legal and practical one, viz., that governments cannot be held liable for the ravages of war, and his speech, brightened by wit and sarcasm, was an able and convincing defense of that principle.

Or take his brief remarks in the course of the free silver debate of 1892, when he took up the partisan aspects of the question and the change in Democratic policies since the last Congress. "I remember how leader after leader took the floor and announced how earnest and vigorous he was for the free coinage of silver. And for the moment it actually seemed as if the Democratic party had actually struck a level which might be called a level of principle."

Another member, Mr. Patterson, of Tennessee, had, he explained, done much to clear up the matter of principle involved. "He has explained to us the real principle which underlies the existence of the Democratic party—only he has somewhat embellished that principle in order to make a quotation. He says the great principle which underlies the Democratic party is public office; and he adds that it is a 'public trust'; and that relieves it from the nakedness of a true principle and it becomes a quotation as well."

But this was merely preliminary to a keen analysis of the forces behind the demand for free silver, the "pioneers of civilization, broadening the paths of empire in this great country," entitled to sympathy whatever their errors in judgment; a second group who would debase the currency in order to pay their debts in a cheaper medium; and a third who were "represented here"—men "who do not believe the doctrine they advocate but who want office."

"I have never," Cannon once remarked, "heard my distinguished friend from Maine take the floor upon any subject but that I did not feel sometimes regretful that I could not crystallize an idea, if I had one, as he does, roll it up with my hands into proper shape and hurl it at the head of my opponent." In an address in Boston another congressional associate, J. H. Walker of Massachusetts, once declared: "I think if the Book of Proverbs should be destroyed by accident, Tom Reed would be called on as the best man in the world to rewrite them. The man doesn't live who can state a proposition—or anything, in fact—so clearly and so effectively in the smallest number of words as Mr. Reed can." [1]

Reed's speeches went into the *Record* as they were delivered, and most of them were extemporaneous. He met in full the requirements which the historian of the House has laid down for "the real leader." He was "the original, daring debater, who seizes the opportune moment, and without apparent preparation, hurls his powerful compact sentences, loaded with destructive arguments, into the midst of his adversaries." Take, for example, the following excerpt from the tariff debate of 1888, which illustrates a number of his striking qualities, his arrogance, his use of the forensic bludgeon on his opponent, the quick rapier-like thrust, and throughout, the mastery of the art of statement.

Mr. Thomas Wilson of Minnesota raised the oft-mooted question as to the effects of the tariff on domestic prices. Lumbermen were making great profits and farmers were barely mak-

[1] New York *Tribune*, October 23, 1897.

ing a living. "Why is poverty continuously compelled to pay tribute to wealth, as the present tariff compels it to do?" Reed's
retort, "You do not seem to see that you beg the question and
assume a fact which does not exist, and then want to know why
it is so," merely brought a plaintive reiteration of his inability
to get a satisfactory answer. The ensuing dialogue is no better
nor more characteristic than many other similar passages scattered through the *Record:*

Mr. Reed. If the discourse of the gentleman from Minnesota (Mr. Wilson) did not illustrate a great many more things,
I should not feel it at all worth while to reply to his oft repeated question. He wants to know why poverty is taxed to pay
money to wealth; he wants to know why it is so; and he has
been unable after two days of consideration to comprehend that
the question implies a statement, namely, that poverty does so
contribute. He assumes that it does, and then wants to know
why. Can he not see the absurdity of asking me to tell him
why a thing is so when I asseverate with all my voice that it
is not so? If he believes it is so he ought to give the reason for
it—not I. I believe it is a lie; and therefore I am unable to
give any reason for it.

Mr. Wilson, of Minnesota, rose.

Mr. Reed. Now, I sincerely hope the gentleman from Minnesota can comprehend a proposition so plain as that, especially
when it is dissected into its two parts. But there are some minds
that seem to be incapable of comprehending that a question
may involve an assertion; and he has paraded that proposition
here, in season and out of season, until he actually believes it
himself, which is astonishing, he being an intelligent man; and
he has actually got some of the other people on that side to
believe it, which is far less astonishing, judging by what I have
heard from them. [Laughter] . . .

Mr. Wilson, of Minnesota. Can you not answer that question?

Mr. Reed. Now, will the gentleman keep quiet and peaceful
a moment? I do not wonder he does not like this, but the

dissection was absolutely necessary to the peace of the country; for he would have been still repeating that question day after day if he had not discovered the answer by the same surgical operation which seems to be necessary to get a joke into a Scotchman's head. [Laughter.]

Now this famous free-trade dilemma—

Mr. Wilson, of Minnesota, rose.

Mr. Reed. Oh, there he is again!

Mr. Wilson, of Minnesota. The gentleman stated, as I understood, that he would answer my question—does or does not the tariff raise the price of lumber?

Mr. Reed. The question which the gentleman asked me just before, which, now that I am about to answer, he seems anxious not to have answered, was whether the tariff does not necessarily raise prices, and if it does not, what is the good of it? Now, that is a pat remark of gentlemen on the other side. I have heard it as many times as I have heard some of the witty remarks of the gentleman from New York. [Laughter.] It has the same sanction of universality and antiquity.

The proposition which we make is that by the encouragement of an industry engaged in the production of a necessary of life, the result in a long series of years will be good wages and low prices, and we prove it by facts and figures; we prove it by the general consensus of mankind; we prove it by the fact that every civilized nation on earth, except one, which is exceptionally situated, is in favor of the principle and practice of protection. Now, if we prove it by figures, if we prove it by theory, if we prove it by the common sense of mankind, as shown by the general adoption of the doctrine, it seems to me that even the gentleman from Minnesota might, by giving days and nights to the matter, get some glimmering of the idea connected with it. [Laughter and applause.]

The members themselves appreciated Reed in full measure and, as Alexander says, his mere presence "encouraged the hope that at any moment his clear, penetrating voice might change the House from a dull, half-weary body to an expectant public meeting. When he rose, a hundred members, catching the words

'Mr. Speaker,' hastened from their seclusion and settled into an attitude of attention." [1] The Washington *Post* of August 30, 1893, gives a vivid picture of such an occurrence.

The House had passed the bill repealing the Silver Purchase Act for which Congress had been called in special session and was now debating the rules. Reed made an able defense of the procedure of the 51st Congress, mercilessly ridiculing the Democratic adherence to old, out-worn practices which facilitated evasion of responsibility. "I tell you, gentlemen, it is a course of that sort, pursued for a century, that has made this House come to be regarded, as I have said of it elsewhere, as the coward center of the United States. You get into the habit of dodging propositions instead of meeting them."

A dramatic incident followed. Speaker Crisp, stung by Reed's comments, left the chair to reply. When Reed began his remarks there were only one or two drowsy occupants on the press benches, and a few scattered members at their desks, semi-somnolent with the heat of a Washington mid-summer afternoon. The galleries were empty. As he proceeded the members began to gather and before the tilt between ex-Speaker and Speaker was over, the floor was filled, the newspaper correspondents were out in force, and the next day's papers spread accounts of the clash throughout the country. The *Post* gives a striking picture of the two leaders, one from Maine, the other from Georgia, as they faced each other across the broad middle aisle, "the one dominant and aggressive, the other positive, defiant and resolute; in beliefs, in training, in lifelong environment, in modes of thought and in conclusions antipodal, yet both showing in figure, face, bearing, name, and speech that they are straight-bred Anglo-Saxons without a tincture of the Latin:"

The difference between their personal appearance is great, and yet as they faced each other it had a strange similarity.

[1] *House of Representatives,* 297.

Mr. Reed is much the larger man of the two. His features as well as his frame are more massive. Yet the countenances of both are clean shaven and strongly marked and both are very courageous men. The Northerner wore his usual negligee suit of "tow," the Southerner was clad in an immaculate black coat and white linen, with the turn down collar relieved only by a narrow black tie. Their clothes were as distinctive of the two sections as their manners. . . . Both of the men are thorough parliamentarians, both experienced debaters, both fluent, both intellectual, and both vitally interested in the question at issue.

Crisp showed considerable feeling in his remarks, and this clash of August 29 was one in a series of incidents which aroused no little ill-will between the participants and which kept Reed in his seat when at the close of the 53rd Congress there was a rising vote of thanks to the retiring Speaker. The debate itself involved an interesting clash of opinions. Crisp argued that the innovations of the 51st Congress, especially the Speaker's usurpations, had proved odious to the country, and that the elections of 1890 had demonstrated the fact.

Reed defended both the rules and his own position with respect to their enforcement. As for the public attitude toward the 51st Congress: "Why! did you make me an issue in the campaign? I thought it was the tariff." However obnoxious the rules might be, the other side would eventually adopt them all. Every effort was being made to reach the results attained by the 51st Congress and at the same time conceal the imitation. It was perhaps unreasonable to expect the Democratic party to catch up entirely within four years. The Speaker had said that this was a hobby. "It is true, it is my hobby; and I had it long before the 51st Congress. And is this hobby unworthy? The method of doing business on the part of the greatest legislative body on the face of the earth—is that an unworthy thing for any man to be interested in? Is that beneath the dignity of a member from any part of this Union?"

Members were arguing for days as to which had had the better of this passage at arms, and the same was true of a similar bout with Bourke Cockran at the next session. The eloquent New York Irishman, a warm personal friend of Reed, was undoubtedly his superior as a platform speaker. When, on January 15, 1894, he assailed the principle of protection as contributory to existing unemployment and distress, he made a deep impression. Reed's reply and the repeated give and take which followed constituted one of the outstanding features of a session which abounded in dramatic episodes.

The Washington *Post* described it as one of the greatest debates ever heard in the House. "At times the uproar on the floor was beyond description. Cheers, howls of derision and counter demonstrations of applause mingled with each other until the chairman ceased pounding the gavel in despair and settled back in his seat until the noisy manifestation had spent itself." It is unnecessary to repeat the arguments offered by either party and honors appear to have been evenly divided. Contemporary comment divided on partisan lines, Republicans considering that their champion had demonstrated his invincibility in rough and tumble debate.

It is sufficient to quote Reed's characteristic remark on taking the floor. In the hush which followed Cockran's speech, while the air still seemed to vibrate with his rolling eloquence, Reed, slowly getting on his feet, interjected the rasping comment: "I am exceedingly sorry that, with all the repertoire of eloquence which the gentleman from New York has at his command, he should resort so frequently to that portion of it which is merely physical." There was a burst of laughter and the audience was ready for argument.

Reed's long speeches were few in number and have been, or

will be, mentioned in connection with the measures on which
they were delivered. As he remarked in his speech on the Wilson Bill, "if anything seems to have been discussed until human
nature can bear it no more it is the tariff." Nevertheless, his
speeches on the Mills Bill and the Wilson Bill can be read
with pleasure and profit, not merely by the special student but
by any person interested in public questions. These two
speeches, together with that on repeal of the Silver Purchase
Act, will bear comparison with any addresses on similar topics
in the history of the House. He could take the dry facts of
economic controversy, and breathe fire into them until they
fairly glowed. Nelson Dingley undoubtedly knew more about
tariff and currency than any man in Congress, but Dingley could
never have made any of these three speeches. As for McKinley,
a comparison of almost any of his longer congressional speeches
on the tariff with Reed's on the Mills Bill of 1888, or the Wilson
Bill of 1894, will fairly indicate the difference between their
capacities.

Reed lacked many of the graces of the finished public speaker
and his success was another triumph of sheer intellect. His nasal
drawl lent greater effectiveness to his retorts or to the running
interchanges in which he so frequently participated, but it would
probably have been a handicap for any but a man of intellect
and character whose words commanded instinctive respect. Certainly, in his campaign speeches and the few long congressional
addresses, he held his hearers from start to finish and won admiration and respect from friend and foe alike. "On his feet,"
says Champ Clark, "in the full tide of speech, with his vast bulk
and vibrant tones, he literally compelled attention, and drove
home his propositions with the force of a pile driver." [1]

Francis E. Leupp, who observed him carefully over a long
period of years, noticed that Reed was stimulated by opposition

[1] *My Quarter Century of American Politics,* I, 278.

and at his best when facing a dangerous opponent. He has left an interesting picture of Reed at the Minneapolis convention of 1892, when the delegates, wearied by the antagonism between the Blaine and Harrison factions, suddenly recognized the ex-Speaker among the spectators and broke into a tremendous ovation. Reed was forced to the platform and made a few platitudinous remarks on the glory of the Republican party, "the poorest apology for a speech," Leupp avers, that he ever heard Reed make in the course of twenty years. Leupp and others always believed that had he risen to the occasion he might have stampeded the convention into a nomination.

The Reed ovation was, he declared, "the sole spontaneous act of the convention, the single tribute which bore no scent of purchase or pledge." The opportunity passed. "The words which might have settled matters remained unspoken, for Reed could not command them. The subsidence of the temporary mania among the delegates left everything where it was before, and Reed realized before he went to bed that night that the best chance he would probably ever have for the presidency had passed beyond his reach." [1]

Whatever may have been the possibilities of the situation, and they were probably not as great as Reed's admirers would have us believe, inasmuch as the convention of 1892 was an office-holders' convention, sophisticated, cynical, and bound to carry out orders like a regiment of regular veterans, it was a good illustration of the fact that Reed's forte was the rough and tumble debate. Opposition stimulated him, but at Minneapolis he was out of his element. He disliked theatricals and would have scorned the tactics which Bryan used so successfully at Chicago four years later. "But to Reed," says Leupp, "for just a little while, it was given to feel a strange sense that he was facing the crisis of his life, but powerless to affect its outcome."

[1] New York *Evening Post,* December 10, 1902.

Reed's retorts, the brutally frank expressions of a mind which had scant tolerance for loquacity or dullness, are scattered through the *Record* in great abundance. While far less significant than many of his contributions, they were better known than more important utterances and undoubtedly heightened the impression that he was a bully, rude, domineering and ruthless.

William M. Springer and Richard W. Townshend of Illinois constantly drew his fire. "Springer," he is reported to have remarked, "is the broader-minded jackass of the two, Townshend altogether the more intense." On one occasion when the latter quoted Garfield's opinion of dilatory motions "for the benefit of gentlemen who are seeking to delay action," Reed retorted: "If you would repeat more of the language of the gentleman from Ohio it would be a great improvement in your speeches." [1] On another occasion, Springer, rising to a question of privilege, complained that the newspapers had attributed to him certain remarks really made by Dolliver. "Perhaps," said Reed, "he was only anticipating you by a year or two."

Of Hewitt's tariff views he once said: "I can remember when my friend from New York was convulsing this country on the subject of free raw material. He never rose in his place, his mouth never opened without free raw material issuing forth." [2] When J. D. Warner took his seat at the conclusion of a speech Reed rose with the introductory statement: "I cannot expect to equal the volume of voice shown by the gentleman from New York. That is only equaled in this world by the volume of things with which he is not acquainted."

During debate on the Wilson tariff a Wyoming member urged an amendment increasing the duty on diamonds, defending his proposal as a statesmanlike effort to equalize the burdens

[1] *Cong. Record,* 46 Cong., 1 Sess., 1745.
[2] *Ibid.,* 49 Cong., 1 Sess., 4442.

of taxation. Reed's response was prompt and to the point. "As the gentleman from Wyoming says, it touches upon some of the domains of statesmanship, that is, the domains of humbug and blatherskite which are a large portion of certain kinds of statesmanship." In the course of debate on the removal of internal revenue duties he remarked to Roger Q. Mills: "The gentleman from Texas does not mean to be believed when he says the Republican party is for free whisky, because he knows there would not be enough Democrats left to make up the electoral ticket in half the States of the Union if they had confidence in his statement." "Oh, the gentleman from Texas is safe," he remarked on another occasion to Kilgore. "His district is Democratic naturally. The common-school system does not prevail there." [1]

Reed was popular and successful on the stump, and especially in the last decade of his public life, was in great demand as a campaign speaker. He had the good sense there to avoid, as in the House, the oratorical flourishes and the professional tricks of the "spell-binder." Always he was Tom Reed, clear-thinking, satirical and convincing. In his earlier campaigns, especially in his own State, he was frequently involved in give-and-take with members of his audiences. His Maine colleague, C. A. Boutelle, told the story of a speech Reed made in Biddeford, Maine, when a large number of Democrats attended. Reed knew they were there, and began his address, after surveying the crowd, with the statement: "If a photographic snapshot could be taken of the Democracy at any time or any place it would reveal them in the act of doing some mean, low-lived and contemptible thing." Thereupon the Democratic portion of his audience stood up as one man, hissing and jeering. "There," said Reed, "I told you so."

People long remembered that it was one of the treats of a

_____
[1] *Ibid.*, 53 Cong., 2 Sess., 4637.

political campaign to hear him deal with Democrats and their works, but in his later years he became more mellow and tolerant. His campaign speeches lacked some of the pungency and force which characterized his earlier efforts but gained in argumentative power. Nevertheless, he was not primarily a campaign speaker and his reputation must rest on his record as a parliamentary debater.

Reed after 1888 became well known as a writer and for some years added considerably to his income by contributing to various magazines. He adopted the rule of refusing formal interviews with newspaper representatives, insisting that if his views on public questions were worth publication he was entitled to payment for them. But he continued to explain his position on pending questions and comment informally on men and measures to the newspaper correspondents.

He contributed an admirable series of articles to the *North American Review* from 1888 to 1902 and in 1897 made fortnightly contributions to the *Illustrated American*. Occasional articles also appeared in the *Saturday Evening Post*, the *Youth's Companion* and other magazines, as well as in various newspapers. Like Cleveland, he never learned to dictate successfully, writing his papers laboriously in longhand and correcting each with infinite care and patience. They are of high quality and in controversial matters display the same characteristic touches which made him the great debater. Unquestionably, in the field of journalism he would have been one of the great editors of the day and it is quite conceivable that, had he had the time, he could have made a still higher reputation in the field of historical and political exposition. As it is, his work as a man of letters is of decided significance and his pen did much to supplement his voice in the creation and guidance of American opinion.

THE CONTEST FOR THE NOMINATION, 1892

(From *Judge*)

IN spite of the disastrous outcome of the congressional elections of 1890, Reed's personal prestige was still high and a few days after adjournment the New York *Tribune,* March 7, 1891, published a lengthy and decidedly significant sketch of the ex-Speaker, in which he was described as "one of the great leaders of thought in this country," "the most active mind, perhaps, to-day in modern politics." "He is today one of the strongest men in the Republican party. He is young and with physical health of the most superb character. He is proud and independent. He acknowledges no man as his master, and yet is a cordial and hearty friend. His future is of better promise than that of most men in American politics." Appearing in the leading organ of the party, and followed by many similar expressions through-out the country, such opinions seemed to indicate that Reed had still greater honors in prospect.

The opening of the 52nd Congress had for Reed and the surviving Republican members of the 51st some elements of anti-climax. The party seats had been emptied by the late debacle like the saddles of the Light Brigade at Balaklava, and the huge Democratic majority flooded over into what had long been considered Republican floor space. Reed was again minority leader, and his followers, he said, "behaved with gentleness and modesty, partly because they were very good men and partly because there were very few of them." C. F. Crisp, of Georgia, who had led the fight against the Reed rules, was chosen Speaker on December 8, and another Congress was under way. Thomas E. Watson received 8 Populist votes for the speakership and the House was generally reported as consisting of 231 Democrats, 88 Republicans, and 14 Populists.

On December 16, Speaker Crisp announced that the Committee on Rules would consist of the Speaker, Messrs. McMillin, Catchings, Reed and Burrows, thereby disregarding the precedent of several preceding sessions, under which the chairmen of Ways and Means and the Appropriations Committee had, with the Speaker, constituted the majority of the Committee on Rules. William M. Springer and William S. Holman respectively headed these latter committees. Apparently this indicated a tendency toward a wider distribution of power and responsibility. Reed, who had also been made ranking minority member of Ways and Means, did not approve the change and in an interview published in the Washington *Post* on December 17, 1891, stated his objections. His remarks throw considerable light on his theory of House control and leadership:

I appointed the Committee on Rules in the last Congress, to consist of four men, two of whom were the chairmen of the Committee on Ways and Means and Appropriations, because both these committees have the right of way in the House, and therefore these chairmen would not want to gain an undue advantage for their committees at the expense of others. Furthermore, the chairmen of these committees are practically the advisers of the Speaker. They know the great legislation which is to come before the House, and they are in a better position to pass on the order of business than are chairmen or members of other committees. Despite the great outcry which was raised against us in the last Congress, there must be a "steering" committee to arrange the order of business and decide how and in what way certain measures shall be considered. That was the sole object of the rules of the last, to do business in a business-like and systematic way, and while this is a great country and it takes the people some time to understand things, I do not believe that has been misunderstood. If the rules of the last Congress were to be an issue, I do not think there would be any doubt as to their being sustained by the country.

Long before Congress met the Democratic members had vociferously proclaimed their intention of obliterating "Reed-ism" and all its works, and on January 26 the new code made its appearance in the House. Catchings, of Mississippi, explained the changes. With some modifications the rules of the 52nd Congress were those of the 50th. The effect of any revolution is seldom wholly lost even when counter-revolutionists seem completely victorious, and Reed's was no exception. Catchings admitted that it seemed desirable to increase the power of the Committee on Rules with respect to special orders by preventing filibustering against its reports. His admission that it seemed nec-essary "to lodge somewhere the power which would enable this House, when a majority desired seriously to have a vote upon important business, to have that vote" sounded very much like the principle for which Reed had contended ever since the days of the 47th Congress. "Some power to arrange the order of business was vitally needed," continued the Democratic spokes-man.

The defective order of business reappeared and worst of all the "Holman amendment," which had been rescinded by the 49th Congress, was restored. It might, as Reed contemptuously remarked, be "dear to the heart of what is called retrenchment and reform," but although first introduced in 1874, it had long since been tried and found wanting. "It is now resuscitated," he continued, "after its features have become so sodden by death that it is hoped nobody will quite recognize them, and it is hoped they may be palmed off upon us as something useful and valu-able." The result was certain to be "that most obnoxious and unhallowed thing, legislative riders upon appropriation bills." Riders were provocative of trouble with the Senate, and "the question of what is germane and what reduces expenditure is as interesting as any variegated landscape that you ever beheld."

The quorum-counting rule was, of course, anathema to the new majority and member after member seized the first opportunity to denounce the conduct of the Speaker of the 51st Congress. Reed had not left the chair during his tenure of the speakership to participate in debate on the floor, but he was now in a position to defend and explain his conduct. On January 26 he made what was at once a brilliant defense of his own reforms and a scathing, merciless attack on the pending code. It was one of the ablest of all his numerous speeches on the subject, in spite of the fact that there was not the slightest prospect of success. "If I could by some miracle transfer to my audience the wisdom and experience they will have at the end of the session," he began, "I would not have the present hopeless task."

He took advantage two days later of an opportunity to point out to the Populist members "that minorities in the House are not always political minorities; that, in fact, the larger part of the business of this House is conducted upon non-partisan lines, and that if you were simply limiting the partisan majority perhaps a feeling of patriotism might induce some of us to assist you in the process. But you are doing more than that. You are limiting the non-partisan majority of the House and in non-partisan matters. You are proclaiming not only contempt for your political majority, which perhaps I could endure, but you are proclaiming a contempt for a large majority of non-political matters which I deem to be, as I deem the other, contrary to the Constitution of the United States and contrary to the principles of democratic or republican government."

In conclusion he pointed out that the Democrats had been clamoring for an opportunity to serve the country. They had often explained that somebody had always balked their efforts in the past, but the 51st Congress had shown that this excuse was forever invalid. Here was a wonderful opportunity and yet they were closing all thoroughfares for the passage of bills except one through the Committee on Rules, and the other through attaching riders to appropriation bills:

You want an opportunity for these great remedial measures that you desire. You want to rescue Kansas from starvation [Laughter]; you want to look after the burial of Georgia citizens. [Laughter.] You want to pass an act for the free coinage of silver and enable this country to be eternally prosperous. You want also to strike down the tariff, that hideous creature of monopolies; you want to strike down all trusts; you want to redeem this country, and make this a great, glorious people, such as you are yourselves. [Great laughter.] That is what you want to do. [Laughter.] And you do not want deliberately to refuse yourselves an opportunity. [Laughter.] [1]

The rules were of course promptly adopted, and the House proceeded to the business of the session. With an overwhelming Democratic majority constantly available, the quorum did not become an issue and with a presidential campaign impending and serious dissension developing within their own ranks, the Democrats had no burning desire to legislate. Parliamentary questions therefore proved of very slight importance in this Congress.

Before the 52nd Congress met, the Silver Purchase Act had begun to show serious results. The gold reserve was steadily dwindling, and there was considerable uneasiness in financial circles. The difficulties of Baring Brothers late in 1890 had embarrassed British finance, and the ensuing liquidation had led to heavy selling of American securities and further withdrawals of gold from New York. How long the Treasury would be able to continue redemption operations in view of the added burdens imposed by the Silver Purchase Act was a serious problem. In December, bills providing for the repeal of the law made their appearance, but so also did that inevitable brand of

[1] *Cong. Record,* 52 Cong., 1 Sess., 648.

political cowardice which prevented both parties from taking a courageous stand on the question.

In the House, Mr. Bland, long the outstanding advocate of silver coinage, introduced a free coinage bill on February 10, 1892. This measure was denounced by numerous Eastern Democrats and enthusiastically supported by others from the West and South. Reed, as leader of a minority which could be overridden at any time, saw the split in the majority and realized its value both to the cause of Republicanism and that of sound money. He fought the Bland bill at every turn, his vast store of parliamentary knowledge and his skill in applying it proving of incalculable value to the cause of sound money.

The contest was close. On March 24, 1892, the Speaker's vote making a tie, the motion to lay the bill on the table was defeated 148–148, filibustering began, and further action was then postponed, Speaker Crisp deciding not to report a closure rule. The Democrats at this juncture were not anxious to commit the party to a radical course. "Ex-Speaker Reed," declared *The Nation*, which for the past three years had seldom found anything to praise in his actions, "has won golden opinions from all sorts of people." He had fought the bill, the editor continued, not for expediency but on principle; to beat a dangerous measure, rather than to put his opponents in a hole. "In this he has shown the highest political wisdom."

On July 13, the House refused consideration for a Senate free coinage bill. Now that Mr. Cleveland had received the presidential nomination, and his attitude on the currency question was clearly understood to be in favor of the gold standard, the immediate danger was over. Reed took advantage of the occasion to offer some ironical congratulations to the Democratic party on its repentance. It had been a different story, he said, when they were in the minority in the last Congress.

In the second session "a bill to increase the circulation of na-

tional banks, and for other purposes" was called up in the House
on February 9, 1893, under a report of the Committee on Rules.
The measure was described by Bland as "a monstrosity, yield-
ing to the national banks further privileges, increasing their
circulation in the interest of the bondholders, to defeat the mone-
tization of silver in behalf of the gold gamblers and speculators." Several Democratic members, however, urged that action
was imperatively needed and that further purchases under the
Silver Purchase Act should be terminated at once, as they were a
peril to the nation's credit.

Reed again explained that the latter measure had been a
compromise. It had been hoped that it would assist in bringing
silver to par, but conditions had changed. Bimetallism could be
sustained only "on the shoulders of the whole world" and the
monometallic nations who were not anxious to change. "We are
now," he continued, "about to perform an act which will have a
certain moral influence, though probably not a legislative influence; because there is another body whose rules are such that
deliberation goes on until deliberation ceases to be an absolute
and unqualified advantage to the community."

William J. Bryan, appearing in Congress for his first term
and already recognized as one of the orators of the House, had
made an impassioned plea for free coinage of silver and the retention of the Silver Purchase Act "as a hostage until they return
to us our own child 'the gold and silver coinage of the Constitution.' " Reed's remarks in the light of subsequent events seem
strangely prophetic:

I sympathize with the gentleman from Nebraska in his feelings. He has been in the habit of listening to the shoutings
of the Democratic party, from the highest citizen to the lowest,
in favor of free silver and what they call the "good of the
people." Well, he finds now that, in power, even the Democratic party has got to obey the everlasting laws of common

sense. [Laughter.] When they are in the minority they can throw their limbs about in all sorts of contortions; they can look any way that they think beautiful.

But when they come into power they have got to act according to the eternal verities, and that is going to be a great shock to him on every occasion. [Renewed laughter.] He is going to see the leader of the House quail on the subject of free trade. He is going to see "patriots" all around him operating as some of them are going to operate today, and I beg of him to summon to his assistance that stoicism which his countenance indicates, in order to help him in his very mournful future." [Laughter and applause.] [1]

Reed made in the course of his address some significant remarks on the currency question in general. He expressed confidence that the country would remain on a sound money basis and that an analysis of the impending vote would disclose a willingness to meet the crisis when it arose. "And whenever we do get fairly at it, I hope for my part (and I am speaking only as an individual) that it will result finally in the establishment of such a banking system as will remove our currency question from the domain of active politics, and that we shall have a sound business system, carried out on sound business principles and automatic in its character. That I believe the wisdom of Congress will be equal to whenever the proper time shall arrive." Two decades were to pass and two panics to work their devastation before this prediction was realized. Reed's apparent expectation that the pending bill would pass proved false. Opponents of repeal had a small majority, the previous question was ordered on the report by a vote of 152 to 143, and it was then recommitted to the Committee on Rules without instructions.

The difference between Democratic professions of economy and their actual practice in handling appropriations gave Reed a

---

[1] *Cong. Record,* 52 Cong., 2 Sess., 1381.

fine opportunity. He upbraided Holman for reporting inadequate appropriation bills which merely transferred to the Senate the responsibility of keeping the public services from starvation. Holman, he once wrote, had long been "a worshipper at the shrine of vocal economy," but in spite of his presence at the head of Appropriations the outlays of the government could not be curtailed and in some instances were further increased. The ex-Speaker had never opposed the spending of money where warranted by results, but he would not have been human had he not remembered the uproar over "the Billion Dollar Congress."

"What I am pointing out to you," he remarked in the course of debate on June 30, 1892, "is the unspeakable and ineffable humbug of your talk two years ago. I am trying to bring Democracy face to face with itself. I am trying to bring its talk into the usual contradiction of its action. . . . You do not do this on purpose; you do not do it intelligently; you have not made these increases on account of your superior intelligence; you have done it because you were driven into it in spite of your ignorance."

The first session of the 52nd Congress accomplished little, and Reed dealt with its shortcomings in one of the most brilliant articles he ever wrote.[1] The House, he wrote, "led a gelatinous existence, the scorn of all vertebrate animals." The Democratic leaders had determined "that the party should enter the next contest unencumbered by principle." For that reason Springer had been placed at the head of Ways and Means, and "the party can contemplate his work of this session with the calm certainty that there is no intellect so subtle, no mind so broad, no sympathy so delicate as to detect therein the slightest trace of a principle of economic science or a system of revenue."

The rules adopted had made it easy to avoid raising issues. Under these rules the leaders had not only abdicated, but nobody

[1] "Two Congresses Contrasted," *North American Review,* August, 1892.

else could reign. "Given a wonderful power by the people, a power which might have enabled them to carry out any plan for the relief of what they called the down-trodden people, they deliberately put the veto into the hands of one-third, and in most cases into the hands of less, and relapsed into imbecility." "In history," he concluded, "it will present all the dead level of a Dutch landscape, with all its windmills, but without a trace of its beauty and fertility."

During the pre-convention campaign, political gossip had been busy with Reed's name as a presidential possibility, many believing that neither Harrison nor Blaine could be nominated and that the ex-Speaker would be an admirable choice. Reed's opinions of Harrison were well known and the Portland collectorship squabble had aggravated matters. Cannon remembered his own embarrassment in dealing with both men, inasmuch as Reed avoided the White House and he himself was frequently there on public business. "Reed," he says, "had the tongue of a wasp and Harrison distilled poison like an adder; the dislike was cordial and undisguised."

Reed's opinion of Blaine was no higher than his opinion of the President. In a letter to Henry Cabot Lodge written from Paris on May 25, 1891, he described him as resembling "the gentleman Sinbad carried," a sufficient index of his view as to Blaine's position in the party. "The Lord gave us B. and H.," he wrote later in the summer, "and the Lord will take them away. Thus far, however, there is no occasion for finishing the quotation." [1]

The Washington *Post* on April 25 stated facts which were well known in political circles when it reported that Reed was strongly opposed to the President's renomination. "His grievances have been nursed for some time, and in private conversa-

[1] *Lodge Papers.*

tion he denounces the President with all the biting wit and merciless satire of which he is so thoroughly a master." Whether or not he expected to receive the nomination himself, the writer went on, was unknown. "Mr. Reed is saying nothing and even his most intimate friends know nothing of his plans." "Well," he had written to Lodge on July 2, 1891, regarding the President, "perhaps he is as good a man to get licked with as anybody. This may sound like repetition and if it does I can only add that I hope he won't get a chance to be even licked. It would be too good for him." "My sorrow has been mellowed by philosophy," he added on April 1, 1892. "If we can't have a President at all we certainly can't have Harrison. Let us not forget this lining of German silver which a contemptuous Providence has flung at us with the cloud." [1]

Whatever Reed's hopes may have been, nothing came of them. Harrison was renominated and a somewhat lethargic campaign was soon under way. Asked if he would mount the Harrison band-wagon, Reed remarked, "I refuse to ride in the ice wagon," and the saying went over the country, much to the edification of Harrison's opponents. Such remarks, however, could have added nothing to the popularity of Reed among the party managers, and there was still a powerful Harrison element in the Republican ranks.

Reed after his own reëlection in September took an active part in the campaign and spoke at various places in New England, New York, Pennsylvania and the Middle West. It attracted considerable attention when, on opening his own congressional campaign at Old Orchard, he did not once refer to the President or his administration, but Reed was too honest to eulogize on the stump a man for whom he did not hesitate to express dislike in private. There was a dull presidential cam-

[1] *Lodge Papers.*

paign and Cleveland won decisively. For the first time since the Civil War the Democrats were to control House, Senate and Presidency.

The short session began December 5, 1892. There were no flowers on Reed's desk on the opening day. "Oh, it is because I am nobody's darling," he remarked when his attention was called to this oversight. While the President's message was being read to a thin House and amid general inattention, he strolled ponderously about and near the Speaker's desk was heard to drawl, "Will the House adjourn at the conclusion of the ceremonies out of respect to the memory of the departed?"

The short session naturally showed no more desire for legislative accomplishment than had the first. There seemed to be a general lethargy in both parties. Business throughout the country was uneasy and the financial condition of the Government caused acute anxiety among those who understood the situation. The Harrison administration was apparently counting the days until its burden of responsibility could be shifted to the sturdy shoulders of Grover Cleveland. Reed took little part in debate, and observers noted that he seemed to have lost some of his rancor toward opponents, made but few sarcastic remarks, and spent a great deal of time at his desk writing letters. On the last day of the session, however, he made a few admirable remarks on the dignity and importance of the speakership as the embodiment of the power of the House and gave a notable exhibition of magnanimity in moving the address of thanks to Speaker Crisp.

In the meantime the question of what constituted a quorum within the meaning of the Constitution was on its way to final adjudication by the Supreme Court. In the adoption of the act of May 9, 1890, classifying worsted cloths as woolens, the Speaker had counted a quorum and an importer promptly contested its constitutionality on the ground that it had not been passed by a quorum within the meaning of the Constitution. On February 29, 1892, Justice Brewer handed down the Court's decision.[1]

The Court made quick work of the argument that a constitutional quorum had not been present. The Journal showed a majority present; under the Constitution a majority constituted a quorum; a majority of that quorum voted in favor of the act and it had legally passed the House. The Court quoted House Rule XV as laying down the procedure required and decided that the question at issue was the validity of the rule. It should be noted that Reed's action of January 29, 1890, in counting a quorum was not before the court, and never was. The validity of the rule by which the Speaker was authorized to count a quorum was tested; not, as some writers have stated, the validity of Reed's original action. That was successful revolution and nothing else.

The decision, however, ended at least one phase of the controversy. It was a distinct triumph for Reed, and another step toward the complete vindication of his actions and policies. That process was to be completed in the course of the next Congress.

Business improved slightly during the early weeks of 1893, perhaps on the prospect that Congress might bring about repeal of the Silver Purchase Act; but when the short session closed without remedial action, conditions went steadily from bad to worse. As described by a contemporary a little later, "a strange blight fell on the country like fog coming out of the sea." There were many circumstances which combined to produce economic demoralization. The repercussions resulting from the failure of Baring Brothers were still in motion; there were serious financial disturbances in the Argentine; bank failures in Australia. In the United States both internal and international forces were

[1] *United States* vs. *Ballin,* 144 United States, 1.

working for disaster and the latter were supplemented by the natural curtailment of credit following a period of undue expansion, together with uncertainties regarding the tariff and currency policies of the incoming administration.

Whatever the causes, there could be no question about the results. Gold was moving steadily to Europe, the reserve was sinking in ominous fashion, and while President Cleveland's inaugural declaration that the executive would exercise every power "to maintain our national credit or avert financial disaster" did something to preserve confidence, panic conditions rapidly developed, reaching a crisis late in June when the Indian government announced the suspension of silver coinage. Banks, manufacturers and commercial houses went under by the thousand, railroad receiverships became commonplace events, and the effect on agriculture was especially disastrous.

Naturally, whatever the political merits of the case—and the Harrison administration cannot be absolved of its full share of responsibility—the Democratic administration had to bear the brunt of criticism. President Cleveland's unflinching courage and determination in face of disaster, assailed by party opponents and by malcontents within his own organization, threatened, as we now know, by fatal disease, hounded by office seekers, and burdened with all the routine business of an incoming administration, constitute one of the finest exhibitions of civic heroism in the history of the presidency. There was considerable criticism of his delay in calling an extraordinary session, but the interim at least afforded public opinion a chance to concentrate on the Silver Purchase Act as one of the chief causes of existing difficulties.

Congress was finally summoned on June 30 to meet in special session August 7, 1893. The President urged repeal in the strongest terms. "This matter rises above the plane of party politics. It vitally concerns every business and calling and enters every household in the land." Repeal, however, was not a simple matter. To the Western farmer, in many instances it meant increased hardships. All the remnants of Greenbackism, augmented by the growing power of Populism, and whipped into savage resistance by economic distress, consolidated in opposition.

There could be no doubt about Reed's position. He had taken a firm stand in favor of repeal during the preceding session and now stated his intention of supporting the President to the utmost. "Do you think, Mr. Reed," he was asked on one occasion, "that President Cleveland will appoint you to the Cabinet?" "He might," was the response, "but please don't mention it. It might hurt me in my district." [1]

When the House assembled on August 7, Reed was in his place and again received the minority vote for the speakership. His followers had increased from 88 in the 52nd Congress to 128. "He was the observed of all observers, an object of awe to the far Western member who saw him for the first time and has been used to regard him as a modern ogre, and was kept busy shaking hands with new acquaintances and old." [2]

While the business interests of the country were clamoring for repeal, the outcome was by no means certain. The free silver advocates were actively canvassing the members. "There is something touching in the implicit confidence which they repose in the ultimate success of the fight for the white metal, and their assurances that the statesmen who fail to board the silver car as it passes by are doomed," reported the Washington *Post* on August 13. Even "that rockribbed Gibraltar of Republican conservatism, Thomas B. Reed," the account went on, had received overtures from the silver men. One of them had approached him at the Shoreham where he sat one evening "wrapped in the profundity of his meditations and a linen suit."

[1] Washington *Post*, February 15, 1893.
[2] *Ibid.*, August 8, 1893.

"Why, Mr. Reed," urged the silver siren, "if you will only vote for free silver you can have the nomination without asking for it."

"Well, I'll tell you," came the drawling reply, "I don't know whether I'll vote for silver or not, and I haven't made up my mind whether I'll be President just yet."

Congress got to work with about the usual amount of preliminary wrangling and delay. The situation of the country had become pitiable. As the same journal remarked on August 21, "The wheels of industry are standing still. Thousands of men are idle and women and children are without food. Mills and factories are closing, railroad earnings are fading away, and every day adds thousands to the ranks of the unemployed."

The repeal bill, the first on the calendars, was soon put on its way to passage. On August 26, in the stifling heat, with the galleries packed and seemingly in motion from the ceaseless waving of fans, Reed, according to observers one of the coolest people in the House "despite the general opinion that it is the fat man who suffers most in such temperatures," closed the debate for the forces of repeal.

It had been a great debate and Reed's speech was worthy of the occasion. It was in fact one of the greatest of his career, and showed all his remarkable power of analysis and presentation of a great and burning issue. His theme was the necessity of restoring confidence, and the vital importance of repeal as contributory to that end.

Human progress, he began, was never continuous, even if the general trend was forward. The United States had been in a decline for some time. It was the same story. After each long period of recuperation confidence reasserted itself, prosperity increased, and there seemed to be no limit to its possibilities. Then confidence disappeared, caution reawakened and some overt occurrence precipitated another crisis:

If the period of prosperity could be expressed in a single word, that word would be confidence; and if the period of adversity, as we call it, could be expressed in a single word, that word would be distrust.

In former times conditions were confined to particular countries; the earth was now bound together by economic ties, but in each country there was also a cause peculiar to itself. There had been a drain of money from London to South America and, as a result, from the United States to London. Last May it was evident that the day of reckoning was approaching. "The stroke of the clock which shows that the time of settlement has arrived is always a surprise; and from the nature of things and of human beings, always will be a surprise." Universal distrust was the present condition. The uncertainty regarding the tariff was aggravating the situation. "We are on the down grade to that period of recuperation, economy, and self-denial which will cause grave suffering, especially to the poor."

Repeal, he went on, would help in the process of restoring confidence, but it would be merely one contributory factor. There could be no restoration of confidence if banks and corporations were the object of indiscriminate hostility. They had an indispensable work to perform. Whatever might be the contempt for foreign capital, the next upturn would be by the assistance of the whole world and aid would depend on our being in accord with the world on the question of money. "Gentlemen sometimes exaggerate the greatness of the United States in flights of eloquence. Nevertheless, there remains the fact that our country is larger than our wealth: that the possibilities of the United States are a thousand fold in advance of any progress which it has yet made." For that process of development it would be necessary to draw upon the capital of the entire world. How could capital be secured unless the lender had confidence in the policies of the country?

Inevitably, he added, his mind went back to the days of the 45th and 46th Congresses, when resumption of specie payments was the subject of the same heated discussion. "Hardly a new idea has been presented, hardly a new prophecy. There was the same attack upon wealth; there was the same laudation of the poor. Everything seems to me, as I sit and listen to the debate here in the House, as if the tide of time had rolled back and I were sitting here a new member, listening to the wisdom of fifteen years ago." How familiar it all seemed! Debtors would be ruined; it was a surrender to England; the poor would be prostrated forever. "And yet I lived to see every one of those prophecies forgotten and every man connected with them forgotten, too." When specie payments were assured the country took an upward start. Property values increased; employment was abundant; production grew rapidly.

No single nation, declared Reed, could maintain bimetallism, however feasible it might be on a world basis. A continuance of the Silver Purchase Act would be interpreted as a declaration that the country expected eventually to be on a silver basis and no one would advance his capital without assurance that his money would be repaid in full:

The proposition to lower the ratio I hail as the one good sign of this discussion. To drop from the bigoted determination that 16 to 1 is a heaven-appointed ratio raised up by the Almighty, and proceed even to discuss market values, seems to give some slight hope that when we really undertake anew the reform of our financial system we may approach it with some reference to existing conditions and to the facts of the universe.

The pathway of duty, he concluded, was clear. Unconditional repeal was essential. The position of the President was especially embarrassing. "What wonder then that he appeals to the patriotism of another party whose patriotism has never been appealed to in vain?" The Republicans had always been champions of true and solid finance. "And when the time comes, as it surely will come, for us to lead this land back to those paths of prosperity and fame which were trodden under Republican rule for so many years, we shall take back with us our ancient glory undimmed by adversity; our ancient honor unsullied by defeat."

Reed sat down in the midst of a tremendous ovation from floor and galleries alike and it was reëchoed from sound money supporters throughout the land. The Washington *Post* on August 28 remarked editorially that Reed's speech was "the broadest and most vigorous statement that has yet been heard on either side." It was, it continued, a great pity that the editors who represented Reed as a sneering and sardonic cynic could not have heard him discuss the situation. "In the presence of a national calamity he was a patriot before he was a Republican, and a statesman rather than a politician." The New York *Tribune* on the 29th declared Reed's speech "decidedly the ablest and most elevated in character" of all the closing speeches and illustrative of "the lofty courage of conviction, the splendid patriotism and the broad statesmanship," of the Republican leader. It was predicted everywhere that the debate would have a profound influence on public opinion, a belief which seems to have been justified by events. "What a superb speech Reed's was!" wrote Theodore Roosevelt to Henry Cabot Lodge on August 28, "I do not suppose that the Republicans here would allow me to go; if they only would I should certainly be a Reed delegate at the next national convention." [1]

[1] *Selections from the Correspondence of Theodore Roosevelt and Henry Cabot Lodge,* I, 131.

On August 28, repeal was carried by 240 yeas to 110 nays and free coinage was voted down by 227 nays to 124 yeas. Newspaper men who gathered around Reed's desk after the vote heard him remark to Bryan and John Allen: "The gold bugs not only got away with the silver bugs, but the straddle bugs as well," a reference to desertions from the free silver alignment. To Bryan, in reference to the plea in his speech that Cleveland "order one more charge," he added, "This is a Marengo, without a Desaix."

The House, in closer touch with public opinion, had performed its duty, but the Senate had still to be convinced. For week after week the struggle continued in the upper chamber until the country began to discuss the absurdity of unlimited debate and to discover unsuspected virtues in the methods which had been applied in the House three years before. On October 25, Reed spoke before the Republican Club of Boston and, perhaps in disregard of the comity obtaining between the two Houses, handled the Senate obstructionists without gloves. The will of the people was obviously for repeal and "there never has been a moment since that bill reached the Senate when, under the Constitution of the United States, the will of the people could not have been obeyed, when all this distress which resulted from that bill might not have been swept away."

Public opinion was for the President and against the Senate. "For the first time in the history of this land that august body is the subject of the flouts and jeers of all mankind." It was all part and parcel of the great struggle for majority rule. The minority had been conquered in one branch of Congress. "But the right of the majority to rule is the farthest from being established in this country today that it ever was. The majority of the people are not ruling; and that encourages every minority to add to the Constitution of the United States . . . this proviso: 'Provided the minority are not persistent and ugly enough

to prevent.' " Not until October 30 did the Senate obstructionists give way, when the bill passed by a vote of 43 to 22, only 20
Democrats supporting it.

The Capitol during these weeks drew throngs of visitors, and
attendants noted that Reed was always the first man asked for by
visiting ladies who at times filled the galleries. "Ever since Tom
Reed sat on the House throne he has been a continued magnet
for gallery women," remarked the Washington *Post* on September 24. When proceedings were dull and uninteresting the
remark was often heard, "It did not use to be that way when Tom
Reed was in the chair." His humor and "the sense of power
about him" were great attractions. "If Mr. Reed wants to run
for President all that is necessary is to give the franchise to
women."

When the repeal bill had finally passed, Reed made a few
general remarks on the national situation, declaring that the delay had robbed the country of much of the benefit of its passage.
Congress adjourned on November 3. "The purpose for which
Congress has been called in extra session is behind us, and to
continue the session would be an idle parade of zeal," said Senator Gray of Delaware. "The sooner this Democratic body ad-
journs," said Reed, "the less mischief it will inflict upon the
country." "Now that Wall Street has no further use for us,"
grumbled Bland, "I suppose we can go home." These remarks,
according to the Washington *Post*, were a fair index of the views
of the various factions. Reed had given a masterly demonstration of leadership.

THE 53rd Congress marked in many respects the most significant epoch in Reed's career. He was at the very height of his
physical and intellectual powers. The situation of the country and
the issues before the national legislature called for statesmanship
and courage of highest type. No other Republican member of
either branch commanded quite the same degree of popular
confidence and interest or combined as many qualities of leadership. Blaine was dead and Harrison had led the party to defeat
in 1892. McKinley was active in the politics of Ohio, where he
was elected Governor in 1893, and his star was rising; but he
had not yet passed out of the obloquy and abuse released during
the great tariff controversy of 1890. No one could realize in
1893 how a fortunate combination of circumstances, utilized to
the full by the organizing genius of Marcus A. Hanna, would
work to his advantage in the next three years, with the White
House as the inevitable climax.

The 53rd Congress convened in regular session on December
4, 1893. McKinley, John Sherman and Reed contributed to an
interesting symposium on the political situation in the Washington *Post* of December 3, the latter predicting a hard winter
due to continuance of distrust and uneasiness, aggravated by
the Senate's delay in repealing the Silver Purchase Act and the
prospect of tariff revision. Of the tariff he remarked: "Protection as a system administered with sense and reason all over the
country is wisdom and prosperity. Protection by districts and as
a reward for votes is robbery."

He had scant confidence in the ability of the Democratic
majority to handle the existing situation. "When Cleveland was
elected, people in general forgot that electing him meant elect-

ing his party just as it was, with all its negations and all its dis-
cordance and its wild ideas." He expressed the latter idea even
more forcibly in an address at Cooper Union some months later.
"A party is made up for an object—to do something, or to stop
something, or merely to criticize the other party. That last function the Democratic party performs pretty well—a little hysterical and inconsistent, perhaps, but vigorous and omnipresent.
But when it came into power the trouble began. It had to get
somewhere, not stand on the sidewalk and find fault with the
driving."

The course of events in the second session demonstrated the
fact that the Democratic party was hopelessly divided. To President Cleveland fell the thankless task of holdings its vagaries
in check, and to Thomas B. Reed, the laborious and also thankless task of restoring the prestige of the Republican minority,
wrecked by the disasters of 1890 and 1892.

The session began in the same manner as usual. Routine business filled the opening days and it was noted by the newspaper
reporters that the lobbyists were gathering around the Ways and
Means Committee room "like flies on a molasses barrel." Reed
was much in the public eye and an interesting portrait of the
ex-Speaker at this time appeared in the Washington *Post* of
December 17, contrasting the dignified figure of December, clad
in "the customary suit of solemn black," with "the external
Thomas B. Reed of last summer" clad in a suit of linen crash.
"The coat of this suit hung about him in folds innumerable, and
to every fold there were a thousand creases; the vest crawled up
to his chin and left exposed a not always immaculate shirt; the
trousers fitted him as stockings would a rooster. He was a sight
to make the heathen rage and kind hearted women weep."

His portrait by John S. Sargent, painted during his visit to
England in the summer of 1891, appeared during the special
session, but it has never been considered one of the artist's master-

pieces. "He is supposed," wrote an irreverent contemporary, "to be in the act of counting a quorum but in fact has just been inveigled into biting a green persimmon, a distinctly rebel and Democratic fruit, tabooed, unclean, and anathema maranatha to all loyal Republicans born north of the fortieth parallel." [1] "Many thought it was a work of destiny manifesting retributive justice in its treatment of czarism," and Reed himself is reported to have remarked, after contemplating it at a respectful distance, "Well, I hope my enemies are satisfied now." Sargent himself appears to have had no illusions about his work, for he wrote: "I found him awfully hard and this is the result of a second attempt different in view and character from the first, which I destroyed. His exterior does not somehow correspond with his spirit and what is a painter to do? I am afraid you and your friends will be disappointed and that I could have made a better picture with a much less remarkable man. He has been delightful." [2]

The 53rd Congress was confronted with important issues and abounded in great debates and dramatic episodes, but of special interest in its bearing on the fortunes of Thomas B. Reed was its adoption of the quorum-counting rule. New rules had been introduced soon after the opening of the special session in August preceding and it was evident that the Reed reforms were still exerting an influence. The power of the Committee on Rules was considerably increased and the quorum in Committee of the Whole was reduced to 100 members, as had been the rule in 1890. Reed spoke at considerable length on the new code on August 29, becoming involved in a notable clash with Speaker Crisp before the debate was over. He expressed his gratification that an adequate means had been provided for suppressing the

---

[1] Washington *Post,* September 17, 1893.
[2] Quoted in letter of Charles Fairchild to Henry Cabot Lodge, July 29, 1891, *Lodge Papers.*

filibusterer, but urged that the majority should be given complete control. The order of business remained defective, and it
was still possible by filibustering and a few roll calls to consign a
bill to "unfinished business," which was "in the nature of the
Greek Kalends." There was possible the familiar misuse of privileged motions for purposes of obstruction.

A few days later he took up the matter of the quorum. The
great dispute in the 51st Congress, he argued, had been regarding the nature of the quorum required by the Constitution. The
United States Supreme Court and every other court which had
ever decided a similar question had decided that the present,
and not the voting, quorum was all that was required.

On September 6 he again argued for "the Reed rules," declaring that when he found Mr. Springer and the Supreme Court
opposing each other "of course it would be a very puzzling matter to me if I did not have some convictions of my own." The
principles of general parliamentary law supplied the power
necessary to check abuses, and it was in his opinion part of the
duty of the presiding officer to refuse to entertain dilatory motions, as the Speaker of the House of Commons had met the
crisis of 1881:

When the action attempted is a stoppage for willful purposes of the business of the House, and that is perfectly apparent, it is the duty of the presiding officer to interpose and
arrest it; and in my judgment it will be the duty of the present
Speaker to do so in the future proceedings of this House, notwithstanding what has taken place upon this report of the Committee on Rules. It is his general parliamentary power.

However, he concluded, considerable progress had been made,
and as the debate progressed less foolishness was being talked.
Even Mr. Springer was becoming more sensible. "His language
is much more moderate and reasonable. This does not result

from his disposition to be on both sides of a great many questions; it is because the slow process of time has infiltrated him with some knowledge of these affairs, as I know it will the rest of you gentlemen. I bid you Godspeed in the progress you have thus far made." [1]

The business of the session proceeded under the new code, and on November 2 Reed took advantage of its provisions to give the majority a foretaste of the humiliation which awaited them at the regular session. As an exhibition of what could be accomplished by a determined leader who understood the parliamentary system and had the backing of a united minority, it was one of his master strokes. The House had voted to adjourn on November 3, at three o'clock; but it was necessary to pass a resolution empowering the Ways and Means Committee to sit during the recess to prepare the new tariff bill. Reed objected to the form of the proposal, and realizing that enough Democrats had left town to deprive the majority of a voting quorum, began to filibuster. The day passed in a dreary succession of roll calls. There was abundant opportunity to twit Speaker Crisp on the merits of the voting quorum. "The Chair must not make any mistake on this. We must not have any tyranny here." Members were brought in under arrest; the doors were locked; one member was led in from the barber shop with lather on his face and a towel around his neck; there were outbreaks of bad temper accompanied by profanity and several personal encounters; the Speaker beat the head off his gavel. "The suggestion might be made that we are quite ready to have the Chair count us," taunted Reed amid the derisive laughter of his followers.

At last, this demonstration of strength having proved sufficient, the minority leader remarked that while it was quite evident that the majority could not produce a quorum, and it was evident furthermore that "these interesting proceedings"

[1] *Cong. Record,* 53 Cong., 1 Sess., 1262.

could be very much further prolonged, "the size of the transaction hardly seems to warrant it." The majority accepted his amendments and the resolution was then permitted to pass. The virtues of their quorum rule could hardly have seemed convincing to Speaker Crisp and his weary followers. Next day Congress adjourned.

"Do you not see that if the House gives permission for piracy," Reed had remarked while the preceding Congress was debating the rules, "some gentleman may choose to go into that interesting and lucrative business?" The demonstration of November 2 had shown the possibilities of piratical enterprise and Reed was biding his time until favorable opportunity was offered for still more extensive operations. It was not long in coming.

On February 7, 1894, Bland introduced a bill providing for coinage of the silver seigniorage in possession of the Treasury. The adoption of this measure, to which free silver advocates rallied with enthusiasm, would still further embarrass the Treasury and constitute a serious threat to the credit of the country. The inflationists were strong in numbers and determined of spirit and it was clear that the bill stood an excellent chance of adoption. Filibustering soon developed, the Republicans and sound money Democrats opposing all efforts to force the bill to passage. "A few more episodes will reconcile the country to a restoration of the Reed rules," declared the New York *World*, assailing the Democrats for "slinking away from the issue like cowards."

There was an ugly scene on the floor on Washington's birthday, when the members several times threatened to get out of hand and the Speaker maintained a semblance of order only with the greatest difficulty. Members were brought in under arrest and at Reed's suggestion the House went through "the regular jail delivery" amid growing evidence of nervous strain and rising ill-temper. For seven days, it was pointed out, Mr.

Bland had tried in vain to get a vote on the seigniorage bill, although there were anywhere from 225 to 275 members always present. The silent members blocked all action. Various expedients for relief were discussed and Joseph W. Bailey of Texas, together with some of the younger leaders, were reported to be in favor of having Speaker Crisp count a quorum. This, however, was precisely what Crisp was determined to avoid at all costs. The struggle continued on the 23rd, Bland making an hysterical attack on the filibusterers and alternately demanding and pleading for a vote. Reed pointed out that the way was plain; a quorum was on the floor—let the Speaker count it. "When a thing is necessary for the procedure of public business in the House the Speaker has a right to perform it, if it is not otherwise delegated, and not otherwise established, and is suitable for him to perform, subject, of course, to the control of the House at all times." Mr. Bland, he pointed out in the course of the discussion, must now realize how the Speaker of the 51st Congress had felt. To Bland's attack on "downright filibustering" he retorted: "Downright? You mean upright." The disturbances continued for some days, and it was not until March 1 that the deadlock was broken and the seigniorage bill passed. Reed voted against it and later to sustain President Cleveland's successful veto of it.

Democratic cohesion had been ruined by the currency issue. Sickness and the ordinary routine absences reduced the majority, which ordinarily had thirty or more above a quorum, to the danger line. Across the aisle sat Reed, always present, always watchful, waiting to take advantage of every favorable opening.

The majority held a caucus on March 6 at which the subject of counting a quorum was discussed, but no action taken. Throughout the rest of the month there was systematic filibustering as opportunity offered, and little business was transacted. Time and again the minority leader kept the House in a succession of roll calls while the Democrats scoured the city in desperate search for missing members. The Republican objective was perfectly plain.

"The leader that they follow without question," said Speaker Crisp on March 29, "has one great thought, one great idea in his mind, and that is to force this side to count a quorum. Every other question, no matter how great, no matter how important it may be, sinks into insignificance." His remarks constitute a unique tribute to Reed's powers as floor leader. None of his friends have put it more forcibly. "Gentlemen on that side blindly follow him," said the Speaker, "no matter how their own convictions may differ from his. He is the great leader on that side. You will hear them privately saying 'Reed ought not to do that,' or 'This is wrong,' but when Reed says 'Do it' they all step up and do it."

On March 30 there was a dramatic episode which served to emphasize the tenseness of the situation. The filibuster was in full swing; and Reed remarked sarcastically, "This is very much like tyranny," when Speaker Crisp repeatedly refused to entertain appeals from the Republican side. When, however, the minority leader had taken a place near the desk to supervise a roll call, he was called sharply to account. The Speaker, as was his right, declined all argument, and ordered his predecessor to be seated, directing the Sergeant-at-Arms to enforce the order.

Amid intense silence and before the shocked countenances of his followers, Reed marched back to his place. "The gentleman always obeys," was his only remark. "See Jumbo go back to his stake," remarked a Democratic member in a stage whisper. It is only fair to state that Crisp himself on March 4, 1890, had figured in a precisely similar incident; but Crisp in 1890 was, after all, not a very conspicuous person. Had Napoleon been marched off the parade ground in the custody of a gendarme, the feelings of the Guard would have doubtless resembled those of the Republicans on this occasion.

The filibuster went on and the majority strove desperately to maintain a quorum. The party whip cracked unsparingly; the officers of the House had never been so busy. The Democratic leaders begged for full attendance. The Speaker resorted to every parliamentary expedient to keep the legislative machinery in motion, but in vain. All the while Reed sat in his place, bland, smiling and implacable, waiting for the time when the Speaker would be obliged to take the final step and count a quorum. He spoke only infrequently, but his occasional sardonic comments peppered the majority leaders like a charge of rock salt from a ten-bore gun.

Early in April the contest entered its final phase. As Springer put it, "two days of actual work had not been accomplished in a month." The Democrats were at last without a quorum and Reed had them completely at his mercy. Under the Constitution one fifth of the members present had a right to demand a roll call. The rules of the House required approval of the Journal as one of the preliminaries of the day's business. The minority course was simple but effective. Approval of the Journal ceased to be a perfunctory matter of routine. When the Journal of the preceding day had been read, one of Reed's lieutenants promptly demanded the yeas and nays and under the Constitution the demand could not be denied. On the resultant roll call the silent Republicans broke the quorum and, with the Journal unapproved, business was at a standstill.

This parliamentary "merry-go-round" revolved slowly while the days passed. It was a time of happy anticipation for the Republicans, of chagrin and humiliation for their opponents. The frequent clashes between Speaker Crisp and the minority leader kept both members and spectators on edge with excitement and the galleries were crowded. The Committee on Rules on one occasion reported an amendment to the rules under which unexcused members were made liable to a fine of ten dollars for failure to vote on the question of approving the Journal. Reed blasted this proposal with the contemptuous comment that it was a mere attempt to turn the House into "a justice of the peace shop, with ten dollars jurisdiction, less than one half what we have in the little State of Maine." [1]

At last the majority held a caucus which decided to surrender to the inevitable, and on April 13 Springer presented a quorum-counting rule. Under its provisions the Speaker was authorized to appoint a teller from each side to note those present but not voting on roll calls, and on the basis of their report he was to declare a quorum. The use of tellers did not alter the essential fact that the present, rather than the voting, quorum was henceforth to be the authoritative source of legislation.

It was a bitter pill for the majority and it was not swallowed without protest. The Republicans of the 51st Congress had, as Russell of Georgia pointed out, been forced to adopt the rule because hard pressed for a majority; the Democrats of the 53rd had an ample majority and the humiliation was all the greater. William J. Bryan, as frequently happened, defended a lost cause, urging that "there is far more safety in giving to the minority the power to delay legislation until a majority have expressed themselves in favor of a law." Kilgore, of Texas, who had taken a spectacular part in the struggle of 1890, declared his unalterable opposition to any rule of which Reed was the parent, reiterating the arguments already long familiar to the older members of the House. The debate closed on April 17. Reed might have been excused had he taken advantage of the occasion to rub salt in the Democratic wounds, but he was satisfied with a few brief remarks. The scene before them was far more effective than

[1] *Ibid.,* 53 Cong., 2 Sess., 3707.

any address which he could make, he declared. "The House is about to adopt the principle for which we contended under circumstances which show its value to the country. I congratulate it upon the wise decision it is about to make." A few minutes later the rule was adopted and the value of one of his great reforms was formally recognized by his party opponents.

Cannon, however, showed less magnanimity than his chief, and taunted Speaker Crisp with surrendering his principles for expediency. In view of the fact that he had been elected largely because of his fervid opposition to the Reed rules he was now, in effect, "holding goods that he obtained under false pretenses." To the country at large, the change was generally acceptable, although *The Nation*, April 26, 1894, declared that "those distrusting representative institutions throughout the world will take comfort from the spectacle." In a few weeks the new system was working so successfully that the controversy seemed to belong to the remote past. Even the use of the tellers was soon dropped by tacit consent. Reed was a revolutionist who saw the results of his work incorporated into the institutions of his country·by the very men who had bitterly opposed it.

In the meantime the tariff bill had been reported by William L. Wilson, chairman of Ways and Means, on December 19. The minority of the committee, of which Reed was ranking member, presented a powerful dissenting report, and another historic contest began. The measure was far from radical in spite of all the free trade talk which had flourished since 1890, but protectionists believed that the bill was a serious threat to American industry and its income tax clauses, intended to meet possible losses in revenue from customs duties, were generally regarded in the Eastern states as a vicious product of Populism and sectional hostility. In the earlier stages of debate, while it was admitted that the Senate would make changes in any bill which passed the

JOSEPH G. CANNON

House, there was little realization of the mangling which the ill-fated measure was to encounter in the upper chamber.

Debate on the tariff bill proceeded throughout the month of January, in the course of which Reed had his most memorable clash with Bourke Cockran. On February 1, the bill passed the House by a decisive majority, and on that date, Reed reached what was perhaps the high point of his career when he closed the debate on behalf of the minority.

It was a memorable day in the history of the House. The only occasions in preceding years which could compare with it were the memorial exercises for President Garfield, when Blaine delivered that magnificent and touching eulogy, or the closing debate on the Mills Bill in 1888; and the crowd was greater than on either of those occasions. Years after, a witness described it as "the grand inquest of a free, sturdy people making an effort to conclude the deliberations of a generation," without pageantry, and heraldry, but with a profound interest in the affairs of government, and comparable with only one other occasion in American tariff history, that of forty-eight years before when George Evans, another man from Maine "greater than Reed, or Blaine, or even Fessenden," had grappled with McDuffie of South Carolina upon the Walker Bill which President Polk so determinedly drove through Congress.[1]

Many of the observers were reminded of historic scenes in the House of Commons, when the great orators of Parliament joined battle and ministries had fallen. The setting, however, was essentially American and no characteristic touches were lacking. The members had given out more gallery tickets than the space accommodated, and every place was occupied within a few minutes of the opening of the doors at nine o'clock. Thousands jammed the House wing of the Capitol and the lobbies were

[1] Washington *Post*, December 21, 1902.

crowded to suffocation. In the long forenoon wait the crowd became increasingly restless. Women fainted and were carried out. Men jammed the doors and tried to bribe the doorkeepers. Pickpockets reaped a harvest. So threatening did the situation become that the Sergeant-at-Arms summoned a squad of city police to assist the Capitol officers.

Within the chamber, in contrast with the turmoil in the corridors, all was peace and quiet, except for a brief diversion when a white man assaulted a negro who encroached on the precious foothold he had secured in the gallery. Members of the diplomatic corps and distinguished visitors appeared as the opening hour approached, and Cardinal Gibbons was noted among the guests in the Speaker's gallery. Most of the Senators were present, among them the venerable Senator Morrill who had fathered the great protective measure of 1861. The pressure for admission had now become so great that friends of the members were admitted to the floor of the House, a most unusual procedure. All but eleven members were present, so that even this measure afforded but slight relief.

The House met at eleven o'clock and the next hour was filled with routine business and discussion of minor points in the pending bill. Promptly at twelve o'clock, however, Reed took the floor amid a roar of cheering from the crowd. His address, contrary to his usual custom, had been carefully prepared, and John Dalzell sat by as prompter, printed slips ready at hand; but it was noted that in the course of the next two hours he had occasion to whisper a word only once or twice. Considering the length of the speech—over 15,000 words—it was a marvelous exhibition of memory, and yet it seemed to have all the fire and vigor of extemporaneous delivery.

"Never before," said the Washington *Post* next day, "had he or any other man faced such an audience in the House. The galleries, the floor, the aisles, the space in front of the Speaker's desk, the cloakrooms, and the area behind the desks were all filled with an intelligent, critical and expectant audience. His voice, as he began, was clear and distinct but not loud. He faced his foe—the Democratic side—and kept his eyes almost entirely upon his colleagues around him, rarely allowing his gaze to wander to the faces that peered over the galleries above him."

While perhaps less brilliant than his speech on the Mills Bill six years before, it was, on the whole, more analytical in tone and a most effective and closely reasoned defense of protection. *The Nation* on February 8, defending the Wilson Bill as a moderate measure which tended in the right direction, hinted that Reed's faith in protection was not altogether sound. He had admitted that the foreigner does not pay the tax, which was heresy; that there were two sides to the question, which was dangerous; he had given credit for national prosperity to resources, Providence and the wit of man, which was impious; he showed study of political economy, which was perilous. He was, however, apparently "sound on the main article, that by taxing ourselves lavishly we will all get rich."

It is unnecessary to discuss the speech at great length, especially as like the best of Reed's speeches it defies successful paraphrase or summary. The Wilson Bill, he began, was odious to both sides, inasmuch as it pretended to give protection without affording it and looked to free trade without attaining it. It would, if passed in its present form, aggravate the uncertainty and depression which prevailed throughout the land.

Protection had justified itself in American history. In spite of a great war and its aftermath, in spite of disordered currency, prosperity had increased until, admitting temporary depression, we were nevertheless the envy of the world. English observers saw no limits to the increase of our national well-being. There had been a great rise in real wages. "I confess to you that this question of wages is to me the vital question. To insure our growth in civilization and wealth we must not only have wages as high as they are now, but constantly and steadily increasing." This was not due to any love for the individual but to interest in the welfare of the whole nation, mere enlightened selfishness. "In my judgment, upon wages and the consequent distribution of consumable wealth is based all hopes of the future and the possible increase of our civilization. The progress of this nation is dependent upon the progress of all. This is no new thought with me."

This was not a civilization of nobles and slaves and there must be a general elevation of the level of the whole group. High wages would tend to obliterate class distinctions. There was no real analogy between British and American conditions, and the fight on the Corn Laws which had so aroused the Democrats was entirely misunderstood by "our wiseacres who are reading British books of forty years ago with the emotions of great discoverers," a shot intended for Bourke Cockran. The Corn Law contest had been a struggle between manufacturers and land owners, the former understanding that a decrease in the cost of food was the equivalent of an increase in wages for their employees. Replying to Bourke Cockran's contention that it was shameful for the high American civilization to confess that it could not meet the competition of lower civilizations, he delivered some pungent and effective sentences:

Now it is a great truth that civilization can successfully meet barbarism, but it must do it with brains and not with rhetoric. How often have I heard this and similar eloquent outbursts about our superiority, and therefore inevitable conquest of the inferior. Survival of the superior! That is not the way the naturalist put it! "Survival of the fittest" was his expression; survival of the fittest to survive, not the superior, not the loveliest, not the most intellectual, but the one who

fitted best into the surroundings. Compare the strong Bull of
Bashan with a salt-water smelt. Who doubts the superiority
of the bull? Yet, if you drop them both into the Atlantic
Ocean, I will take my chances with the smelt. [Laughter.]
A little tomtit, insignificant as a bit of dust in the balance, cannot compare with the domestic swan either in grace, beauty,
or power. Yet if both were dropped from a balloon hung high
in the air, I would rather be the insignificant tomtit than the
graceful swan. If I had a job to dig on a railway, the com-
petitor for that job whom I should fear would not be my
friend from New York (Mr. Cockran) [laughter], but some
child of sunny Italy so newly imported that he had not grown
up to the wages of this adopted country.

Again and again he reverted to the matter of wages. The question of their maintenance, he declared, was an all important
factor in consumption. "All production depends on consumption.
Who are the consumers? In the old days, when the products of
manufactures were luxuries, the lord and his retainers, the lady
and her maids, were the consumers, a class apart by themselves;
but today the consumers are the producers. Long ago the laborer
consumed only what would keep him alive. Today he and his
wife and their children are so immeasurably the most valuable
consumers, that if the shop had to give up the wealthy or those
whom it is the custom to call poor, there would not be a moment's
hesitation or a moment's doubt." The Democrats, he added, were
working on the idea that producers were in one class and consumers in another. The Wilson Bill proposed in effect to lower
wages and so lessen the market, but "men in America demand
high and higher wages because their surroundings create what
used to be luxuries into necessities."

The tariff, Reed argued, promoted diversification of industry.
Diversified industry educated people, raised the level of civilization, and encouraged invention. There were always induce-

ments to inventors in a land of high wages, for invention is born of necessity and there was always pressure for lower costs of production. Again his speech became pungent:

To hear the discussion in Congress you would suppose that invention dropped from Heaven like manna to the Jews. [Laughter.] You would suppose that James Watt reached out into the darkness and pulled back a steam-engine. It was not so. All invention is the product of necessity and of pressure. When the boy who wanted to go off to play so rigged the stop-cocks that the engine went itself, he was not only a true inventor, but he had the same motive—personal advantage—that all inventors have, and like them was urged on by business necessities.

As for the farmer, "if, with cities growing up like magic, manufacturing villages dotting every eligible site, each and all swarming with mouths to be filled, the producers are worse off than when half this country was a desert, I abandon sense in favor of political economy."

When he concluded his speech Reed left the hall at once, amid a tremendous ovation, and a page who hurried forward with a huge floral tribute from admirers was obliged to place it on an empty desk. Honors of the day were divided with Wilson, who followed, making an address on behalf of his bill so able that many listeners considered it superior even to Reed's. His stirring plea for party unity aroused vast enthusiasm and at its conclusion Bryan, John Sharp Williams, and other followers carried the orator from the scene of his triumph upon their shoulders, while the Democrats joined in a frantic demonstration of approval. All in all, it was a great scene in the annals of revenue legislation. A few days later, the Washington *Post* made some ironical comments on the Wilson triumph, declaring that while Mr. Reed might easily create a furore in the next Congress "he

will be lifted on no man's shoulders and be made ridiculous by
no unnatural elevation. Mr. Reed's bulk protects him. He may
be the Moses, the Solomon, the David, and the Joshua of his
party, but never at his present weight, its Balaam."

It is unnecessary to follow the tortuous legislative course of
the unfortunate Wilson Bill. Month after month passed while
the lobbyists got in their work and the Senators bargained and
wrangled, finally passing the measure on July 3. The bill as
it emerged from the upper chamber with over six hundred
amendments was hardly recognizable. On July 7 the House
voted to non-concur in the Senate amendments, Reed objecting
strenuously to the drastic limitations which the majority imposed
on debate. The Senate amendments had, he argued, made great
changes in principle, introducing a larger element of protection
and abandoning the principle of free raw material. The limitation on debate in the case of the McKinley Bill did not constitute
a precedent, for in that case the Senate changes were merely in
matters of detail.

He had little comfort for the chairman of Ways and Means.
"I am glad to have him utter this note of defiance to the Senate,
and yet I am perfectly confident, as is every member of this
House, that it is the last outcry that will be uttered by him or
by his side." His insistence on free raw material was an absurdity. Free raw material was not to be found on the face of the
earth:

It is a mere chimera; a mere illusion of the schoolmen, which
the moment it got before these practical gentlemen in the Senate, men of business, "men with difficulties," vanished, leaving
not a wrack behind. And when they get into the conference
committee those practical business men, with their "difficulties," will confront the gentleman from West Virginia, and
confront him at shorter range, and will obliterate him more ef-
fectually than they have already done.

On July 19, Wilson reported that the conferees were unable to agree and the House voted to insist on its disagreement. It was on this occasion that Wilson read into the record President Cleveland's famous letter on "party perfidy and party dishonor," giving Reed an opportunity for some sarcastic comments on the internal harmony of the Democratic party. He had no expectation that the House conferees could accomplish anything, for, as he put it in one of his characteristic comments, "they are contending not with idealists, not with individuals with a theory, but with individuals who have definite purposes, definite aims, definite motives; gentlemen who know precisely on which side their provisions are buttered."

Three weeks passed in futile discussion and equally futile conference, the Senate stubbornly refusing to give way. Finally the House became alarmed when the Senate showed signs of breaking off the conference, and on August 13 adopted a special rule providing for concurrence in the Senate amendments and immediate action on the bill. There was a somewhat complicated parliamentary situation, and the anxiety of the House to claim possession of the measure led Reed to remark to a friend: "I have heard of people eating crow, but I never heard of people stealing the crow in order to eat it."

The adoption of the special rule meant that the fight for tariff reform was practically over. The Senators had acted precisely as Reed had predicted they would act. Wilson made a somewhat pathetic attempt at palliation, declaring that in spite of the amendments, the bill afforded some relief to the taxpayers, and did something to "clip the wings of the gigantic monopolies" that were blocking legislation. Not much can be said, however, for the introduction and passage of "pop-gun bills" for free sugar, coal, iron and barbed wire, which everybody knew had not the remotest chance of ever becoming law.

Reed gave no quarter and in the whole course of twenty-two

years in the House he probably never appeared to greater advantage than in the last hours of this great tariff debate; and it was noted that he at times imparted special solemnity to his words by sinking his voice "almost to a whisper without impairing the distinctness of his enunciation. The effect was electric." [1]

But as usual he was at his best in his satirical comments on Democratic policy. As he rose to reply to Wilson, pointing out that the majority was about to enact a bill which they believed to be dishonest, in spite of all protestations and threats of resistance to the end, there was considerable disturbance on the other side, and demands for the vote. "I think your feeling is perfectly natural," he remarked in his usual drawling tone. "The job that you have got to do is such that the sooner you get it over the better you will feel. [Laughter and cries of Vote! Vote! on the Democratic side.] But at the same time you will have to listen to a plain statement of what you are doing, and you will recognize it yourselves, and it is because you recognize it in advance that you are crying, 'Vote! Vote! Vote!' Your class of people in the latter day will be crying, in similar fashion, for the mountains to fall on them."

Debate continued throughout the day, the "pop-gun bills" giving Reed a wonderful opportunity for characteristic thrusts. His opponents on one occasion became so enraged that he was moved to comment on the fact that the majority members were not "in their usually sweet temper," and to express his concern lest "something they have eaten has perhaps disagreed with them." "I remember well," he declared some months later, "how every time I rose that day I thought how much they looked like a grainfield devastated by a hailstorm." The free sugar bill was finally reached. It was, said Reed, "the last of the air-cushions which the statesmen of this little kingdom of Lilliput,

[1] Washington *Post*, August 14, 1894.

in which we are now living, have arranged for themselves to tumble on this evening."

The tariff reform fiasco was over and the party was shortly afterwards turned out to wander in the wilderness for almost twenty years. "Why," asked Reed, as the debate closed, "cannot the Democratic party once in a while at least be middling honest?" For the estimable William L. Wilson the outcome was disastrous. As Reed said in his Cooper Union speech on October 13, the Democratic Senator from Maryland [Gorman] "had stripped him of his armor and dragged him about the walls of Troy."

While Reed's course on the repeal of the Silver Purchase Act and currency questions in general had been thoroughly statesmanlike and consistent with his own record on previous issues, before the close of the second session he committed what, both from the personal and political standpoint, can only be considered a serious blunder. In June, 1894, the *Fortnightly Review* published under the title "Silver and the Tariff at Washington" an interview with the ex-Speaker. The significance of Mr. Reed's utterance was stressed. There was a strong probability, said the English editor, that the next administration would be Republican and "Mr. Reed's popularity, great services, and strong individuality distinguished him as the candidate of his party for the Presidency." The interview, he added, "indicates an important development in the economic policy of his party."

According to the interviewer, Reed suggested that if England desired the United States to lower the tariff she should be willing to give something in exchange. "Will you open your mints to the free coinage of silver by international agreement?" The Republicans, he explained, would not be found ready to turn the other cheek as the Democrats had done. The latter were proposing to lower the customs duties in spite of the fact that the Indian mints had been closed to free coinage and a duty imposed on imports of silver bullion to that country. The exports of Asiatic countries were stimulated by cheap silver and the result was especially detrimental to the American farmer.

It was important for the debtor nations, and the United States was the leading one, to raise the price of silver and thereby reduce "the bounty on Asiatic exports." The silver and tariff were not two distinct issues but a single one, and it would be a desirable thing for those states which were friendly to bimetallism to form a tariff union with reciprocity as the reward for free coinage of silver. By raising the tariff against those nations which rejected the monetary agreement, the debtor states would eventually secure a favorable balance of trade.[1]

Henry Cabot Lodge, who at this time had leanings toward international bimetallism, had already made a similar suggestion, *The Nation* of May 3, 1894, declaring that nothing could be "crazier or more anarchical." This journal, then at the height of its influence and the leading organ of intelligent conservative opinion, promptly turned its fire on the *Fortnightly* article, declaring the free silver-reciprocity suggestion on a par with that of Æsop's fox who wanted all his fellows to cut off their tails. Reed's deliverance, in view of "his excellent reputation on financial questions," had been a great surprise to the country. As Speaker, the editor continued, he had used his power to prevent the adoption of a silver bill and as minority leader he had promptly suppressed Burrows's suggestion that the Republicans keep silent and permit the adoption of bad measures.

The Washington *Post* on June 1 reported that the *Fortnightly* article was the subject of much interesting discussion by members of the House and quoted Bryan as remarking: "If Mr. Reed is really interested in the restoration of silver he might show it in ways not so obviously intended to benefit the protected industries." In an editorial on June 8, the *Post* declared that the coun-

[1] *Fortnightly Review*, LV, 837–38.

try was not proving responsive to Reed's scheme, that the Maine platform ignored it, that the Republican press was cautious in receiving it, and "what he probably hoped for was the unification of his own political household."

In view of Reed's subsequent fortunes in the presidential contest and the Republican stand on the currency question in 1896, it is worth noting that *The Nation* on June 28, 1894, reported that at that date not a single Republican State Convention had made a straightforward declaration in favor of sound money and against further trifling with "the disastrous and dangerous free silver delusion." Kansas, Maine and Vermont had adopted "various degrees of bimetallic nonsense adapted to the respective localities," California was for free silver, and Ohio and Indiana for the Lodge-Reed plan. On August 2, however it reported that the latter was "visibly wilting" and "the author was reported to be sick and ashamed of it." In any case, the First Maine District in renominating him had adopted a thoroughly good financial plank.

While Congress was wrangling over the Wilson Bill and the miscellaneous business of the session, the maintenance of national credit had become increasingly difficult. Business prostration continued and the revenues were entirely inadequate. The third and last session of the 53rd Congress began amid intense gloom and with opinions of members hopelessly divided on currency questions. The Senate majority was committed to free silver.

In spite of heavy borrowing by the Treasury the drain of gold continued and in January, 1895, the situation again became acute. On January 28, President Cleveland in a special message urged that Congress authorize the issue of fifty-year bonds at three per cent, payable principal and interest in gold. "We should," said the President, "be relieved from the humiliating process of issuing bonds to procure gold to be immediately and repeatedly drawn out on these obligations for purposes not related to the benefit of our Government or our people." He therefore urged the redemption and cancellation of the United States legal tender notes and of the Treasury notes issued under provision of the Silver Purchase Act. On the following day Springer introduced a bill giving effect to the President's recommendations, and the measure was made a special order on February 4.

Reed's position in the matter of national credit was entirely orthodox. "A nation's credit is its great stronghold. Disasters may happen to a nation. Democratic Administrations may occur to it. Everything is possible within human affairs. Under such circumstances the most precious thing in this world is a nation's credit, and it ought always to preserve it if it can." [1] He was not, however, satisfied with the Springer Bill and offered a substitute providing for the redemption of United States notes by the issue of three per cent bonds payable in "coin" and with "like qualities, privileges and exemptions" provided for bonds under the Specie Resumption Act of January 14, 1875. For the payment of the current expenses of the Government, the substitute proposed to authorize the issue of interest bearing certificates of indebtedness.

In defending his proposal Reed attributed much of the existing demoralization to unwise legislation which had produced a great deficiency in the revenues. The Treasury was really engaged in two distinct activities. It was at once a banking and an ordinary business establishment. The misfortunes of the second had affected the first. The business department had been obliged to take the money of the banking department and reissue it; hence the "endless chain" by which "the United States has been made the furnisher of gold for the rest of the world, a condition of things never contemplated by our system of finance." He did not consider it necessary to go into general financial and currency legislation as the Springer Bill did.

The remedy which he proposed was, he continued, simple,

[1] *Cong. Record,* 53 Cong., 3 Sess., 2199.

and it avoided many of the most serious difficulties. A more favorable state of affairs would inevitably result when the two main transactions of the Government were separated and the people of the United States and the rest of the world could see what was going on. The Republicans might be in favor of making revenue equal to expenditures but they were willing to forego that. "These difficulties in the way of raising revenue arise from a pride, if I can call it pride, in the present advantageous tariff bill. A proposition to raise revenue would be, in a certain sense, a confession, and confession would perhaps be suicide."

The main thing, he concluded, was to keep the deficiencies in revenue from running into the gold account, and the issue of certificates of indebtedness would achieve that end. It would also, in the long run, prove more economical than the long time gold bonds for which the Government would eventually be obliged to pay a heavy premium when it was in a position to begin retirement. "Now, why is not that the solution of our problem without raising vexed questions which we know cannot be solved?" The substitute bill was rejected, however, and the Springer Bill itself met the same fate.

Reed's friends always believed that his bill could have passed the Senate and claimed authoritative assurances to that effect. Cannon, in the debate on February 14, declared that the Reed substitute bill, "the only one which had the remotest chance to pass Congress, and which would have wrought the necessary cure to the Treasury," had been done to death at the command of the Secretary of the Treasury and the President.

The failure of the Springer Bill was followed by announcement of the famous contract between the Treasury and the Morgan-Belmont banking syndicate. President Cleveland in his message of February 8, announcing the terms of the contract, pointed out that "there never should be a doubt in any quarter as to the redemption in gold of the bonds of the Government which are made payable in coin," and that the discrimination made by investors in favor of those specifically payable in gold was "very significant." "The sentiments or preferences of those with whom we must negotiate in disposing of our bonds for gold," he added, "are not subject to our dictation." The discrimination in favor of "gold" three per cent bonds as compared with the four per cent "coin" bonds authorized under the Act of 1875, amounted to more than half a million per annum in interest charges.

On February 13, the Ways and Means Committee introduced a resolution authorizing the Secretary of the Treasury to issue the necessary amount of three per cent bonds "payable in gold coin of the present standard of weight and fineness." The resolution started a protracted debate, much of it irrelevant, in which the coinage question and the conduct of the administration were discussed at length. There was a hopelessly complicated struggle of opinions in Congress. Inflation, in one form or another, was the object of many members, who were sufficiently numerous to make effective opposition to any act which implied recognition of an inferior status for silver.

The basic cleavage of opinion was brought out by William J. Bryan in the course of debate when he declared that the existing union of Eastern Democrats and Republicans would force the rest of the country into a new alignment "to preserve their homes and welfare." He was speaking against a form of oppression. "The demand of our Eastern brethren, both Republicans and Democrats, is for a steadily appreciating monetary standard. They are creditors; they hold our bonds and mortgages, and as the dollars increase in purchasing power, our debts increase and the holders of our bonds and mortgages gather in an unearned increment. They are seeking to reap where they did not sow; they are seeking to collect that to which they are not entitled; they favor spoliation under the forms of law."

Reed replied defiantly to Bryan's threat of a union of West and South, and gave somewhat grudging support to the proposed gold bond resolution. The government had always paid in gold or its equivalent and would continue to do so, he declared. He apparently felt, however, that the issue of these special gold bonds might have some adverse effects on the other issues outstanding. Yet he voted for the resolution. It was decisively beaten. Bryan's prediction as to the collapse of existing party lines seemed in process of fulfillment, for only 31 Republicans followed Reed in support of the resolution and 63 voted against it. The Democrats were more evenly divided with 89 for and 94 against.

While Reed's record on the currency question had been distinctly creditable and entirely consistent with views which he had always expressed, his attitude toward international bimetallism and his "coin" substitute for the Springer Bill created an element of doubt in various quarters which was to work to his political injury for some months to come.

On July 30, 1895, Theodore Roosevelt wrote to Senator Lodge: "I regret more and more all the time that Tom Reed did not make a strong anti-free coinage speech when he voted for the Gold Bonds. Had he done so, and come out in a ringing speech as the champion of sound money, there would not now be the slightest opposition to him in New York. . . ." Roosevelt was a better politician than Reed.

President Cleveland remained the great and redoubtable champion of the gold standard. "There was never a more brutish Congress than the one now in session," said *The Nation* on February 21, 1895, and it is hard to find fault with this judgment. Like all things mortal it at last came to a close. It had accomplished little or nothing to relieve the country's distress, and March 3 probably brought a sense of relief to a great majority of thinking people throughout the land.

"THE Democratic mortality will be so great next Fall," Reed predicted during the spring of 1894, "that their dead will be buried in trenches and marked 'unknown.' " [1] Later he amended this prediction by adding "until the supply of trenches gives out." He took a prominent part in the campaign, speaking at various places in the Eastern States and, in October, throughout the Middle West, being received with great enthusiasm wherever he appeared. The press followed his progress watchfully and his speeches were reported with considerable care. He was of course regarded everywhere as a potential candidate for the presidency in 1896.

Reed's speeches during this campaign were decidedly conservative in tone, especially in regard to the tariff. In an interview published in an Ann Arbor, Michigan, newspaper he was reported to have repudiated certain features of the McKinley tariff of 1890, and while he denied some of the printed allegations, there was widespread feeling that the next presidential election would see the tariff issue relegated to a much less prominent place and that Reed's attitude was highly significant.[2]

On November 15, *The Nation* quoted Senator John Sherman to the effect that recent election results were not to be considered as an indorsement of the McKinley tariff or as constituting a demand for radical action, his views being "substantially what Reed admitted in the campaign." The Hawaiian issue, the editor declared, was likely to die out; the tariff issue was moribund; since after thirty years the Republicans had learned that force

[1] Washington *Post,* April 14, 1894.
[2] For comments see New York *Times,* October 18, 19, *Tribune,* October 20, *World,* October 20, 23, *The Nation,* October 25, 1894.

could not give the black man his rights in the South, the sectional question was unlikely to constitute an important issue from now on. What could take their places? The currency question. Let the Republican party dispense with the mining camps. It did not need them. Let it have a platform for rational currency reform.

Looking back on the situation after the lapse of almost forty years the wisdom of this recommendation is evident, but to contemporaries in 1894 the situation hardly seemed as simple as it now appears.

The result of the elections of 1894 proved the soundness of Reed's prediction, and when all was over it was seen that the next House would contain 245 Republicans and 104 Democrats, together with 8 Populists and "Silverites." When the members of the 54th Congress began to gather toward the end of November a year later, Reed was a center of attraction and his quarters at the Shoreham were thronged. He had spent the summer on the seashore and was in fine health and spirits. He had shaved his mustache and there was speculation as to whether its disappearance had some mysterious political significance. Another explanation, however, was to the effect that he had gone to sleep in the House barber-shop and the barber, taking advantage of his helpless condition, had waxed the points of the cherished mustache. Reed, according to this story, took one horrified glance at his reflection in the glass and commanded: "Shave that mustache off, you've made me look like a darned catfish."

When the caucus met on November 30, he was renominated for the speakership. Representative Foss of Chicago, on behalf of the Hamilton Club, presented him with a new gavel and in the course of his remarks explained that its bands of gold and silver represented "that other great principle of Republican faith—bimetallism. Protection and bimetallism have always been the watchwords of the Republican party." [1] The reference to this symbolism is not without significance.

Next day Reed was formally elected Speaker and once more took his place in the chair. A great crowd had gathered expecting, in all probability, that the Speaker would make some characteristic references to the circumstances under which he had last appeared in that position, or that he might let fall some remarks which would have a bearing on the presidential campaign. If so, they were disappointed, for he confined himself to a few general statements appreciative of the honor conferred and expressing hope for a productive and harmonious session.

The end of the long fight for reform of the rules passed almost unnoticed when, on the same day, the rules of the 51st Congress were adopted practically without debate. It marked, however, the successful conclusion of the struggle which Reed had begun in 1882 and had waged unceasingly for the past thirteen years.

The committees were announced on December 21, and the membership was carefully scanned in order to discover their political significance. Dingley became chairman of Ways and Means, Cannon of Appropriations and Henderson of Judiciary. There was little criticism of the assignments, and the Washington *Post* on December 23 reported that opinion was general that "as working committees they could hardly be improved." The appointment of Dingley attracted considerable attention, and speculation was rife as to why John Dalzell of Pennsylvania or Sereno E. Payne of New York had not received this important place in view of the power of those States in the nominating convention. The Speaker, however, had every confidence in Dingley because of the latter's long experience in handling revenue matters and his deserved reputation as a master of the subject.

[1] Washington *Post,* December 1, 1895.

Where, other things being equal, political advantage might result from an appointment, Reed would make it, but on the whole his primary consideration was always to secure an effective working organization of the House.

With Cleveland still in the White House and a presidential campaign impending there was little likelihood that the 54th Congress would initiate a legislative program of importance. The Venezuelan flurry caused by the President's message of December 17, 1895, disturbed the opening weeks of the session. More than a year before Reed had made an ironical reference to "Hawaii and a firm foreign policy" in one of his published articles criticizing the administration, but no obstacle was interposed to a resolution authorizing the appointment of the boundary commission requested by the President. The Venezuelan affair was unfortunate in its effects on business and Reed afterwards wrote of it as "the Venezuelan war cloud" which brought "a chilling frost" on reviving prosperity.[1]

Reed's second speakership, however, is merely a background for the story of the presidential campaign of 1896, and the 54th Congress had little more constructive work to its credit than had the 52nd. The Republican majority was so large that the Speaker was confronted with few of the problems he had been obliged to face six years before. In some respects this result was unfortunate. Reed had made a reputation as a daring, resourceful leader and there was now little opportunity for him to display his peculiar abilities. It was also difficult to keep the unwieldy majority in line, and more than once party cohesion was seriously threatened.

Reed was watched carefully by the Washington correspondents and he soon found that, like all potential candidates, his smallest action and his slightest utterance were weighed in the light of his presidential ambitions. It was not a situation in which

[1] New York *World*, September 12, 1897.

the Speaker was likely to appear at his best, and it was not long before the newspaper men and others noted a change. The representative of the St. Louis *Globe-Democrat* dealt with it at some length. Reed, he wrote, was no longer frankly humorous and sarcastic; he no longer commented freely on current affairs for the correspondents who questioned him. He was as friendly as ever, but caution was apparent in all that he did and said. There was evidence that he felt "a necessity of taking himself seriously, of presenting an impressive aspect, of looking as wise as he can with that cherubic countenance," and if for several months he was "to play a sober and taciturn part," it would be a matter of national regret that he ever allowed the presidential bee to get into his bonnet. It was to be expected, however. "He does not dare to indulge his remarkable drollery when a crisp joke may cost him a delegate or a fine bit of irony turn a State against him. It is a great pity and a public loss that this could not have been avoided. At most there is little brightness in our politics, and the suspension of Mr. Reed's surpassing service in that relation leaves us poor indeed, and at a time, too, when we particularly need that sort of thing as a relief from the dull and tiresome speeches that are sure to be made during the present session of Congress."

The Washington *Post* on February 23 described him as having gone through a "remarkable metamorphosis," being now inclined to "Harrisonian exclusiveness," cracking no jokes, avoiding his colleagues, and "stalking along the Avenue, all by himself, thoughtful, unobserving, wrapped in solemn grandeur and his own greatness." As a matter of fact, Reed's conduct in 1895 was as free from pose as it had been in 1890. He refused to do anything which might remotely resemble solicitation of influence or support. The course of congressional business offered no opportunity for the display of those qualities which had made him the man of the hour six years before.

Reed had apparently adopted "business as usual" as his guiding maxim, and the House followed the routine of a quiet session. It was not entirely smooth sailing and Cannon, with all his courage and his devotion to sound finance, found that his earnest demands for economy made little impression in spite of the fact that continued business depression rendered extravagance dangerous. Before the session was over he paid a deserved tribute to the Speaker, declaring that "except for his strong restraining influence" Congress would appropriate more than ever before. "He does not stop to think about his candidacy at all. If he did, he would not day after day deny the appeals of members who say they must have certain appropriations or they cannot be reelected, and cannot cultivate in their districts any sentiment favorable to the nomination of Mr. Reed." [1]

It was a matter of common note around the Capitol that Congressmen who sought to secure promises of recognition for private bills got little encouragement from the Speaker. "I reserve the right to see you or not," was his usual response. "The bill will not be allowed to come up even with that Reed button in your coat," was the blunt reply to another member who applied for favor. [2]

Reed undoubtedly desired the presidency. He was entirely free from vanity in the ordinary sense of the term, but he was also conscious of his own power and capacity. He had by his sheer ability and strength of character secured a dominant place in American public life. He could not but have realized to the full how greatly his services in the 52nd and 53rd Congresses had contributed to the sweeping Republican victory of 1894. Party rehabilitation owed more to him than to any other leader. Whether or not he had strong hopes of securing the great prize

[1] Quoted in *Kennebec Journal,* April 2, 1896.
[2] Washington *Post,* May 1, 1896.

is uncertain, but one of his remarks on the subject has often been quoted. To a friend who inquired whether he expected to receive the Republican nomination he replied: "They might do worse, and they probably will."

Taking his career as a whole and considering his long service to the country, the contest for the nomination in 1896 is little more than an episode, unfortunate in some respects, but illustrating in admirable fashion some of Reed's essential qualities. As a party leader he had elements of strength and weakness and both appeared in the course of the two years preceding the decision of the St. Louis convention on June 18, 1896.

On June 12, 1896, when the delegates had begun to gather in St. Louis, and when McKinley's nomination was everywhere accepted as inevitable, the Washington *Post* raised the question as to why Reed's boom had gone awry. At the close of the last Congress, "the field was his alone"; he had been "the strongest candidate" inasmuch as "the leading issue was to be financial." He had the backing of many men in Congress and others throughout the country who had been notably successful in political management. From first to last, however, the Reed campaign had disregarded "all that tends to give political status preliminary to a convention." While criticizing Reed's friends and managers the *Post* suggested that it was doubtful just how far Reed himself was to blame for the outcome.

There can be little doubt, however, when the history of the campaign is examined. Reed had won his place in Congress by sheer ability and not by political manipulation. He had never been conciliatory, he had never cultivated sentimental ties, he had often been criticized as lacking warmth and geniality. "But he commands everything," as a departing Congressman put it after adjournment in March, 1895, "by the brutality of his intellect." Contemporary opinion was very general that if the nomination or election had depended on the House of Representatives, Reed would have won the presidency as readily as the speakership.

But to win the support of a national party organization was a very different matter. That party organization represented a vast array of local and personal interests, often discordant and usually greedy and self-seeking. Reed could handle such a situation in the House. He might concede, he might accept decisions of which he did not wholly approve, but he always retained the whip hand, and always he endeavored to follow a course which would best serve the interests of the country. To win a presidential nomination, however, required pledges and commitments. Furthermore, it required money and money could be secured only by multiplying and strengthening those same pledges and commitments. For work of this type Reed was constitutionally disqualified, nor would he allow others to do it for him.

His philosophy of government and his views on economic issues would have made him eminently satisfactory to the business interests of the country. He believed in protection and no man, in Congress or out, had defended it more effectively. His record in financial matters had been excellent. His keen mind had grasped the causes of the recurring periods of distress, and his sharp tongue had mercilessly exposed the futility of the nostrums which political quacks were peddling throughout the country as remedies. In political availability, however, Reed's status was not so secure. He lacked a national following among the voters. He was well known and respected, and he drew great audiences while on the stump; but more was needed to produce a following which could muster votes in the national convention. Mark Hanna grasped this essential fact, and as his latest biographer has pointed out, gave no little time to learning the impression which Reed had made on the rank and file of the Western Republicans. That they believed Reed "stuck-up" might be merely a colloquial acknowledgment of his intellectual superiority, but from the standpoint of practical politics it had immense possibilities, and Hanna proceeded to utilize them for the benefit of William McKinley.

From a strictly rational and objective standpoint, Reed, from 1893 to 1896, had vastly more to recommend him for the presidency than McKinley, but that is never the standpoint of party managers or of the voters at large. The panic of 1893 and the depression which followed had produced a remarkable revulsion in public sentiment. The McKinley tariff of 1890 had been a thoroughly unpopular enactment; sentiment was then running strongly against protection. As the depression continued, however, protection and prosperity became more and more associated in the popular mind. The currency issue was less clearly understood and until late in the pre-convention campaign there were many who expected, at the most, merely an ambiguous plank in the Republican platform. McKinley had made a name for himself as a protectionist, and his backers used every art in stimulating public sentiment in his favor. He had the personal qualities which made him understandable to the mass of the voters, and when these advantages were supplemented by a powerful organization, commanded by a veritable Napoleon of practical politics, the outcome was certain.

At the beginning of 1895 Reed's prospects seemed excellent. Party magnates like Quay and Cameron of Pennsylvania, Platt of New York, Carter of Montana, Samuel Fessenden of Connecticut, William E. Chandler of New Hampshire and others, were reported to be sympathetic. Senator Henry Cabot Lodge was an early and vigorous promoter of Reed's campaign. Joseph H. Manley of Maine, secretary of the Republican national committee, declared himself in favor of Reed, stating, however, that his position on the committee, being wholly executive, could not be used to push any man's candidacy. Senators Frye and Hale came out in his favor, although he had not been on friendly terms with either. As late as October 16, 1895, a contributor to the Washington *Post* declared that Reed was well ahead of McKinley, Allison, Sherman, Harrison and all other candidates, and that while his strength was sure to breed bitter opposition, he "could not be beaten in fair and open fight." Theodore Roosevelt published articles in *The Century* and *The Forum*, recounting the Speaker's great services in the cause of sound money and parliamentary reform, which attracted widespread attention and were considered direct contributions to Reed's campaign. Scattered throughout the country he had some journalistic support and influential personal followers, but the campaign which was now under way was to be decided not by literary efforts or appeals from the stump, but by the sheer force of carefully planned and ruthlessly executed organization, coupled with one of those tidal movements of public opinion which nothing could stay.

As a matter of practical politics the "favorite son" movements also promised some advantage to Reed. Senator Allison of Iowa, Senator Cullom of Illinois, Levi P. Morton of New York and Senator Quay of Pennsylvania were all convention possibilities and on April 19, 1895, Reed wrote to Senator Lodge asking if he would consider it wise to encourage a favorite son movement in Minnesota.[1] Cushman K. Davis was popular in the latter State. Could Reed secure the united support of New England, a majority of the delegates from the Pacific slope, where his chances for a time seemed promising, and scattering support from other parts of the country, there would be an opportunity for the combinations and strategic operations which had been effective in so many preceding conventions. As early as May, 1895, however, it was reported that McKinley sentiment was growing rapidly even in New England and that both New Hampshire and Connecticut were wavering.

[1] *Lodge Papers.*

While Joseph H. Manley was in general direction of Reed's interests, the active management of his campaign was in the hands of Representative J. Frank Aldrich, an energetic Chicagoan then serving his second term in the House. His committee room in Washington was Reed's headquarters during the months preceding the convention. It was, Aldrich says, "a labor of love"; his father had been a colleague of Reed's in the House in the late seventies and early eighties, and both father and son were devoted admirers of Reed. Probably no manager has ever, in all our presidential campaigns, been confronted with quite the same conditions.

It is easy to explain Reed's loss of the nomination by putting the responsibility on Hanna, in much the same fashion as a group of former Union officers once decided, after protracted debate upon the loss of Chancellorsville, to lay the blame on Stonewall Jackson. Reed, however, contributed to the outcome by the standards which he set for the conduct of his own campaign, and, as is now evident, by his failure to realize in time the importance of seizing the currency question as the leading issue, and driving home to the American people, as no one else was so well qualified to do, the incalculable evils which would accompany any deviation from the gold standard. "I was familiar with all the incidents of his candidacy," wrote Henry Cabot Lodge, "and I know how he declined to promise offices from the cabinet down or to spend money to secure Southern delegates. He lost the nomination, but he kept his honor pure and his high conception of public duty unstained and unimpaired." Lodge believed that McKinley had made improper promises of office in exchange for support.

It followed, naturally enough, that if Reed refused to accept financial assistance, or to make pledges in return for political support, any elaborate organization or large-scale campaigning activities were precluded from the very beginning. He did per-

mit a very few intimate friends to contribute to his cause and a
fund of about $12,000 was raised. He often told his Portland
friends and associates in after years that he could have had several hundred thousand had he cared to accept. He refused to
make the nomination a matter of bargain and sale and years later
Mr. Aldrich vividly remembered some occurrences during these
months which cannot be better stated than in his own words.[1]

In the campaign of 1896 Collis P. Huntington sent for me
three times—that is to say he asked his "man Friday," a Mr.
Boyd, who was the recognized lobbyist of the Huntington
(Southern Pacific Railroad) interests in Washington, to request
me to call upon him at the Normandie Hotel. I paid no attention to it until the third request came. I then went to Mr. Reed
and told him that Huntington had for the third time asked
me to call upon him. "Why don't you go and see him?" drawled
Reed. "Well, I think I know what he wants of me," said I.
"What do you think he wants of you?" drawled Reed again.
"I think he wants to make a contribution to your campaign
fund," said I. "Well, now, if I were you, I'd call on him. You'll
find him interesting in many ways; he'll talk to you of art and
music and a variety of things. I regard Mr. Huntington as one
of the brainy men of the country, one of the biggest men in
the country; go and see him but remember," and he held up
his index finger, pointed it at me and continued, "Not one
dollar from Mr. Huntington for my campaign fund!"

I did find him, as Reed said I would, most entertaining. He
talked of a number of things and finally blurted out, "How
are you getting along with Mr. Reed's campaign?" "Oh," I
said, "about as well as can perhaps be expected under all the
circumstances." "Have you got any money?" said he. "No,"
I replied, "none to speak of. You know Mr. Reed is—well,
you know him I guess—he doesn't believe in these large campaign expenditures and wouldn't permit us to accept anything
but a few paltry contributions by a few of his very personal
friends." As a matter of fact our expenditures were just about

[1] Letter to author, November 7, 1929.

$12,000, and I suppose Mark Hanna spent a million. Mr. Huntington was disgusted. "Why, you can't run a campaign without money," he said. "I know it, but Mr. Reed will not sanction it." "Why," interrupted Mr. Huntington, "the others [the McKinley and Allison managers] have taken it"; and then the cat was out of the bag—he had already contributed to those who were managing these two candidacies, and now proposed to do the same for Reed. He was taking no chances!

Another incident. One day John Corliss, member of Congress from the Detroit district, called on me at my committee room and said: "Governor Pingree is down stairs and wishes to meet the Speaker." "Bring him right up here," said I. "I'll endeavor to get Mr. Reed down here to meet him." He did so. I was presented to the Governor and said, "Make yourselves at home, gentlemen. I'll go up to the House (then in session) and see if I can't get him to come down—as I think he will be glad to do so." I sneaked up behind the Speaker and whispered, "Governor Pingree is down in my room and wants to meet you." No answer. I repeated the statement. No answer save a grunt. "Well, will you come down?" said I. "What-does-he-want-to-see-me-for?" Reed drawled. "Well," said I, a bit impatiently, "You are a candidate for President, aren't you? And you know Governor Pingree carries the delegates from Michigan in his vest pocket." Another grunt, and I was uncomfortable. I finally turned and tried once more before leaving him. "Well, will you come down?" "Tell him I'll be down in a few minutes," was the reply. I returned to my room, told how the Speaker was busy in the chair, but would be down shortly. I knew Reed had no patience with Pingree's voluble utterances—free silver, or at least "double standard," and various isms, so I expected a possible unpleasant result. Reed lumbered in after a time, and was presented to the Governor, whom he met cordially, but who proceeded to enumerate his undigested doctrines to the Speaker—telling what ought to be done, etc. Reed listened patiently, and then lit into the Governor, but kept his temper while he lambasted him in a manner that was his own. It's too long a story, but Pingree wanted to be for Reed. He went away and espoused the cause of McKinley.

Another case was the visit of Mike De Young of California, who spent *hours* in Reed's office room at the Shoreham Hotel one evening trying to tie up with the Speaker on the proposition that he and his papers would be for him—but wanted the assurance that California would be represented in the Cabinet. (He didn't say that he was a receptive candidate for a portfolio, but Reed so understood it.) It is unnecessary to say that De Young made no headway, and when he left the Speaker he walked right into the McKinley camp.

The pre-convention campaign which gave McKinley the nomination is a familiar story. Mr. Hanna's labor on behalf of his friend was in many respects pioneer work, and excites less reprobation in a generation familiar with large scale publicity and propagandist operations than it once did. He saw that it was entirely feasible to conduct his campaign on a nation-wide scale, disregarding sectional comity and the preserves of favorite sons, and eventually to enter the convention with a mass of pledged delegates which did away with all necessity of bargaining and arrangement in the convention itself.

All through 1895 the wretched business of rounding up the Southern delegates, for the most part ex-holders of Federal office and venal negro politicians, went on. McKinley's visit to the South in the spring of that year greatly strengthened his candidacy, and in any case his organization had an overwhelming advantage in this somewhat sordid business. Reed did secure some delegates in the South, but the number was not large and his support was never dependable. "They were for me," he once said, "until the buying started." In the convention he actually received 18½ votes from the South. He always felt resentment in regard to this phase of the contest and Robert Underwood Johnson tells how, on a later occasion, after discussing a matter of pending legislation with the Speaker, he stated his intention of visiting President McKinley to enlist his support. Reed, says

Johnson, replied as follows, dwelling with particular contempt upon the word "niggers": "Well, have you ever bought any Southern delegates for McKinley? I do not mean ordinary delegates, I mean niggers, niggers! If you ever bought any niggers for McKinley then you will probably get what you want; otherwise I don't think there's much of a chance." [1]

As the winter of 1895–96 wore away the results of Hanna's work became apparent, although Reed's friends continued to make claims and counter-claims on his behalf, the press tabulating delegate totals from time to time. On February 24, General Charles H. Grosvenor of Ohio, a McKinley supporter, issued a statement in which he pointed out how sentiment for that candidate had been growing steadily and rapidly "ever since the country has felt the industry-smashing influence of Democratic policies," and declaring that "in spite of efforts to make the money question paramount, the tariff issue is the greatest." He claimed that McKinley was already assured of 433 votes, that the favorite son booms would collapse, and that his candidate would be nominated on the first ballot, all of which claims, with the exception of that regarding the currency, subsequently proved correct.

Early in March, Hanna's methods began to provoke sharp criticism from supporters of various candidates. Senator Allison's backers were reported to be especially disgruntled as the Western delegates in increasing numbers were brought into the McKinley fold. The country suddenly woke up to the fact that the three-year campaign in behalf of the Ohio man was now showing its natural results.[2]

On March 16, Senator Chandler made a sensational contribution to the campaign, declaring that the canvass was being carried forward by the levy of contributions on the manufacturing in-

[1] *Remembered Yesterdays,* 410.
[2] See Washington *Post,* March 7, 13, 15, 1896.

terests of the East. He denounced the "fat-frying methods" of
Hanna and asserted that it was a "boodle campaign" with general use of money to manipulate State conventions. Next day, in
reply to a defense of the McKinley campaign by General Grosvenor, he stated that the Republican party would have to face
the charge that it had received boodle in return for a tariff and
had put up for the presidency of the United States a man who
made a failure of his own affairs. On March 19 Hanna made a
flat denial of the Senator's charges, declaring that it had not
been necessary to create McKinley sentiment inasmuch as it was
spontaneous in every State.

Chandler's action probably injured the Reed cause more than
it helped. He himself had been none too scrupulous a politician,
and a cartoon in the Washington *Post* on March 27 with the
ironic caption, "The truly good Mr. Chandler bitterly bewaileth
the wicked ways of politics," undoubtedly expressed the sentiments of many good Republicans. Hanna was reported at this
stage of the campaign to have informed various state bosses that
he was indifferent to what they thought and could get along
without their good will or their services. Chandler's fulminations were considered merely the ill-natured utterances of a
beaten man, and his conduct probably caused a certain reaction
in favor of McKinley. There were actually stories in circulation
that the Senator's action constituted deliberate treachery to the
Speaker.

Events moved rapidly from now on. The action of the Massachusetts convention, which adopted a sound money plank and
elected Reed delegates, brought some temporary encouragement. Manley gave out a statement predicting that the McKinley
campaign would repeat the history of the Blaine campaign of
1876, ending in failure in the convention. It was immediately
pointed out, however, that essential factors were different in
McKinley's case. Blaine had had bitter and vindictive enemies in

MARCUS ALONZO HANNA

the party, and the Grant administration was determined to thwart him, while McKinley had never been the object of personal prejudice and dislike.

The result of the New Hampshire convention on March 31 was a serious blow and expectations that it would write a sound money plank and indorse Reed were both disappointed. The convention was reported to be at heart for McKinley, although the delegates elected eventually voted for Reed in the national convention. The convention straddled on the presidential question, declaring that the electoral vote of New Hampshire would be given "to any nominee who worthily represents the party, but we prefer Reed or McKinley," and the financial plank was a meaningless jumble of words about gold, silver and paper.

The news caused a sensation and Reed's backers were seriously alarmed. There was considerable discussion as to whether he was any longer in the running and the outcome in this State was reported to have given great encouragement to the McKinley sentiment in Connecticut. Senator Chandler wrote to Lodge denouncing the platform and its "mongrel resolutions," and declaring his belief that the convention was really for Reed. Chandler's letter, however, contained an implication that Reed was for bimetallism, and in view of the fact that Lodge had just issued a statement that the Speaker was for gold, did not help matters in the least.

When the Vermont convention on April 28 declared for McKinley, Reed's cause was doomed. With the New England alignment broken, he was no longer even a sectional candidate. Senator Redfield Proctor denied that he had influenced the situation and declared that the action of the convention merely reflected the McKinley sentiment which had been growing rapidly throughout the State for months past. The latter part of this statement, at least, was undoubtedly correct. Senator Frye had been unable to appear to speak on behalf of Reed, while Senator

Thurston of Nebraska was there and delivered an address for McKinley. But the somewhat slippery Proctor was suspected of active intervention on the McKinley side. He admitted sending a dispatch to Hanna stating the result, and Reed forever after entertained a lively resentment toward the Vermont senator.

"Vermont is a nice state where I hope you will have a good time," he wrote to Senator Lodge on August 21, as the latter left for a campaign trip. "If Proctor should die while you are there telegraph me at Portland, Farmington, and Grand Beach. Be sure, however, that he is really dead." "The morning paper shows that Wellington the faithful and true has been beaten in Maryland," he wrote on August 27, a year later. "If the Lord oftener took scamps in hand it would be easier to be a saint. I cannot expect Proctor next. He is too carefully oiled for moth and rust to corrupt very soon. *Mais ça ira*." [1]

"When it comes to political loyalty," said the Washington *Post* on May 12, "New England produces a fine line of coop-flyers." The result in Vermont was followed a day later by a sweeping victory for McKinley in Illinois. The latter state was of the utmost importance for McKinley and Charles G. Dawes had conducted a vigorous and skillful campaign in his behalf. McKinley delegates were chosen after a closely contested struggle in the state convention. The "favorite son" movement for Shelby M. Cullom had collapsed and there was still less likelihood that any anti-McKinley combination could be arranged in the convention. McKinley's nomination was now generally conceded and *The Nation* on May 7 declared that it was time to put forth every effort for the adoption of a gold standard plank at the St. Louis convention. "No one doubts that McKinley would stand on any kind of a platform offered him. The despondent anti-McKinley leaders cannot do better than struggle to put him

[1] *Lodge Papers.*

on a gold plank. He would look just as picturesque and be a good deal safer."

In the meantime there had begun a long succession of desertions from the Reed cause. House committee chairmen who in some instances owed their places to the Speaker's appointment, editors and party leaders scattered throughout the country, began to go over to the Ohio candidate. It was this feature of the campaign that left an indelible impression on the Speaker, and to the end of his life he was unable to suppress his feeling in regard to the desertion of those whom he had trusted.

All through the pre-convention campaign the currency issue kept appearing, like Banquo's ghost, and it was in this matter that the Speaker's course, however justifiable in his own eyes, however understandable in view of the inchoate condition of Republican opinion on the subject, and however consistent with his own unwillingness to engage in a scramble for support, was politically unwise. Everything considered, Reed's course during the last session of the 53rd Congress had had unfortunate results. His record on the currency question from the days when in his first term he had voted to sustain President Hayes's veto of the Bland-Allison Act, while McKinley had voted to override it, had been absolutely firm on the side of sound money. His proposal for a bond issue payable "in coin" had been a practical measure calculated to meet a dangerous public emergency, though it had aroused some suspicion among the powerful business interests of the Eastern states.

Theodore Roosevelt, who later in his career was to demonstrate an uncanny ability to catch the drift of popular sentiment and utilize it for personal and party advantage, wrote to Lodge on June 5, 1895, that he found "a very widespread feeling among good solid Republicans" in New York that Reed had straddled on the currency question, and expressed the opinion that an emphatic stand for sound money would have insured him the nomination. It was not too late, he wrote, even then. "He can't keep the silver fanatics with him and undoubtedly the sound money men at present feel that he is luke-warm in the matter, and is trying to play politics for the silver vote."

Roosevelt had urged Lodge to impress upon Reed the importance of a firm stand on the currency question and it was apparently in answer to such a letter that Reed wrote the Senator on June 29. "I presume what you say is true about the currency question," he stated, "but I am in a state of profound disgust over the whole attitude of the banking crowd towards me." He was, he continued, "the only man who ever took any risks on this silver question," and he disliked "to admit there is any excuse for the attitude of these people. I have made a plain simple record and to be called up like a schoolboy simply because somebody has been stupid and have weapons put into the mouths of enemies is very distasteful." "I wish I had a dollar and a half surplus," he added, "wherewith to roam the world. I would tell the whole lot to apply for consulates in warm climates." [1]

The Nation on June 6 in a caustic editorial had demanded that Reed declare his position on the currency question, and throughout the next nine months the demand was repeated with increasing insistence in various quarters. It was in answer to such an editorial, sent him by E. L. Pierce of Boston, that he wrote to the latter on August 23, 1895, a letter marked "strictly personal." In this he declared that, having a decided and unvarying record on the subject, he was not properly to be called upon by stray newspapers to make a declaration of faith. He was not, he wrote, "one of those patriots who as soon as they announce their views are supposed to change them unless hourly bulletins of health are issued." Opponents would merely say, "At last these Republicans have been forced to declare. They were really bad

[1] *Lodge Papers.*

but we bold courageous men have driven them into helping the Lord." "Silver," he went on, "is settling *itself*, no thanks to these 'courageous' but to the facts of life, as I supposed it would. This letter is strictly personal, for I don't mean to yield to the ideas expressed in the editorial sent, especially as they are dying a natural death. . . ." [1]

It is evident from the above that Reed, like so many of his contemporaries, failed to grasp the fact that silver would inevitably prove the great issue in the next campaign. His own views were well known, and he intended to maintain them; but why antagonize important elements in the party by adopting what they would certainly consider a provocative attitude? As it turned out this was defective strategy. He would have done well to remember the maxim which had guided him in the prolonged battle for reform of the rules. "Virtue in this world gets on not merely by sound statement but by reiteration of sound statement. It gets on by means of men having the idea driven into them that something is wrong." [2]

"In that contest," records one of his admirers, "Reed lost the opportunity of his political life when he failed to come out boldly and plainly for the gold standard which at heart he favored." [3] On May 2, 1896, downcast over results in Vermont and Illinois which had made McKinley's success a certainty, Roosevelt wrote to Lodge, "Oh! if only Reed would have made an aggressive and striking fight for sound finance, beginning at least six months ago."

If Reed had seized some psychological moment to speak on the currency question as he had spoken on the Mills Bill, with all the same persuasiveness and fire, showing as no one else could have done more effectively how free coinage of silver would

---

[1] From *E. L. Pierce Papers* in Widener Library, Harvard University.
[2] *Cong. Record,* 48 Cong., 2 Sess., 1290.
[3] Robert Underwood Johnson, *Remembered Yesterdays,* 410.

affect American standing in the commercial world, how it would strike at all property values, all securities, all insurance policies, all savings accounts, in short, how it would carry its blighting influence into every home in the land, his position would have been vastly strengthened. If he had continued to spray the straddlers, cowards, and ignoramuses with the sulphuric acid of ridicule and contempt, he might have rallied the great business interests of the country so strongly behind him that eventual success in the convention would have been the result.

Hindsight, however, is a much more common gift than foresight and there remains the question, which Hanna undoubtedly considered, whether the candidacy of any other man than McKinley could have prevented serious party disintegration in the Western states. And there still remains the question whether Reed could have carried the country in November. His very intellectual strength might have been a handicap, and as he himself always recognized, brilliant qualities of leadership are not necessarily the most effective in securing results where the conflicting interests of great masses of men are concerned.

The result in Illinois was everywhere taken to mean that the fight was practically over. There were repeated rumors that Reed would receive the nomination for Vice President and in spite of contradictions by Mr. J. Frank Aldrich, Mr. Amos Allen, Senator Lodge, Mr. Murray Crane and others who were in the Speaker's confidence, these reports continued until almost the day of nomination. A widely circulated statement that Reed might round out his career as parliamentarian and become "emancipator of the Senate" was not without humor.

When on May 14, the Speaker counted a quorum and squelched an Illinois member in a manner reminiscent of the 51st Congress, the item was telegraphed over the country as indicating that "Reed was himself again" and that his presidential ambitions were over. *The Nation* a week later mentioned the fact that Reed's wit was growing brighter as his prospects dimmed, and apropos of the clamor over McKinley as "the advance agent of prosperity" quoted the Speaker's comment on the advance agents of the circus, whom he remembered as a boy, covering the barns with colored lithographs setting forth the glories of the coming show. "It never came up to the show-bills, but there was always at least one first-class acrobat who rode two horses at once." "What a pity," continued the editor, "Speaker Reed invested this acrobat with the tinsel that now makes him such a glittering attraction to all the small boys of the countryside." "McKinley isn't a gold-bug, McKinley isn't a silver-bug, McKinley's a straddle-bug," was also attributed to the Speaker.[1] "I *know* these Ohio men!" he once remarked to Mr. J. Frank Aldrich.

From May 1 until the opening of the convention on June 16, there was undoubtedly growing concern among the business interests of the country lest the party waver on the currency question. McKinley's record on currency matters had been unsatisfactory and his repeated efforts to make the tariff appear the dominant issue began to arouse intense suspicion in the financial centers of the country. As early as April 4, the New York *Sun* in an elaborate analysis of McKinley's congressional record on financial questions pointed out that his course had been uncertain and contradictory with bimetallism apparently his dominant interest.[2]

[1] New York *Sun*, May 13, 1896.
[2] Cf. *Ibid.*, May 15, "The Straddle-Bug":

> My words have been for silver,
> My silence stood for gold,
> And thus I show the teaching
> Of some great sage of old.
> And if there is a question
> As to just what I meant,
> I'll answer that quite fully—
> When I am President!

Reed's only hope lay in the possibility of a violent upheaval in the convention on the currency question, and anything of the sort was extremely unlikely. The prevailing uncertainty on the whole matter, however, shows that his own course may have appeared wiser at the time than it does at present. "I don't know of any instructions to give you except what you don't need, to be brave and not lower the flag," he wrote to Senator Lodge on June 10. "Don't let them get off on the money question. Fight it clear out."

But as far as Reed was concerned, all was over when on June 10 Manley announced his belief that McKinley would be nominated on the first ballot. Manley's statement followed the decision of the national committee, in the first contests brought before it, to seat McKinley delegates. In April, both Manley and Quay had intimated that the anti-McKinley forces would control the committee and that the McKinley claims as to delegates controlled would be found deceptive when the committee completed his work on the convention roll. Hanna was too great a strategist to have overlooked such a possibility, and the first hearings before the committee showed that his control was complete. There were one hundred and sixty contests, and the seating of McKinley delegates in the great majority of cases was a certainty. All doubt as to the outcome of the nomination was ended. Manley, however, appears to have been panic stricken at the first tooting of the steam roller. Furthermore, he gave out the statement without consulting the other Reed backers in the convention, and naturally enough, in view of his relations with Reed in the pre-convention campaign, his conduct was generally denounced as treachery. "Mr. Reed's candidacy," said the Washington *Post* on June 12, "seems to have been sadly handicapped by a set of managers who are inclined to break ranks at the sight of a pie counter." Three days later appeared a cartoon featuring "Cassius Proctor" and "Brutus Manley."

Manley's action, however, was not "treachery," and Mr. J. Frank Aldrich remembers that he and other Reed men advised the Speaker against having Manley deposed as committeeman, an action which the Maine delegation was willing to take provided Reed approved. "We advised Reed not to give the word to do it, having more or less sympathy with Manley after his explanation to us, and because he was literally heartbroken when he realized what he had done." [1] Manley wrote contritely to Reed on June 12, expressing profound regret for his "great mistake" and declaring that he had "never been disloyal in thought, word, or deed." [2] The affair simply confirms contemporary opinion that Manley was hardly qualified to handle an important campaign. "Tom Reed," the Washington *Post* had declared on June 17, 1895, when the nominating campaign was in its early stages, "can well afford to pay all the expense which may be incurred by an indefinite prolongation of Joe Manley's European trip." On December 13, 1897, came the sardonic comment: "It is a real pleasure to observe that no one is so foolish as to indulge in any promiscuous poking about the hole into which Hon. Joe Manley has retired."

The St. Louis *Republic*, after Manley's blunder occurred, published a long and circumstantial story of the "betrayal" of the Speaker who in "intellectual grandeur, purity of character and strength of will" stood "head and shoulders above any Republican of his time." This story bears all the earmarks of having been furnished by disgruntled and embittered partisans of the defeated candidate. But it performed one service for posterity by recording the remarks which General Samuel Fessenden of the Connecticut delegation addressed to the unfortunate Manley. "Joe, God Almighty hates a quitter. I have been a soldier in actual war, and am a faithful soldier of Reed now, but my gen-

[1] Letter to author, June 16, 1930.
[2] McCall, *Reed,* 224.

eral has deserted." Erroneously attributed to Reed himself by many subsequent writers, Fessenden's "God Almighty hates a quitter" has outlived the brilliant nominating speeches in which Henry Cabot Lodge and Charles E. Littlefield put Reed's name before the convention. For almost forty years it has worked for the strengthening of hearts in the face of discouragement, and it should be remembered alike to the credit of the follower who made it and the leader who inspired it.

There was little enthusiasm around Reed headquarters, although his followers staged a torchlight procession and proclaimed their intentions of fighting to the last. With the nomination of McKinley assured, Hanna was conciliatory. Reed men were accorded recognition on committees and played an important part in securing adoption of the all-important gold plank in the platform. Much recent evidence has come to light in regard to the origin of the gold plank, and creditable as were the services of Senator Lodge and other Reed supporters, there is no doubt that Hanna himself was sound on the main issue and no other result was to be seriously considered.

On the first ballot McKinley received 661½ votes, Reed 84½, Quay 60½, Morton 58, Allison 35½. Sixty-two of Reed's votes were from New England. Manley's prediction was verified by the course of events. Statements were freely made in hotel lobbies, state headquarters and about the convention hall itself that a majority of the delegates, if free agents, would have preferred Reed, and many of the latter's friends to this day have retained the belief that had it been possible to hold off the nomination for a few ballots Reed would have won. Such speculations are entirely futile. Hanna's campaign from its very inception had been directed to prevent just such a possibility. McKinley was backed by Republican opinion throughout the country and questionable as were the agencies through which public will actually operated, those same agencies undoubtedly gave it the man it wanted.

No one can examine the political news which filled the press during the first six months of 1896 without perceiving the tremendous ground swell of McKinley sentiment. *The Nation* might cavil at the fact that his support was coming chiefly from the farmers, that "the farm mind associated the tariff with good crops," and that the candidate was the beneficiary of a fortunate coincidence of tariff legislation and prosperity. It might rail at him as "a silver man" not "through fraud or selfishness" but "probably through sheer stupidity and ignorance," having "no more idea of the laws of currency than one of his negro delegates at St. Louis will have of the higher mathematics." It might sneer at his campaign as "a country wide advertising dodge" which had drawn "the wondering admiration of all the undersized intellects in the country." This might all be true, but it could not obscure the fact that McKinley had the delegates and the delegates, often against their personal views, were fairly representative of popular sentiment.

It was absurd, declared the St. Louis *Globe-Democrat* on June 19, discussing the outcome of the convention, to blame Mr. Reed's managers. He had not been defeated; he had simply never had a chance. "There has been no time in the past six months when the best that any human being could do would have defeated Mr. McKinley. The nomination . . . was simply a formal ratification of a choice already made by the people. There can be no question about the fact that he is the preference of a large majority of the Republican voters of the country. The sentiment in his favor extends all over the country and among all classes of citizens." After thirty-five years there is little to add to this verdict. Reed was penalized for mistakes of omission and commission but also for his very greatness of intellect and character. When James Bryce explained "why great men are not chosen president" and listed among the defects of the presidential system the fact that it offered "too great a stimulus to ambition," he said about all there was to say on the subject.

There had been frequent rumors in the weeks preceding the convention that Reed planned to retire from politics. He had in recent years been offered advantageous opportunities for private legal practice and his defeat in 1896 undoubtedly led him to serious consideration of such a possibility. On June 20, an editorial in the New York *Sun* took cognizance of these reports and extended an invitation. "New York will be glad to receive him. Glory and fun and wealth are waiting for him here. The Hon. Joseph Hodges Choate is waiting for him too. A wit and genius on a par with his will take from him his present lonely preëminence. And busy as New York is, Mr. Reed will be allowed to read his little French novel in the elevated train every morning and night."

Whatever may have been Reed's chagrin at the outcome of the St. Louis convention, he soon dropped the idea of retirement and took up the duties of the campaign. "My best consolation," he wrote Senator Lodge on June 20, "is that you won so much for yourself in the fight on the platform." The Republican party had taken its stand for gold and the nomination of Bryan on a free silver platform made a clean-cut issue. Reed made a notable contribution to the literature of the campaign in the October number of the *North American Review,* appealing for support of the Republican ticket as the only method of averting the dire calamities inherent in success of the free silver cause. It was plain that it was to be one of the most momentous campaigns in American history and although, as he wrote Dalzell, "politics is mostly pill-taking," he threw himself into the contest with full vigor.

He was renominated on July 29 and opened the Maine campaign with an address which was received with approval by advocates of sound money. *The Nation* on August 6, described it as "the first one on either side that can be considered a thoughtful argument appealing to human reason," and one of the first signs that there was to be a genuine campaign of education. "The tone which he has adopted ought to be the tone of the Republicans throughout. If it is so, the happiest results may be expected." The speech was printed and widely circulated as a campaign document.

The result of the Maine election on September 14 was decisive and strengthened Republican morale throughout the country. Reed himself received a plurality of over 12,000, a great increase over that of any preceding year. On October 5 he addressed an immense meeting at Boston and after speeches in New York and Connecticut traveled throughout the West, winding up his campaign with a speech at Oakland a few days before election. The California Republicans afterwards asserted that it was Reed's speeches that saved California for McKinley. Never had he been in such demand as a campaign speaker and he was able to accept only a small fraction of the engagements offered. But he expressed a growing distaste for the stump. "I regret the tendency in our elections toward blare and display. I object to being exhibited from the tail end of a train like a criminal on his way to jail. . . . I object to having my testimony put into a newspaper with a border round it like a patent medicine advertisement." [1]

It was noticeable in this campaign that his style had changed considerably and there was less of the clashing sarcasm and caustic wit which had once delighted his audiences. This was not merely due to an evident desire to enlist sound money advocates of all party affiliations, but was characteristic of most of his later utterances. He had become more philosophical and decidedly less partisan. He was heard to say on one occasion: "We have

[1] Washington *Post*, September 27.

not been wholly righteous ourselves in times past, and there is nothing to be gained by painting the other fellow all black."

It was noticed that while he had much to say regarding the issues he had little to say regarding McKinley, but there was general agreement that he did tremendous service toward the latter's election. He was without question the outstanding Republican on the stump and as the Washington *Post*, October 27, said of his speeches in Kansas:

After the tempestuous howlings of Mrs. Lease, the shrill noise of Jerry Simpson, and the muffled expostulations of the much bewhiskered Peffer, Kansas should rejoice in the clean-cut satire, the strenuous logic and the breezy good-humored argument of a man like Reed. People feel better and more wholesome after an hour with Reed. He stirs the blood, he stimulates the fancy, he actually flatters men by making them believe they have real minds.

McKinley received 271 electoral votes to Bryan's 171, but the popular vote in many states was by no means so decisive and a few shifts would have made a great change in election totals. The result showed that the tremendous exertions of the Republican organization were justified by the situation. It showed, furthermore, that McKinley with his conciliatory temperament and Middle Western background was probably the most effective candidate to meet the special conditions of this memorable campaign.

THE election of 1896 gave the Republican party not only the presidency but a comfortable majority in Congress. For the first time in years the way was clear for important legislation. The tariff was first on the program and the 55th Congress met in special session on March 15, 1897, with a bill on which the Ways and Means Committee had been laboring during the preceding winter as the first item on the calendar. Reed was renominated for the speakership by acclamation and elected over Joseph W. Bailey by a vote of 200 to 114.

There had been much gossip around the Capitol as to the attitude which he would adopt toward the McKinley administration. Reed had never disguised his resentment toward Hanna's tactics in the pre-convention campaign of 1896 and his opinion of the President's character and capacity was well known. It was suggested in certain quarters that Reed and Dingley, who again headed Ways and Means, could cause considerable embarrassment by thwarting the distribution of tariff favors among the interests which had contributed so lavishly to the party war chest. But there was no likelihood whatever of such a development. Not only was the Speaker thoroughly in sympathy with a restoration of the protective system, but he was too good a party man to permit his personal feelings to interfere with its interests. He had disliked Harrison intensely but had taken the responsibility of throttling the free silver bill of 1890. Had he permitted it to reach the President, either acceptance or veto would have had embarrassing political consequences for the latter. There was, said the Washington *Post* on January 12, 1897, no likelihood of a feud between President and Speaker. But on February 2, commenting on the outlook in the next Congress the *Post* pointed out that "if Tom Reed were several sizes smaller in statesmanship he would step to one side and allow the pork-hunting Congressmen to pile up some very embarrassing legislation for the McKinley administration to wrestle with."

Thanks to the industry of Nelson Dingley and his colleagues, the tariff bill was ready for prompt action, passing the House on March 31. It had been determined by the party leaders that tariff legislation was the main business of the session and the Speaker made only such committee appointments as were absolutely necessary. While the bill was in the Senate the House proceedings were for the most part merely a series of daily meetings and adjournments. The members became restive. The Speaker was of course held responsible for the lack of opportunity to secure legislative action and the situation soon called for the exercise of all his powers of control. As Amos J. Cummings described the work of this Congress, the absence of House committees meant that nine tenths of the Senate legislation had no hopper in which to fall, and the Speaker, when members protested, merely "stared at them with open-mouthed nonchalance," and nothing was done. "The Senate was fully organized and its digestive organs were in full play. Hundreds of bills were passed—some of them very important—and sent over to the House. They fell into the hands of the Clerk and could not be distributed because there were no committees. Among them was a resolution recognizing Cuban belligerency whose consideration might have prevented war with Spain." [1]

The really able and redoubtable Kansan, Jerry Simpson, proved the most vehement objector to the Speaker's policy, but Reed in the face of considerable provocation kept his temper in spite of repeated clashes. "Tom and Jerry," he is reported to have remarked to a friend, "may mix in a bar-room, but not in

[1] Washington *Post,* March 5, 1899.

REED, McKINLEY, AND HARRISON, 1896
(From *Judge*)

the House of Representatives." On April 7, Simpson secured the floor on a question of privilege, reading into the record a savage editorial denouncing the Speaker for his failure to appoint committees, as "a political cannibal autocrat." Incidentally, he mentioned the fact that in the last campaign Reed had told his Kansas constituency that for four years past "it had been represented by chaos." Simpson unquestionably represented a considerable body of opinion when he declared that the country had been undergoing a quiet constitutional revolution and the House of Representatives was on the way toward extinction. "Without any formal change in the Constitution, that body has practically ceased to exist, and in its place we have been supplied with a more concrete, simple, and unanimous institution. The body and other personality are one Reed." [1]

To this Speaker Reed replied with entire good humor that more time was necessary to study the situation and the new members before making assignments. Ordinarily he had had from March to December to make such a study. Apparently to clear the air, Nelson Dingley on May 3 introduced a resolution calling on the Speaker to appoint the committees at once. This session, Dingley pointed out, had been called for one particular purpose; the nation expected the performance of the main task and an early adjournment. The resolution was decisively beaten and the question settled. Not until the last day of the session were the committee assignments announced.

On July 8, with the return of the tariff bill from the Senate, the House went back to work. Sharp differences of opinion developed in regard to some of the Senate amendments, and especially the sugar schedule. The House in 1894 had made a humiliating surrender to the demands of the Senate, and the sugar schedule had been one of the unhappy features of the Wilson Bill. In the present instance Reed and Dingley made a notable

[1] *Cong. Record,* 55 Cong., 1 Sess., 650.

fight and their stand against the excessive Senate rates attracted considerable attention. "It is refreshing," said the Baltimore *American* in regard to the Speaker, "to have a great leader come to the rescue of the people." In any case, Reed and Dingley prevailed, the conference committee at length agreed, and the Senate abandoned its opposition to the House sugar schedule.

"The House," says the leading historian of the tariff in discussing this feature of the Dingley Bill, "had adopted the plan of leaving things as they were, and had successfully resisted the effort of the refining monopoly to secure more. The result was due mainly to greater party cohesion and more rigid party discipline, enforced by the genial despotism of the autocratic Speaker of the House." [1] There was abundant material for criticism in the Dingley tariff, but it proved one of the more satisfactory measures of its type and was destined to have a longer life than any of its predecessors. A number of factors were responsible for a great business revival in the last years of the century, and interested parties worked to attribute an undue share of the credit to the tariff. Reed repeatedly defended it, although admitting that no tariff, considering the vast complexity of the interests involved, could ever be entirely satisfactory. Congress adjourned on July 24.

In the meantime there had been developing, its full significance inadequately appreciated by the country in general, the issue which was destined to result in the Speaker's abandonment of public life. In February, 1895, chronic discontent in Cuba had again flared up in general insurrection. It was evident that the trouble was too widespread and too deep-seated for prompt military suppression, and the temper of both sides precluded a peaceful adjustment. Naturally the struggle aroused intense interest in the United States. Various interests were adversely affected by

[1] F. W. Taussig, *The Tariff History of the United States*, 1923, 352.

conditions on the island, while popular sentiment interpreted the contest as a great struggle for freedom and self government by an oppressed people. Fanned by yellow journalism, the feeling in favor of intervention steadily increased.

General Weyler arrived in the island on February 10, 1896, and the severity of his policy further inflamed American resentment. Both parties adopted resolutions of sympathy for the Cuban cause at their national conventions, and when the 54th Congress met for the short session in December, 1896, there was a considerable element in both Houses which frankly desired recognition of Cuban independence. On December 21, a resolution recognizing Cuban independence appeared in the Senate, but Secretary Olney's brief statement that recognition was a matter for the Executive, and the fact that a new administration would assume office in a few months, prevented further action. Unquestionably the spirit of jingoism was abroad in the land, and congressional fulminations on Cuba and Venezuela were indicative of the state of a considerable section of public opinion. *The Nation* on March 12, 1896, made a scathing attack on jingoism in general, congressional jingoism in particular, and on Secretary Olney as putative author of the Venezuela note, for having "suggested to a body of idle, ignorant and not very scrupulous men an exciting game" which involved inestimable danger to the country. "To have an assembly of breech-clouted warriors, who are daily shaking their tomahawks at all strangers, presiding and legislating for a nation which has a stock exchange and banks in every town, and in which the poorest man is interested in the conditions of the money market, is an absurdity. No such régime can last. But we shall have no change for the better as long as our leading men are afraid to let the warriors know that we have definitely broken with the old savage life, live by trade and industry, and take no scalps."

Reed seldom discussed foreign policy either on the stump or

in Congress, but his views were well known. He detested jingoism and all forms of national aggression with the same fervor that his English contemporary William Vernon Harcourt was displaying during this same period in the House of Commons. He had always admitted that war, human nature being what it was, seemed unavoidable under some conditions, but as he grew older he hated it more intensely than ever. To provoke trouble, especially in dealing with weaker lands, seemed to him unworthy of a great nation, and with all his cynicism and occasional flippancy Reed loved his country and was jealous of its dignity and honor.

"We have very little to do with foreign nations," he once wrote, "and there is nothing which troubles us less than our foreign affairs. Judging from what has happened in the little sphere in which we do move, it is lucky for us that rolling oceans, for the most part, divide us from the rest of the world." [1] Years later one of his newspaper friends remembered his disgust at President Harrison's handling of the Chilean embroglio of 1891. He had expressed himself in vigorous terms coupled with the warning, "If you publish what I have said tomorrow, I'll come to your office and kill you." What he had said was that "I do not think the President ought to have written such a message to those little Chileans. They do not wish to fight us, we do not want to fight them. What we ought to do is to charter a ship, not too large or too safe, put Harrison on board of it, and send him down to fight the Chileans. He's just about their size." [2]

The Cuban situation remained serious throughout 1897, and during the extra session an incident occurred which is of interest both as an illustration of the methods by which Reed handled

[1] "The Present Administration of National Affairs," *North American Review,* July, 1894.
[2] New York *Sun,* December 14, 1902.

the business of the House and as showing the dangerous tendency of members to meddle in what was undoubtedly a critical matter of foreign policy. The Senate had passed a resolution recognizing Cuban belligerency, but because of the Speaker's policy regarding committee assignments, no action had been taken by the House. In the ordinary course of business on July 7, 1897, Benton McMillin inquired whether it was in order to make a motion to suspend the rules and pass bills, "today being a continuation of the legislative day of Monday," and when the Speaker answered in the affirmative, the Tennessee member promptly moved to suspend the rules and pass the resolution recognizing Cuban belligerency. It was a dangerous moment, for many members desired its passage; but the Speaker, fumbling with the gavel, at last caught Dingley's attention with "the gentleman from Maine is recognized," and amid laughter the latter at once moved to adjourn. Party discipline was excellent, the motion was carried, and the baffled McMillin could only remark: "I thought the gentleman from Maine had been moved to move in that direction."

It is a matter of regret that Reed's position as Speaker prevented his participation in debate on the Hawaiian and Cuban questions. His attitude, however, was perfectly well known and reported in the newspapers from time to time. In addition, he touched on several aspects of the general situation in articles published during the course of the year. The country, he wrote in a discussion of naval affairs, should avoid foreign complications, "grow up to the territory we have already," and strive to create a fully united nation. There was, he added, no serious danger of foreign attack, and while naval power might be a necessary form of insurance, over-insurance should be avoided because "that is costly and makes a moral hazard and a danger of a conflagration which might burn what we have not protected." [1]

[1] "The New Navy," *Illustrated American*, September 25, 1897.

Again, in an article which attracted widespread attention he pointed out how all the great empires of history had demonstrated "the need of union and the tendency to discord," how the genius of war and statesmanship had wrestled vainly with the problem, how American expansion had resulted in great variations in the thought and needs of the country, and how, because of the mode of representation in the Senate, we would actually be governed by a minority until the thinly populated areas were filled. Not every opportunity for aggrandizement should be seized, and unassimilated communities were always a strain on institutions of government.[1]

The familiar Reed touch appears in his last *Illustrated American* article in criticizing the partiality of the public for crime news and the willingness of the press to gratify it. "It might be well," he wrote, "to give some thought to this and to contemplate this, along with our method of administering justice by the discriminating aid of a mob, before we undertake the purification of the world and the civilization of other lands. It may be that after we have ceased to enjoy prurient details of crime and have become content with justice administered under the law of the land we would have a greater influence over the world at large as well as over Turkey and Spain—an influence which would have its origin in character as well as in strength." To Senator Lodge he wrote on August 27, 1897, denying that he was "pro-Spanish" and declaring that he would prefer "not to spill any American blood" unless there should be some clear advantage to America. "As I have said to you before, let us assimilate Pettigrew and Teller before we try something harder." On September 13, he wrote again pointing out the dangers of recognizing Cuban belligerency. "If some man with a real American name, not Sanguilly but Murphy or Shaughnessy were killed war would be sure. And our wars cost. As to their government

---

[1] "Empire Can Wait," *Ibid.*, December 4, 1897.

being like ours in the Revolution, I yield to your superior knowledge but with a slight shake of head. But that does not matter. As for gratitude of nations that is not worth counting. If we help another people to liberty we either do it for our own interests or it will seem so when their interests become diverse. In fact until the federation of the world let each nation look out for itself." [1]

President McKinley was anxious to secure a peaceful solution of the Cuban question and Reed gave him a full measure of support. When the regular session opened in December, 1897, it seemed likely that all dangerous resolutions from the Senate would be safely buried in the files of the House Committee on Foreign Affairs and that there would be no opportunity for agitators in the lower chamber to create unwelcome disturbance. Dingley, after a conference with the Speaker, had publicly stated that the Cuban question should be left in the hands of the President without congressional meddling. The despotism of the Committee on Rules was sufficient to insure inaction unless an unexpected crisis solidified congressional and popular opinion in favor of intervention. That, unfortunately, was precisely what happened. Weyler had been recalled October 9, 1897, and temporarily at least, the tension relaxed. Throughout the opening weeks of the session the Speaker held the House to routine business, and in spite of disturbing incidents and the continued uproar of war-mongering newspapers and politicians there seemed a reasonable prospect of peaceful adjustment.

Then on February 15, 1898, the *Maine* blew up at her moorings in Havana harbor and the clamor for action arose with redoubled vehemence. To the end of his life Reed refused to accept the popular view that the warship was the victim of Spanish treachery and he frequently expressed skepticism as to the correctness of the findings of the board of inquiry which reported

[1] *Lodge Papers.*

that the *Maine* had been destroyed by an external explosion. Whatever its source, the explosion shattered the hope of preserving peace as completely as it had shattered the vessel itself.

Events moved rapidly and on March 8, Cannon as chairman of Appropriations, acting on the request of President McKinley, introduced his famous bill appropriating fifty million dollars for national defense. The temper of the House was evident in the almost unanimous support accorded the measure. Cannon himself was opposed to war and had recently remarked that "many of the gentlemen who are loudly shouting for war are agonizing to shed their blood in selling supplies to the government." He believed, however, that the pressure of public sentiment rendered war inevitable and that common sense demanded that preparation be furthered before the jingoes got completely out of hand. Reed, whom he had not consulted in the matter, Cannon writes, walked to the street car with him that evening and asked, "Joe, why did you do it?" Cannon explained his reasons. " 'Perhaps you are right. Perhaps you are right,' the Speaker commented and we never discussed the matter afterwards." [1]

There was still a slight chance that war could be averted, and Reed continued to hold the House in check. On March 26, the time allotted to general debate was reduced, thereby curtailing opportunity for discussion of the Cuban question but causing considerable restlessness and opposition among the members. On March 30, Bailey tried to push through a resolution recognizing Cuban independence, but the Speaker, quoting Democratic precedents, ruled that the resolution was not privileged and the effort failed. Public excitement grew and the House debates were conducted in the presence of a hostile and excited crowd in the galleries.

The Speaker's firmness aroused considerable resentment

[1] Busbey, *Cannon*, 192.

throughout the country and he was assailed with a violence which was reminiscent of the quorum controversy of 1890. Here and there, however, there was an appreciative note. Thus the Omaha *Bee* remarked:

The part of Speaker Reed in this juncture is not so generally understood or appreciated as it should be. He has exerted an influence hardly less potent and valuable than that of the President in repressing the bellicose spirit and passion engendered by the Cuban question. . . . He has kept the House of Representatives from becoming the hotbed of warlike declarations, and while it was not possible to wholly repress the spirit of jingoism that so largely prevades that body, the Speaker, assisted by other Republican leaders, has so kept it in check that it has worked little harm in the public mind. There has been quite enough of war talk in the House . . . but there would have been vastly more but for the Speaker.

Whether even at this late date war might still have been averted by a different line of action on the part of the President is a controversial matter on which it would be unprofitable to enter. In any event, on April 11 the President sent in his war message asking for the necessary authority "to secure a full and final termination of hostilities between the government of Spain and the people of Cuba, and to secure in the island the establishment of a stable government capable of maintaining order . . . and to use the military and naval forces of the United States as may be necessary for these purposes." It was apparent that the members were overwhelmingly in favor of prompt action, but a sharp difference of opinion developed over the question of recognizing the independence of the Cuban republic. The Senate resolutions, introduced in answer to the President's request, accorded such recognition and there was the prospect of an embarrassing delay.

The conservatives controlled the House and while agreeing

on armed intervention they refused recognition of the Cuban government. Feeling ran high. In the course of debate on April 13, there was an outbreak on the floor in which blows were struck and order was restored with difficulty by the Sergeant-at-Arms. Two days later Bailey, who was steadily demonstrating his growing incapacity as Democratic floor leader, severely criticized the Speaker and received a brief castigation such as, the Washington *Post* stated next day, had made Reed "famous the country over as the most dangerous antagonist in public life." On April 14th the House voted down an amendment recognizing the Cuban government and a bitter contest developed with the Senate. Many members were desirous of accepting the Senate resolutions and it was with difficulty that Reed and his lieutenants kept the party ranks unbroken. After protracted wrangling in conference, a compromise was reached April 19 and the report was promptly adopted by both Houses. The President signed the resolution on April 20 and the war was on, the formal declaration passed a few days later dating its existence as of April 21. To one of the six members who had voted against it, Reed remarked a little later: "I envy you the luxury of your vote. I was where I could not do it." [1]

While giving support to revenue bills and other measures necessitated by the war, Reed was disgusted with the outcome. He felt that with a firmer and more intelligent handling of the situation the war could have been avoided in spite of all contributory influences which seemed to render it inevitable. His alleged statement that McKinley had "the backbone of a chocolate éclair" probably expressed his real opinion of the President. The conduct of the war itself, the bungling and incompetence and the resultant suffering of the troops alternately depressed and embittered him. Among his intimate friends he occasionally let fall remarks which indicated his growing dissatisfaction with public

[1] McCall, *Reed*, 234.

life. Before the war had closed the settlement of another issue convinced him that his day in politics was over.

Hawaiian annexation had bulked large in the affairs of the Cleveland administration, and the project was renewed under President McKinley. American investors in the islands, with visions of increased profits to be made by growing sugar and other tropical products under conditions of cheap production, with the world's greatest market available behind the barriers of a protective tariff, supplied an active lobby for annexation. Naval authorities saw the desirability of great strategic base in the mid-Pacific. Some were interested in Hawaiian missions, others were confident that the extension of American rule had beneficent possibilities not merely for the islands but for the world at large. The old expansionist spirit which had carried American institutions across the wilderness, from the Alleghenies to the Pacific, in little more than a century, was still a force to be reckoned with.

On June 16, 1897 Secretary of State Sherman signed a treaty of annexation and on September 16, this instrument was ratified by the Hawaiian legislature. Strong as was annexationist sentiment in the United States Senate, however, it soon became apparent that the two-thirds majority necessary for ratification could not be obtained. Thoughtful people realized that the proposal marked a radical innovation in American policy and *The Nation*, best representative of this point of view, on November 25, 1897, commenting on the report that all the senators from New England favored annexation, took occasion to declare that "no community on either side of the ocean has, within the century, turned its back so completely on the traditions of its own political and social life," and that it must be a source of regret to those who "remember what were the fundamental professions of the Republican party." Reed was a New Englander who remembered them. He made no attempt to conceal his views in the interests of party harmony. He stated them again and again, declaring that the addition of such territory would be a source of weakness rather than strength.[1]

Although the exciting prospect of intervention in Cuba and war with Spain furnished a more favorable atmosphere for the operations of the annexationists, it was still more evident by the middle of March that the treaty could not be ratified. There was then recourse to that old weapon, a joint resolution, which made its appearance in the Senate on March 16.

A joint resolution, however, required coöperation from the Speaker. Such resolutions had before now passed the upper chamber only to die obscurely in the pigeon-holes of a House committee because the Speaker refused opportunity to bring them before the House. All through April, amid the excitement accompanying the outbreak of war and the redoubled clamor of the annexationists, the Speaker remained unshaken in opposition. Then came Dewey's victory in Manila Bay on May 1. "This is a serious matter," Reed is reported to have said when he received the news. "Dewey ought to sail right away from that place. It'll make us trouble for all time to come if he does not." [2] The battle at Manila settled the fate of Hawaiian annexation and wrecked all hopes which the Speaker and his supporters may have had of blocking a project which they detested.

Reed had been at the very height of his power as Speaker in the early days of the 55th Congress. There were frequent protests from minority members at the ruthless control of the Committee on Rules, and Republicans grew restive at times. Even in the Senate, there was some caustic comment on the situation, Senator Morgan on one occasion describing the members of the House as "standing about and waiting for a word from the lips of a single man to determine whether they shall have a voice and exercise it in the government of the United States," while meas-

---

[1] Washington *Post,* December 8, 1897, New York *Tribune,* February 8, 1898.
[2] Champ Clark, in New York *World,* December 14, 1902.

ures passed by the Senate were ignored because the Speaker considered it inadvisable to act.[1]

"We have a horrid example before us constantly," said Senator Allen of Nebraska on February 10, 1898, "like a nightmare, in another end of the Capitol building, where one man transacts the business of 357, which absolutely paralyzes one branch of Congress, a thing which, to my way of thinking, is an absolute, positive, inexcusable, bold, and open disgrace to the American people. . . . Forty-five States of this Union, with their Representatives numbering 356, all held metaphorically speaking, by the throat as a highwayman would treat you when he wanted you to deliver your money. Your legislation may pass if it meets his stamp of approval, and it is rejected if it does not."

The Nation on January 21, 1897 under the caption "Our Ruler the Speaker," illustrated the tremendous power exercised by Mr. Reed by citing the case of the Nicaragua Canal Bill, which the Speaker refused to allow to come to a vote in spite of a special request from the entire Pacific coast delegation and a petition signed by a majority of the members of the House. "We are bound to say," continued the writer, "that the Speakers have as a rule, exercised their autocratic power for the public good. The Blair Bill could not be brought to a vote in the House as long as Mr. Carlisle was Speaker. Mr. Reed throttled the free silver bill of 1890. His killing of the Nicaragua Canal Bill is an undoubted benefit. Almost anything, in fact, which the Speaker prevents Congress from doing is a cause for rejoicing. The presumption is that the thing Congress wants to do is a bad thing. If we could only be sure of always having a benevolent tyrant as Speaker, the system would not be a bad one."

It is worth note that on March 9, 1899, the same journal again took up the canal bill, declaring that "Speaker Reed never won

[1] *Cong. Record,* 55 Cong., 1 Sess., 1348.

a greater triumph than the one he scored in the Nicaragua Canal matter. He succeeded in heading off a piece of rash and confused and suspicious legislation and in substituting a rational measure without the smell of jobbery upon it." The compromise measure finally adopted provided only for inquiry by competent engineers on competing routes and plans to be reported to Congress. If the country wanted a canal across the Isthmus it wanted it wisely and honestly constructed. "This has now been made possible and we owe it to Speaker Reed, whose firm and skilful opposition to a band of desperate speculators has not been displayed in the eye of the public but has been deserving of the highest praise." In spite of the Speaker's disapproval, however, the 55th Congress was an extravagant one, particularly in its appropriations for public buildings.

"The approval of the House is the very breath in the nostrils of the Speaker," had long been one of Reed's maxims, invoked when opponents became especially vehement in charging tyranny and oppression. Proponents of Hawaiian annexation were quick to take advantage of the new situation in the Philippines, and Reed was soon to discover that his course no longer had the approval of the House. Annexation might have been defeated on its intrinsic merits, given sufficient time, but as a war measure it proved invincible.

The Newlands resolution providing for annexation was introduced in the House on May 4, but for three weeks the Speaker refused to permit a rule for its consideration. In close touch, as always, with the trend of House opinion, he realized that the demand for action was growing rapidly and that annexation sentiment would soon have to take its course. On May 24, a petition for a caucus was actually circulated and signed by many Republican members. The petition took the unusual form of requesting Chairman Grosvenor to summon a caucus "to consider the Hawaiian resolution with a view to its prompt and speedy consideration and to transact such other business as may be necessary." [1] Reed surrendered to the inevitable and on June 2 it was announced throughout the country that the annexation resolution would be passed before adjournment.

On June 10, Chairman Hitt of the Committee on Foreign Affairs asked unanimous consent that the order of business set for the following day be vacated and that debate on the Hawaiian resolution proceed until June 15 when at five o'clock a vote should be taken. There was no objection, and under this special order, which, incidentally, spared the Speaker the humiliation of having to interpose with a report from the Committee on Rules, the joint resolution providing for annexation came before the House.

Opinion was overwhelmingly in its favor although in the course of debate the dangers of this departure from American traditions were forcibly presented. It passed the House on June 15 by a vote of 209 to 91. Reed was absent, ill, but when the result was announced Dalzell rose and stated that he was authorized to say that the Speaker would have voted "no" if present.[2]

As *The Nation* on June 30 pointed out, the long contest between the Speaker and the annexationists had ended with the former "standing almost absolutely alone, so far as party friends are concerned, and as one of a feeble minority, nearly all Democrats." His course, however, received a measure of praise which that critical journal had seldom accorded him. "Courage to oppose a popular mania, above all to go against party, is not so common a political virtue that we can afford not to pay our tribute to the man who exhibits it. Speaker Reed has already

[1] Washington *Post,* May 24, 25, 26, New York *Tribune,* June 2, 1898.
[2] *Cong. Record,* 55 Cong., 2 Sess., 6019.

had, we cannot doubt, evidence of approval which, next to that of his own conscience, he must value highest, and we believe that time will vindicate his political sagacity."

After Congress adjourned on July 8, Reed spent the rest of the summer in his cottage at Grand Beach, Maine. He was, according to reporters who occasionally sought him out, apparently without a care in the world. He had given up his bicycle, but walked a good deal and was apparently in excellent health.

He was renominated on August 2, and the district convention refrained from any comment on his recent relations with the administration, a fact which was interpreted in some quarters, however, as a rebuke. He addressed the delegates briefly, responding to shouts of "Take the platform," with "No, let me have my own way once." There was, he pointed out, a dearth of political feeling throughout the country, and never in his political career had a campaign promised as little excitement. "The problems after the war will be the most troublesome, and will demand the most earnest efforts of us all. For my part, I hope that all these problems may be worked out consistently with our time-honored and dearly bought institutions, and with the traditions of our wise forefathers." He closed with an expression of appreciation for "the large liberty you have always given me in interpreting your wishes." He was reëlected by a somewhat reduced majority, but there was no evidence that his hold on the district was weakened to any perceptible degree.

He had become reconciled with Senator Hale, who like himself was bitterly opposed to expansion, and in October visited the senator at his Ellsworth home. The nomination of Reed's candidate as collector of customs at Portland the following February attracted considerable attention as marking the final triumph of the Speaker in a controversy which had begun in the early eighties. It was generally attributed to his renewal of friendly relations with Senator Hale.[1] Outside his own district, however, he was reported to have been largely disregarded by the administration in matters of patronage.

Congress opened for the short session on December 5, 1898. The aftermath of the war, as Reed had foreseen, was a series of vexatious problems in the immediate foreground, involving ultimate possibilities which no one could estimate. The glamour had passed. The noble army of Cuban martyrs had become an armed rabble as unchivalrous as it was unsanitary. Inflated reputations had collapsed. Secretary Alger was busy explaining the failures of the War Department, the heroes were squabbling like prima donnas over their share of public favor and over all hung the smell of the "embalmed beef." The proposed annexation of Porto Rico and the Philippines promised to cause a lively fight, although it was confidently expected that the Hawaiian precedent would carry great weight and the expansionist program would succeed.

It was common knowledge long before Congress convened, that Reed was as anti-expansionist as ever and that he regarded the prospective acquisitions as merely additional liabilities of a useless and unnecessary war. President McKinley, however, rightly or wrongly, was convinced that public opinion demanded the retention of the Philippine Islands. For some time the outcome was not altogether certain and old-line Republicans like Senators Hoar and Hale, together with ex-Senator George F. Edmunds, threatened to rally considerable opposition. Reed's sarcastic remark that "we have bought 10,000,000 Malays at $2.00 a head unpicked, and nobody knows what it will cost to pick them," went all over the nation. He stirred unfavorable comment among sentimentalists by his contemptuous references to the "yellow-bellies" of our trans-Pacific conquests, although it was not long before "civilize 'em with a Krag" became a march-

[1] Washington *Post*, February 16, 1899.

ing song of American soldiers in the islands and "Hell-roaring Jake" Smith was showing, as Reed ironically pointed out, that General Weyler's methods were by no means a monopoly of the Spaniard and that cruelty was an inevitable concomitant of imposing a colonial system on an unwilling people.

There was widespread feeling that if the Speaker took the lead there were enough independent Republicans, in combination with anti-expansionist Democrats, to carry a hostile resolution through the lower House with defeat of the treaty by the Senate as the inevitable result. The Speaker, however, was and always had been a strict party man. He probably believed that the majority favored the President's program although he was equally firm in the belief that that majority was wrong. He declined to lead an organized revolt against the President's policy. He neither wrote nor spoke officially on the subject but never hesitated to give his opinions. "Reed is terribly bitter," wrote Theodore Roosevelt to Henry Cabot Lodge on December 20, 1898, "saying all sorts of ugly things about the administration and its policy in private talks, so I keep out of his way, for I am fond of him and I confess that his attitude is painful and disappointing to me beyond words." "To those willing to listen," wrote the correspondent of the New York *Tribune*, April 23, 1899, "he would discourse last winter by the hour almost" against imperialism. More than once, according to Champ Clark, he refused recognition for private bills carrying small appropriations on the ground that "the money is needed to pay for the Malays" and when Congress appropriated $300,000 for the Philadelphia Commercial Museum he remarked with a sigh, "This seems like a great waste of money. We could buy 150,000 naked Sulus with that." [1]

Unwilling to break with the party which he had served so long and equally unwilling to accept its new policies, he was

[1] New York *World*, December 14, 1902.

steadily being forced into a position of isolation. But he still retained his hold on the House. The respect of that body as a whole and the affection and admiration of those who knew him best never wavered. He was no longer contented in his position, however, and Amos J. Cummings gives a glimpse of him during what proved to be his last month of service: "The Speaker of the House looms up colossal above all other figures. He has no intimate associates. On pleasant days he lumbers along the Avenue on his way to the Capitol, silent and alone, occasionally stopping to gaze at something attractive in the store windows. . . . He lives upon a column far more lofty than that of Simon Stylites, enwrapped in his own personality, placidly surveying the political herd below him; and no earthquake has yet overthrown the column." [1]

The treaty was ratified, the necessary appropriation was voted, March 2, 1899, and the United States embarked on its colonial ventures. "I think I can see a sardonic smile on Joe Chamberlain's face this morning," Reed remarked when the momentous decision had been made. Years before when the English statesman visited Washington, Reed had told him, in response to a suggestion that the United States should formulate and carry out a Far Eastern policy, that we had too much trouble in governing our own territory to help pull John Bull's chestnuts out of the fire.

There was a wealth of incident in those spacious days of the Spanish War and some of it furnished the Speaker with splendid targets for his satiric wit. When General Shafter published a newspaper article casting reflections on Reed's loyalty to the administration, the item was forwarded to him by another officer with the suggestion that such language called for a court martial. "I suppose General Shafter was looking for a furlough on full pay," was the Speaker's sole response. Apparently he had

[1] Washington *Post,* February 26, 1899.

in mind the President's recent action mitigating the sentence of General Eagan, who in the course of the "embalmed beef" investigation had called his superior officer General Miles a liar and threatened to cram the contents of a camp latrine down his throat. Another anecdote of the same sort which caused great glee in Washington was his remark to Congressman Lacey of Iowa, whose appearance was supposed to suggest that of Secretary Alger. The alleged resemblance was called to the Speaker's attention while Lacey was addressing the House and at the conclusion of his remarks, Reed strolled over to the member's seat:

"Brother Lacey, they tell me you look like Alger. There is a faint resemblance, I admit; but if you care to increase it, why don't you get yourself white-washed?" [1]

To the Schley-Sampson controversy he also made a characteristic contribution: "I don't see what the row between these two naval heroes is about. As far as I can see one of them wasn't in the fight at all and the other was doing his damnedest to get out of it."

Reed's prestige as a parliamentary officer remained unaffected by the course of events even though, as Amos J. Cummings wrote, the appropriation for carrying out the peace treaty was put through "beneath the beady eyes of the Imperator" who was known to detest it, and in spite of rumors that in the next Congress "the rule of the Imperator may end in the revolt of the Pretorians." [2]

There were continued protests from the minority at his arbitrary rule, Bailey of Texas and James Hamilton Lewis, then representing a Washington district, taking the lead against the Speaker in these parliamentary wrangles. Bailey was frequently suppressed by characteristic Reed methods, but in the case of

[1] New York *Tribune,* April 23, 1899.
[2] Washington *Post,* March 5, 1899.

Lewis, who by his industrious study of rules and precedents probably caused the Speaker more embarrassment than any other opponent, there seems to have been a great measure of mutual respect. Of Reed, Lewis once remarked:

"My increasing acquaintance has developed my admiration. He has not let himself grow stagnant with mere legislative routine as have many men in Congress. He has kept up his letters and sciences and seems to emulate Edmund Burke. In my opinion, compared with any other Republican he stands as Saul did among his people, head and shoulders above them all."

But it was concerning Lewis that another characteristic story went the rounds. One morning he rose in the House on a question of personal privilege to complain that a New York newspaper had described him as "a thing of beauty and a joy forever." *Sotto voce* came the Speaker's comment, "They should have called you a jaw forever."

When on December 14, 1898, a Missouri member delivered a scathing attack on the Committee on Rules, Reed made a brief reply which, as the Washington *Post* remarked next day, was "only a few words, but the Speaker vindicated himself as the Terrible Turk of political debate." John Randolph, Reed pointed out, had made much the same complaint about curtailment of debate as early as 1816, but in actual practice "the House may have noticed that, however much despotism is exercised by the rules, there is no subject in the heavens above or in the earth beneath that has not been discussed, even in this present Congress."

During his last years as Speaker, Reed was constantly called upon for information or opinions on the parliamentary tangles of various organizations throughout the country. His little manual of parliamentary law published in 1894 was widely used and in spite of the pressure of his official duties he gave courteous attention to the requests which continually poured into his office, his assistant, Asher C. Hinds, often devoting considerable research to the technical points involved. To the *North American Review* of June, 1897, he contributed his last and one of his ablest articles on parliamentary matters, "How the House Does Business," which gave an admirable picture of the duties and responsibilities of the Speaker's office when it was at the very summit of its dignity and power.

But possession of such power had its disadvantages and it was noticed that Reed was steadily becoming more watchful and less sociable. A trifling incident reported by one of the correspondents shows one of the embarrassments of his position. According to the story the Speaker one morning stopped in the lobby and was soon surrounded by a group of friends chatting and joking in high good humor. Suddenly they were interrupted by the appearance of an elderly woman who timidly made her way to the Speaker with an appeal that he appoint the committees so that her claim against the government might receive consideration. Reed glanced around and saw other suppliants preparing to waylay him. A look of weariness came over his face and he hurried off to the quiet of his own room, pushing through the groups of members without a word. 'They won't let him be amiable," said a friend. "If he smiles someone must take advantage of it." [1]

A somewhat different touch appears in the story of his reply to Joseph Washington, a Tennessee member who tried in vain to secure recognition on a bill paying the claim of a Methodist publishing house for the destruction of its building in Atlanta during the Civil War. In a personal appeal the Representative asked in vain that he be accorded recognition.

"Mr. Speaker, what can I tell my constituents to show that I am doing something on their behalf?"

Imperturbably the Speaker quoted the refrain of two popular

[1] New York *Tribune*, July 22, 1897.

songs of the gay nineties: "Joseph, just tell them that you saw me," and, "Tell them, sometimes you think I will, and sometimes you think I won't." [1]

As the short session drew to a close hostility toward the Speaker steadily mounted, accompanied by reports that his days of leadership were numbered, phenomena which had often been noted in the past. But, in the words of a shrewd observer, "The hostile of mid-March becomes the disciple and censer-swinger of December. The stormy vernal equinox is changed into a perfumed zephyr. And Reed, large, bland, cynical, observant, knowing the whole game and appraising the players at their genuine worth, resumes his gavel with a placid wink." [2] This time however, Reed's long term of public service was drawing to a close, although at his own initiative.

March 3 at last arrived, the day which, Reed wrote, the distracted Speaker always welcomes "as the saint ought to welcome death and paradise." Bailey, in spite of the frequent castigations he had received, made some appreciative comments on the Speaker's services and moved the customary resolution of thanks. Reed, for what was to be the last time, stood up behind the Speaker's desk. The stillness, the correspondents noted, was impressive and the Speaker "fairly towered over his surroundings." Slowly and deliberately he returned his thanks.

"In laying down for the third time the insignia of an office which has but one superior and no peer, I might perhaps fairly congratulate myself upon having had a great opportunity to administer a great office in the fashion indicated by the noble words known to our law, 'without fear, favor, or hope of reward.' [Applause.] Where I have succeeded I am sure to have your final approval; where I have failed I am sure you have given me credit for honorable intention. [Applause.]

[1] *Ibid.,* May 4, 1897.
[2] Washington *Post,* March 11, 1899.

"With pleasant memories of our past, which I shall always cherish, and best wishes for your future, which I shall always entertain, I now declare this House adjourned without day."

That same evening the Speaker was the guest of the New York Republican delegation, which presented him with an inscribed loving-cup. Representative Wallace T. Foote made the speech of presentation, in the course of which he paid tribute to "the courage and true patriotism he showed when he defied the storm of criticism and abuse from puny politicians, whose creed is present success to themselves—men who cannot comprehend the broad principles of a nation's ultimate good nor discern the true statesman whose sole motive is to establish them."

Reed's public career was over.

Soon after adjournment Reed took a trip South accompanied
by his daughter, and at Jekyll Island had a brief meeting with
President McKinley. He had sedulously avoided the White
House since the latter's inauguration, Dingley and Cannon
maintaining the necessary connection between the Representatives and the chief executive. In view of this well-known situation the Jekyll Island meeting, brief as it was, attracted considerable attention and there were many reports in circulation
as to its political significance. No authoritative statement was
forthcoming on either side, and Reed himself told a reporter
who questioned him after his return that the chief significance of
the trip was that he was still on friendly terms with Mrs. Reed,
who had been obliged to remain in Washington during his absence.

There had been recurrent rumors during the last year that his
retirement was imminent and there was little surprise in inner
political circles when it was announced on April 19 that he would
soon enter the law firm of Simpson, Thatcher and Barnum of
New York as senior partner with a guarantee of $50,000 a year.
Reed had been in more comfortable circumstances in recent years.
As Speaker he received a salary of $8,000 a year, his writings
and occasional speaking engagements brought him a considerable
return, and in 1896 he had succeeded Governor William E.
Russell of Massachusetts as referee for twenty-eight of the
principal life insurance companies of the country, a responsible
post with a generous salary and no very onerous duties. Although
living simply and avoiding extravagance, he had never possessed
the ability to accumulate. His rigorous principles of official

propriety prevented his taking advantage of the money-making opportunities always available to a man in his position. His expenses, in view of his political and social responsibilities, had been considerable and his retirement was publicly stated to be due to a desire to make provision for his family in view of his advancing years and limited means.

It was everywhere admitted, however, that there were additional factors in the situation. Reed had obviously become dissatisfied with existing conditions in the Republican party and the new policies resulting from the war with Spain. He might jeer at the colonial enterprises of the McKinley administration but at heart he honestly regarded them as betrayal of a national trust and flagrant disregard of a great tradition. To a friend who mentioned that he planned a visit to our insular possessions but was undecided as to the route, he once remarked: "Well, if you travel westward you'll reach the Philippines by way of Hawaii, and if you travel eastward you'll reach Hawaii by way of the Philippines. The whole question is whether you prefer to take your plague before your leprosy, or take your leprosy before your plague." [1]

His deeper feeling was apparent however, in his statement to Asher C. Hinds: "I have tried, perhaps not always successfully, to make the acts of my public life accord with my conscience, and I cannot now do this thing." Still more striking and effective was an unpublished arraignment of the new policies found among his papers and apparently written during the course of the Paris peace negotiations. There is evident in this document the loyal adherence to the principles of a generation which believed that "our fathers did not make their Declaration of Independence as a piece of rhetoric but as a guide of national life," and the burning indignation of the Civil War Republican that a new

[1] F. E. Leupp, "Personal Recollections of Thomas B. Reed," *The Outlook*, September 3, 1910.

generation should cheerfully and apparently with a minimum of thoughtful consideration assume "the great risk of forgetting the foundation principles of our government. Our Fathers forgot them once, and Lincoln's Second Inaugural tells the solemn story in words as stately and sublime as ever flowed from lips inspired by God. I do not compare our possible governing of others without their participation to the sin of human slavery; but, as I remember the story of the Indians whom we have governed at home and of the negroes we are governing at home, that time may come when I can claim the credit of great moderation speaking of the government of people utterly unknown four thousand miles away." [1]

While the report of his impending retirement brought a flood of protests and expressions of loyalty from his House colleagues coupled with assurances that the speakership was his as long as the Republicans held the House, Reed was well aware that his position, in view of his feeling toward the administration, was certain to be embarrassing. There was nothing of the Mugwump in him. He believed in party government. "A good party," he once wrote, "is better than the best man that ever lived." He was a Republican and had lived and worked forty years under its traditional tenets. He could not lead a revolt nor could he go over to the opposition. There was only one course he could follow and that was to abandon political life. "It is a very lonely life that a man leads," he once remarked in a public address delivered after his retirement, "who becomes aware of truths before their time." That of the man who keeps the faith when others abandon it is no less so. The death of Nelson Dingley on January 13, 1899, was another factor and the loss of this intimate friend and loyal lieutenant, had, he informed members of the latter's family, removed the last inducement to remain in Congress.

[1] McCall, *Reed*, 259.

Before assuming his new duties Reed spent the summer in Europe with his wife and daughter, being received everywhere with the respect and consideration due one of the most distinguished citizens of the American republic. He returned in August and the lingering hopes of some of his friends that he might combine a New York law practice with continued service in Congress were dashed by his formal resignation addressed to Governor Powers on September 4, 1899. "Congress without Tom Reed!" said an editorial in the New York *Tribune*. "Who can imagine it?"

He had always been averse to displays of sentiment, but now issued a brief address to his supporters of the district he had so long represented. "Words alone are quite inadequate," he admitted, "and I must appeal to your memories. During three and twenty years of political life not always peaceful, you have never questioned one single public act of mine. Other men have had to look after their districts, but my district has always looked after me." To those who had supported him, Republicans and Democrats alike, he could express honest appreciation, for "no sail has been trimmed for any breeze nor any doubtful flag ever flown." His commission was now returned. "Office as 'a ribbon to stick in your coat' is worth nobody's consideration. Office as opportunity is worth all consideration. That opportunity you have given me, untrammeled, in the fullest and amplest manner, and I return you sincerest thanks. If I have deserved any praise it belongs of right to you."

On October 18, he was admitted to the New York bar, his fellow-alumnus Thomas H. Hubbard moving his admission as a practicing lawyer and member of the bar of another State. Judge Van Brunt of the Appellate Division approved the application, administered the oath, and the last phase of Reed's career had begun. On November 17, he appeared for the defendants in a suit brought by William J. Logan against J. G. Moore,

William Rockefeller, Henry Rogers and others for an accounting of the affairs of the consolidated Brooklyn gas companies.

Reed could not but be a striking figure under any conditions,
but Reed the prosperous corporation lawyer lacked some of the
picturesqueness of Reed the Speaker or floor leader of the House
Republicans. His friends noted with affectionate regret that the
slouchy loose-fitting clothes disappeared and that he now pa-
tronized a fashionable tailor. He was surrounded by a circle of
devoted friends, some old, some new, and entered with zest
into the social life of the city. Mark Twain, with whom he had
much in common, was now one of his closest associates. Ranking
with Chauncey Depew and Joseph H. Choate as a popular after-
dinner speaker, he was bombarded with invitations, most of
which he declined. The occasional addresses reported during
these years are almost wholly on non-political topics. Once or
twice his name was "mentioned" as a possible candidate for New
York office, but his professional work absorbed an increasing
amount of time and he remained unresponsive to such overtures.
He received the honorary degree of Doctor of Laws from Columbia University in 1900. If he had retained any lingering
presidential ambitions they must have been dissipated by the
death of McKinley and the succession of Roosevelt, young, vigorous and intensely ambitious.

When Reed resumed the practice of law it had been freely
stated that his value to his firm would consist chiefly in his political prestige and the confidence he commanded generally
among men of affairs. These were great assets undoubtedly and
an increase of business followed his accession to the firm, but he
threw himself vigorously into professional work.

He was in his sixty-first year, his career for more than twenty
years had been political, and while maintaining connection with
his Portland practice he had given it little active attention. He
frankly admitted to his friends in these last years that he was

deficient in his knowledge of law. With expert assistance always available in matters of detail, his old-time ability as·a debater to grasp the essentials of any issue stood him good stead in the court room. "Mr. Reed was not a great master of legal technicality," wrote Thomas H. Hubbard. "He was not a great student of obsolete cases. He was great in his comprehension of legal principles and of their use to promote the ends of justice." His most important case was that of the Carnegie Steel Company vs. the Cambria Iron Company (183 United States, 403), an involved and difficult patent case which he won after thorough and conscientious personal study, donning overalls and watching minutely the manufacturing processes concerned in order to strengthen his mastery of the facts as well as the law. "There seemed to be no character of court proceedings into which ex-Speaker Reed could not infuse some humor," wrote another observer of his work. "Instead of declining," declared the New York *Sun,* December 9, 1902, in an editorial on this phase of Mr. Reed's career at the bar, "his distinction increased, even under the test of the fierce competition of New York. So far from being lost, he stood out all the more prominently because of the great mass of ability above which he rose."

If the main object of his retirement from politics had been the accumulation of a competence for his family, he succeeded to an unusual degree in the limited time at his disposal. His friends often noted that he had a decided speculative bent and believed, in some cases at least, that his lack of surplus income in the past had meant little after all, inasmuch as he would probably have lost it in business or investment projects. In his New York position, however, he had the benefit of expert advisers, and thanks to their friendly interest he invested his surplus earnings to advantage and was reported to have profited greatly from the Northern Pacific corner of 1901. In three years he accumulated a considerable estate and left his family comfortably provided for.

He wrote little except a few brief magazine articles, but often discussed the possibility of some more extended literary work when in a position to retire from legal practice. His name appeared as editor of the compilation *Modern Eloquence*, published in 1900, but the bulk of the work was done by others. His mind was as keen and his tongue as sarcastic as ever and his comments on men and events occasionally found their way into print by indirect routes, although he gave practically no interviews to the press.

In 1899, soon after his retirement, one of Reed's classmates remarked to Frank L. Dingley, "I predict Reed will not live three years," basing this prediction on the danger involved in changing environment and activity for a man of Reed's years and regular habits. As a matter of fact, he began to fail in health, though not seriously, early in 1902. He had greatly reduced his weight by dieting and the use of Turkish baths, looked well, and judging from ordinary appearances had many years of active life still before him. He delivered the centennial address at Bowdoin College in June and spent a great deal of time during the summer with old friends and associates in Portland and vicinity.

Resuming work in New York in the fall, he attended Mark Twain's birthday dinner on November 28, where he made what proved to be his last speech. Next day he went to Philadelphia and from there to Washington. On Monday afternoon, December 2, he visited the Capitol and was soon in the Ways and Means committee room surrounded by old friends. Congress was just assembling for the short session, and he had an opportunity for some caustic comments on President Roosevelt's Philippine and anti-trust policies. It was on the latter phase of public business that he uttered his last recorded epigram while in conversation with Sereno E. Payne, who, when Reed suggested the desirability of amending the Constitution during the coming session, inquired as to the object:

"Why, an indefinable something is to be done, in a way nobody knows how, at a time nobody knows when, that will accomplish nobody knows what. That, as I understand it, is the program against the trusts. The opportunity is so broad and so long that I wonder that you will not take advantage of it."

From the committee room he went on to the Senate wing of the Capitol, and in the Marble Room suddenly collapsed in severe pain. He was removed to his room at the Arlington Hotel where the doctors, hurriedly summoned, found that he was suffering from appendicitis, and, more serious, from chronic Bright's disease. His apparent good health, as one of them pointed out, was really a misfortune. A thorough physical examination and careful diagnosis, had he been ill enough to resort to them in recent years, would certainly have had beneficial results. The kidney involvement would have been detected and his life, under a proper regimen, might have been prolonged for years. As it was the discovery came too late; his condition moved rapidly from bad to worse; his wife and daughter were summoned from New York, and by Friday afternoon the attending physicians, reënforced by a Philadelphia specialist, admitted that there was little hope for recovery. He was delirious at intervals, sometimes imagining himself in the chair; again, debating on the floor. At other times he argued in legal phraseology with the attending physicians.

On Saturday evening he became unconscious and the end came soon after midnight. In the hotel banquet room the Gridiron Club, of which he had so often been an honored guest, was holding the first dinner of the winter season. The members and their guests were immediately informed that Mr. Reed had passed away. Justice Brewer stopped in the middle of an address

THE MONUMENT AT PORTLAND, ME.

and all joined in singing one of Mr. Reed's favorite songs. Then the gathering dispersed, and in the words of one who was present, "there was hardly a word spoken; there was many a wet cheek, and there was a feeling in the breast of every one that the life of one of our greatest Americans had closed." [1]

On Sunday afternoon, under a lowering winter sky his body was removed to the Pennsylvania Station. There was no ceremony; the streets were almost empty; and as the hearse moved past the Treasury and along Pennsylvania Avenue, the route he had so often followed in the days of his congressional service and where his giant figure had long been familiar to the newsboys, the shop-keepers and passers-by, there were few who gave the cortège more than a passing glance. Here and there, however, a spectator who realized its significance stood with head bared in farewell to one of the great leaders of his time.

Interment took place at Portland on December 9, after services at the State Street Unitarian Church. There was a great throng anxious to do honor to one of the greatest men the State had produced, but more significant was the fact that, without any pre-arrangement, when the noon hour struck, business was suspended and a Sabbath-like quiet rested over the city.

The passing of the great parliamentarian attracted attention all over the world and there was general recognition of the important part he had played in the development of modern legislative institutions. In the American press there appeared a great mass of eulogies, estimates critical and uncritical, reminiscences and anecdotes, indiscriminate praise, and here and there a carping reminder of the tyranny of the "Czar." Among his contemporaries in American public life there was general agreement that Reed was a great man. The tone of the press was similar. "He was one of the really great men of the times," declared the Washington *Post*, "in the view of those who knew him best,

[1] Samuel L. Powers, *Portraits of a Half Century,* 272.

one of the greatest in native intellect of his generation." "Too great a man to be President" is a comment frequently found in contemporary editorials.

The judgments of 1902 can hardly be accepted in their entirety thirty years later, but the opinions of Reed's contemporaries have stood the test of time remarkably well. In the history of the last quarter of the nineteenth century he still stands among American public men, to use the simile which was overworked by admirers in his lifetime, towering like Saul, head and shoulders over all but one or two of his contemporaries.

A mere glance at the record of his congressional career is sufficient to show that he was not a great legislator, although as Speaker he influenced the legislative program to a greater degree than any party leader of his time. Jonathan P. Dolliver of Iowa, one of his House colleagues and later a distinguished Senator, an excellent judge of matters political, asserted that had Reed identified himself directly with some great legislative measure he would certainly have secured the presidency. He was responsible for suppression of countless ill-advised and extravagant bills. As an enemy of jobs and jobbery he saved the Treasury an incalculable amount, but while Presidents and Governors have gained fame by the vigorous exercise of the veto power, the Speaker who applies the same weapon to embryonic measures wins more hostility than fame.

His opinions on questions of public policy were usually sound and have in general been vindicated by the course of events, but no thoughtful person would maintain today, as Frank L. Dingley did, that he was "one of the profoundest students of economic and social phenomena that ever sat in Congress." He had, it is true, an acute mind which enabled him to see issues in their entirety, to grasp their broader significance, to judge the ultimate as well as immediate effects of proposed enactments. But his political economy was, after all, that of the New England protectionist school, and his intense partisanship which made the Green-backer, the Democrat or the Populist too often appear in his eyes as an enemy of his country, frequently blinded him to evils which those opponents, however blunderingly, were endeavoring to remedy. Theodore Dreiser, then a young reporter on a St. Louis newspaper, remembered the Speaker's somewhat heartless attitude when he questioned him about the grievances which had produced "Coxey's army." "It doesn't matter what their grievance is," was Reed's testy answer. "This is a government of law and prescribed political procedure. Our people must abide by that." [1] His reliance on the forces of social evolution as the ultimate remedy for existing ills prevented his realization of the effectiveness of governmental action in expediting and controlling, in a measure at least, that evolutionary process. He could ironically congratulate Theodore Roosevelt on his discovery of the ten commandments, but Roosevelt had perceived, as Reed had not, the need of attacking deep-seated evils in our economic and social structure.

Reed was both indolent and industrious. He was capable of tremendous exertion under pressure but, with the exception of parliamentary procedure, few subjects held him to more than temporary and somewhat spasmodic activity. Nevertheless, as Speaker and minority leader he handled, with exacting fidelity to his trust, an enormous amount of routine business. His desk in the Speaker's room, observers often noted, seemed to be in hopeless confusion, but work proceeded according to schedule and the Speaker displayed an almost uncanny familiarity with the multitude of bills and resolutions on the calendars. Even more important, he knew the members, their abilities, their foibles and their weaknesses, and could judge to a nicety the condition of that somewhat erratic and unmanageable force "the mind of the House."

[1] *A Book about Myself,* 408.

His greatest concrete achievement was in the field of parliamentary procedure. He established beyond dispute the principle of party responsibility in the lower chamber. The party became a compact disciplined body, the interests of individual members were subordinated to those of the group, and the Speaker became a functionary of power and influence unique in legislative annals. The system was not a product of usurpation. Representative Hepburn of Iowa, who had tried to secure changes in the rules during the 55th Congress and who took part in the movement which at length produced important modifications in the 61st, stated the facts soon after Reed had laid down the gavel for the last time:

There was no ground for calling Mr. Reed a tyrant or a Czar. He never usurped any authority or power. He simply administered the rules as we gave them to him. In my judgment it was very foolish for members to place the political power of their constituencies in the hands of any one man but we did it. We gave Mr. Reed the absolute power to determine who should speak for the House. I think he exercised that power as fairly and evenly as any man could. We gave him the power to select the Committee on Rules, and then we gave that committee wonderful power. Mr. Reed had his own ideas about legislation and he used his power to promote or retard measures, but it was the power we gave him.

The weakness of the Reed system lay in the very extent of the Speaker's powers. Given the courage, will-power, experience and integrity of Reed, his rare qualities of leadership, and dominating ability, the system worked. Reed could handle the horses of Diomedes. With his firm hand on the reins and the lash ready for emergencies, the party steeds might sweat and champ the bit but the legislative chariot moved forward steadily. His immediate successors were able drivers, but neither possessed the master touch of the reins, and the lash irritated but did not cow. In 1910 the horses turned upon the driver.

Much of the Reed system is still in operation, but the speaker-ship, shorn of its power over committee assignments and especially over the Committee on Rules by the revolution of that year, is no longer the speakership—dignified and powerful though the office still remains—of 1899.

As a party leader and debater he has had no successor, and it is impossible to leave this phase of his career without pointing out how his career was circumscribed by the American presidential system and separation of powers. As a parliamentary leader he was the greatest ever produced by the Republican party, perhaps by any party in American history, but his qualities were not those which rendered probable or even possible the attainment of the presidency. No caucus can make a real party leader, a fact which was vividly illustrated by the failure of Joseph W. Bailey in the 55th Congress. Reed's position was practically unquestioned throughout eight Congresses. In Great Britain or Canada he would have been Prime Minister, with long and successful tenure. Reed, whether on the Treasury Bench or leader of the opposition, would have been a superb figure.

But in the last analysis the personal qualities of the man were such that his place in American public life is secure for all time. Few men have risen so high or held power so long in a democratic country who had such disdain for the arts of demagogy or even for ordinary conciliatory tactics. He scorned flattery in all its forms and at times seemed to take a perverse satisfaction in provoking antagonism. Pitman Pulsifer, clerk of a Senate committee, once related an incident which was typical of this side of Reed's temperament. Pulsifer was a Maine court reporter in his youth and on one occasion a lawyer who was opposing Reed in a pending trial paused at the reporter's table and playfully smoothed down his hair. Reed observed the act, strolled across the room, and deliberately rubbed his hair back the wrong way.[1]

[1] New York *Sun*, December 8, 1902.

He was as ready to ridicule popular fallacies as those of his colleagues in Congress. In his dealings with the latter he relied on reason and intellectual force and not on love and admiration to produce results, and while he won love from many and admiration from all, it was always the dominant force of his intellect and will which made his leadership so effective. "The unquestioning loyalty of the Republicans to Reed," Speaker Crisp once remarked, "reminds me of the Hindu, who, kneeling in prayer before his idol, consoles himself with the idea that he knows his God is ugly and thinks he is great."

His sarcasm made him feared, and undoubtedly his use of this weapon—"the language of the devil," as it has been called—worked to his political hurt. Applied to Democrats it aroused amusement and admiration among his Republican colleagues. His retort to Springer's "I would rather be right than President" is perhaps best known of all his sayings: "The gentleman need not worry. He will never be either!" "I have read and heard much of the wild ass's colt of the desert," he remarked of a South Dakota member, "but I never had any clear conception of what manner of animal it really was till I saw Pickler in action." In the same category was his suggestion that the Democratic party adopt as its slogan in 1892, "The prophet and the ballot-box—both stuffed." But he was also reported to have described Blaine as "the great white elephant of our party," and Harrison, McKinley, and many other party colleagues served as targets for his arrows. "Reed's wit is enjoyable," McKinley once remarked, "especially if you do not happen to be the person at whom it is directed."

"The fact was," wrote Henry Cabot Lodge, "that Mr. Reed had a mind of remarkable originality. He not only was an eminently independent thinker and a very strong and sound one, but he thought in his own way and framed his conclusions in a manner peculiar to himself. Every fact, every occurrence, important or unimportant, common or uncommon, was returned or reflected from his mind at an angle quite different from that of other people." As a result, his retorts, his whimsical comments on persons and events, his aphorisms, have become part of the American political tradition. These sayings, recorded in the press and the memoirs of his contemporaries, would fill scores of pages.

The most commonplace incidents were given a special color wherever he was involved. When he hurried into the House one morning as a Democratic tariff bill was being called up for debate and forgot to remove his gloves, Boutelle whispered to him that they would attract attention unless removed quickly. "Charles," answered his colleague, "why do you speak with so little consideration? Can't you see that I can't trust myself yet to handle this thing without gloves?" On another occasion he had an argument in the cloak room with Representative Bynum as to which of their colleagues, Berry or Curtis, was the tallest. Berry, who had been slouched down in his chair, got to his feet and straightened up for measuring. "My God, Berry," exclaimed Reed, "how much of yourself do you keep in your pockets?" When he stated to several cronies that his weight was one hundred and ninety-nine pounds, he met their skeptical rejoinders with the solemn pronouncement, "No gentleman ever weighs more than two hundred pounds." Asked his opinion of a Papal message, he remarked: "The overpowering unimportance of this makes me speechless. I have nothing to say." An editor who was preparing a symposium on "the greatest problem now confronting the American people," sent a reporter to get Reed's opinion. "How to dodge a bicycle," was the response.

Samuel G. Blythe tells a story of an attempt on the part of several newspaper correspondents to secure Reed's opinion on Speaker Henderson's retirement, a topic giving rise to much gossip and speculation in its day. Reed was in Washington at the time and the reporters surrounded him on a street corner while one of them made a tactful and carefully worded request, pointing out the great value to the country of the ex-Speaker's opinions on every subject. Reed listened courteously, gazed meditatively at the sky, and at last turned to his questioners with an air of great solemnity. "That cloud indicates that we are going to have rain," and that was all the satisfaction they got.

A Washington *Post* reporter has recorded a somewhat similar experience. An important opinion on political matters, purporting to come from Mr. Reed, had that day appeared in a New York paper. The reporter asked the Speaker, whom he discovered in front of a haberdasher's window on Pennsylvania Avenue, if he had made the statement in question.

"Does So-and-So say I said it?" asked Mr. Reed in his anxious, high pitched voice.

"Yes, Mr. Reed," said the reporter, "he says you told him so."

Mr. Reed turned his attention again to the neckties.

"Well," said he dryly, "one of us is a liar."

To another reporter who visited him at his summer home to secure an opinion on recent resolutions of a Grand Army post condemning the Speaker for his refusal to accord recognition on certain pension legislation, he gave a strikingly accurate and vivid summary of the reasoning behind such protests. Every post, he pointed out, was likely to have in its membership a less desirable element. These members, "whose war record isn't always a thing to be paraded, get together and resolve three things. First, we saved the country; second, the country wouldn't have been saved if it hadn't been for us; third, we want it."

Many of his comments in the course of business on the floor are matters of record, but the student of proceedings during his congressional service must note with regret the occasional entry

in the *Record:* "Mr. Reed made a remark inaudible to the reporter." E. L. Lampson, one of the House clerks, related how
from their vantage point, they heard occasional comments from
the Speaker that were not intended for the *Record.* "When Bailey
was the Democratic leader," he recalled soon after Reed's death,
"he advised Jerry Simpson one day to go and inform himself.
'The gentleman from Texas should not make so unreasonable a
request,' commented the Speaker."

On another occasion, after the reading of the Journal, a member from Kansas, a Populist, arose to correct the record, and in
a hesitating manner, said: "Mr. Speaker, I want to call your attention to an omission—in my mind." "That is unnecessary,"
said Mr. Reed in an undertone, "you are a 'Pop.' " [1]

William L. Lorimer, on one occasion rose to ask for the correction of the record of a yea and nay vote. "Mr. Speaker, it appears that I am not recorded, although I distinctly voted 'no'
twice."

"The gentleman from Illinois is entitled to only one vote,"
was the Speaker's comment as he admitted the correction, and
the House roared at the embarrassment of the Illinois member.

During one of the stormy sessions of the 51st Congress a
Southern member, startled by one of the Speaker's decisions at
the moment when he had just cut a morsel from a large plug of
chewing tobacco, jumped to his feet and shook the plug at the
chair, shouting, "This is damnable, suh! Damnable!" "It looks
it," answered Reed mildly, and turned his attention elsewhere.

But such incidents show only one side of Reed's personality.
No Speaker was more punctilious as to the dignity and decorum
of the House or more meticulous in enforcing the rules. Where
smoking was forbidden, the rule was enforced and Reed himself
observed it to the letter. He banished the venders' fruit and

[1] Washington *Post,* December 17, 1902.

cigar stands from the House wing of the Capitol. While courtesy personified to visitors and persons with legitimate business, he insisted that the doorkeepers and other officers permit no intrusion on the part of unauthorized persons.

He demanded that members observe proper decorum on the floor. "The Czar commands you to haul down those flags of truce," was the message carried by a page to an ex-Confederate, who had elevated his feet on his desk, thereby displaying his white socks in what seemed to the Speaker an unseemly manner. A Massachusetts member, during the long debate on the McKinley tariff in sweltering midsummer weather, once took off his coat in Committee of the Whole when the Speaker was absent, and finished his speech in his shirt-sleeves. Reed heard of the incident, and next day when a member who noticed that the Speaker remained in the chair beyond his usual luncheon hour inquired the reason, replied, "Well, I'm afraid if I leave the chair some graceless scamp may get up and take off his trousers. It's hotter today than it was yesterday."

His command of the House, especially during his last four years in the speakership, was remarkably effective and occasionally received illustration in unexpected ways. On March 29, 1897, an exciting incident took place. James S. Sherman of New York was in the chair and became involved in a parliamentary wrangle with an Indiana member. The latter refused to take his seat and in an instant the House was in a turmoil, the members crowding forward, shouting and shaking their fists. When the uproar was at its height, as an onlooker described the scene, "suddenly the doors burst open, and the large form of the Speaker came into view. The effect of his appearance was electrical. It was like a big country school. In the teacher's absence the pupils had thrown all discipline to the winds. With the teacher's return all was quiet." The Speaker proceeded to lecture the delinquent member in a fatherly manner on the inherent reasonableness of the rules, which were intended for the general good even if they sometimes seemed oppressive to the individual. The storm was over almost as suddenly as it began.

The vigilant reporter of the Washington *Post* on February 10, 1896, noted an incident which he declared was "an interesting illustration of the potency of the leadership which Reed exercises." The Speaker had left the rostrum and dropped into a seat on the floor. A score of "lesser Republicans" immediately found their way to the neighborhood "as tacks are drawn to a magnet," and it was noticeable that whenever Reed smiled their faces irradiated laughter. In the meantime a Democratic member was expatiating at wearisome length on "the crime of '73." The Speaker, forgetting the electric call-bell system, suddenly clapped his hands to summon a page, and "as though pulled by one string," there was a prolonged and enthusiastic outburst of applause from his neighbors.

He could be blunt enough with fellow members when occasion demanded it. "You are too big a fool to lead, and you haven't got sense enough to follow," he once told a colleague who mismanaged a certain measure then before the House. A member once pestered him for recognition and finally got it, only to have his bill killed by an objection from Cannon. He sought the latter in high dudgeon.

"What do you know about the bill?" asked the member.

Cannon admitted that his knowledge was limited.

"Then why did you object?" was the next demand.

"Because the Speaker asked me to," said Cannon, not caring to shoulder the blame.

"What do you mean by granting me recognition and getting Cannon to kill my bill?" next demanded the member of the Speaker.

Reed showed not the least bit of disturbance but said in his usual tone: "To get rid of you." [1]

To another member, who called his attention to the fact that a ruling just made was contrary to the principles laid down in his own *Rules*, he calmly returned the volume with the terse comment, "The book is wrong."

But at the same time he could be exceedingly considerate and generous, especially toward new members, and the Speaker's room was often filled with an admiring group of younger men. "He is one of the most benevolent and kindly men in assisting new legislators," Representative Walker of Massachusetts declared in 1896, "in giving information patiently and in helping them in every way that he can, above any other man in the House that I have ever met." "I am indebted to him for kindness, promotion, instruction, and commendation," recorded Champ Clark. "Though no two men ever sat together in the House who differed more radically in politics than he and I, I am proud to have counted him among my friends." "He was generous in recognizing merit," he also wrote. "The green-eyed monster did not bother him." For the clerks and other House employees he invariably showed the utmost consideration and no Speaker was more popular and respected among these officials.

But intellect, wit, leadership, and all the other qualities which Reed possessed in such abundance could never have given him his place in public life in the absence of one essential—integrity. He was honest in every sense of the word. His viewpoint, it is true, was usually that of those corporate interests which a later generation realizes had, for the most part, an evil influence on American politics. But through it all, while he supported policies which too often involved exploitation of men and resources for the benefit of minorities or special interests, he acted from honest convictions and he kept his hands clean. There were no "Mul-

[1] Washington *Post*, December 21, 1902.

ligan letters" to cloud his career. He could no more have written about "not being a dead head in the enterprise" than he could have attempted to steal the dome of the Capitol.

Amos Allen told of his refusal to make use of the franking privilege once accorded members at the telegraph office in the Capitol, insisting that his messages should be sent from the Pennsylvania Avenue office of the company properly prepaid. "The time may come," he said, "when I shall want to hit one of these telegraph companies a wallop, and I don't want to put myself in a position where I shall be charged with ingratitude." So general was his reputation for incorruptibility that the lobby, the official world of Washington, and the country at large accepted Reed's honesty as one of the undisputed facts of American politics. His friends even expressed surprise that it was mentioned in his obituaries. It was something to be taken for granted like the existence of the ocean.

But his honesty was not merely negative. He declared on one occasion, during a sharp clash with Townshend of Illinois: "If I have at any time been found upon the side of a railroad corporation, which is a term of reproach on his part, it has been because I was defending the cause of justice upon the floor of this House; and while I stand here a member of this House there is no man on the face of the earth so poor nor any corporation so rich that I will prostitute myself to injustice for the sake of that temporary advantage which comes of maintaining a false position because some dishonest men are clamoring against me. It is the duty of every member of this House to act upon his conscience and his sense of duty. It is his business to stand up for what he believes to be right, careless of what may happen to him in consequence thereof." [1] He meant exactly what he said. He never hesitated to take the unpopular side and his contempt for sham, humbug and demagogy was never more effective than in

[1] *Cong. Record*, 48 Cong., 1 Sess., 2049.

exposing the shifts and artifices of popularity-seeking members, who were willing to starve the public services, disregard the findings of the Court of Claims, or cheat the honest creditors of the nation in order to prate of economy on the stump. That there was political advantage in a certain course and political hurt in another, meant nothing to him; he depended on nobody; he formed his own conclusions and shaped his conduct accordingly.

Murat Halstead wrote at the time of Reed's death that "he did not look when Speaker of the House as though it could be worth while for another member ever to be Speaker." In a sense he has had no successor. But for those who knew him or those who have studied the history of the period, his figure is still present:—perhaps on the rostrum, placid and imperturbable, his features, as a humorous admirer once described them, "so strangely reminiscent of Raphael's cherub looking out in baby wonder upon a strange and unknown world," as though shaped for the express purpose of making his rulings seem more definitive or his retorts more incisive; or perhaps on the floor, as Henry Cabot Lodge described him, waiting for an opponent to conclude, "with every trace of expression banished from his face, and looking as if he had not an idea and hardly heard what was being said," when in an instant, by epigram or retort, he would illuminate the entire question or clear the national vision on a pending issue as other men could not do in hours or days of dreary exposition. "The wit of Reed," wrote Halstead, "was like the sudden broad gleam of a saber, and his deliberate drawl like the dull roar of high pressure steam in a firm boiler."

There is a temptation to extend the list of his sayings and epigrams, to repeat familiar anecdotes, and to add others now scattered in the obscure recesses of old periodicals, newspapers and almost forgotten memoirs. The recorded impressions of his contemporaries deserve far more extended quotation and comment than they have received, but it is time to close. After all, he told his own story, gave his own opinions, never posed, and feared nothing. He stands on his record and his place in the history of our polity is secure.

Thomas W. Laffan of the New York *Sun* wrote a brief tribute which may well stand as the verdict on the man and his career. The passing years have as yet brought no need of revision and it is unlikely that they ever will.

"Tom Reed was a great man and a good man. A quarter of a century of warm friendship taught us to know him in that close and personal aspect that is commonly destructive of the abstract and public apprehension of a man. Did it detract from his figure? Not a bit of it. He grew bigger and broader and greater and more lovable with each succeeding year. . . . Never, never again, shall we look upon the like of Tom Reed.

"He was a splendid character and there was nothing in all the length and breadth of our land that was more American than he. . . . He was a politician, but we always thought he was a poor politician. He never drew a dishonest breath. The man was the soul of honesty. He was a statesman in spite of himself."

BIBLIOGRAPHY

Alexander, De Alva Stanwood. History and Procedure of the House of Representatives. Boston. 1916. A useful and interesting work containing many incidental references to Reed's achievements in procedural reform.

Andrews, E. Benjamin. The history of the last quarter-century in the United States. 2 vols. New York. 1896. A useful general history.

Andrews, E. Benjamin. The United States in our own time. New York. 1903.

Barry, David S. Forty years in Washington. Boston. 1924.

Beer, Thomas. Hanna. New York. 1929. An interesting portrait, containing, in spite of much irrelevant material, some information not available in other biographies.

Bigelow, John. The life of Samuel J. Tilden. 2 vols. New York. 1895.

Bishop, Joseph Bucklin. Theodore Roosevelt and his time, 2 vols. New York. 1920.

Blaine, James G. Twenty years of Congress. 2 vols. Norwich, Conn. 1884.

Bowers, Claude. The tragic era. New York. 1929. The best history of the reconstruction period.

Boutwell, George S. Reminiscences of sixty years in public affairs. New York. 1902.

Brown, George R. The leadership of Congress. Indianapolis. 1922.

Brownson, W. H. Thomas B. Reed. *New England Magazine*, April, 1890.

Busbey, L. White. Uncle Joe Cannon: The story of a pioneer American. New York. 1927.

Chiu, Chang-Wei. The speaker of the House of Representatives since 1896. New York. 1928. Useful for study of parliamentary procedure in the House.

Clark, Champ. My quarter century of American politics. New York. 1920. Somewhat diffuse and repetitious but containing valuable sidelights on persons and events.

Clark, Francis E. Thomas B. Reed as a neighbor. *The Independent*, January 8, 1903.

Congressional Record, 1877–1902. The chief source of the present study.

Connelley, William Elsey. The life of Preston B. Plumb. Chicago. 1913.

Coolidge, Louis A. An old-fashioned senator: Orville H. Platt of Connecticut. 2 vols. New York. 1910. Valuable.

Croly, Herbert. Marcus Alonzo Hanna: his life and work. New York. 1919. An able biography.

Cullom, Shelby Moore. Fifty years of public service. Chicago. 1911.

Cumberland Club of Portland, Me., scrap-book. Contains large collection of newspaper clippings, mostly obituaries and reminiscences, on Thomas B. Reed.

Day, Holman F. Tom Reed among his neighbors. *Saturday Evening Post*, January 3, 1903.

Dewey, Davis R. National problems. New York. 1907.

Dingley, Edward Nelson. The life and times of Nelson Dingley, Jr. Kalamazoo, Mich. 1902. A biography of the filiopietistic type but containing considerable valuable information on Maine politics, the course of congressional business, and the relations of Reed with his Maine colleague.

Dingley, Frank L. Reminiscences and comments of a Bowdoin College student of the sixties, incidental to reading McCall's biography of the great speaker. Eight articles, Lewiston *Weekly Journal*, January–March, 1915. Contain valuable information on Reed's early life and incidental comments on his personality and career by one of his intimate friends.

Dunn, Arthur Wallace. 2 vols. From Harrison to Harding. New York. 1922. Valuable.

Dunning, W. A. Reconstruction political and economic. New York. 1907.

Eckenrode, H. J. Rutherford B. Hayes: statesman of reunion. New York. 1930.

Exercises at the unveiling of the statue of Thomas Brackett Reed, at Portland, Maine, August 31, 1910. Contains addresses by several of Reed's former colleagues and friends.

Fessenden, Francis. The life and public services of William Pitt Fessenden. 2 vols. Boston. 1907. Throws some light on Maine politics at the opening of Reed's career.

Follett, M. P. The Speaker of the House of Representatives. New York. 1896. The best book on the subject.

Foraker, Joseph Benson. Notes of a busy life. 2 vols. Cincinnati. 1916. Useful.

Ford, Henry Jones. The Cleveland era. New Haven. 1919. A useful survey which emphasizes the importance of procedural conditions in the House of Representatives.

Foulke, William Dudley. Life of Oliver P. Morton. 2 vols. Indianapolis. 1899.

Fuller, H. B. Speakers of the House. Boston. 1909.

Griffin, Solomon Bulkley. People and politics observed by a Massachusetts editor. Boston. 1923.

Hamilton, Gail. Biography of James G. Blaine. Norwich, Conn. 1895. Uncritical but full of valuable information.

Hamlin, Charles Eugene. The Life and times of Hannibal Hamlin. Cambridge. 1899. A eulogistic study of one of Maine's ablest politicians.

Hasbrouck, Paul De Witt. Party government in the House of Representatives. New York. 1927.

Haworth, Paul L. The United States in our times. New York. 1920.

Haworth, Paul L. The Hayes-Tilden election. Indianapolis. 1927.

Hepburn, A. Barton. A history of currency in the United States. New York. 1915.

Hinds, Asher C. Precedents of the House of Representatives. 8 vols. Washington, D. C. 1907–08. Essential in any study of congressional procedure.

Hinds, Asher C. The Speaker of the House of Representatives. *American Political Science Review,* May, 1909.

Hoar, George F. Autobiography of seventy years. 2 vols. New York. 1903. Useful.

Hubbard, Thomas H. Memorial of Thomas Brackett Reed. Annual report of the association of the bar of the City of New York. 1904. Contains valuable information on Reed's career as a lawyer.

Johnson, Robert Underwood. Remembered yesterdays. Boston. 1923.

Kennebec Journal, The. Augusta, Me. 1868–70. Contains considerable information and comment on the proceedings of the Maine legislature.

Kerr, Winfield S. John Sherman. 2 vols. Boston. 1908.

Knight, Enoch. Thomas B. Reed: an appreciation. *New England Magazine,* April, 1904.

La Follette, Robert M. La Follette's autobiography: a personal narrative of political experiences. Madison. 1913.

Laughlin, J. L. The history of bimetallism. New York. 1886.

Lingley, Charles R. Since the Civil War. New York. 1926.

Lodge, Henry Cabot. The democracy of the constitution and other addresses and essays. New York. 1915. Contains a valuable essay on Thomas B. Reed.

Lodge, Henry Cabot. Early memories. Boston. 1913.

Lodge Papers. Collection at present in custody of Massachusetts Historical Society. Contains some correspondence between Reed and the late Senator Lodge.

Long, J. C. Bryan the great commoner. New York. 1928.

Leupp, F. E. Personal recollections of Thomas B. Reed. *The Outlook*, September 3, 1910.

Luce, Robert. Congress: an explanation. Cambridge, Mass. 1926.

Luce, Robert. Legislative procedure. Boston. 1922.

Luce, Robert. Legislative assemblies. Boston. 1924.

Luce, Robert. Legislative principles; the history and theory of law-making by representative government. Boston. 1930. Mr. Luce's books contain a vast amount of valuable material on the general subject of legislative procedure and parliamentary law.

McCall, Samuel W. The life of Thomas Brackett Reed. Boston. 1914. Contains valuable material drawn from Reed's personal papers but neglects some of the most important aspects of his congressional career.

McElroy, Robert. Grover Cleveland the man and the statesman. New York. 1923.

McElroy, Robert. Levi Parsons Morton, banker, diplomat and statesman. New York. 1930.

MacFarland, Henry B. F. Thomas Brackett Reed. *Review of Reviews*, January, 1903.

Mitchell, Edward P. Memoirs of an editor: fifty years of American Journalism. New York. 1924.

Nation, The. 1876–1902. Indispensable for any study of the period.

Nevins, Allan. The emergence of modern America, 1865–1878. New York. 1928.

Nevins, Allan. Henry White: thirty years of American diplomacy. New York. 1930.

New York *Tribune*, 1884–1902. A strongly partisan journal but ably represented by its Washington correspondents. An index of editorials and important articles renders its materials readily accessible.

New York *Sun*. 1896.

North American Review, 1876–1902. Contains valuable

contributions on the leading issues of the period. Reed was a frequent contributor from 1888 until his death.

Oberholtzer, E. P. A history of the United States since the Civil War. 3 vols. New York. 1917–1926.

Olcott, Charles S. The life of William McKinley. 2 vols. Boston. 1916.

Orations and addresses delivered by Thomas Brackett Reed. Privately printed. Portland, Maine. 1911. Contains many of Reed's non-political addresses not available elsewhere.

Paine, Albert Bigelow. Mark Twain, a biography. 4 vols. New York. 1912. Much material on the friendship of Reed and Mark Twain after Reed left Congress.

Peck, Harry Thurston. Twenty years of the republic, 1885–1905. New York. 1906.

Platt, Thomas Collier. The autobiography of Thomas Collier Platt. New York. 1910.

Porter, Robert P. Thomas B. Reed of Maine. The man and his home. *McClure's Magazine*, October, 1893. Throws light on Reed's personality and interests.

Portland *Press*. 1867–1876. The chief journalistic supporter of Reed in the First District.

Powers, Samuel Leland. Portraits of half a century. Boston. 1925. Contains an interesting sketch of Thomas B. Reed.

Roosevelt, Theodore. Autobiography. New York. 1916.

Roosevelt, Theodore. Thomas Brackett Reed and the fifty-first Congress. The *Forum*, December, 1895.

Roosevelt, Theodore. Selections from the correspondence of Theodore Roosevelt and Henry Cabot Lodge, 1884–1918. New York. 1925.

Sherman, John. Recollections of forty years. 2 vols. Chicago. 1895.

Smalley, George Washburn. Anglo-American Memories. 2nd Series. London. 1912. Contains sketch of Reed.

Smith, Theodore Clarke. The life and letters of James Abram Garfield. 2 vols. New Haven. 1925.

Stanwood, Edward. James Gillespie Blaine. (American statesmen series). Boston, 1905.

Stealey, O. O. Twenty years in the press gallery. New York. 1906. Contains valuable material on events in Washington during the greater part of Reed's activity there as well as an important character study by A. Maurice Low.

Stoddard, Henry Luther. As I knew them; presidents and politics from Grant to Coolidge. New York. 1927.

Taussig, F. W. The tariff history of the United States. New York. 1923.

Thompson, Charles Willis. Presidents I've known and two near Presidents. Indianapolis. 1929.

Washington *Post* 1885–1902. A valuable source of information on the day-to-day course of business in Congress. The column "Under the Capitol Dome" is a mine of anecdote and incident.

Watterson, Henry. "Marse Henry," an autobiography. New York. 1919.

White, Andrew D. Autobiography of Andrew D. White. 2 vols. New York. 1905. Contains a flattering estimate of Reed.

Wilson, Woodrow. Congressional government; a study in American politics. Boston. 1885.

INDEX